US HEGEMONY AND INTERNATIONAL ORGANIZATIONS

D1567114

US Hegemony and International Organizations

The United States and Multilateral Institutions

Edited by
Rosemary Foot,
S. Neil MacFarlane,
and
Michael Mastanduno

OXFORD
UNIVERSITY PRESS

OXFORD
UNIVERSITY PRESS

Great Clarendon Street, Oxford OX2 6DP

Oxford University Press is a department of the University of Oxford.
It furthers the University's objective of excellence in research, scholarship,
and education by publishing worldwide in

Oxford New York

Auckland Cape Town Dar es Salaam Hong Kong Karachi Kuala Lumpur
Madrid Melbourne Mexico City Nairobi New Delhi Shanghai Taipei Toronto

With offices in

Argentina Austria Brazil Chile Czech Republic France Greece
Guatemala Hungary Italy Japan South Korea Poland Portugal
Singapore Switzerland Thailand Turkey Ukraine Vietnam

Oxford is a registered trade mark of Oxford University Press
in the UK and in certain other countries

Published in the United States
by Oxford University Press Inc., New York

© the several contributors, 2003

The moral rights of the authors have been asserted

Database right Oxford University Press (maker)

First published 2003

British Library Cataloguing in Publication Data

Data available

Library of Congress Cataloging in Publication Data

US hegemony and International Organization : the United States and
multinational institutions / edited by Rosemary Foot, Neil MacFarlane,
and Michael Mastanduno.
p. cm.
Includes bibliographical references and index.
1. United States–Foreign relations–1989-   2. International agencies.
3. International organization.   I. Foot, Rosemary, 1948-   II. MacFarlane, S. Neil.
III. Mastanduno, Michael.
JZ1480.U813 2003   341.2–dc21   2002035570
ISBN 0-19-926142-3 (hbk.)
ISBN 0-19-926143-1 (pbk.)

7 9 10 8 6

Typeset by Newgen Imaging Systems (P) Ltd., Chennai, India
Printed in Great Britain on acid-free paper by
Biddles Ltd., King's Lynn, Norfolk

ACKNOWLEDGEMENTS

This book is the outcome of a collaborative project between the Centre for International Studies at the University of Oxford and the Dickey Center for International Understanding at Dartmouth College. It has brought together participants from three continents in a fruitful effort that has lasted many months. We are grateful to all our authors for their dedication to this project over a period which saw a number of significant developments in their respective areas of expertise, as well as a change in US administration. We offer our warm thanks for their willingness both to stick with the project and to respond to calls to revise and update chapters.

The first stage of this enterprise comprised a workshop at Dartmouth where outline papers were discussed. The next stage involved a conference at Oxford where full papers were presented and debated with the valuable aid of the following discussants: Amitav Acharya, James Mayall, Kalypso Nicolaidis, Stewart Patrick, Adam Roberts, Monica Serrano, and Andrew Walter. These additional participants made a major intellectual contribution to the project and we record our thanks to them.

We are particularly grateful for the administrative and editorial assistance that has been given to us from staff at Dartmouth as well as at Oxford. Special thanks go to Donna Chung for her help with preparing the papers for publication. We are grateful too to Dominic Byatt, Senior Editor at Oxford University Press, for his unstinting encouragement and for commissioning external reviews of the project. And we thank Dr Michael James for his calm and efficient work as copy-editor for the Press.

Financial support for this undertaking has been given by the Dickey Center and by the Norwegian and Swedish foreign ministries who have generously contributed to the Research Programme of the Centre for International Studies. We could not have drawn upon such a wide range of perspectives and specialist argument without those vital sources of funding.

Rosemary Foot
S. Neil MacFarlane
Michael Mastanduno

Oxford, June 2002

CONTENTS

viii *Contents*

NOTES ON CONTRIBUTORS

RALPH A. COSSA is President of the Pacific Forum CSIS, which is based in Honolulu, and affiliated with the Center for Strategic and International Studies (CSIS) in Washington, DC. He is a founding member of the Steering Committee of the multinational Council for Security Cooperation in the Asia Pacific (CSCAP) and co-chairs a CSCAP working group on confidence and security building measures. He has written widely on Asia-Pacific security relations, including his edited text *US-Korea-Japan Relations: Building Toward a 'Virtual Alliance'* (CSIS Press, 1999).

ROSEMARY FOOT is Professor of International Relations and the John Swire Senior Research Fellow in the International Relations of East Asia, St Antony's College, University of Oxford. In 1996 she was elected a Fellow of the British Academy. Her most recent books are *Rights Beyond Borders: The Global Community and the Struggle Over Human Rights in China* (Oxford University Press, 2000), and, co-edited with John Lewis Gaddis and Andrew Hurrell, *Order and Justice in International Relations* (Oxford University Press, 2003).

DR DAVID G. HAGLUND is Professor in the Department of Political Studies, Queen's University, Kingston, Ontario. His research focuses on transatlantic security and on Canadian and American international security policy. He is currently researching a book on the France–US security relationship, tentatively titled *Sister Acts: America, France, and the Antinomies of Strategic Culture.*

DR STEPHEN HOPGOOD is Lecturer in International Politics at the School of Oriental and African Studies, University of London. He is the author of *American Foreign Environmental Policy and the Power of the State* (Oxford University Press, 1998) and 'Reading the Small Print in Global Civil Society', *Millennium: Journal of International Studies*, 29/1 (2000). Between September 2002 and March 2003 he undertook a constructivist analysis of the International Secretariat of Amnesty International funded by a Social Science Research Council Fellowship in Global Security and Cooperation.

G. JOHN IKENBERRY is Peter F. Krogh Professor of Geopolitics and Global Justice at Georgetown University. He is also Non-Resident Senior Fellow at the Brookings Institution. He previously taught at Princeton and the University of Pennsylvania. He is the author of *After Victory: Institutions, Strategic Restraint, and the Rebuilding of Order after Major War* (Princeton, 2001), co-author of *States and Markets: The International Political Economy* (Norton, 2003), and editor of

America Unrivaled: The Future of the Balance of Power (Cornell University Press, 2003).

HAL KLEPAK is Professor of Latin American History and International Relations at the Royal Military College of Canada. Professor Klepak is an adviser to Canada's Departments of Defence and Foreign Affairs and International Trade. He publishes extensively on foreign and defence policies of Latin American states and the inter-American security system.

EDWARD C. LUCK is Professor of Practice in International and Public Affairs and Director of the Center on International Organization of the School of International and Public Affairs, Columbia University. Formerly President and CEO of the United Nations Association of the United States (UNA-USA), Dr Luck's most recent book is *Mixed Messages: American Politics and International Organization, 1919–1999* (Brookings Institution Press, 1999).

S. NEIL MACFARLANE is the Lester B. Pearson Professor of International Relations and a Fellow of St Anne's College, Oxford. Until October 2002, he was also Director of the Centre for International Studies, University of Oxford. He is also a non-resident faculty member of the Geneva Centre for Security Policy. He writes on regional and international organization, and security relations within the former Soviet Union. Recent publications include *Intervention in Contemporary World Politics* (Adelphi Paper 350, 2002).

DAVID M. MALONE, on leave from the Canadian Foreign Service, is President of the International Peace Academy in New York. A former chair of UN negotiations on peacekeeping issues, he has been successively Director General of Policy, International Organizations and Global Issues in the Canadian Foreign Ministry. He is an adjunct professor in the New York University School of Law and in l'Institut des Etudes Politiques in Paris.

MICHAEL MASTANDUNO is Professor and Chair of the Department of Government at Dartmouth College in Hanover, New Hampshire. He has written numerous articles and essays concerning US foreign policy, the politics of the world economy, and the relationship between economic and security affairs. He is the author of *Economic Containment: CoCom and the Politics of East-West Trade* (Cornell University Press, 1992) and co-editor of *Beyond Westphalia?* (Johns Hopkins University Press, 1995), of *Unipolar Politics: Realism and State Strategies after the Cold War* (Columbia University Press, 1999), and of *International Relations Theory and the Asia Pacific* (forthcoming).

PHILIP NEL was until 2002 Chair of the Department and Professor of Political Science at the University of Stellenbosch, South Africa. He is editor and co-author of books on South African foreign policy and multilateralism, and on public participation and foreign policy. With Pat McGowan he edited

Power, Wealth and Global Equity: An International Relations Textbook for Africa (2nd edn, University of Cape Town Press, 2002). His current research focuses on global welfare inequalities, the theory and practice of deliberative and redistributive democracy, and global governance. In February 2003 he joined the University of Otago, New Zealand, as Professor of Political Studies.

DR GAUTAM SEN is Lecturer in the Politics of the World Economy, Department of International Relations, London School of Economics and Political Science. His teaching and research interests are in international political economy, economic development, and defence economics. He is author of *The Military Origins of Industrialisation and International Trade Rivalry* (2nd edn, Cassell, 1995), and has been writing on globalization and the poor, and the internationalization of China's economy. A forthcoming co-authored book is on the political economy of trade, money, and foreign investment.

NGAIRE WOODS is Fellow in Politics and International Relations at University College, Oxford. Her next book will be on the politics of the IMF and the World Bank. Her other recent publications include *The Political Economy of Globalization* (Macmillan, 2000), *Inequality, Globalization and World Politics* (with Andrew Hurrell: Oxford University Press, 1999), *Explaining International Relations since 1945* (Oxford University Press, 1996), and numerous articles on international institutions, globalization, and governance (see http://users.ox.ac.uk/~ntwoods).

LIST OF ABBREVIATIONS

ABM	Anti-Ballistic Missile (Treaty)
ACRI	African Crisis Response Initiative
AD	Anti-dumping
AFTA	ASEAN Free Trade Area
AGOA	African Growth and Opportunity Act
AMU	Arab Mahgreb Union
ANZUS	Australia, New Zealand and the United States
APEC	Asia Pacific Economic Cooperation
ARF	ASEAN Regional Forum
ASEAN	Association of Southeast Asian Nations
ATRIP	African Trade and Investment Program
AU	African Union
CFCs	Chlorofluorocarbons
COMESA	Common Market for Eastern and Southern Africa
CRS	Congressional Research Service
CSCAP	Council for Security Cooperation in the Asia-Pacific
CSSDCA	Conference on Security, Stability, Development, and Cooperation in Africa
CTBT	Comprehensive Test Ban Treaty
CVD	Countervailing duties
DPRK	Democratic People's Republic of Korea
DSB	Dispute Settlement Body
DSM	Dispute Settlement Mechanism
EAEC	East Asia Economic Caucus
EASR	East Asia Strategy Report
ECA	Economic Commission for Africa
ECCAS	Economic Community of Central African States
ECOMOG	ECOWAS Military Observer Group
ECOWAS	Economic Community of West African States
ESDP	European Security and Defence Policy
EU	European Union
FPDA	Five Power Defence Arrangement
FSC	Foreign Sales Corporation
G 77	Group of 77
GAO	General Accounting Office
GATT	General Agreement on Tariffs and Trade
GCC	Global Climate Coalition
GPA	Government Procurement Agreement

HIPC	Heavily Indebted Poor Country
IBRD	International Bank for Reconstruction and Development
ICC	International Criminal Court
IDA	International Development Association
IFI	International Financial Institution
IGAD	Intergovernmental Authority on Development
ILO	International Labour Organization
INC	Intergovernmental Negotiating Committee
INTERFET	UN-Sponsored International Force for East Timor
IPCC	Intergovernmental Panel on Climate Change
IPR	Intellectual Property Rights
IRBD	Independent Review of Bangladesh's Development
ISG	Intersessional Support Group
ITA	International Trade Administration
ITC	International Trade Commission
ITO	International Trade Organization
IUCN	International Union for Conservation of Nature
KEDO	Korean Peninsular Energy Development Organization
LDC	Less Developed Country
LWR	Light Water Reactor
Mercosur	*Mercado Comun del Sur* (Common Market of the South)
MINURSO	UN Mission for the Referendum in Western Sahara
NAFTA	North American Free Trade Agreement
NATO	North Atlantic Treaty Organization
NEACD	Northeast Asia Cooperation Dialogue
NEPAD	New Partnership for Africa's Development
NGO	Non-governmental organization
NIEO	New International Economic Order
NMD	National Missile Defence
OAS	Organization of American States
OAU	Organization of African Unity
ONUCA	UN Observer Group in Central America
ONUMOZ	UN Operation in Mozambique
ONUSAL	UN Observer Mission in El Salvador
ONUVEN	UN Observer Mission for the Verification of Elections in Nicaragua
OPCW	Organization for the Prohibition of Chemical Weapons
OSCE	Organization for Security and Cooperation in Europe
PAU	Pan American Union
PDD	Presidential Decision Directive
PKO	Peacekeeping Operation (UN)
PMC	Post-Ministerial Conference
PRC	People's Republic of China
RIMPAC	Rim of the Pacific Exercise
ROK	Republic of Korea (South Korea)

RTAA	Reciprocal Trade Agreements Act
RUF	Revolutionary United Front
SADC	Southern African Development Community
SADCC	Southern African Development Coordinating Conference
SCR	Security Council Resolution
SEATO	Southeast Asia Treaty Organization
SWAPO	South West African People's Liberation Organization
TAA	Trade Adjustment Assistance
TPA	Trade Promotion Authority
TRIMS	Trade-Related Investment Measures
TRIPS	Trade-Related Aspects of Intellectual Property Rights
USPACOM	US Pacific Command
UN	United Nations
UNAMIC	UN Advance Mission in Cambodia
UNAMIR	UN Assistance Mission in Rwanda
UNAVEM	UN Angola Verification Mission
UNEP	UN Environment Program
UNESCO	UN Educational, Scientific and Cultural Organization
UNGA	UN General Assembly
UNGOMAP	UN Good Offices Mission in Afghanistan and Pakistan
UNIMOG	UN Iran-Iraq Military Observer Group
UNIKOM	UN Iraq-Kuwait Observation Mission
UNMIH	UN Mission in Haiti
UNMUR	UN Mission in Uganda-Rwanda
UNOMIG	UN Observer Mission in Georgia
UNOMIL	UN Observer Mission in Liberia
UNOSOM	UN Operation in Somalia
UNPROFOR	UN Protection Force
UNRWA	UN Relief and Works Agency for Palestine Refugees in the Near East
UNTAC	UN Transitional Authority in Cambodia
UNTAET	UN Transitional Authority in East Timor
UNTAG	UN Transitional Assistance Group in Namibia
URA	Uruguay Round Agreement
USAID	US Agency For International Development
USTR	United States Trade Representative
VER	Voluntary Export Restraint
WMO	World Meteorological Organization
WTO	World Trade Organization

Introduction

ROSEMARY FOOT, S. NEIL MACFARLANE, AND MICHAEL
MASTANDUNO

US attitudes towards multilateral organizations once again have become matters of intense debate. Although that debate has been a perennial one since
America's founding, it reached a particularly high level of intensity in the
1990s. That decade began with US officials promoting a renewed and more
prominent role for the United Nations (UN). It ended with an increasingly
assertive US Congress refusing to ratify the Comprehensive Test Ban Treaty
(CTBT) and calling into question the US commitment to other multilateral initiatives. The US debate has become more passionate still in the twenty-first
century as a result of various Bush administration decisions, including those
to withdraw from the Anti-Ballistic Missile (ABM) treaty and the Kyoto
Protocol on Global Climate Change. The deliberation resumed with the US
response to the terrorist attacks of 11 September 2001. Many observers both in
the United States and abroad urged the Bush administration to address these
security threats through multilateral measures. The administration proved
eager to enlist the support of other countries but also made clear its belief that
unilateral military action was appropriate in the face of a direct attack on
American territory.

One Bush administration spokesperson, Director of the Policy Planning Staff
Richard Haass, has described his colleagues not as advocates of unilateralism but
as proponents of 'hard-headed multilateralism'. According to Haass, this hard-
headed variety combines American leadership with a division of labour in dealing with foreign policy problems; it sometimes results in the creation of formal
institutional structures, sometimes not; and, in light of America's 'unique global
responsibilities', it involves a willingness to risk unpopularity by not always
going along with others. With these understandings, he concludes, 'multilateralism need not constrain our option[s], done right, it expands them'.[1]

Other commentators have been more explicit in extolling the virtues of unilateralism, perhaps none more so than the influential political journalist

---

[1] Speech to a conference sponsored by the Carnegie Endowment and the Center on
International Cooperation, New York (14 November 2001).

Charles Krauthammer. In Krauthammer's view, withdrawal from the ABM treaty in December 2001 'unashamedly reasserts the major theme of the Bush administration's foreign policy: unilateralism'. Approvingly, he explains: 'The essence of unilateralism is that we do not allow others, no matter how well-meaning, to deter us from pursuing the fundamental security interests of the United States and the free world. It is the driving motif of the Bush foreign policy. And that is the reason it has been so successful.'[2] The sentiments expressed by Krauthammer, not surprisingly, have generated a reaction from the more multilaterally inclined US elite. Secretary of State Colin Powell argued publicly and consistently for a multilateral approach in the US response to 11 September. The central argument of the Harvard professor and former Defence Department official, Joseph Nye's, book is that the United States cannot 'go it alone', notwithstanding its dominant power position. The United States, Nye asserts, has little choice but to collaborate with others in order to realize its foreign policy objectives.[3]

Wherever one stands on the benefits or drawbacks of multilateral engagement, and whatever one's perceptions of where the Bush administration itself stands on these questions, there is no denying a long-standing US ambivalence towards multilateral organizations. It is an ambivalence that is manifested towards those organizations of which America is a part and those which it influences even by its absence.

This volume is a response to the intensification of this debate about the place of multilateral organizations in US foreign policy. Its primary aims are twofold: to describe and explain US behaviour in and towards a wide range of significant global and regional organizations, and to examine the impact of US behaviour on the capacity of each organization to meet its own objectives. We have not entered into this examination convinced that all multilateral behaviour is to be applauded, and bilateralism and unilateralism invariably to be opposed. However, we do think it of value to explore and to advance the public's understanding of US behaviour at a time when globalizing trends in the context of US hegemony are creating a particular set of tensions in world politics. Global society has become increasingly institutionalized, greater interdependence and manifestations of transnational harm have resulted in intensified efforts to coordinate outcomes at the global level, yet the US position as sole superpower increases the temptation for it to act unilaterally.

Indeed, one glance at the annual *Yearbook of International Organizations* should be enough to convince all but the most sceptical observer of the extent to which our lives have become increasingly entwined with multilateral international

---

[2] Charles Krauthammer, *The Washington Post*, reprinted in the *Guardian Weekly* (20–6 December 2001).

[3] Joseph S. Nye, Jr, *The Paradox of American Power* (Oxford: Oxford University Press, 2002).

organizations.[4] More notable still has been the rise to prominence of these bodies since the 1990s across a broad range of issue areas from security to economics, the environment, human rights, health, culture, and science. Specialist and non-specialist writings now give ample and regular space to explaining the activities of, and often the crises faced by, universal or regional international bodies. Frequent media reference to such institutions as the UN, the World Trade Organization (WTO), the European Union (EU), the Organization of American States (OAS), or Organization of African Unity (OAU) has widened understanding of the additional channels that exist for addressing policy matters seemingly beyond the capacity of the state.

If membership of such bodies is any guide, few states—even the most powerful—perceive they can afford to avoid, or want to avoid, interaction with multilateral organizations. And such understandings clearly had influenced the United States as it rose to power over the course of the twentieth century. US administrations demonstrated through their efforts in creating multilateral institutions that they recognized their worth as instruments of policy, particularly at times of fundamental structural change at the close of the two world wars. Perhaps they recognized, too, a compatibility between multilateral approaches and the prized domestic cultural value of pluralism. In the first phase of the post-cold war era, a time when America stood out as the only truly global power with global interests and with concerns about global order, it involved itself again in institutional innovation, raising expectations that it would continue to turn to such bodies, as it had in the past, to advance national and milieu goals. This interest and involvement showed itself even in instances where the United States was not a member of a particular organization, as with the OAU, for example, where US preferences played a major role in the design of regional approaches to peacekeeping in an attempt to ward off pressure for direct US involvement in the management of African conflicts.

Indeed, the Clinton administration came into office initially wedded to 'assertive multilateralism' in the security field, and quickly built on the previous Bush administration's agenda in expanding the scope of major multilateral organizations such as the UN and North Atlantic Treaty Organization (NATO). Clinton also showed a commitment to the advancement of trade liberalization, promoting this aim via the WTO, as the successor to the General Agreement on Tariffs and Trade (GATT), and regionally through the establishment of the North American Free Trade Agreement (NAFTA) and the enhancement of the visibility and importance of the Asia-Pacific Economic Cooperation forum (APEC). Multilateral organizations thus initially came to

---

[4] For example, see Union of International Associations (ed.), *Yearbook of International Organizations*, Edition 36 (Munich: K. G. Saur, 1999–2000). We mean by 'multilateral international organizations', or in this work 'intergovernmental organizations', formally organized bodies of three or more members, characterized by permanent locations and reasonable longevity.

be projected as essential tools in the post-cold war landscape. They were regarded as even more important to the United States in this era because threats and interests were not as clearly defined as during the cold war, although they were understood to be much broader in range. Adding to the attraction for the US administration and for large sections of domestic opinion was that these formal groupings of states could help the US to spread burdens, control risks, and promote its values. They could also legitimize and universalize its interests at a time when it needed to reassure others about the way it would use its dominant position in the global system.

Although these positive perspectives on international organizations are sometimes advanced in the United States at the beginning of the twenty-first century, they were in fact views that were more widely held in the early 1990s. The combination of post-cold war US preponderance and the prominence of multilateral organizations generated a backlash in the United States by the middle of that decade. Important, too, to the creation of that negative reaction was the apparent failure of multilateral efforts in such wrenching instances as Somalia and Bosnia which, together with the fact of US hegemony, reinvigorated well-honed arguments about the threats multilateralism posed to US national sovereignty and capacity for autonomous action. Presidential Decision Directive (PDD) 25, which set strict conditions for US participation in UN peacekeeping operations, encapsulated this thinking. The criticisms that helped bring this new directive about pointed up Congressional willingness to challenge Executive branch policies, exacerbating relations that had already become troubled for other reasons.

As is well understood, the structure of the US political system, with its diffusion of power and lack of party allegiance, provides ample opportunity for blocking a president's policy initiatives. On some occasions during the Clinton era, these challenges in the field of foreign relations were mounted plainly for partisan political reasons; at other times, the fear seemed genuine that international bodies had accrued sufficient power to force US foreign policy in directions that were deemed inimical to the country's values and interests. The Clinton administration came under attack from predominantly Republican Party opponents for 'subcontracting' US foreign policy to international organizations.[5] An ever-expanding mass media, across a broad ideological spectrum, and concerned to maximize audience share, stood ready to latch on to these debates, often providing platforms for the administration's critics to present dramatic and simplified arguments in support of one position or another.[6] This activity served to raise to the highest levels of the US foreign policy agenda questions relating to the proper place of multilateral international organizations in the conduct of US policy, reminiscent in some ways of those debates in previous decades about the relative merits of isolation or entanglement.

---

[5] As quoted in John Gerard Ruggie, *Winning the Peace: America and World Order in the New Era* (New York: Columbia University Press, 1996), 22.

[6] A point made in W. Michael Reisman, 'The United States and International Institutions', *Survival*, 41/4 (1999–2000), 76.

US exceptionalist arguments, embracing deeply held beliefs in the validity and universality of America's political experiment, led to calls for international institutional reform in directions that brought them more closely in line with US values, or to demands that the United States leave institutions that not only constrained but also tainted the country through their inability to reform.

US critics of multilateral organizations typically have described such bodies as a drain on US resources, as predominantly hostile to its objectives, and as obstacles to the US ability to take rational, self-interested decisions. The United States, in this view, should not allow itself to be constrained by institutions that reflect the least common denominator of world public opinion, especially when that opinion tends to be hostile to US power and the purpose to which it is put. Those who have disagreed with this depiction, especially America's foreign critics, have described US behaviour in these bodies in precisely opposite terms: as increasingly self-serving and based on a willingness to use US power to achieve the outcomes it has desired, even in the absence of compromise with its major allies.[7] The critics of unilateralism also fear that, because the United States is such a powerful actor, its defiance of multilateral organizations constitutes a threat to the effectiveness and in some cases to the very existence of those organizations.

1. Perspectives on the US and Multilateral Organizations

Despite the importance of this debate and the centrality of America to multilateral cooperation, there is a relative scarcity of general studies of the relationship between the United States and multilateral organizations. This seeming neglect of a major global issue has provided further impetus to this project. Certainly, the matter has been central to some of the key theoretical debates in international relations.[8] Realists, liberal institutionalists, and constructivists, among others, have debated the extent to which international organizations have affected the advancement of American objectives. John J. Mearsheimer, for example, has argued that institutions are dependent variables that reflect the distribution of power in the world. NATO, he avers, 'was essentially an American tool for managing power in the face of the Soviet threat', and it and other such institutions were 'based on the self-interested calculations of great powers' with 'no independent effect on state behavior'. For a liberal institutionalist such as Robert O. Keohane, however, institutions matter because they offer a range of resources; they provide information, monitor for compliance, facilitate issue

---

[7] For one discussion of the instability in external perceptions of the United States see François Heisbourg, 'American Hegemony? Perceptions of the US Abroad', *Survival*, 41/4 (1999–2000).

[8] Examples of a number of these works can be found in our select bibliography.

linkage, and help reach solutions to collective action problems, thereby changing state preferences and state behaviour and contributing substantially to the
maintenance of a stable peace.[9]

The writings of John Ruggie have been crucial in helping students of this topic
to clarify the relationship between multilateralism and multilateral organizations, as well as that between the United States and the multilateral world order
it helped to create. Important to examine, too, is Ruggie's argument that US identity, principles, and beliefs have acted as potent sources of its commitment to a
multilateral order.[10] Edward Luck, in his 1999 book, holds a less sanguine view.
He focuses on the US approach to the League of Nations and its successor, the
United Nations, and provides a detailed exposition of the range of factors that,
rather than attracting the US to collective action, has contributed to US ambivalence towards these two bodies.[11] Notable, too, however, is his remark, made with
some understandable surprise, that his 1999 study was the first to trace the
evolution of US attitudes and policies towards these two major organizations.

Two broad-based studies that have provided important points of comparison for our project are, first, the text by Margaret Karns and Karen Mingst,
undertaken over a decade ago, and that by Stewart Patrick and Shepard
Forman, published in 2002.[12] The context of the Karns and Mingst study is
very different from our own in its attention to a relative *decline* in US power
and America's decisions to withdraw from major international organizations.
From the perspective of the late 1980s, a period that witnessed a diminution
in US power, the two authors investigated an apparent erosion of America's
willingness and ability to exert its influence in institutions, and even actual
departure from a major post-war international organization—the UN
Economic, Social, and Cultural Organization (UNESCO)—and temporary
withdrawal from another—the International Labour Organization (ILO).
Karns and Mingst concluded, however, that relative decline in fact had not led
the United States to abandon international institutions. They also undertook to
measure *change* in US behaviour over the period from 1945 to the late 1980s:
change in US use of intergovernmental organizations as instruments of policy,

[9] John J. Mearsheimer, 'The False Promise of International Institutions', *International
Security*, 19/3 (1994/95), 7, 14; Robert O. Keohane, *International Institutions and State
Power* (Boulder, CO: Westview Press, 1989); and see too the special issue of *International
Organization*, 52/4 (1998), with an editorial essay by Keohane, Peter J. Katzenstein, and
Stephen D. Krasner, 'International Organization and the Study of World Politics'.
[10] For three major statements see John Gerard Ruggie (ed.) *Multilateralism Matters: The
Theory and Praxis of an Institutional Form* (New York: Columbia University Press, 1993);
Winning the Peace; and *Constructing the World Polity: Essays on International
Institutionalization* (London: Routledge, 1998).
[11] Edward C. Luck, *Mixed Messages: American Politics and International Organization,
1919–1999* (Washington, DC: Brookings Institution, 1999).
[12] Margaret P. Karns and Karen A. Mingst (eds), *The United States and Multilateral
Institutions: Patterns of Changing Instrumentality and Influence* (Boston: Unwin Hyman,
1990); Stewart Patrick and Shepard Forman (eds), *Multilateralism and US Foreign Policy:
Ambivalent Engagement* (Boulder, CO: Lynne Rienner, 2002).

and change in the nature of the constraints imposed by, and the influence of, multilateral bodies on the United States. Their conclusions suggest that the international distribution of power did not especially matter. Even as US power declined relatively, multilateral organizations remained important to the United States for regime and rule creation throughout the cold war period. Karns and Mingst found that domestic politics figured prominently in shaping behaviour across both time and with respect to a given issue area. Yet it was variations in the level of ideological congruity between the United States and dominant groupings within particular international organizations, together with the salience of the particular problem area, they found, that had the greatest effect on the evolution of the patterns of instrumentality and influence.

Patrick and Forman are interested in explaining the causes of US ambivalence towards multilateral cooperation. Their conclusions are that US behaviour stems from such sources as US exceptionalism, America's domestic institutional structure, and its global dominance. Our text is complementary to theirs in that we seek to weigh the relative importance of a number of explanatory factors for US behaviour. One key difference is that whereas they are especially concerned about the costs and benefits to the United States of that ambivalence, we are less interested in the specific effects on America, and have given more explicit attention to the consequences of US behaviour for various multilateral organizations themselves. Another key difference involves case selection. Whereas they have chosen to examine US behaviour via a focus on issue areas, we have sought out multiple points of comparison. We examine US behaviour towards regional as well as global organizations, towards security as well as economic and environmental issues, and towards multilateral organizations in various regions of the world in a test of the proposition that geographical location matters when it comes to exploring the quality of US engagement.

These various earlier studies obviously remain important for us to compare with our main findings, and as will become apparent they stand up well on the basis of the conclusions reached here. However, it is worth reiterating that our study is interested both in explaining US behaviour and in understanding the impact of US behaviour on the organizations themselves. Because of the power and prominence of the United States, its behaviour is of major concern to America's allies as well as its enemies, and is perceived as a matter of major consequence to the organizations to which the United States is linked, as well as to those which it is not.

2. Explaining US Behaviour Towards Multilateral Organizations

The US behaviour that is our central focus covers a wide range of possibilities. We are interested, for example, in the level and extent of US participation in multilateral organizations. Under what circumstances does the United States take on a leadership role, acting as the prime mover in establishing and furthering the agenda of a particular organization? At the other extreme, when and why does it adopt a posture of benign neglect or even hostility towards an organization? We are equally interested in the style of US participation. US officials sometimes operate in a consensual manner, accepting compromises and deferring to the sentiments of other states even when the United States finds itself in the minority. Alternatively, the United States frequently behaves unilaterally and coercively, asserting its own will or going its own way in defiance of a multilateral consensus.

This section provides an overview of a variety of factors with the potential to explain US behaviour. For purposes of analytic convenience, we divide these factors into domestic and international, that is, those internal and those external to the United States, although we recognize that these two levels are interpenetrated.

Internal Factors

Domestic sources of US behaviour may be found at the level of society or of the state, or at the intersection of the two. A prominent societal explanation focuses on the preferences and power of interest groups. As multilateral organizations have come to play a greater and more intrusive role in the politics of the United States, the stakes that interest groups have in the operations of these organizations naturally have risen. The evolution of the GATT/WTO offers an apt illustration. In the early decades of the post-war era, the GATT was rather narrow both in membership and in the scope of its substantive activities. By the 1990s it had evolved into the more global WTO and, by focusing on non-tariff barriers to trade liberalization, took on an increasing role in areas central to the political economies of its member states. Societal forces in the United States mobilized in response to the greater prominence of the multilateral trade organization. Some US interest groups—for example, in agriculture, financial services, and high technology—viewed these developments as an opportunity and sought to shape the trade liberalization agenda in the Uruguay Round and beyond. Other groups—environmental and labour interests—have perceived the more prominent WTO as a threat and have sought either to constrain its reach or to force it to accommodate their priorities.

Political scientists generally consider the United States to be a 'weak' state in the sense that interest groups enjoy significant access to and influence over the central government.[13] The fact that interest groups have both a stake in the

---

[13] Stephen Krasner, *Defending the National Interest* (Princeton: Princeton University Press, 1978); Helen Milner, *Resisting Protectionism* (Princeton: Princeton University Press, 1988); and Helen Milner, *Interests, Institutions and Information: Domestic Politics and International Relations* (Princeton: Princeton University Press, 1997).

activities of multilateral organizations and access to US decision making suggests that the societal level is a plausible place to look for explanations of US behaviour. Interest-group influence is likely to be most significant in the economic or environmental areas. But we should not assume its absence in the security area: ethnic groups in sensitive electoral locations—for example, Polish-Americans in the Midwest—helped to push the Clinton administration towards NATO expansion during the 1990s.

The structure of the US political system offers a second promising explanatory factor. The US state is decentralized and fragmented, with the Executive and Congress sharing decision-making authority. During the early decades of the cold war, members of Congress tended to defer to the Executive on matters of foreign policy. Since the Vietnam War, Congress has become far more assertive. Members have demanded not simply greater oversight of the Executive but a central role in the co-determination of foreign policy. This more engaged Congress has simultaneously become more decentralized as an institution. The seniority system has broken down, and committees and subcommittees with a voice in foreign affairs have proliferated. Individual members have augmented their staffs and acted more autonomously, leading critics to charge that the United States has '535 secretaries of state' to complement and more often confound the work of central foreign policy decision-makers in the Executive.

Inter-branch struggles have taken on additional importance since the end of the cold war. The absence of a central strategic threat and the widespread perception of the United States as relatively insulated from international influences, until the onset of the struggle against terrorism after 11 September, had encouraged some in Congress to use foreign policy routinely as an instrument of partisan politics. The Senate rejection of the Comprehensive Test Ban Treaty in 1998 is a striking example. Republican opponents of President Clinton used the rejection of the treaty to embarrass him politically, notwithstanding that the decision placed the United States in defiance of an overwhelming international consensus.

Executive branch officials, particularly in the State Department, tend to take a broader and more supportive view of the US role in multilateral organizations. Members of Congress generally tend to be more parochial and more suspicious of the impact of participation on US sovereignty and autonomy. Co-determination of foreign policy by the two branches thus can have a major impact on US behaviour towards multilateral organizations. It can force the United States to be less consistent and predictable in its dealings with other member states. But it can also afford bargaining leverage to Executive branch officials to the extent they can point credibly in international negotiations to a more hostile Congress waiting in the wings, a tactic that Clinton used, as Philip Nel notes in Chapter 7, when explaining delays in his African policy initiatives.

A third source of internal explanation concerns divisions *within* the Executive branch. In the familiar pattern of bureaucratic politics, different

Executive agencies share foreign policy responsibility yet possess distinctive institutional interests and commitments. Graham Allison's oft-quoted aphorism 'where you stand depends on where you sit' captures the potential for conflict and even stalemate in intra-Executive decision-making. The National Security Council (NSC) staff, lodged in the White House, has responsibility to coordinate the positions and preferences of various Executive agencies. Yet during and after the tenure of Henry Kissinger—with the possible exception of the current Bush administration—the National Security Advisor and staff more frequently have become advocates for particular foreign policy initiatives rather than effective coordinators of the foreign policy process.[14] The coordination that does take place tends to be limited in other ways as well. Mac Destler has argued that the US government possesses an 'economic complex' and a 'security complex' in foreign policy decision making.[15] These two clusters of Executive agencies work along separate tracks with little coordination, even though an increasing number of issues fall at the intersection of the two issue areas.

Bureaucratic politics within the Executive can affect US behaviour towards multilateral organizations, especially in issue areas that cut across the concerns of different agencies. The environment offers a clear example. In Chapter 6 Stephen Hopgood makes much of the 'divided state' and the struggle between activists and sceptics within the US government in accounting for the pattern of US behaviour towards environmental multilateralism.

A fourth explanation centres on the political culture or national character of the United States. Political culture is pervasive across the state and society. It reflects a shared set of attitudes, beliefs, or world views that are so deeply ingrained and closely held that they have the potential to shape foreign policy decisively. Different analysts are likely to stress different components of US political culture. Americans, for example, place great emphasis on the importance of the individual and the protection of individual liberties. This belief is often projected outwards in campaigns for the protection or promotion of human rights abroad. Americans also are sceptical of centralized political authority; the framers of the US constitution sought ways to constrain and diffuse political power rather than assure its efficient mobilization and use. Yet another component of US political culture with foreign policy relevance is the deeply held conviction that American political and economic institutions are a model for others to emulate, a theme that is taken up by Edward Luck in Chapter 1. To many Americans, a world in which other countries look 'more like us' is a safer and more prosperous world.

US political culture, to the extent it influences the US approach to multilateral organizations, paradoxically could lead the United States to lurch between over-commitment and under-commitment. Edward Luck's and David

---

[14] James Nathan and James Oliver, *Foreign Policy Making and the American Political System* (Boston: Little, Brown, 1987).
[15] I. M. Destler, 'Foreign Policy Making with the Economy at Center Stage,' in I. M. Destler and Daniel Yankelovich (eds), *Beyond the Beltway* (New York: Norton, 1994).

Malone's chapters in this volume illustrate these two end points of the continuum to good effect. Over-commitment results from American policy-makers and citizens having excessively optimistic expectations regarding the transformative power of international institutions. Disillusionment, and the tendency to reduce commitments, typically sets in when it becomes apparent that multilateral organizations cannot meet the high expectations Americans set for them. Under-commitment also results from the concern many Americans share that international organizations are nascent world governments with the potential to strip the United States of its sovereignty. In this way, the pervasive yet very parochial American concern over the suffocating power of 'big government' is carried over into the international arena.

External Factors

It is also plausible to expect US behaviour towards multilateral organizations to be shaped by the external environment, that is, by the international context within which the United States is situated. Four factors merit special attention: the international distribution of material capabilities, the international normative context, the diplomatic efforts of other governments, and the performance of multilateral organizations themselves.

The position of a state in the global distribution of power will likely shape its approach to multilateral organizations. The analytic challenge is to determine precisely how, and that challenge is especially difficult in the case of the United States. The United States is the dominant power in the current international system, and dominant powers act with considerable freedom of choice. International structure shapes the options and behaviour of weaker states more than stronger ones. Strong states, and in particular a unipolar power, typically enjoy the luxury of a relatively unconstrained foreign policy.

With due regard for this problem of indeterminacy, we can offer two contrasting hypotheses on the link between US hegemony and its behaviour towards multilateral organizations. One argument anticipates that a hegemonic United States will treat these organizations with a 'take it or leave it' attitude. A dominant power is sufficiently strong and secure not to rely on international institutions. It can afford to act unilaterally and arbitrarily; its preponderant power will insulate it from the negative consequences that would befall more ordinary states acting in this fashion.

A second argument, however, suggests that multilateral organizations will be important to a dominant state precisely because of its privileged position. Dominant states seek to preserve the international status quo in which they benefit most. Multilateral organizations can assist in that task. By providing weaker states a say in international decision making—a benefit that in part explains the desire of such states for membership in bodies like the ASEAN Regional Forum (ARF), discussed by Ralph Cossa in Chapter 8—they help to allay the natural concern weaker states have that the dominant state will exploit them. Multilateral organizations also enable a hegemonic state to institutionalize or 'lock in'—to use G. John Ikenberry's phrase—its dominant position so that its preferences have the potential to endure even after power relations have become less asymmetrical.[16]

Although these arguments point in different directions, together they may capture a sense of US behaviour towards multilateral organizations in the period since the 1990s. On the one hand, a hegemonic United States has retained some commitment to promoting and strengthening international institutions and seeking to shape a multilateral consensus within them. On the other hand, US officials seem incapable of resisting the temptation, bestowed by their dominant power position, to act arbitrarily, to avoid multilateral engagement, or to operate in defiance of consensus positions when the United States finds itself in the minority within multilateral organizations.

The international normative context is a second external source of US behaviour. International norms help to establish what constitutes legitimate and acceptable behaviour in relations among sovereign states. As states have become more interdependent over the post-war era, they have come to conceive of themselves increasingly as members of an international community. A strong expectation has emerged that members of this community decide and act collectively rather than individually. Multilateral organizations are the institutional expression of this contemporary norm, and thereby they create incentives for all states, even the most powerful, to join and participate actively in them.

Two examples suffice to illustrate. Great powers have always intervened in the affairs of smaller and weaker ones. Today, that intervention is considered far more legitimate if it is undertaken collectively with the imprimatur of some institution representative of the international community.[17] The United States proved sensitive to this during its planning of the Persian Gulf War: US officials carefully constructed an international coalition and sought the support of the UN Security Council for intervention. Domestic critics even complained that the Bush administration placed greater priority on an international consensus than a domestic one. The international coalition provided valuable political support to the US-led operation. In contrast, the United States was roundly criticized during the Kosovo intervention of 1999 for failing to obtain Security Council approval. The United States was forced to absorb that political cost, but did ensure that it had the support of the key regional organization, NATO. America proved sensitive to the benefits of international approval again when, immediately after the events of 11 September, it sought UN, NATO, and APEC resolutions of support.

---

[16] See Chapter 2 and also, for an extended treatment, G. John Ikenberry, *After Victory: Institutions, Strategic Restraint, and the Building of Order After Major Wars* (Princeton: Princeton University Press, 2000).

[17] Gene Lyons and Michael Mastanduno (eds), *Beyond Westphalia? State Sovereignty and International Intervention* (Baltimore: Johns Hopkins University Press, 1995).

In the trade area, during the nineteenth century it was common for states to raise or lower market barriers unilaterally rather than through a process of multilateral bargaining. In the United States, Congress routinely sets tariff levels with little regard for the concerns of US trading partners. Today, the raising and—more often—lowering of trade barriers is largely a multilateral process, as Gautam Sen demonstrates in Chapter 5 on the GATT/WTO process. Attempts by states to raise barriers unilaterally—see the discussion in Chapter 5 of the 2002 case of US tariffs on steel—are treated as violations of international norms. Multilateral organizations, whether global or regional, set the rules of the international trade game and thereby demand the active participation of all key trading states, even though they may not in all circumstances gain that participation.

Third, US behaviour towards multilateral organizations may be shaped by the diplomatic efforts of other governments, in particular close allies of the United States. Due to its size and power, US unilateralism is a major concern to other states. They have an interest in a more consistent and predictable US foreign policy, and one that reflects at least to some degree their own preferences. An important means to achieve these objectives is to ensure that US foreign policy initiatives are channelled through collective decision-making mechanisms. During the 1980s, America's major allies worried about 'aggressive unilateralism' in US trade policy and lobbied hard to ensure US compliance with multilateral procedures.[18] Similar concerns existed and a similar lobbying effort took place in 2002 over US plans to construct a national missile defence, and in response to its decision in February 2002 to impose tariffs on steel imports, apparently in defiance of WTO rules.

Foreign governments have the potential to voice their concerns effectively because they enjoy access to US decision-making procedures. The United States is a somewhat unusual dominant power in the extent to which it is open to and penetrated by the lobbying efforts of foreign governments. The same decentralized structure that affords ready access to US interest groups also offers access to foreign officials, as Canadian and Mexican officials have learned in reference to their NAFTA interests.

Finally, the performance of multilateral organizations—more accurately, how that performance is perceived in the United States, thus making this factor as much internal as external to the US—may have a significant impact on the US approach to these organizations. US Treasury officials believed that the IMF played a key role in the successful resolution of the Latin American debt crisis of the 1980s. This belief helped to shape US reliance on the IMF during the 1990s in response to the Asian financial crisis and as the principal international instrument to encourage market reforms in Russia. In contrast, the widespread belief—correct or not—that the UN failed during the early 1990s in

---

[18] Jagdish Bhagwati and Hugh Patrick (eds), *Aggressive Unilateralism: America's 301 Policy and the World Trading System* (Ann Arbor: University of Michigan Press, 1990).

peacemaking efforts clearly affected the level of enthusiasm and support that US officials offered to UN operations in the latter half of the decade—a point that David Malone makes in Chapter 3.

3. The Impact of the United States on Multilateral Organizations

The second major theme of this study is the impact of US policy on multilateral organizations. The power of the United States to determine outcomes in multilateral organizations is generally assumed to be considerable. The United Nations and all regional organizations, with the exception of NATO, lack substantial military capability of their own in responding to threats to international peace and security. In the single case of NATO, which possesses such forces, state members retain a veto power over their use. As such, international organizations considering the use of force are dependent on the willingness of state members to allow the forces they have made available to the organization to be used in a cooperative (peacekeeping) or coercive (peace enforcement) mode.

Where the United States stands on these questions of use is, then, likely to be crucial. The liberation of Kuwait in 1990–1 was rendered possible by the deployment of substantial land, naval, and air forces from the United States and from US bases in Europe. In the early 1990s, American forces formed the core of the UN-mandated coalition (UNITAF) that intervened in Somalia's civil war to provide support for the delivery of humanitarian assistance. In mid-decade, American forces again provided the core and much of the logistics for the NATO-led, UN-mandated force (IFOR) that ended Bosnia's civil war. And at the end of the decade, NATO action against the Federal Republic of Yugoslavia over Kosovo depended heavily on US logistics, ordnance, and air power. On the other hand, the United States was not willing to provide such forces in Rwanda and the Democratic Republic of Congo—a decision that may well have stymied efforts to develop a multilateral response in these instances. Yet there are examples where peace enforcement operations have proceeded without significant US participation: Opération Turquoise in the last stages of the war in Rwanda, Operation Alba in Albania, and INTERFET in East Timor. The chapters by Luck and Malone help us to obtain a better understanding of the conditions under which the United States will agree to participate in such operations and when US decisions regarding involvement are consequential for the outcome.

As a member of the UN Security Council, UN peacekeeping operations do require, of course, US approval or at least acquiescence. The same is true of 'Petersberg task' operations that might be conducted by forces under NATO command. The US is the largest single contributor—in theory, anyway—to the UN peacekeeping budget, which is why its reluctance, until 2001, to pay assessed contributions has been deemed significant to the UN's ability to respond to emerging security issues.

The potential for the United States to have a significant impact on multilateral organizations is equally evident in the area of international financial cooperation, as is clear from Ngaire Woods's contribution in Chapter 4 of this volume. The decisions of the IMF and the World Bank are based on a weighted voting formula and the United States enjoys the largest share of votes. Nevertheless, as Woods also shows, these institutions depend for their legitimacy on being able to demonstrate both technical expertise and some autonomy from the political environment of decision making. The relationship between power and outcome is not straightforward where there is a desire to contribute to the longevity and authority of multilateral institutions.

Experience in other functional areas also warrants investigation. In multilateral efforts to manage environmental problems, as Stephen Hopgood argues in Chapter 6, the US decision to participate might depend on domestic interest groups: for example, the extent to which US domestic industries dominate the market in alternative and cleaner technologies. Certainly, as by far the single largest emitter of carbon dioxide, both in total and per capita, the pressure on America to participate in multilateral efforts to control greenhouse gases is considerable. An effective deal cannot be struck in the absence of US involvement. On the other hand, in the area of international legal instruments the success of the effort to negotiate a convention on the International Criminal Court was drawn into question by the unwillingness of the United States to sign and, once President Clinton did sign in January 2001, by the reluctance of the US Senate to ratify. However, in fact the treaty has attracted the 60 or more ratifications needed to bring it into existence, several years before this was expected to occur.[19]

In assessing possible effects of US policy on multilateral organizations, several distinctions are necessary. In the first place, one should distinguish between specific policy consequences and broader effects on the institution in question or on multilateralism as a general project. An example of the first might be the effect of American reluctance to engage on the UN Security Council's approach to the crisis in Rwanda in 1994 or on multilateral responses to the Yugoslav crisis in 1991–4. An example of the second, as provided by David Haglund in Chapter 9, would be the effect of US ambivalence on the capacity of the EU to translate its security and defence aspirations into concrete operational capability, given the interpenetration of NATO and European national force infrastructures.

At a still wider level, a further illustration might well be the consequences of the American preference to act outside the UN Security Council in Kosovo for the legitimacy of the United Nations as the authoritative body for multilateral responses to threats to international peace and security. Such effects go beyond

---

[19] The 60th ratification occurred on 11 April 2002, after less than four years.

the capacities of institutions to pursue specific actions or their efforts to define their functional roles. At the ideational level, American ideas concerning the appropriate relationship between the state—and state sovereignty—and multilateral institutions are also likely to affect the identity of multilateral institutions, as are American ideas on the appropriate organization of states themselves.

The measurement of the American impact on multilateral organizations at one level involves an assessment of the motivated application of American power.[20] As in domestic settings, there are several dimensions to the use of power in international relations. The first concerns the deliberate application of power to get an entity to change its behaviour. This application may involve incentives and/or penalties. One pertinent example is the adoption by the US Congress in 1985 of the Kassebaum-Solomon amendment mandating the withholding of 20 per cent of US dues until UN institutions adopted the principle of weighted voting on budgetary questions. As noted below in the chapter by Edward Luck, this ultimately produced a compromise whereby budgetary decisions would be made on the basis of consensus, enhancing thereby the influence of major contributors such as the United States over spending decisions.

A second prominent example concerns the non-reappointment of former UN Secretary-General Boutros Boutros-Ghali in 1996. In this instance, there was a consensus minus one within the Security Council on reappointment, and this was supported by a strong majority in the General Assembly. The United States, however, took advantage of the Charter provision requiring Security Council nomination of candidates for the office to the General Assembly and the necessity of unanimous support amongst the veto-bearing members of the Council to prevent his re-election. At the regional level, NATO's choice of the strategic air bombardment option in the former Yugoslavia over the Kosovo dispute in 1999 is an instance of the exercise of American power to obtain a specific policy outcome in the face of resistance from other member states.

The first dimension of power may be enabling as well as disabling. To what degree was the success of international efforts to manage the 1997 Asian financial crisis influenced by the American desire to restore stability to the international financial system and its willingness to organize and participate

---

[20] By 'power' we mean at this point the capacity of an actor to get another actor to do what the latter would not otherwise choose to do. In this sense, the application of power is in essence relational and coercive. For discussions of the nature of power, going beyond this relational form, see Steven Lukes, *Power: A Radical View* (London: Macmillan, 1974) and William Connolly, *The Terms of Political Discourse*, 3rd edn (Oxford: Blackwell, 1993). The discussion of power has evolved to consider more substantially non-coercive forms of its application, based on ideational hegemony. See Robert Cox, *Production, Power and World Order: Social Forces in the Making of History* (New York: Columbia University Press, 1987); and Joseph Nye, *Bound to Lead: The Changing Nature of American Power* (New York: Basic Books, 1990).

in rescue packages for the affected economies? Absent strong American support, would negotiations leading to the establishment of the WTO have been successful? If the United States had not decided that a forceful response to Iraqi aggression against Kuwait was desirable, would the United Nations have been mobilized to provide the necessary mandates? In each of these cases, it appears likely that the eventual outcome depended substantially on the US position.

The capacity of the powerful to impose their preferences is closely linked to a propensity on the part of the weaker to forgo certain policy options as a result of the belief that the penalties imposed by a powerful actor would exceed any possible benefits of the action in question: that is, to surrender in advance. Anticipatory surrender also weighs in both at the level of specific policy choice and at that of the evolution of institutional roles in a larger sense. For example, under Article 99 of the Charter the Secretary-General and his secretariat have the right to bring issues to the Security Council if they believe them to constitute a risk to international peace and security. The secretariat had forewarning of the genocide in Rwanda in 1994, but it chose not to highlight the issue for the Security Council. Some UN officials have claimed that the warning received, like much other information on potential crises, was inconclusive. However, the secretariat was also aware of the deep reluctance of the United States to contemplate new peace enforcement missions so soon after the October 1993 debacle in Somalia.

Anticipatory surrender is closely linked to a second dimension of power: the ability to control agendas.[21] Control of the agenda of issues discussed and options that are considered in response to a particular problem, defining what an organization considers and what it does not, was recognized as an important aspect of power within the UN as early as the negotiations on the Security Council, where the USSR sought to extend the veto rights of permanent members to procedural matters. As E. E. Schattschneider put it: 'All forms of political organisation have a bias in favour of the exploitation of some kinds of conflict and the suppression of others . . . Some issues are organised into politics while others are organised out.'[22]

The capacity to construct barriers to the discussion of particular policy problems and disputes is a form of power available for US use in multilateral organizations.[23] It is widely agreed that American reluctance to contemplate the existence of standing multilateral peacekeeping forces, and the provisions of the Helms-Biden Act prohibiting payment of US arrears in the event that the UN reaches agreement with any country on the earmarking of forces for use by the UN, have effectively prevented serious consideration of the creation

---

[21] See Lukes, *Power*, 16; and Peter Bachrach and Morton Baratz, *Power and Poverty: Theory and Practice* (New York: Oxford University Press, 1970).

[22] E. E. Schattschneider, *The Semi-Sovereign People: A Realist's View of Democracy in America* (New York: Holt, Rinehart and Winston, 1960), 71.

[23] Bachrach and Baratz, *Power and Poverty*, 8.

of such capabilities. A second example is the unwillingness of the United States to contemplate the development of alternatives to state-based financing of UN activities. In contrast, the US desire to replicate its own understandings of macroeconomic theory and its normative preferences with regard to the international economy has served to shift the agendas of international financial and development institutions towards economic neo-liberalism. Similarly, African leaders, Nel argues, have come to accept that neo-liberal economic solutions provide the only viable route to economic advancement. And, as discussed by Hal Klepak in Chapter 10, the growing salience of democratization on the agenda of the OAS is related to American preferences. The same is true of the profile given to eastward enlargement on the agenda of NATO.

The analysis above has focused on rational agency: the observable application of power directly or through constraint on the range of issues and options considered by multilateral organizations in order to achieve particular outcomes. Yet the application of power may not be limited to situations of observable or latent conflict. To the extent that a powerful state is successful in promoting its ideas as universal and legitimate,[24] others will 'choose' to do what it prefers. This may prevent conflict from arising at all. In such situations, there would be no observable application of power. As Lukes notes: '[I]s it not the supreme exercise of power to get another or others to have the desires you want them to have—that is, to secure their compliance by controlling their thoughts and desires?'[25] The wide acceptance of the legitimacy of liberal democratic conceptions of governance and property relations, at least at a procedural level, coupled with the absence of compelling ideological alternatives, considerably diminishes the scope for contestation in multilateral forums.

There is, however, a second and substantial type of impact that powerful states can have on multilateral organizations. This concerns the inadvertent consequences for multilateral organizations of policies adopted or actions taken by such states for other reasons. Here too the impact may be enabling or disabling. For example, the levels of tension or amity in bilateral relations between the United States and Japan, or between the US and China, can influence the use that these states make of bodies such as the ARF, as Cossa argues. In the environmental sphere, the quest for a global agreement on ozone depletion was smoothed by *prior* passage of domestic legislation regulating CFCs inside the United States. This changed the incentive structures for the domestic lobbies and thus their willingness to promote an international agreement. On the other hand, Luck's chapter provides illustration of the ways in which a president committed to a particular action—in this case Clinton's willingness to make up significant portions of US funding arrears to the UN—was stymied by the

---

[24] As Lukes puts it: 'A may exercise power over B by getting him to do what he does not want to do, but he also exercises power over him by influencing, shaping, or determining his very wants.' *Power*, 23. See also Joseph Nye, *Understanding International Conflicts* (New York: Longmans, 2000), 57.   [25] Lukes, *Power*, 23.

addition to the legislation of amendments preventing the use of US contributions for the support of family planning programmes. President Clinton felt he had to veto the legislation, choosing to deny the UN funds and instead to support those domestic constituencies that he considered to be important to him.

Thus, there are various ways in which the powerful can shape multilateral institutions in world politics, through observable and less observable means, using consensual or coercive methods, and even inadvertence.

4. The Structure of the Study and Chapter Outlines

In the chapters that follow, we seek in the first place to determine which factors carry the most explanatory weight and whether there is any meaningful variation in US behaviour towards organizations based regionally as opposed to globally, or among those based in different regions of the world. We also explore the extent to which US behaviour differs across issue area, from security to economics to the environment. Second, we seek to assess in a more detailed way the nature of the US impact on multilateral organizations and what forms of impact are particularly salient, whether this varies across cases, and why. In our conclusion we revisit the candidate explanatory factors, in light of the empirical evidence offered by our authors, to provide an overall assessment of the forces shaping US practice. We then assess the impact of US policy towards multilateral organizations across the range of cases.

In exploring these themes, this study focuses on the contemporary period, but our chapters seek to embed contemporary issues in an historical framework. In Part I we begin with consideration of how domestic political processes affect American behaviour in and towards multilateral organizations. Edward Luck addresses the ways in which what he describes as a deeply-ingrained sense of American exceptionalism coupled with its pragmatism affects the country's approach to multilateral institutions. Luck examines US policies towards peacekeeping, the creation of the WTO, and UN arrears, noting far more positive attitudes towards the WTO than the UN, the latter being perceived as a riskier venue for the promotion of US interests. He concludes that, while the United States is generally reluctant to defer to multilateral processes, it cannot be accused of being hostile to all forms of multilateral organization: it is pragmatic and case-specific in its choice of foreign policy tools.

G. John Ikenberry complements this analysis with an international perspective. He explains that US ambivalence towards multilateral institutions reflects certain choices that it is called upon to make. The United States weighs the attractions of institutions as groupings that lock other states into stable and predictable policy orientations, thus reducing the need for coercion, against the reduction in its own policy autonomy and ability to use power that comes as the price of that institutional bargain. Ikenberry concedes that the actual costs and benefits behind the trade-off are difficult to specify in advance, leading him to conclude that his model is better at identifying the dilemma that the US faces and less effective at specifying in advance how the trade-off will be made. The Bush administration is grappling with these long-standing dilemmas as it develops the policy against terrorism.

In Part II, the study turns to consideration of American approaches to global organizations. David Malone examines the evolution of US behaviour in the UN Security Council since the 1990s and notes an inconsistency in that behaviour born out of a general suspicion of the organization, particularly the General Assembly. He argues that US historical experience of the UN largely explains that suspicion. From the 1960s, the UN's shifting demographics reduced Western dominance of the General Assembly, which in turn led to a number of negative developments from the US perspective, including the 'Zionism as racism' resolution of the mid-1970s and developing-country promotion of a 'New International Information Order' and 'New International Economic Order'. Although the US can find the UN helpful to the promotion of its interests, this legacy of hostility and suspicion is difficult for any administration, Republican or Democrat, to overcome, reinforcing a preference for 'picking and choosing' very carefully among the occasions when it might use multilateral means to meet its objectives.

The next two chapters deal with the major global economic organizations. In Chapter 4 Ngaire Woods takes up the role of the United States in international financial institutions. She concludes that the United States is extraordinarily influential, and that its influence is a function of both formal means—for example, US financial contributions—and informal practices and conventions that have developed within the IMF and World Bank over time. The informal mechanisms of influence are often more important than the formal ones. Woods also argues that, notwithstanding the weight of US influence, it would be inaccurate to consider international financial institutions as mere instruments of US power and policy. The credibility and legitimacy of these institutions rest in part on their ability to create some political distance between themselves and their most powerful state patron. Domestic political conditions are also important. Within the United States, the division of authority between Executive and Congress sometimes enhances and at other times constrains US influence. The effective exercise of US power also requires interlocutors in host governments who share the technical mind set and ideological predispositions of the United States and international financial institutions. The United States shapes the behaviour of these institutions profoundly, but not completely.

Gautam Sen examines the relationship between the United States and the GATT/WTO system. He addresses the crucial question of the likelihood that the United States will exit or through its behaviour undermine the multilateral trade organization in favour of regional or bilateral alternatives. Sen concludes that the probability of a US-inspired weakening of the WTO is low. He does argue that incentives for protectionism in the United States are strong and growing as a result of globalization and the changing international division of labour. The domestic political system gives voice to protectionist interests through a set of administrative and legal remedies that are reinforced by principles such as reciprocity and 'fair trade'. Yet he also points to various countervailing factors that diminish the likelihood of new legislation similar to the Smoot-Hawley Act of 1930. The growing power of US export interests and the effectiveness of the Executive in deflecting the protectionist tendencies in the US Congress are two such factors. Perhaps most importantly, he emphasizes the exceptional power and influence of the United States over the multilateral regime. The United States is a rule maker rather than a rule taker in the WTO. As such, it enjoys the power to bend the rules selectively to serve its interests, thereby diminishing the temptation to break away from the regime completely. Sen concludes that, since the WTO tends to reflect and reinforce US economic interests, the United States will continue in overall terms its efforts to comply with and generally strengthen the multilateral organization.

Stephen Hopgood broadens the analysis beyond economic and security multilateralism. Focusing on the issues of ozone depletion, biodiversity, and climate change, he argues that the evolution of US perspectives on environmental multilateralism reflects a fundamental split in the US policy arena. On one side are activists who seek to promote multilateral regulation of environmental issues and to deepen the US role therein. On the other are sceptics, hostile to state and international regulation of environmental issues and preferring market solutions. He suggests that, although sceptics have scored repeated short-term successes, the longer-term momentum favours the activists. The United States is gradually becoming more deeply embedded in multilateral environmental regimes.

In Part III, the study turns to American relations with regional organizations. It deals both with organizations of which the US is a member—for example, the ARF, NATO, the OAS—and with those where the US is not a member—for example, the EU and the OAU. Philip Nel's chapter, which begins this section, suggests that US policy towards Africa since decolonization has vacillated between accommodationist and rejectionist perspectives. During the Clinton administration, the pendulum swung towards accommodation in numerous initiatives to engage African states and their multilateral institutions. This engagement embraced economic reform and openness, democratization and human rights, and conflict management and resolution. Deliberate and sustained efforts were directed at strengthening regional and sub-regional institutions in this context. American neo-liberal preferences were accepted by newer African leaders. Although America's post-cold war agenda reflected the domestic political interests of the administration as well as Clinton's personal interest in Africa, its content was quite consistent with the effort to maintain and strengthen US neo-liberal hegemony. In this respect, it is no surprise that the transition to the Bush administration has involved little change in the basic thrust of US policy towards the region and its multilateral institutions.

In the next chapter, Ralph Cossa examines US behaviour as it encounters the relatively undemanding agendas of the ARF and APEC. Cossa argues that the fact that the ARF does not pose any challenge to long-standing US security arrangements in the region helps explain the retention of US support for this body, since it is America's key bilateral alliances that are at the foundation of its Asia-Pacific strategy. Nevertheless, he also notes that neither the ARF nor APEC could have been established without Washington's support and that, on balance, both organizations are seen as helpful rather than detrimental to certain US security and economic objectives, such as confidence-building and trade liberalization. Were the United States to find that these organizations did start to constrain US goals, then they would be rejected by Washington, Cossa argues, a position that places constraints on the future development of the agendas of such organizations.

The third chapter in this section, by David Haglund, takes up the relationship between the United States and multilateral organizations in Europe, in particular NATO. US relations with Europe, he suggests, are an indicator of the US commitment to multilateralism more generally. Haglund argues that the US approach to NATO has been driven by a combination of international structural factors—that is, the distribution of capabilities—and the key domestic factor of national character—that is, the liberal identity of the United States. These very same factors hold important consequences for NATO because the United States is the decisive actor in NATO. NATO is a hybrid. As a political entity it reflects the multilateralism that has its foundations in US national character. But as a military instrument it reflects the dominant power of the United States. The resulting tension in NATO was finessed more easily during the cold war, in the face of a common enemy. These tensions are more significant in the current unipolar system, which exaggerates both the incentives for the United States to act unilaterally and the frustration of European states who are less able to constrain the United States yet unwilling to act independently. Haglund expects NATO to become less rather than more important to the United States in the years ahead, and thus to matter less as a multilateral organization.

The next chapter, by Hal Klepak, focuses on American approaches to multilateralism in the Americas, a particularly interesting case given the longstanding preponderance of the United States in the region and the deep historical effort of the United States to construct and maintain multilateral institutions reflecting and reinforcing that preponderance. Klepak focuses on the evolution of security institutions—the Pan-American Union and the OAS—but includes substantial discussion of economic institutions, notably NAFTA and Mercosur. He establishes the significance of the distribution of power in the definition of multilateral institutions, agendas, and norms in the region, while underlining the fact that the less powerful have also seen multilateral institutions as a means of constraining the hegemon.

The conclusion summarizes our findings.

I

PERSPECTIVES ON THE US AND MULTILATERAL INTERNATIONAL ORGANIZATIONS

1

American Exceptionalism and International Organization: Lessons from the 1990s

Edward C. Luck

Despite the sweeping claims of some commentators, history did not start anew either with the turn of the millennium or with the terrorist assaults on the United States of 11 September 2001. In gauging the sources and course of American foreign policy, the lessons of the 1990s are as apt as ever. Though the war against terrorism underlined the value of the transatlantic alliance, it only temporarily muted European complaints about the unilateralist tendencies of the United States.[1] Surely the context has changed since September 11, but Washington policy-makers still have to weigh the often competing claims of exceptionalism and of pragmatism in deciding what mix of unilateral and multilateral policy options would best advance US priorities. In Afghanistan, as in Kosovo, both the superiority of American fire-power and the political advantage of acting in concert with others were once again demonstrated, as had been the case when former President George Bush called for the forceful expulsion of Iraqi forces from Kuwait in 1991.

More than a decade later, the patterns of American ambivalence toward multilateral rules and organizations, born of a deeply ingrained sense of exceptionalism, remain a defining characteristic of US foreign and security policy. A close look at the record of the 1990s provides a sense not only of how the divergent tendencies toward exceptionalism and pragmatism once interacted, but also of how they continue to shape US responses to a changed world. With the collapse of the Soviet Union and the end of the cold war, the 1990s offered unprecedented opportunities both for the expression of American exceptionalism within international organizations and for a testing of its limits. It was a time for building new international institutions while flouting the rules of old

---

[1] See Chris Patten, 'Jaw-jaw, Not War-war,' *Financial Times* (15 February 2002); Rosemary Righter, 'Why It Is Right to Join America's Fight', *The Spectator* (16 March 2002); and William Wallace, 'U.S. Unilateralism: A European Perspective', in Stewart Patrick and Shepard Forman (eds), *Multilateralism and U.S. Foreign Policy: Ambivalent Engagement* (Boulder, CO: Lynne Rienner, 2002).

ones, for preaching globalization while fearing its domestic implications. How these contrary impulses interacted to shape US policies toward international institutions during that turbulent decade is the subject of this chapter.

During these years, the United States proved more willing than any other major power to go it alone in international bodies, whether in denying Boutros Boutros-Ghali a second term as UN Secretary-General, declining to become a party to the Convention on the Rights of the Child, the Rome Statute for the International Criminal Court, the Ottawa Landmines Convention, and the Comprehensive Test Ban Treaty, refusing to pay a substantial share of its assessed UN dues, or demanding a long list of concessions from other member states before consenting to pay off a portion of its accumulated arrears to the world body. Yet it continued to make substantial voluntary payments to the UN system, voted for a record number of peacekeeping operations around the world, and supported a major expansion of international institutions in trade, arms control, and European security. With some justification, it was possible both for critics of the Clinton administration to charge that its embrace of 'assertive multilateralism' was insufficiently attentive to American national interests and for its partisans to charge the Republican-controlled Congress with espousing a 'new isolationism' as destructive to the prospects for international cooperation as anything seen since the Senate's rejection of the League of Nations four generations earlier.[2]

The lessons of the 1990s roller-coaster, however hard to decipher, do matter. Given America's unsurpassed power inside and outside of international bodies, how it expresses its deeply ingrained sense of exceptionalism and whether it resolves its internal political contradictions could well decide the course and character of international organization in the new century. Following a brief discussion of the nature of American exceptionalism, this chapter tracks: (1) the ups and downs of US policies toward UN peacekeeping over the course of the decade; (2) the contrasting politics of the 1994 decision to join the newly created World Trade Organization (WTO); and (3) US financial withholdings over these years and the steps towards partial payment of its arrears to the UN in 1999–2000.

---

[2] For an articulation of the philosophy of 'assertive multilateralism,' see the statement of Madeleine Albright, US Permanent Representative to the United Nations, before the Subcommittee on International Security, International Organizations, and Human Rights of the House Committee on Foreign Affairs, 24 June 1993. Among the scores of partisan critiques, see Bob Dole, 'Shaping America's Global Future', *Foreign Policy*, 98 (Spring 1995), John R. Bolton, 'The Creation, Fall, Rise, and Fall of the United Nations', in Ted Galen Carpenter (ed.), *Delusions of Grandeur: The United Nations and Global Intervention* (Washington, DC: Cato Institute, 1997), and Charles Krauthammer, 'A World Imagined', *The New Republic* (15 March 1999). For a blast at 'the new isolationists' in Congress, see remarks by Samuel R. Berger, Assistant to the President for National Security Affairs, 'American Power: Hegemony, Isolationism or Engagement', Council on Foreign Relations (21 October 1999).

These three stories caution against sweeping or simplistic explanations of what motivates US policy-making. Frequently, for example, the exceptionalist impulse can be seen bumping into the demands of pragmatism, another trait for which Americans are well known.[3] At no point did either impulse triumph across all three issue areas. Nor could either international or domestic politics long predominate without reference to one another. It is their interaction, in fact, that provides the central theme of this chapter.

1. Exceptionalism

What makes a member state exceptional? In the context of international organization, four related characteristics stand out:

(1) a willingness to go it alone on a variety of issues, along with apparent immunity to the pressures and criticisms of others;
(2) an assumption that its national values and practices are universally valid and its policy positions are moral and proper, not just expedient;
(3) a strong tendency to look inwards, to domestic political considerations and processes, when determining how to act in international forums, in some cases coupled with a willingness to adopt national legislation that contradicts the rules and responsibilities imposed by international arrangements; and
(4) a belief by national policy-makers and legislators that they have other options for pursuing their nation's interests and that acting through multilateral institutions is only an option, not an obligation.

Exceptional states are therefore less willing than others to compromise in multilateral forums for the sake of approval or to maintain consensus.

Under these criteria, four states stood out as exceptional at different points during the UN's first half century: the Soviet Union, China, France, and the United States. Each combined a distinct political culture with an allergy to certain issues on the UN agenda. All were permanent members of the Security Council. Three were large continental powers. And each has disputed the amount of money it has been assessed by the UN.[4]

---

[3] For a nation of America's unsurpassed power, what appears to others to be exceptional behaviour in multilateral bodies may actually be quite pragmatic in terms of advancing certain national goals, at least in the short run.

[4] Edward C. Luck, *Mixed Messages: American Politics and International Organization, 1919–1999* (Washington, DC: Brookings Institution Press for the Century Foundation, 1999), 233–8, 295. Given its economic difficulties, the Russian Federation has achieved a reduction in its assessment rate to just 1.077 per cent of the UN regular budget in 2000, while China did not top 1 per cent until 2001. General Assembly resolutions 52/215 of 22 December 1997 and 55/5B-F of 22 January 2001.

So what makes the American brand of exceptionalism special? As I noted in *Mixed Messages*:

The scope and reach of American power, as well as of its interests, are without precedent. Combined with deep strains of idealism and ideology, shaped by a singular history, and conditioned by a political system defined by the separation of powers and by partisan differences over foreign policy, American relations with the League of Nations and the United Nations have proven more persistently problematic than those of any other nation, large or small. For most Americans, moreover, the sense of exceptionalism has been so much a part of their outlook, values, and national character that it has received only occasional question or critical comment.[5]

Unlike the other exceptional member states, the position of the United States is more exceptional in the real world outside international meeting halls than within them. At this point, no other country comes close to matching the US in any of the core components of national power, and in recent years the gap has widened.[6] By spurring a resurgence of national unity and sense of purpose, the terrorist attacks on the United States of September 2001, if anything, have reconfirmed the centrality of American power.

The separation of powers in Washington and Congress's readiness to trump major international initiatives and treaties are also unique. During the 1990s, the results were inconsistent policy outcomes and an embarrassing disjunction between Washington's power and its ability to act decisively. The split between the Clinton administration and the Republican-led Congress was so sharp that at times it was hard to tell who was speaking for America.[7] Adding to the impression of divided government, Senator Jesse Helms, when Chairman of the Senate Foreign Relations Committee, told the UN Security Council in January 2000 that 'we in Congress are the sole guardians of the American taxpayers' money' and that 'we have not only a right, but a responsibility, to insist on specific [UN] reforms in exchange for their investment'. Were the UN to reject these conditions, he warned, 'it would mark the beginning of the end of US support for the United Nations'.[8] It is only when the US is confronted by an imminent external

[5] Luck, *Mixed Messages*, 15–16.
[6] See Stephen G. Brooks and William C. Wohlforth, 'American Primacy in Perspective', *Foreign Affairs*, 81/4 (2002). Kenneth N. Waltz argues, however, that 'the present condition of international politics is unnatural' and that the relatively modest US population 'cannot sustain present international burdens indefinitely'. 'Globalization and American Power', *The National Interest*, 59 (Spring 2000), 46–56. Lawrence F. Kaplan, noting that many of the 'declinists' predicting the demise of American power are conservative Republicans, warns that these 'false prophets in our midst' represent 'the most formidable challenge to that power.' 'Fall Guys: Guess Who Hates America? Conservatives', *The New Republic* (26 June 2000), 22–5.
[7] Citing UN arrears as one example, Sebastian Mallaby cautioned that the presidency had been so weakened by its struggles with Congress that it could no longer pursue a coherent foreign policy. 'The Bullied Pulpit', *Foreign Affairs*, 79/1 (2000). Michael Hirsh placed much of the blame for decreased US support for the UN on what he saw as a weak-kneed Clinton administration. 'The Fall Guy', *Foreign Affairs*, 78/6 (1999).
[8] Address by Senator Jesse Helms Before the United Nations Security Council, 20 January 2000, available at www.senate.gov/~helms/FedGov/UNSpeech/unspeech.html;

threat, such as terrorism, that partisan and executive-Congressional differences tend to fade, only to reappear when the threat recedes.

American actions in multilateral bodies—and those of other exceptional member states—cannot be explained without reference to the domestic determinants of foreign policy. The downturn in US relations with the UN in the 1990s could not have been predicted on the basis of international events. In essence, the US turned its back on the world body just as its economic and political principles had finally gained ascendancy in UN agendas, programmes, and priorities. Paradoxically, Congress failed to withhold funds during the 1970s and early 1980s, when American values were under persistent siege in the General Assembly and when management and financial reforms were even more needed. Through the years, Republicans in Congress have been most sceptical of international organization and of US multilateral diplomacy when Democrats occupied the White House.[9] More than other people, Americans remain deeply divided about the benefits and risks inherent in participation in global organizations.[10] This polarization has given an ambivalent and mottled appearance to US policies towards these bodies, while making it much more difficult to sustain anything approaching a coherent strategy in them. Delegates from other member states continue to search in vain for a consistent line or an organizing theme to explain what the world's most powerful nation wants and expects from their collective intergovernmental bodies.

In focusing on domestic determinants of policy, however, this chapter also highlights ways in which beltway politics have been affected by global developments, by the actions of other states, and by the performance of the international organizations themselves. US policies toward peacekeeping, the creation of the WTO, and UN arrears are products of the interactions between these two levels of politics—domestic and international—and between the urges toward exceptionalism and pragmatism.

2. Peacekeeping

The end of the cold war permitted an unprecedented expansion of UN peacekeeping efforts, whether measured in missions, soldiers, or expenditures. The

see also Barbara Crossette, 'Helms, in Visit To U.N., Offers Harsh Message', *New York Times* (21 January 2000).

[9] For example, Republicans in Congress went along with votes to make substantial payments of arrears to the UN during the two Bush administrations rather than during the two terms of the Clinton administration that separated the two Republican White Houses.

[10] Cross-national comparisons of public opinion surveys concerning the UN suggest that, while the aggregate views of Americans are quite similar to those in other developed countries, the divide between supporters and hard-core sceptics is much wider in the US. See Luck, *Mixed Messages*, 35–9.

United States enthusiastically supported this trend. A decade after the last new peacekeeping operation, 1988 saw observer missions approved for the Soviet withdrawal from Afghanistan (UNGOMAP) and for the Iran-Iraq border (UNIIMOG). The pace quickened the next year with new peacekeeping operations in Angola (UNAVEM I), Namibia (UNTAG), and Central America (ONUCA). Observer missions were undertaken in Nicaragua (ONUVEN) in 1989 and Haiti in 1990, followed by five new peacekeeping operations in 1991: El Salvador (ONUSAL), Kuwait-Iraq border (UNIKOM), Western Sahara (MINURSO), Angola (UNAVEM II), and Cambodia (UNAMIC). Added in 1992 were major peacekeeping operations in the former Yugoslavia (UNPROFOR), Cambodia (UNTAC), and Mozambique (ONUMOZ), and the deceptively modest UNOSOM I in Somalia. All told, 16 observer or peacekeeping missions were launched during the five-year period between 1988 and 1992.

Two other features of this period stand out: (1) all of this unprecedented activity came with a Republican in the White House, and (2) none of these steps generated much Congressional or public controversy. Washington even welcomed UN peacekeeping operations on the ground in Central America, long regarded as Monroe Doctrine territory from which transatlantic interventions should be excluded. The first Bush administration undertook a series of steps to strengthen UN peacekeeping capacities.[11] Though quite prepared to use force unilaterally if necessary, it placed a high priority on gaining Security Council authorization for the use of force to expel Iraqi forces from Kuwait, seeing this as a means of rallying support both from a Democratic Congress and from potential coalition partners.[12] Indeed, popular enthusiasm for the United Nations peaked following the success of the Security Council-authorized enforcement operation in 1991.[13] Support for the UN rose most markedly among conservatives, Republicans, whites, and men, traditionally the groups most sceptical of the world body.[14]

The incoming Clinton administration, despite some signs of creeping unease on Capitol Hill, had reason to expect that its embrace of UN peacekeeping could be built on the political foundation laid by its Republican predecessor. After all, one of the last international initiatives of the Bush administration had been to make a unilateral commitment of American forces

---

[11] Many of his administration's initiatives to strengthen peacekeeping capacity were laid out in President Bush's speech to the UN General Assembly on 21 September 1992.

[12] George Bush and Brent Scowcroft, *A World Transformed* (New York: Knopf, 1998), 356, 415–16, 446, 491. On the first Bush administration's willingness to use force unilaterally in Panama and the Gulf, see Edward C. Luck, 'The United States, International Organizations, and the Quest for Legitimacy', in Patrick and Forman (eds), *Multilateralism*.

[13] For a detailed comparison of public opinion data over time and by country, see Luck, *Mixed Messages*, 260–71, 34–40.

[14] See the results of 1989 and 1992 Roper polls conducted for the United Nations Association of the USA (UNA-USA), as analysed in Jeffrey Laurenti, *Directions and Dilemmas in Collective Security: Reflections from a Global Roundtable* (New York: UNA-USA, 1992), 18–19.

to Somalia—a place where the US had no strategic interests—to take over the protection of relief supplies from the overwhelmed UN operation. Most of the new peacekeeping operations proceeded reasonably smoothly during the early months of the new administration, but the missions in Bosnia-Herzegovina and Somalia encountered serious obstacles and growing doubts in Congress. In some cases, parties to the conflicts may have been tempted to test the mettle of an inexperienced administration preoccupied with domestic issues. Even a more determined and seasoned president might well have become frustrated by the intransigence of the parties, the complexity of the crises, and the inadequacy of the resources available for the job. Many of these factors are beyond Washington's control, but the president and Congress can shape the way the public perceives what is at stake and what are the nation's options. It is at this juncture that domestic politics come most prominently into play, as the president and Congress decide how to react to unfavourable developments overseas. In this case, both the White House and Congress allowed the future of peacekeeping to become mired in partisan and Executive-Congressional differences. While it would be tempting to blame the CNN effect and public opinion, following the gruesome television pictures of American Rangers being dragged through the streets of Mogadishu, in truth the Clinton administration had already started to back-pedal months before the October 1993 Mogadishu disaster.[15]

During the presidential campaign, candidate Clinton had called for the establishment of a small UN force for rapid deployment in a crisis to deter a potential aggressor, such as on the Kuwait side of the border with Iraq in the summer of 1990.[16] Upon taking office, the President called for an inter-agency study of peacekeeping options and capacities.[17] He also approved, in 1993, US support for six more peace operations: observer missions in Georgia (UNOMIG), Uganda-Rwanda (UNOMUR), and Liberia (UNOMIL); peacekeeping deployments in Haiti (UNMIH) and Rwanda (UNAMIR); and, fatefully, a more robust Chapter VII operation in Somalia (UNOSOM II).[18] None of the undertakings was on a large scale individually or initially. But, when added to the ongoing UN operations scattered around the world, including high-cost, high-risk missions in the former Yugoslavia and Cambodia, the cumulative

---

[15] The Clinton administration's initial steps on peacekeeping are described in Ivo H. Daalder, 'Knowing When to Say No: The Development of US Policy for Peacekeeping', in William J. Durch (ed.), *UN Peacekeeping, American Politics, and the Uncivil Wars of the 1990s* (New York: St Martin's Press, 1996) and Michael G. MacKinnon, *The Evolution of US Peacekeeping Under Clinton* (London: Frank Cass, 2000).

[16] Remarks Prepared for Delivery by Governor Bill Clinton (New York: Foreign Policy Association, 1 April 1992).

[17] The review addressed four basic questions: 'When to engage in peace operations?; Who should conduct peace operations—the UN, regional organizations, or ad hoc coalitions?; How can UN peacekeeping be fixed?; and How can the US system to support peace operations be improved?', Daalder, 'Knowing When to Say No', 36, 42–4.

[18] For authoritative information, see United Nations, *The Blue Helmets: A Review of United Nations Peace-keeping*, 3rd edn (New York: United Nations Department of Public Information, 1996).

weight began to worry many Americans. Few US combat forces were involved on the ground, but in 1993, for the first time, Congress was billed over $1 billion for UN peacekeeping.[19]

A number of commentators from both parties began to question the priorities and strategies of the Clinton administration.[20] They contended that the sole superpower was obsessed with developments in places of marginal strategic significance, while relations with other major powers languished. Rather than easing Washington's burdens, multilateral cooperation seemed to be dragging American power and prestige into an unending series of distant and intractable disputes.

Meanwhile, the administration's quick review of peacekeeping policies had itself become a victim of the growing controversies, its completion delayed time and again. Addressing the General Assembly for the first time weeks *before* the Mogadishu incident, President Clinton already sounded sceptical: 'The United Nations simply cannot become engaged in every one of the world's conflicts. If the American people are to say yes to U.N. peacekeeping, the United Nations must know when to say no.'[21]

Coming from one of only five governments with the capacity to say 'no' to new Security Council mandates, the statement had a perverse ring. The President also called for a lowering of US peacekeeping assessments and for a series of measures to give the world body 'the technical means to run a modern world-class peacekeeping operation'.

By this point, it was all too evident that the President was seeking to distance himself from the peacekeeping tool he had so recently championed.[22] With the deaths of the Rangers in the Mogadishu firefight in October 1993, the President's first inclination was to blame the UN, even though the Rangers were acting fully under the US chain of command.[23] By falsely blaming the incompetence of UN

---

[19] William J. Durch, 'Keeping the Peace: Politics and Lessons of the 1990s', in Durch (ed.), *UN Peacekeeping*, 14.

[20] See, for instance, Michael Mandelbaum, 'Foreign Policy as Social Work', *Foreign Affairs*, 75/1 (1996); Stephen John Stedman, 'The New Interventionists', *Foreign Affairs*, 72/1 (1993); Paul D. Wolfowitz, 'Clinton's First Year', *Foreign Affairs*, 73/1 (1994); and Linda B. Miller, 'The Clinton Years: Reinventing US Foreign Policy?' *International Affairs*, 70/4 (1994).

[21] Address by President Clinton to the 48th Session of the United Nations General Assembly, 27 September 1993.

[22] For a UN perspective on these simultaneous crises, see William Shawcross, *Deliver Us from Evil: Peacekeepers, Warlords, and a World of Endless Conflict* (New York: Simon and Schuster, 2000), 82–123.

[23] The most detailed and graphic account of the incident can be found in Mark Bowden, *Black Hawk Down: A Story of Modern War* (New York: Atlantic Monthly Press, 1999). For the US-UN politics at this point, see Stanley Meisner, 'Dateline U.N.: A New Hammarskjöld?', *Foreign Policy*, 98 (1995). See also Robert B. Oakley, 'Using the United Nations to Advance U.S. Interests', in Ted Galen Carpenter (ed.), *Delusions of Grandeur* (Washington, DC: Cato Institute, 1997); Robert Oakley and John Hirsch, *Somalia and Operation Restore Hope* (Washington, DC: U.S. Institute for Peace, 1995); and Senate Armed Services Committee, U.S. Military Operations in Somalia, Hearings, 12 May 1994, 103d Cong., 2nd sess. (US Government Printing Office, 1994).

commanders, he opened the door to the UN's most strident critics. The notion of putting US troops under the command of foreign officers had been an extremely sensitive domestic political issue since the conception of the League of Nations, and no president, not even Woodrow Wilson or Franklin Roosevelt, had agreed to relinquish US command authority.[24]

The administration's tortured review of peacekeeping, Presidential Decision Directive (PDD) 25 of May 1994, firmly stressed the difference between temporary operational control by UN commanders and the integrity of the US chain of command, which is never broken.[25] The technical distinctions and lukewarm language of PDD 25, however, did little to quell the political firestorm that the President had helped to fuel in the first place. During the autumn 1994 Congressional campaign, the Republicans' 'Contract with America' included a promise never to put US troops under a foreign command.

In this case, an international event had sparked a domestic political reaction, but it was Washington politics that had provided the lens, albeit distorted, through which the events in Mogadishu were perceived and interpreted. These warped lessons then almost derailed the Haiti mission and certainly discouraged an effective response to the genocide in Rwanda the following spring.[26] America's foot-dragging as the death toll rose in Rwanda was justified by some as a demonstration of PDD 25 in action—or, more accurately, inaction. At this point, President Clinton decided to sign legislation unilaterally imposing a 25 per cent ceiling on US peacekeeping payments to the UN, well below the 31.7 per cent then assessed by the world body.[27] Acknowledging that this move represented a violation of US treaty obligations, the President nevertheless decided to forgo his option of vetoing the bill, thereby accelerating the accumulation of arrears to the UN.

American support for UN peacekeeping, therefore, had already begun to ebb by the spring of 1994, *before* the Republicans took control of both houses of Congress the following January.[28] With the Republican victory of 1994, many

[24] For a discussion of the historical roots of this sensitivity, see Luck, *Mixed Messages*, 184–93.   [25] Luck, *Mixed Messages*, 190–1.

[26] The best account of the events surrounding the Haiti operation can be found in David Malone, *Decision-Making in the UN Security Council: The Case of Haiti, 1990–1997* (Oxford: Clarendon Press, 1998). The most compelling assessments of the international community's failings in Rwanda are in the *Report of the Independent Inquiry into the Actions of the United Nations During the 1994 Genocide in Rwanda* (New York: United Nations, 15 December 1999); Philip Gourevitch, *We Wish to Inform You That Tomorrow We Will Be Killed With Our Families: Stories From Rwanda* (New York: Farrar, Straus, and Giroux, 1998); and Samantha Power, *'A Problem from Hell': America and the Age of Genocide* (New York: Basic Books, 2002).

[27] Public Law 103–26, signed 30 April 1994. Peacekeeping assessments, which are higher for the five permanent members of the Security Council than their regular budget assessment, vary somewhat over time.

[28] This was only the third time in the twentieth century that the Republicans controlled Congress with a Democrat in the White House. US relations with international organizations were problematic each time. In 1920–1, the Senate frustrated Woodrow Wilson's dream of American leadership in the League of Nations. In 1948, the new

commentators saw the spectre of a rebirth of isolationism,[29] or at least what Senator Helms' aide Marc A. Thiessen praised as 'old-fashioned American exceptionalism'.[30] Yet what is most striking, in retrospect, is how little of the exceptionalist legislation introduced by the new majority actually became law. Somewhat different bills inspired by the spirit of the Contract with America were introduced into the House (the National Security Revitalization Act) and the Senate (the Peace Powers Act).[31] While the former passed the House, the two bills were never reconciled or presented to the President, who had already conceded an unprecedented degree of oversight to the Congress on peace-keeping matters in any case.

While the sceptics in Congress wanted to increase Congressional oversight to put the brakes on what they saw as the uncontrolled expansion of UN peace-keeping ambitions and to limit the exposure of American forces in hostile environments, they did not seek to block all new peacekeeping initiatives. As a first step toward rethinking US peacekeeping policies, they commissioned a series of studies by the General Accounting Office (GAO) and the Congressional Research Service (CRS).[32] At a 1997 hearing on the results of these studies, the Chairman of the House Committee on International Relations, Benjamin A. Gilman of New York, called on the permanent members of the Security Council to 'ensure that the United Nations conducts only peacekeeping and not peacemaking operations, and that they be done on a cost-efficient basis fully consistent with their mandate', and on the administration 'to more closely review the open-ended commitments and the lack of clear exit criteria now prevailing in a number of longstanding U.N. operations'.[33]

Republican leadership in the Senate killed President Truman's plan for the creation of an International Trade Organization (ITO) only three years after the Senate had over-whelmingly agreed to US participation in the UN.

[29] See, for example, Arthur Schlesinger, Jr, 'Back to the Womb? Isolationism's Renewed Threat', *Foreign Affairs*, 74/4 (1995) and Robert S. Greenberger, 'Dateline Capitol Hill: The New Majority's Foreign Policy', *Foreign Policy*, 101 (Winter 1995).

[30] Marc A. Thiessen, 'The Candidates' Foreign Policies: It's Bush's American Exceptionalism Versus Gore's Liberal Multilateralism', *The Weekly Standard* (12 June 2000), 16.

[31] For a fuller discussion of these legislative initiatives, see House Committee on National Security, *H.R. 7—National Security Revitalization Act*, Hearings, 19, 25, 27 January 1995, 104th Cong., 1st sess. (US Government Printing Office, 1996); House Committee on International Relations, Hearing and Markup, *National Security Revitalization Act*, 24, 27, 30, 31 January 1995, 104th Cong., 1st sess. (US Government Printing Office, 1995); and Senate Committee on Foreign Relations, Hearing, *The Peace Powers Act (S. 5) and the National Security Revitalization Act (H.R. 7)*, 21 March 1995, 104th Cong., 1st sess. (US Government Printing Office, 1996).

[32] For three examples see House Committee on International Relations, *Does U.N. Peacekeeping Serve U.S. Interests?*, Hearing, 9 April 1997, 105th Cong., 1st sess. (US Government Printing Office, 1997) and House Committee on International Relations, *Does U.N. Peacekeeping Serve U.S. Interests?—Part II: Administration Witnesses*, Hearing, 17 April 1997, 105th Cong., 1st sess. (US Government Printing Office, 1997).

[33] 9 April 1997 Hearing, 3.

The genocide in Rwanda posed a considerable dilemma for all but truly isolationist Republicans as well as for the Clinton administration. For example,
Representative Christopher H. Smith of New Jersey convened hearings in 1996
and 1998 'to examine the causes and possible solutions of one of the greatest
and longest-lasting humanitarian crises in the history of the world'.[34] The testimony from experts, who warned of the likelihood of further rounds of violence if the US and the UN did not become more engaged, had to be sobering.
When the Subcommittee on Africa held hearings in February 2000 on the proposed peacekeeping force for the Democratic Republic of the Congo,
Chairman Edward R. Royce of California declared that the operation should
proceed despite the evident risks, because 'in 1994, the international community sat on the sidelines as nearly one million men, women and children were
slaughtered in Rwanda'.[35] Likewise, Congress's reaction to the May 2000 debacle
in Sierra Leone, when hundreds of UN peacekeepers were taken hostage
by the rebels of the Revolutionary United Front (RUF), was remarkably
temperate—no doubt in part because American forces were not involved.[36]
While Chairman Helms cautioned that 'the United Nations can ill afford
any future failures', the July 2000 Senate Foreign Relations Committee
Hearings on Africa focused on how to strengthen, not scuttle, the peacekeeping operations there.[37]

Washington's views of peacekeeping remain mixed: cautious but markedly
less negative than in the mid-1990s.[38] The US did put its forces on the ground
in Bosnia-Herzegovina and Kosovo, though only under a NATO command
structure and with conservative rules of engagement. In late 1999 and the first
half of 2000, the US consented to new UN peacekeeping initiatives in East
Timor, Sierra Leone, and the Democratic Republic of the Congo and to
an enlargement of the UN mission in southern Lebanon, as well as indicating
support for a likely mission on the contested Ethiopian-Eritrean border.

[34] House Subcommittee on International Operations and Human Rights, *Rwanda:
Genocide and the Continuing Cycle of Violence*, Hearing, 5 May 1998, 105th Cong., 2nd sess.
(US Government Printing Office, 1998).
[35] House Subcommittee on Africa, *Peacekeeping in the Congo*, Hearing, 16 February
2000, 106th Cong., 2nd sess. (US Government Printing Office, 2000).
[36] A Senate appropriations subcommittee chair, Judd Gregg (R-NH), initially blocked
the transfer of funds to four peacekeeping missions because of his objection to including RUF leaders in the Sierra Leone government, but he released the funds when assured
that this was government policy. See Tim Weiner, 'G.O.P. Senator Frees Millions for U.N.
Mission in Sierra Leone', *New York Times* (7 June 2000).
[37] Hearing Before the Senate Committee on Foreign Relations, *The United Nations
Policy in Africa*, 12 July 2000, 106th Cong., 2nd sess.
[38] In Afghanistan, Washington has preferred a mix of unilateral, coalition, and UN
measures, with the latter limited to post-conflict nation-building. More broadly, in mid-
2002 the Bush administration's strong opposition to putting US peacekeepers under the
jurisdiction of the International Criminal Court led it to veto a renewal of the UN's mandate in Bosnia-Herzegovina, though US participation in the NATO-led SFOR operation
was not affected. Colum Lynch, 'Dispute Threatens U.N. Role in Bosnia; U.S. Wields Veto
in Clash Over War Crimes', *New York Times* (30 June 2002).

The new burst of peacekeeping activity led to a rapid rise in the number of UN deployed peacekeepers—including soldiers, observers, and police—from a low point of 12,084 in June 1999 to 36,605 in June 2000 and to 47,575 in October 2001, the highest level since November 1995.[39] How to share equitably the costs of these missions, however, remains controversial, despite General Assembly agreement in December 2000 that the US assessment would be cut from 30.3 per cent to 25 per cent, as demanded by the Helms-Biden legislation. Ominously, the bill would ban further arrears payments if the UN reaches an agreement with *any* member state under Article 43 of the Charter, which calls for the earmarking of stand-by forces.

During the 1990s, two opposing trends emerged concerning American politics and UN peacekeeping. Over the first half of the decade, international ambitions had to be trimmed to fit US domestic political realities. Over the second half, the more partisan and rejectionist elements in Congress had to reconcile their views both to the demands of international events and to their new responsibilities as leaders of Congress. This suggests that the interplay between domestic and international factors is a continuous one, with neither level able to predominate for long without reference to the other.

3. World Trade Organization

In the 1940s, the US threw its support behind the creation of the UN but forsook the new architecture for world trade. In the 1990s, the opposite occurred. During the closing months of the Second World War, a Democratic administration, with bipartisan support from a Democrat-led Congress, negotiated and ratified the United Nations Charter, the most ambitious multilateral undertaking in history. Just three years later, and as Chapter 5 in this volume details, a then-Republican Congress killed the new International Trade Organization (ITO), presented by President Truman as an essential component of the new global economic structure. In 1994, with support for the UN ebbing and partisanship rising on Capitol Hill, Congress, with strong Republican backing, approved the creation of a powerful World Trade Organization. The Republican leadership—most critically Bob Dole—chose not only to throw its weight behind the WTO but to allow its consideration by the lame-duck Democratic Congress in late 1994. If domestic political considerations doomed

---

[39] *Monthly Summary of Military and Civilian Police Contribution to United Nations Operations*, United Nations Department of Peacekeeping Operations, at www.un.org/Depts/dpko/dpko/contributors/31-10-01.pdf. The totals include soldiers, military observers, and police. Though fewer than 2 per cent of these peacekeepers were Americans, even fewer were provided by any of the other four permanent members of the Security Council.

the ITO, then they worked, on balance, to save its functional successor, the WTO, more than two generations later.

Since the early days of the Republic, trade issues have been every bit as contentious as questions of peace and security. Battles between free-traders and protectionists have often, in times of peace, taken centre stage in the national political debate and even defined presidential contests. William Jennings Bryan, the former populist presidential candidate, opposed the League of Nations in part because of his fears that it would interfere with domestic economic freedoms and development. More recently, the third-party candidacies of Ross Perot, Pat Buchanan, Pat Robertson, and Ralph Nader were propelled by strong anti-globalization platforms. So the passage of the WTO, which followed the divisive struggle over the North American Free Trade Agreement (NAFTA) by only a year,[40] cannot be attributed to its having less political salience than peacekeeping issues. In fact, for the public as a whole trade arguably cuts much deeper as a domestic pocketbook issue, given its diffuse effects, than does the more distant question of peacekeeping.

Americans on the whole have retained positive feelings towards both peacekeeping and the WTO through all of these intra-beltway squabbles.[41] Two months after the disruptions at the Seattle ministerial conference, respondents to a February 2000 Pew Research Center poll said by a 62 per cent to 22 per cent margin that participation in the WTO was 'good for the United States'.[42] However, US policies toward international institutions are not decided through public opinion surveys.[43] If they had been, then there would have been no accumulation of arrears or the retreat from peacekeeping in the mid-1990s. Moreover, while the survey numbers still look quite good for the WTO despite the anti-globalization protests, they have also been strong for peacekeeping, even during the difficult months following the Mogadishu incident. So polls do not explain why there was political backing for the WTO and not for peacekeeping during these critical years.

---

[40] NAFTA came into effect on 1 January 1994, following approval in the House on 17 November 1993 by a vote of 234 to 200 and in the Senate on 20 November 1993 by a margin of 61 to 38.

[41] For extensive poll results on peacekeeping, foreign assistance, and, to a lesser extent, international trade, see Steven Kull and I. M. Destler, *Misreading the Public: The Myth of a New Isolationism* (Washington, DC: Brookings Institution Press, 1999).

[42] Among the most supportive groups were more affluent and younger people. Democrats (63%) and Republicans (62%) were equally supportive, as were those in households with union members (65% to 31%). See 'Doubts About China, Concerns About Jobs: Post-Seattle Support for WTO', *Pew Research Center Report* (March 2000), at www.people-press.org/feb00rpt2.htm. Also see Richard K. Herrmann, Philip E. Tetlock, and Matthew N. Diascro, 'How Americans Think About Trade: Reconciling Conflicts Among Money, Power, and Principles', *International Studies Quarterly*, 45 (2001) and Steve Kull, 'Public Attitudes Toward Multilateralism,' in Patrick and Forman (eds), *Multilateralism*, 109–11.

[43] See Jeremy D. Rosner, 'The Know-Nothings Know Something,' *Foreign Policy*, 101 (Winter 1995/96).

Among the reasons why the WTO fared better than peacekeeping are those set out below, which move from the more international to the more domestic factors:

1. *Perceptions of success.* What works? Most members of Congress have had an unduly negative impression of the results of peacekeeping operations through the years, as the failures stand out and the successes fade from view. Their expectations and standards for success have been, in most cases, unrealistically high. The international trade regime, on the other hand, has been broadly supported by both the public and legislators as an engine of growth and a key to prosperity. The US has prospered, in the aggregate, under its rules, though sceptics, such as Ralph Nader, have contended that some have benefited much more than others.[44]

The main argument against the WTO, in fact, was that it was not needed because its predecessor, the General Agreement on Tariffs and Trade (GATT), was working well. In testifying against the WTO, Pat Choate, later to become Ross Perot's running mate, asserted that GATT had succeeded as 'a contractual relationship . . . based on power relationships' and that it should not be replaced by a more formal international organization in which the US would have less clout.[45] Republican Senators Strom Thurmond, Jesse Helms, and Larry Craig—no fans of multilateralism—called for splitting the legislation so that GATT could be extended without approval of the WTO, 'a powerful new international organization' that should be considered a treaty requiring a two-thirds vote in the Senate.[46]

2. *National interests.* Most peacekeeping missions are perceived as having indirect or marginal impact on US national interests. During the cold war, the danger of escalation seemed higher and the likelihood of US forces serving as peacekeepers was lower. By the mid-1990s, the risks of US involvement seemed higher and the potential benefits lower. The way global trade is managed, however, directly affects Congressional constituents. There is no ambivalence about the desirability of trade or, especially, of increasing exports. Testifying about the Uruguay Round, of which the WTO was a part, former Republican Congressman Bill Frenzel told his former colleagues that 'what you are looking at is a lot of money for the United States . . . If the NAFTA, the critical symbol, was for show, Uruguay is for dough'.[47]

---

[44] Among the dissenters, see the testimonies of Charles McMillon, 96–113 and Lori Wallach, 215–36, Senate Committee on Commerce, Science, and Transportation, *S.2467, GATT Implementing Legislation*, Hearings, 4, 5, 13, 14, 18 October, and 14, 15 November 1994, 103rd Cong., 2nd sess. (US Government Printing Office, 1994).

[45] House Committee on Ways and Means, *The World Trade Organization*, Hearing, 10 June 1994, 103rd Cong., 2nd sess. (US Government Printing Office, 1994), 97–100. Similarly, Michael Lind, another conservative commentator, suggested that GATT and NATO have been the two most successful of the post-war organizations, *S.2467, GATT Implementing Legislation*, Hearing, 118–21.

[46] Letter from Senators Strom Thurmond, Jesse Helms, and Larry Craig to Senator Robert Dole concerning GATT implementing legislation, 10 November 1994.

[47] House Committee on Ways and Means, *The World Trade Organization*, Hearing, 137.

Free trade is treated as a matter of US national security. As Charlene Barshefsky, the US Trade Representative, phrased it:

In the 1930s, they had seen a cycle of trade protection and retaliation, beginning with the Smoot-Hawley Tariff in the United States and continued through European colonial preference schemes, which had cut global trade nearly 70 per cent. Within a few years, the world was transformed into something like a series of island economies, deepening the Depression, intensifying political tensions, and contributing to the political upheavals of the era.[48]

According to Newt Gingrich, 'the United States withdrawing from this agreement would be the economic equivalent of nuclear war'.[49]

3. *It's the economy, stupid.* Bill Clinton's winning slogan was not lost on the members of Congress from either party. In comparison, peacekeeping appeared unpleasant, inconclusive, and politically marginal, while trade was seen as central to the redefined priorities of the post-cold war era. For Clinton's political balance sheet, whatever losses were incurred in Mogadishu or Bosnia could be more than compensated by gains in trade and prosperity. The President was building a new international architecture, but his legacy was to be tied to NAFTA, WTO, and the Internet rather than to the old-fashioned UN peace and security agenda. In any case, the immediate step was to build a record of accomplishment on which to get re-elected. Potential Republican opponents in the 1996 race, like Bob Dole and Newt Gingrich, preferred to go along with the new agenda rather than to be left on the wrong side of the curve.[50]

4. *Confidence.* Americans are supremely confident of their economic, as well as their military, prowess. Given fair rules or free trade, they believe that they can out-produce and out-trade any competitor. As Republican Senator Robert Packwood put it in announcing his support of the pact, 'the United States, on a level playing field, can beat anybody'.[51] President Clinton strongly agreed: 'this agreement requires all trading nations to play by the same rules. And since the United States has the most productive and competitive economy in the

[48] US Trade Representative Charlene Barshefsky, Remarks on US Trade Policy and the WTO, 2 March 2000.
[49] House Committee on Ways and Means, *The World Trade Organization*, Hearing, 135.
[50] More recently, Bill Archer, Texas Republican and Chairman of the House Committee on Ways and Means, commented: 'try to imagine what it would be like if the U.S. was no longer a member of the World Trade Organization. A U.S. without trade would be a nation with 12 million less jobs and millions more displaced or laid off.' Hearing Before the Committee on Ways and Means, US House of Representatives, 'The Future of the World Trade Organization', 106th Cong., 2nd sess., 30 March 2000, 5. A bill to compel the US withdrawal from the WTO was defeated by a 363 to 56 vote in the House in June 2000 (House Joint Resolution 90, 'Withdrawing the Approval of the United States from the Agreement Establishing the World Trade Organization', 6 March 2000).
[51] Remarks by President Bill Clinton, Senator Robert Dole, Senator Daniel Moynihan, Senator Robert Packwood, and Ambassador Mickey Kantor on support for the GATT, White House, Washington, DC, 23 November 1994.

world, that is good news for our workers and our future.'[52] Members of Congress from both parties had more confidence in the President's steward-ship of global economic issues than of geo-political ones. The contrast with peacekeeping—an arena in which neither Congress nor the President felt self-assured—could not be sharper.

5. *Constituencies.* Both peacekeeping and the WTO have their share of critics; the difference is that only one has politically active and influential friends. Some missions, as in Haiti or the former Yugoslavia, have pockets of public support. But the advocacy communities for generic peacekeeping, as for most UN activities, tend to be transnational in scope. They neither carry much clout in the US nor do they orient their arguments to show how US interests would benefit from specific peacekeeping missions.[53]

The debate over the WTO, in contrast, involved powerful interest groups cap-able of mobilizing their members, buying media space and time, conducting public outreach campaigns, lobbying Congress regularly, and placing pro or con advertisements in the next election campaign.[54] Among those testifying for the WTO were the US Chamber of Commerce, the National Association of Manufacturers, and the Consumers Union, as well as prominent economists and trade lawyers. Among its influential detractors was an unusually broad array of labour, consumer, and environmental groups. The WTO was a political issue of real consequence that could not be sloughed off to a legislative assistant. In announcing his support, Bob Dole, the Senate Republican leader, claimed that he had been 'getting about 2,000 phone calls a day' on the subject.[55] In contrast, a few years later Republican Senator Richard G. Lugar, a UN supporter, com-plained that his constituents were not 'beating down the doors for the United States to pay its share at the U.N. There's even grudging toleration of it'.[56]

6. *Parties divided, partisanship ebbs.* The politics of trade issues cut across party lines. President Clinton's centrist inclinations and impassioned advocacy of free trade, economic growth, and productivity put him on the opposite side of this issue from his natural allies in big labour. He brought big business, a traditional pillar of the Republican Party, to his side. Consumer and environmental critics

---

[52] Ibid. Jeffrey M. Lang, a former Senate staffer, testified that the US, as the largest exporter and importer, has great economic leverage in trade issues, though he contended that its relative economic power was declining, so that it made sense to lock in the WTO at that point. See House Committee on Ways and Means, *The World Trade Organization,* Hearing, 65.

[53] See also Edward C. Luck, 'The Enforcement of Humanitarian Norms and the Politics of Ambivalence', in Simon Chesterman (ed.), *Civilians in War* (Boulder, CO: Lynne Rienner, 2001) and Edward C. Luck, Review of William Shawcross, *Deliver Us From Evil: Warlords and a World of Endless Conflict,* for the *American Journal of International Law,* 94/3 (2000).

[54] As noted in the next section, a similar, though more modest, political campaign underwritten by the Ted Turner-financed Better World Fund helped to break the Congressional deadlock on payment of UN dues in 1999.

[55] Remarks by President Bill Clinton, Senator Robert Dole, Senator Daniel Moynihan, Senator Robert Packwood, and Ambassador Mickey Kantor on support for the GATT, 23 November 1994.

[56] Quoted in Eric Schmitt, 'Aid Dresses Up in a Uniform', *New York Times* (10 May 1998).

of the WTO and of the influence of transnational corporations are primarily drawn from progressive or liberal Democratic circles.[57]

Thus, the anti-WTO forces constitute a minority in both parties, mostly on the left of the Democratic Party and on the right of the Republican Party,[58] with little else in common. Nor do they have a broadly attractive candidate. In 1994, the results were bipartisan victories for WTO on both sides of the Capitol: the House vote was 288 to 146—Republicans 121 to 56 in favour, and the Democrats 167 to 89—and the Senate margin was 76 to 23—Republicans 35 to 11 in favour, and the Democrats 41 to 12.[59] Overall, a higher percentage of Republican than Democratic legislators voted for the WTO. In the end, it was often more reliable to predict a vote based on how the export/import economy of a legislator's State or district would be affected than on the basis of his or her party affiliation. Thus, the President's biggest nemesis in the Senate was his Democratic colleague Ernest 'Fritz' Hollings, from textile-producing South Carolina.

Though the WTO was deliberately set up outside of the UN system, its detractors tried on many occasions to suggest that its decision-making procedures and bureaucratic features were no better than those of the world body.[60] Yet these arguments did not seem to carry as much weight as they had in debates about the UN. The context was different: the functions and activities of the WTO, unlike those of the UN, were perceived to relate directly to vital US national interests, or at least to the interests of influential segments of the American body politic. The controversies engulfing the WTO are integrally embedded in core issues of American domestic politics and, as such, cannot be ducked by the White House or treated in a cavalier fashion on Capitol Hill. Except in rare circumstances, the same cannot be said for most peacekeeping operations or UN activities. Americans tend to support or reject the UN for largely symbolic reasons, making it vulnerable to rhetorical assaults, while the WTO is more likely to be judged on the basis of practical results with domestic consequences.[61]

[57] See testimony of Ralph Nader, Senate Foreign Relations Committee, *Uruguay Round of the General Agreement on Tariffs and Trade*, 14 June 1994, 103rd Cong., 2d sess. (US Government Printing Office, 1994). In addition to her testimony cited above, see interview with Lori Wallach in *Foreign Policy*, 118 (Spring 2000).

[58] For a recent discussion of this split, see Kimberly Ann Elliott and Gary Clyde Hufbauer, 'Ambivalent Multilateralism and the Emerging Backlash: The IMF and the WTO', in Patrick and Forman (eds), *Multilateralism*, 405–6.

[59] David E. Sanger, 'The Lame-Duck Congress: The Vote; House Approves Trade Agreement by a Wide Margin', *New York Times* (30 November 1994); 'Senate Seems Set to Approve Trade Accord', *New York Times* (1 December 1994); 'Senate Approves Pact to Ease Trade Curbs; A Victory for Clinton', *New York Times* (2 December 1994).

[60] Some fretted that, unlike in the Security Council, the US would not have a formal veto over WTO actions. Others complained that the WTO's one-nation, one-vote formula would lead to domination by developing countries, as in the UN General Assembly. And Newt Gingrich stressed the need for close and continuing oversight, since 'nothing would be worse than to have the WTO somehow drift off and become another UNESCO'. House Committee on Ways and Means, *The World Trade Organization*, Hearing, 144.

[61] Down the road, however, for those most critical of the opaqueness of WTO procedures the relative and growing transparency of the UN secretariat and

4. Arrears

During the 1990s, US arrears to the UN more than doubled to well over $1 billion,[62] leaving the principle that dues payments are binding treaty obligations badly, perhaps irreparably, frayed. Most of this erosion stemmed from legislation introduced by Republican legislators determined to reduce the American financial commitment to the world body, to compel the UN to accept their vision of reform, and to embarrass a Democratic President whose stewardship of foreign affairs they found lacking. But, as noted above, when President Clinton signed in April 1994 a bill to cap unilaterally US peacekeeping payments at 25 per cent, he essentially opened wide the door to future withholdings.

The only halfway encouraging developments concerning US payments to the UN occurred at the very beginning and end of the decade. In each case, the US began to repay a portion of its arrears in return for reforms adopted by the UN following Congressionally mandated financial withholdings. In the late 1980s, as in the late 1990s, the world body confronted a major financial crisis due, in large part, to growing US arrears.[63] The largest withholdings stemmed from the August 1985 Kassebaum-Solomon amendment, which stipulated that one-fifth of US dues were to be withheld until the General Assembly and the specialized agencies adopted the practice of financially weighted voting on budgetary matters.

After some rather difficult tugging and hauling among the member states, aided by a detailed reform study by a UN-appointed group of experts, the General Assembly agreed that budgetary questions would be decided by a consensus process, which in effect would require the consent of the major contributors— and others. This step, plus some personnel and management reforms, sufficed to persuade the sponsors of the legislation and the Reagan administration that the intent, if not the letter, of the amendment had been achieved. The bill was amended to mandate monitoring, not further withholdings. During his final

intergovernmental bodies may be appealing. The UN's broader-based agenda, which places trade and economic development in the larger context of environmental, labour, and human rights considerations, may also offer a better match for their concerns. See the Secretary-General's initiative to develop a Global Compact with transnational corporations: Transcript of Press Conference by Secretary-General Kofi Annan at UN Headquarters, UN Press Release SG/SM/7496, 27 July 2000, Executive Summary and Conclusion of High-Level Meeting on Global Compact, UN Press Release SG/2065, 27 July 2000, and Joseph Kahn, 'Multinationals Sign U.N. Pact on Rights and Environment', *New York Times* (27 July 2000).

[62] Status of Contributions as at 31 December 1989, United Nations, ST/ADM/ SER.B/325 and Status of Contributions as at 31 December 1999, United Nations, ST/ADM/SER.B/554.

[63] For an account of the financial crisis and reform efforts of the late 1980s, see Tapio Kanninen, *Leadership and Reform: The Secretary-General and the UN Financial Crisis of the Late 1980s* (The Hague: Kluwer Law International, 1995). Also see Luck, *Mixed Messages*, 213, 239–41, and Rosemary Righter, *Utopia Lost: The United Nations and World Order* (New York: The Twentieth Century Fund Press, 1995), 231–5.

months in office, President Reagan congratulated the world body on the 'sweeping' and 'extremely important' reforms and mandated an inter-agency study, led by Colin Powell, to 'work out a multi-year plan to pay our arrearages to the United Nations'.[64] During the second and third years of the subsequent Bush administration, Congress did agree to make partial payments of US arrears.

With the advent of the Clinton administration and the peacekeeping foibles described above, the withholding habit soon returned. Inventive members of Congress—mostly Republican—found all sorts of reasons, some more valid than others, to withhold funds.[65] Some sensible things were achieved, such as the creation of an inspector-general's office for the UN and greater discipline on spending and hiring. But key Senators and Representatives came to see financial leverage as their only means of influencing the world body. The more the UN responded to their withholdings with reform steps, the more they became convinced of the utility of the withholding tactic. Meanwhile, other member states, including most pointedly America's allies, were becoming increasingly annoyed by Washington's unilateralist tactics. As John Weston, then the British Permanent Representative to the UN, complained in 1997, 'American exceptionalism cannot mean being the exception to the laws everyone else has to obey'.[66]

By 1996, the Clinton administration had concluded that a new approach was needed. It began to float the idea of a 'grand bargain' consisting of a broad package of UN reforms that it would seek at Turtle Bay in return for a bipartisan commitment on the Hill to repay most or all of the growing arrears. Though the administration had relatively little leverage over either Congress or the other member states by that point, it was the only actor in a position to try to manage the required two-level domestic-international game. Initially this new strategy made little progress on either front. The unilateral effort to deny Boutros Boutros-Ghali a second term as Secretary-General added to the resentment other member states felt about American exceptionalism, though it demonstrated to Congress that the administration was willing to get tough with the organization. The appointment of the more engaging Kofi Annan as Secretary-General at the end of 1996, moreover, offered the symbolism of a new beginning and the prospect of bridge-building between the UN's 38th floor and Capitol Hill.

By July 1997, the new Secretary-General had cobbled together a broad and sensible, though hardly radical, plan for management reform.[67] What President Clinton deemed the 'most far-reaching reform of the United Nations in its history', however, was initially dismissed as a 'meager package' by

---

[64] Department of State, *United States Participation in the United Nations, Report by the President to the Congress for the Year 1988* (US Government Printing Office, 1989) and the *Washington Weekly Report*, 14–30 (Washington, DC: United Nations Association of the USA, 16 September 1988). [65] See Luck, *Mixed Messages*, 238–43.

[66] 'U.S. Debt Called "Indefensible"; Weston Says It's Catch-22', *Diplomatic World Bulletin*, 28 (April–May 1997), 1.

[67] See Report of the Secretary-General, *Renewing the United Nations: A Programme for Reform*, A/51/950 (14 July 1997) and Luck, *Mixed Messages*, 211–13.

Senator Rod Grams, the influential Chairman of the International Operations Subcommittee.[68] Meanwhile, Senators Helms and Biden, respectively the Chair and ranking minority member of the Senate Foreign Relations Committee, were struggling to put together a list of 'benchmarks' that the UN would have to meet to gain Congressional approval for the payment of a portion of the arrears. The initial legislation, including three dozen benchmarks, was eventually vetoed by President Clinton in October 1998. His reasons for blocking the bill, however, had little to do with the UN but much with unrelated language that had been attached on the House side concerning funding for family planning programmes. Once again, it was evident that key domestic constituencies—in this case abortion rights advocates—mattered far more in the Washington political calculus than more distant international obligations.

Finally, in late 1999 a revised version of the Helms-Biden legislation, this time with 'only' two dozen benchmarks and with watered-down family planning language, was passed and signed into law. It would repay about two-thirds of the arrears over a three-year period in return for a reduction in the US assessment rate—25 per cent to 22 per cent for the regular budget and 30.5 per cent, at the time of the legislation, to 25 per cent for peacekeeping—the placement of the rest of the arrears in a 'contested arrears account'—essentially to be forgiven—the extension of a number of the reforms to key specialized agencies, the guarantee of a US place on the budget committee (ACABQ), freedom of GAO investigators to inspect the UN's books, and the prohibition of UN taxes or fees, of a UN standing army, or of Article 43 arrangements with other member states, and the introduction of various other management and financial reforms. The first modest tranche of arrears payments was made in December 1999 upon the administration's certification that the initial conditions—the easiest and vaguest—had been met.

Why did the two ends of Pennsylvania Avenue finally find some common ground on these contentious issues? By all accounts, by this point many members of Congress were tired of hearing about the details of UN reform and the intricacies of its financing, neither a big issue in their constituents' eyes. Senator Helms—eager to show that he could be an effective chairman, not just a flamethrower, and that he could tame both the UN and the Clinton administration—worked hard for its passage. Once Richard Holbrooke was finally confirmed by the Senate to become Permanent Representative to the UN in August 1999, he lobbied for the bill with his usual gusto. The Ted Turner-financed Better World Fund underwrote a national advertising and letter-writing campaign, focused on key Congressional districts, which encouraged a spate of pay-the-arrears editorials.[69] Allied governments and UN officials kept up a steady chorus of complaints about US behaviour and the worsening financial crisis, and there was positive

[68] Clinton's speech to the 52nd Session of the UN General Assembly, 22 September 1997; Grams, quoted in Barbara Crossette, 'U.N. Chief Promises to Overhaul Organization from the Top Down', *New York Times* (17 July 1997).
[69] Sebastian Mallaby, 'To the U.N.'s Rescue', *The Washington Post* (18 November 1999).

news at the UN as well. With much high-level arm twisting, the US got its seat back on the ACABQ, and the GAO reported that real reform was under way at the world body.[70]

In the end, however, it may have been the UN Charter itself that cast the deciding vote. Under Article 19, any member state two full years behind in its dues payments is to lose its vote in the General Assembly, a penalty that has been invoked against dozens of countries. For several years, the US had managed to pay just enough at year's end to sneak under this bar. Over the course of 1999, however, it became increasingly apparent that the only way to avoid this embarrassment in January 2000, at the onset of the new century, was to adopt the Helms-Biden package.

By January 2000, Senator Helms, Senator Biden, and Ambassador Holbrooke were heralding—prematurely—a new era not only in relations between the UN and its most powerful member but also in terms of a bipartisan approach to the world body.[71] Though persuading other member states to pay more so that the US assessment could be lowered to 22 per cent for the regular budget and 25 per cent for peacekeeping proved to be a difficult and lengthy process, a new assessment scale was finally agreed in December 2000. While the Senate responded with a 99–0 vote on 7 February 2001 to release the next $582 million tranche of the arrears to the UN, the Republican-controlled House hesitated, despite encouragement by the new Bush administration to meet its side of the US-UN bargain. Meanwhile, a series of setbacks at the UN—including the loss of the US seat on the UN Human Rights Commission and US isolation at the UN conferences on small arms and on racism—further soured relations between Washington and Turtle Bay.[72] Sadly, it took the tragic events of September 11 and the Bush administration's efforts to insure full-fledged UN support for the war on terrorism to get the House to go along with the $582 million arrears payment and for the Senate to confirm John Negroponte to be US Permanent Representative to the UN.[73] Whether these extraordinary developments will

[70] Betsy Pisik, 'Lobbying May Pay Off', *Washington Times* (4 October 1999) and Barbara Crossette, 'U.S. Likely to Regain a U.N. Finance Seat', *New York Times* (28 September 1999). 'United Nations Reform Initiatives Have Strengthened Operations, But Overall Objectives Have Not Yet Been Achieved', United States General Accounting Office Report, GAO/NSIAD-00-150 and Barbara Crossette, 'U.S. Report Says the U.N. Has Improved With Changes', *New York Times* (29 May 2000).

[71] Senate Foreign Relations Committee, *Implementation of United Nations Reforms*, Hearing, 21 January 2000, 106th Cong., 2nd sess. (US Government Printing Office, 2000). Testifying at the same Hearing, this author expressed a number of caveats about the prospects for the relationship.

[72] Derek Chollet and Robert Orr, 'Carpe Diem: Reclaiming Success at the United Nations', *The Washington Quarterly*, 24/4 (2001), 7–18; Margaret P. Karns and Karen A. Mingst, 'The United States as 'Deadbeat'? U.S. Policy and the UN Financial Crisis', in Patrick and Forman (eds), *Multilateralism*, 267–94; and Suzanne Nossel, 'Retail Diplomacy: The Edifying Story of UN Dues Reform', *The National Interest*, 66 (Winter 2001/2002).

[73] Lizette Alvarez, 'House Approves $582 Million for Back Dues Owed to the U.N.', *New York Times* (25 September 2001); Stephen Kinzer, 'Approval on U.N. Post', *New York Times* (19 September 2001); and 'A New Presidency', *Wall Street Journal* (19 September 2001).

make more than a temporary dent in America's historic ambivalence toward international institutions, however, is questionable. The unsustainability of the last 'breakthrough' a decade ago suggests that the highly interactive but often destructive interplay between Congress and the UN could well continue for years to come, because future presidents, whether of a Bill Clinton or George Bush variety, are unlikely to treat relations with the UN as a matter of high political priority except in specific cases or under unusual circumstances.

5. Conclusions

Though it is common in internationalist circles to assert that it is hopeless to try to influence Congress these days, since they claim that it is dominated by neo-isolationists who know little and care less about foreign affairs, these cases suggest that such caricatures and conclusions are off the mark. Conservative Republican leaders played pivotal roles in gaining Senate approval of the WTO and in developing a package, albeit an awkward unilat-eralist one, for repaying most of the US arrears to the UN. The gradual and begrudging acceptance of peacekeeping, if largely performed by others, appears to be following a similar path.

Congress, moreover, is not completely immune to pressures from the inter-national community, nor does it always ignore developments, positive or neg-ative, within international bodies. In the arrears case, some Congressional critics followed the financial and management practices and reforms of the UN quite closely over the years. Likewise, though the perception of the UN as a risky place for American interests and values may reflect a lag in appreciation of the political evolution that has taken place within the organization since the mid-1980s, it does reflect an understandable hangover from some very dif-ficult years. While the record of the WTO so far has not justified the worst fears of its critics, these could be refuelled at any point by a series of unfavourable or arbitrary decisions. Again, though the warnings about the risks inherent in UN peacekeeping may have been exaggerated, even supporters warn of debil-itating management flaws and of the growing risks and demands confronting peacekeepers in this turbulent era.[74]

There appears to be, in other words, a substantial degree of interaction between political developments on the international and domestic planes. Each helps to define the context for the other, as illustrated most vividly in the post-September 11 reactions on both levels. Both national and international political players pick up cues from the attitudes and policies displayed by their

---

[74] See, for example, the Report of the Panel on United Nations Peace Operations, A/55/305 (21 August 2000), the so-called Brahimi report mandated by the Secretary-General.

counterparts on the other plane. American policy choices, at least on the strategic level, are ultimately decided, of course, within a domestic policy context, especially when Congress's control of the purse strings comes into play. Because national policies and strategies are determined in Washington, not at the headquarters of international organizations, even those foreign policy choices that are largely dictated by international developments will be played out ultimately among domestic political forces. On the other hand, if one focuses on US behaviour within international bodies, for example on voting patterns in the General Assembly, the Bretton Woods institutions, or the Security Council, then the tendency will be to interpret these solely as the products of interactions with other national governments. Either way, appearances can be deceiving.

The cases above also suggest that, for all its exceptionalism, the United States is capable of learning from experience and of adjusting its policies in response to changing conditions, while pursuing distinct tactics from one forum or issue to another. The US has not adopted either a rejectionist or a 'one-size fits all' strategy toward international organizations. Nor can its philosophy be properly described as unremittingly either unilateralist or multilateralist, since both elements emerge from time to time, place to place, and issue to issue. As the Bush administration has demonstrated, the US finds it perfectly natural to reject the International Criminal Court, the Kyoto Protocol, and the ABM Treaty at the same time as it is asking multilateral institutions to play a larger role in the struggle against terrorism. The US is pragmatic and case-specific in its choice of foreign policy tools, even as its reluctance to defer to multilateral processes and its insistence on maintaining maximum flexibility reflect its innate sense of exceptionalism.

Should other member states permit their resentment of America's exceptional power and unilateralist tactics to lead to efforts to restrict its prerogatives and position in global bodies, however, then their doubts could well become self-fulfilling prophecies.[75] US relations with the UN, in particular, remain precarious. These days, America, the only truly exceptional power, fits awkwardly at best into global bodies such as the UN, which profess sovereign equality as a political rather than legal principle and which express it in one-nation, one-vote rules. While most Americans prefer to have the endorsement and support of international institutions, they are more likely to look to domestic than to international sources of legitimacy.[76] Though Coral Bell praised the Clinton administration for understanding that 'the unipolar world should be run as if it were a concert of powers', these case studies suggest that the approaches of the Clinton and Bush administrations to multilateral institutions have differed more sharply on the

---

[75] Many American commentators have predicted that other countries will seek ways of banding together to try to counterbalance US power. See, for example, Peter W. Rodman, 'The World's Resentment: Anti-Americanism as a Global Phenomenon', *The National Interest*, 60 (Summer 2000), 34.

[76] Luck, 'The United States, International Organizations, and the Quest for Legitimacy'.

rhetorical than substantive levels.[77] Others would do well to focus more on the latter than on the former.

At the same time, it will be important to bear in mind that American policies also do not fit a simple rational actor model in which the US follows a coherent strategy for advancing its self-evident national interests in each forum. Counter-terrorism aside, Washington still lacks a bipartisan consensus either on the content of American national interests or on what strategies would maximize them. There appear to be, for example, fundamental differences over whether the role of multilateral organizations should be expanded or contracted in the conduct of US foreign policy, and whether they represent a threat to American national sovereignty and values or an opportunity to project its power and beliefs. It is to the resolution of such core questions, fortuitously, that other member states can make their most consequential contributions to the shaping of Washington policy-making towards international organization. In the end, other states and international secretariats will largely determine whether US policy-makers and legislators find international bodies to be places where America's exceptional potential is welcomed and embraced or is resented and restrained. Either way, this will be the ultimate test of whether the interplay between global and domestic politics can be productive and mutually reinforcing.

[77] Coral Bell, 'American Ascendancy and the Pretense of Concert', *The National Interest*, 57 (Fall 1999), 60.

2

State Power and the Institutional Bargain: America's Ambivalent Economic and Security Multilateralism

Paradoxically, the United States has been the greatest champion of multilateral institutions in the twentieth century, urging on the world all sorts of new organizational creations, but it has also tended to resist entangling itself in institutional commitments and obligations. Across the century—and in particular at the major post-war turning points of 1919, 1945, and 1989—the United States has pursued ambitious strategies that entailed the use of an array of multilateral institutions to remake international order. No other great power has advanced such far-reaching and elaborate ideas about how institutions might be employed to organize and manage the relations between states. But despite this enthusiasm for creating institutions and a rule-based international order, the United States has been reluctant to tie itself too tightly to these multilateral institutions and rules.

After 1919, the United States put the League of Nations at the centre of its designs for world order; collective institutions were to play an unprecedented role in organizing security and providing mechanisms for dispute resolution and the enforcement of agreements. After 1945, the United States pushed onto the world a breathtaking array of new institutions—multilateral, bilateral, regional, global, security, economic, and political. After the cold war, the United States again pursued an institutional agenda: the expansion of NATO and the launching of NAFTA, APEC, and the WTO. But at each turn the United States also resisted the loss of sovereign authority or the reduction of its policy autonomy. The League of Nations in 1919, the International Trade Organization in 1947, and the more recent decisions by the Bush administration to walk away from treaties on global warming, arms control, trade, and the International

This chapter builds on *After Victory: Institutions, Strategic Restraint, and the Rebuilding of Order After Major War* (Princeton: Princeton University Press, 2001); 'Institutions, Strategic Restraint, and the Persistence of American Postwar Order,' *International Security*, 23/3 (1998/99); and 'Constitutional Politics in International Relations', *European Review of International Relations*, 4/2 (1998).

Criminal Court are all monuments to America's reluctance to bind itself to international institutions.

The puzzle is to explain the logic and variation in the extent to which the United States has agreed to establish binding institutional ties—particularly multilateral ties—with other states. Why did the United States at the zenith of its hegemonic power after the Second World War and again after the cold war seek the establishment or expansion of multilateral institutions and agree to insert itself within them? Why did it agree to bind itself to Europe in a 1949 security pact, deepen that commitment in the years that followed, and seek the expansion of NATO in the 1990s, even after the Soviet threat that prompted security cooperation disappeared? Why did the United States seek to establish order after the Second World War in Western Europe through multilateral commitments and pursue a series of bilateral security agreements in Asia?

An obvious hypothesis is that the United States organizes and operates within international institutions when it can dominate them and resists doing so when it cannot. But a slightly more complex set of calculations seem to be involved. This chapter argues that American ambivalence about multilateral institutions, and variations in its institutional relations with Europe, reflect a basic dilemma that lies at the heart of international institutional agreements. The attraction of institutional agreements for the leading states is that they potentially lock other states into stable and predictable policy orientations, thereby reducing its need to use coercion. But the price that the leading state must pay for this institutionalized cooperation is a reduction in its own policy autonomy and its unfettered ability to exercise power. The central question that American policy-makers have confronted over the decades after 1945 in regard to its economic and security ties with Europe, and elsewhere around the world as well, is: how much policy lock-in of such states—insured by the institutionalization of various commitments and obligations—is worth how much reduction in American policy autonomy and restraints on its power?

The result is a potential institutional bargain, a bargain that lies at the heart of America's multilateral ties to Europe and the wider array of post-war multilateral institutions championed by the United States. It is a bargain that is most fully available when the old order has been destroyed and a newly powerful state must engage weaker states over the organization of the new order. In the institutional bargain, the leading state wants to reduce compliance costs and weaker states want to reduce their costs of security protection, or the costs they would incur trying to protect their interests against the actions of a dominating lead state. This is what makes the institutional deal attractive: the leading state agrees to restrain its own potential for domination and abandonment in exchange for the long-term institutionalized cooperation of subordinate states. Both sides are better off with an institutionalized relationship than in an order based on the constant threat of the indiscriminate and arbitrary exercise of power. The leading state does not need to expend its power capabilities to coerce other states and the other states do not need to expend resources seeking to protect themselves from such coercion. It is the mutually improving nature of this exchange that makes the institutional deal work.

The first section of this chapter develops the logic of the institutional bargain that has informed America's post-war order building experience and continues into the new century. The succeeding sections explore various aspects of this institutional strategy as it appears in America's relationship with Europe in the 1940s and again after the cold war. In the conclusion I assess the relevance of the institutional bargain in an era of American unipolarity.

1. State Power and Institutions

Why would a leading state surrounded by a world of weaker states want to establish multilateral institutions? The answer is that institutional agreements can lock other states into a relatively congenial and stable order.[1] The institutions help create a more favourable and certain political environment in which the leading state pursues its interests. This is possible because institutions can operate as mechanisms of political control. When a state agrees to tie itself to the commitments and obligations of an inter-state institution, it is agreeing to reduce its policy autonomy. A leading state that has created an institutionalized order that works to its long-term benefit is better off than a leading state operating in a free-floating order requiring the constant and costly exercise of power to get its way.[2]

Institutions can serve at least two purposes in international relations. First, as neo-liberal institutionalists argue, institutions can help solve collective action problems by reducing the commitment problems and transaction costs that stand in the way of efficient and mutually beneficial political exchange.[3] But institutions are also instruments of political control. As Terry Moe argues, 'political institutions are also weapons of coercion and redistribution. They are the structural means by which political winners pursue their own interests, often at the expense of political losers'.[4] A winning political party in Congress

---

[1] This discussion of state power and institutional strategies simplifies enormously the political context in which government leaders make choices. Domestic politics, cultural traditions, bureaucratic struggles, and many other factors also shape the way states act. The goal in this section is to isolate the international logic of state choice and generate hypotheses that can be explored across historical cases.

[2] See W. Michael Reisman, 'The United States and International Institutions', *Survival*, 41/4 (1999–2000).

[3] The classic statement is Robert Keohane, *After Hegemony: Cooperation and Discord in the World Political Economy* (Princeton: Princeton University Press, 1984).

[4] Terry M. Moe, 'Political Institutions: The Neglected Side of the Story', *Journal of Law, Economics, and Organization*, 6 (Special Issue 1990), 213.

will try to write the committee voting rules to favour its interests. Similarly, in international relations, a powerful state will want to make its advantages as systematic and durable as possible by trying to rope weaker states into favourable institutional arrangements.[5]

The attraction of institutional agreements for the leading state is twofold. First, if the leading state can get other states to tie themselves to a multilateral institution that directly or indirectly serves its long-term interests, it will not need to spend its resources to constantly coerce other states. It is the most powerful state, so it is likely that it would win many or most of the endless distributive battles in a non-institutionalized relationship with subordinate states, but locking these lesser states into institutional agreements reduces these costs of enforcement.[6] Second, if the institutional agreement has some degree of stickiness—that is, if it has some independent ordering capacity—the institution may continue to provide favourable outcomes for the leading state even after its power capacities have declined in relative terms. Institutions can both conserve and prolong the power advantages of the leading state.

But why would weaker states agree to be roped in? After all, they might calculate that it is better to not lock themselves into an institutional agreement at T1 and wait until T2 or T3, when the power asymmetries did not favour the leading state as much. Weaker states have two potential incentives to buy into the leading state's institutional agreement. First, if the institutional agreement also puts limits and restraints on the behaviour of the leading state, this would be welcome. In a non-institutionalized relationship, these lesser states are subject to the unrestrained and unpredictable domination of the leading state. If they believed that credible limits could be placed on the arbitrary and indiscriminate actions of the leading state, this might be enough of an

---

[5] Institutions are potentially sticky for at least three reasons. First, they can create difficult and demanding legal or political procedures for altering or discontinuing the institutional agreement. Second, the institution can itself over time become an actor, gaining some independence from states and actively promoting institutional compliance and continuity. Third, growing vested interests—groups with stakes in the success and continuation of the institution—along with other positive feedback effects produce 'increasing returns' to institutions that raise the costs of ending or replacing the institutions. This view of institutions can be contrasted with two other perspectives. One is a more narrowly drawn rationalist account that sees institutions as contracts—agreements that remain in force only so long as the specific interests that gain from them remain in place. It is the interests and not the institutions that are sticky. The other, constructivist view sees institutions and the institutionalization of inter-state relations as built upon shared ideas and identities.

[6] To the extent that the locking-in of institutional commitments and obligations is mutual—that is, the leading state also locks itself in, at least to some extent—this makes the asymmetrical relationship more acceptable and legitimate to the weaker and secondary states. This, in turn, reduces the enforcement costs. See G. John Ikenberry and Charles A. Kupchan, 'Socialization and Hegemonic Power', *International Organization*, 44/4 (1990); and Lisa Martin, 'The Rational State Choice of Multilateralism', in John Gerard Ruggie (ed.), *Multilateralism Matters: The Theory and Praxis of an Institutional Form* (New York: Columbia University Press, 1993).

attraction to justify an institutional agreement at T1. Second, when the leading state does in fact circumscribe its behaviour it is giving up some opportunities to use its power to gain immediate returns on its power: it settles for fewer gains at T1 by operating within institutional rules and obligations than it could otherwise achieve with its brute power. It does this with an eye towards longer-term gains that are specified above. But weaker states may have reason to gain sooner rather than later. The discount rate for future gains is potentially different for the leading and the lesser states, and this makes an institutional bargain potentially more mutually desirable. So the leading state is faced with a choice: how much institutional limitation on its own policy autonomy and exercise of power is worth how much policy lock-in of weaker states?

Several hypotheses follow immediately from this model of state power and institutions. First, a leading state should try to lock other states into institutionalized policy orientations while trying to minimize its own limitations on policy autonomy and discretionary power. This is the story that Michael Crozier tells about politics within large-scale organizations. Each individual within a complex organizational hierarchy is continually engaged in a dual struggle: to tie his colleagues to precise rule-based behaviour, thereby creating a more stable and certain environment in which to operate, while also trying to retain as much autonomy and discretion as possible for himself.[7] Similarly, leading states will try to lock other states in as much as possible while also trying to remain as unencumbered as possible from institutional rules and obligations. Second, the leading state will make use of its ability—to the extent the ability exists—to limit its capacity to exercise power in indiscriminate and arbitrary ways as a 'currency' to buy the institutional cooperation of other states.

The availability of the institutional bargain will depend on several circumstances that can also be specified as hypotheses. First, the amount of 'currency' available to the leading state to buy institutional cooperation of weaker states is determined by two factors: the ability of the leading state to potentially dominate or injure the interests of weaker states and its ability to credibly restrain itself from doing so. Although all states might offer to restrain and commit themselves in exchange for concessions by other states, the willingness and ability of powerful states to do so will be of particular interest to other states. Chad may offer to lock itself into an institutional agreement that lowers its policy autonomy and makes its future policy orientation more predictable, but few states will care much about this offer to bind itself and they are not likely to offer much in return to get it. But if a powerful state with the capacity for serious domination and disruption offers to restrain itself, this will get the attention of other states and they are likely to be willing to offer something to get it. But it is not just the domination and disruption potential of the leading

[7] Michael Crozier, *The Bureaucratic Phenomenon* (Chicago: University of Chicago Press, 1964).

state that generates 'currency' to buy the institutional cooperation of other states. It is also the capacity to actually make good on restraint and commitment. If a powerful state cannot credibly limit its power, its currency will amount to very little.

Two other factors will determine whether the leading state—if it has the 'currency' with which to buy institutional cooperation—will in fact want to do so. One is the degree to which the leading state is interested in locking in the policy behaviour of other states. This is a question about the extent to which the actions of other states actually impinge on the interests of the leading state. The security policy orientation of European states would tend to qualify as important but other policy orientations of European states—and the wide range of policy orientations of other states around the world—are not significant enough to justify efforts by the leading state to lock in stable and favourable policy behaviour, particularly if the price of doing so entails a reduction of policy autonomy. The other factor is simply the ability of weaker states to be locked in. The United States may want to lock in the policy behaviour of other states, particularly the security policy behaviour, but may not have enough confidence that these institutionalized commitments and obligations can be effectively locked in.

Taken together, these considerations allow us to see how a leading state and weaker states might make trade-offs about binding themselves together through multilateral institutions. The more the leading state is capable of dominating and abandoning weaker states, the more weaker states will care about restraints on the leading state's exercise of power—and the more likely they are to make some concessions to get leading state restraint and commitment. Similarly, the more a potentially dominating state can in fact credibly restrain and commit itself, the more weaker states will be interested in pursuing an institutional bargain. When both these conditions hold—when the leading state can dominate and abandon and when it can restrain and commit itself—that state will be particularly willing and able to pursue an institutional bargain. From the perspective of the leading state, the less important the policy behaviour is of weaker states—that is, the less consequential it is to the leading state—the less the leading state will offer restraints on its own policy autonomy to achieve policy lock-in. Likewise, the less certain the leading state is that policy lock-in of weaker states can in fact be accomplished, the less the leading state will offer restraints on its own policy autonomy.

2. American Institution Building

This model is useful in making sense of the broad sweep of American institution building in the twentieth century, particularly in its relations with Western Europe. The major patterns of American policy toward multilateral institutions can be sketched.[8] It is not only that the United States has tended to support the creation of multilateral institutions when it can dominate them. This is the most straightforward hypothesis, and there is a great deal of evidence to support it. But there is also a slightly more complicated calculation in American institutional thinking. The United States has tended to weigh the costs of reducing its policy autonomy in relation to the gains that it would realize by locking other states into enduring policy positions.

Post-war Institution Building

The United States has been most active in seeking institutional agreements after the major wars in the twentieth century—1919, 1945, and 1989.[9] The reason why is made clear in the foregoing model. There are several distinctive features of post-war moments that lend themselves to new institutional initiatives. First, the old institutional order has been cleared away by the war and therefore, in contrast to more 'normal' moments in international relations, basic issues of order are on the table. It is difficult simply to fall back on the *status quo ante*. Second, wars tend to create new winners and losers—and ratify a new and often heightened asymmetrical distribution of power. As a result, the new leading state will be faced with the question of how to use its new power assets. It has, in effect, received a windfall of power. Should it simply use these new power assets to win in the endless distributive struggles after the war or use them to invest in an order that serves its long-term goals? The leading state does have incentives at these junctures to act in a relatively far-sighted way. Institutional agreements are potentially a form of investment in the future—but only if they are in fact capable of playing a shaping and constraining role even in the face of shifts in the distribution of power.

Third, because the leading state is newly powerful, secondary states will be particularly eager to gain assurances about the actions of the leading state. They will be interested in agreements that reduce the ability of the leading state to dominate or abandon them. The more powerful and potentially disruptive the new leading state is, the more they will worry about this problem and the more they will be willing to concede in order to get credible restraints and commitments. Fourth, the war itself also tends to disrupt the domestic institutions of both the new leading state and the new secondary states. Often the leading state is actually in a position to occupy and help rebuild the

---

[8] The goal in the following sections is to explore the plausibility of the hypotheses and see how the institutional bargain discussed earlier is manifest in various settings.

[9] Important explorations of American policy toward multilateral institutions include John Gerard Ruggie, *Winning the Peace: America and World Order in the New Era* (New York: Columbia University Press, 1996); and Margaret P. Karns and Karen A. Mingst, 'The United States and Multilateral Institutions: A Framework', in Margaret P. Karns and Karen A. Mingst (eds), *The United States and Multilateral Institutions: Patterns of Changing Instrumentality and Influence* (Boston: Unwin Hyman, 1990).

secondary states. As a result, the post-war moment may be particularly congenial to the establishment of institutional agreements that actually lock weaker states into a long-term policy orientation. Put differently, the lock-in capacity is particularly high after major wars.

Finally, if the leading state does want to create an order that is legitimate, it will be attracted to institutional agreements that not only lock weaker states into a desirable order but that also render the post-war order legitimate, that is, mutually acceptable or desirable. To the extent the institutional agreements restrain and commit the power of the leading state, this may be an attractive option. The institutional agreement lowers its costs of enforcement. After wars, newly powerful states are confronted with these sorts of dilemmas and trade-offs.

Variations in Post-war Institutional Outcomes

The United States pursued a much more elaborate and wide-ranging institutional agenda after 1945 than it did after 1919. The proposal for a League of Nations was an ambitious and demanding institution that sought to establish a global system of collective security. But the hard work of building these institutions was not in the institutional concessions and obligations that the United States and the other countries were to agree to but in the democratic revolution that President Woodrow Wilson saw as ensuring the success of the League of Nations.[10] In contrast, the scope and depth of the post-1945 proposals and the ambition with which the United States sought to remake Europe and Asia entailed a more fully institutionalized post-war order than Wilson could imagine. Why did the United States pursue a much more far-reaching institutional agenda after 1945?

The model presented earlier is helpful in untangling this post-war variation. The US power relationship with Europe after 1945 was far more asymmetrical than it was in 1919. This had a major impact on the ability and willingness of the leading and the weaker states to seek an institutional bargain. More so than in 1919, the United States was a full fledged hegemonic power after 1945 and because of this the Europeans attached a premium to harnessing and restraining this newly powerful state. Europe was more willing to accept institutional agreements in return for a more restrained and committed America. Likewise, the United States had tremendous 'currency' with which to buy the institutional agreement of other states, particularly the Europeans.

Other factors also facilitated the unprecedented post-1945 institutionalism. The United States ended the Second World War with a sophisticated understanding of what had caused the world war and what would be necessary to ensure a peaceful and stable post-war order. In 1919, the Wilson administration did have a strong view about how Europe needed to transform itself. It made stark contrasts between its new thinking and the militarism and

---

[10] See Thomas J. Knock, *To End All Wars: Woodrow Wilson and the Quest for a New World Order* (New York: Oxford University Press, 1992).

balance-of-power thinking of the Old World. The leaders in France and Britain also felt threatened by Wilson's crusade to remake the world. But the American position after the Second World War entailed a more comprehensive critique of European and world politics. Europe needed to integrate itself more fully. Wider social and economic reform would be needed to sustain liberal-democratic regimes, and these reforms would need to be embedded in regional and global multilateral institutions. Just as importantly, the domestic systems in Japan and Germany would need thoroughgoing reform, made possible by the unprecedented opportunity of the American and allied occupation.[11] Compared with 1919, in 1945 the United States saw both more lock-in importance and lock-in opportunity in Europe. As a result, it was willing to give more to get it. Likewise, the Europeans were more willing after 1945 to give concessions in order to get institutionalized American restraints and commitments.

This analysis suggests that three of the four variables that bear on the incentives and opportunities for an institutional bargain were more evident in 1945 than in 1919. What about the fourth variable: the ability of the leading state to make credible restraints and commitments? It is difficult to argue that the institutional character of the United States was radically different after 1945 in a way that facilitated the establishment of credible restraints and commitments. But there was a difference. The sheer density of post-1945 institutional initiatives provides more 'strings' with which to tie the United States down and to Europe. American restraint and commitment to Europe in 1919 was based on the fragile tie of a single treaty. After the Second World War, it was based on dozens of intergovernmental agreements, most importantly NATO.

Variations in American Policy Towards Europe and Asia

American institution building after 1945 took different forms in Europe and Asia.[12] The United States pursued a multilateral strategy in Europe—with

---

[11] Tony Smith, *America's Mission: The United States and the Worldwide Struggle for Democracy in the Twentieth Century* (Princeton: Princeton University Press, 1994), Chapter 6.

[12] There is a growing literature on variations in regional patterns between Europe and east Asia and on America's divergent post-war institutional strategies in the two regions. See Joseph M. Grieco, 'Realism and Regionalism: American Power and German and Japanese Institutional Strategies During and After the Cold War', in Ethan B. Kapstein and Michael Mastanduno (eds), *Unipolar Politics: Realism and State Strategies After the Cold War* (New York: Columbia University Press, 1999); Joseph M. Grieco, 'Systemic Sources of Variation in Regional Institutionalization in Western Europe, East Asia, and the Americas', in Edward Mansfield and Helen Milner (eds), *The Political Economy of Regionalism* (New York: Columbia University Press, 1997); Vinod K. Aggarwal, 'Comparing Regional Cooperation Efforts in the Asia-Pacific and North America', in Andrew Mack and John Ravenhill (eds), *Pacific Cooperation: Building Economic and Security Regimes in the Asia-Pacific Region* (Boulder, CO: Westview Press, 1995); Andrew Hurrell, 'Regionalism in Theoretical Perspective', in Louise Fawcett and Andrew Hurrell (eds), *Regionalism in World Politics: Regional Organization and International Order* (Oxford: Oxford University Press, 1995); and Peter J. Katzenstein, 'Regionalism in Comparative Perspective', *Cooperation and Conflict*, 31 (June 1996).

NATO as the anchor—while in Asia it pursued a series of bilateral security agreements with Japan, Korea, and several south-east Asian states. This contrast amounts to an important puzzle that can sharpen the logic of American multilateralism.

The first observation is that the United States actually did float the idea of a multilateral security institution in Asia in the early 1940s and during 1950–1 that was to be a counterpart to NATO.[13] The second observation is that some of the elements that allowed security multilateralism to be embraced in Europe did not exist in Asia—quite apart from American interests or intentions. Europe did have a group of roughly equally sized and situated states that were capable of being bound together in a multilateral security institution tied to the United States, while Japan was alone and isolated in east Asia. The third observation is that the countries in east Asia that might have been party to a multilateral security pact—South Korea, South Vietnam, and Taiwan—were all interested in national reunification. The NATO pact in Europe seemingly made permanent the division of Germany. This was a development that these Asian states sought to avoid.[14]

The model presented earlier adds to these explanations. The basic difference between Asia and Europe is that the United States was both more dominant in Asia and wanted less out of Asia. This meant that as a practical matter it was less necessary for the United States to give up policy autonomy in exchange for institutional cooperation in Asia. In Europe, the United States had an elaborate agenda for uniting the European states, creating an institutional bulwark against communism, and supporting centrist democratic regimes. It had ambitious lock-in goals. These goals could not simply be realized through the brute exercise of power. To get what it wanted it had to bargain with the Europeans and this meant agreeing to restrain its exercise of power.[15] In Asia, the United States did not have goals that were sufficiently important to purchase with an agreement to restrain its power. Bilateralism was the desired strategy because multilateralism would have required more restraints on policy autonomy. Put differently, the United States had much more unchallenged hegemonic power in Asia than in Western Europe, and therefore it had fewer incentives to secure its dominant position with international institutions. Peter Katzenstein argues that

[i]t was neither in the interest of the United States to create institutions that would have constrained independent decision making in Washington nor in the interest

---

[13] See Donald Crone, 'Does Hegemony Matter? The Reorganization of the Pacific Political Economy', *World Politics*, 45 (July 1993).

[14] See Barry Buzan and Gerald Segal, 'Rethinking East Asian Security', *Survival*, 36 (Summer 1994); and Rosemary Foot, 'Pacific Asia: The Development of Regional Dialogue', in Fawcett and Hurrell (eds), *Regionalism in World Politics*.

[15] On the ways in which NATO multilateralism restrained the American exercise of power, see Steve Weber, 'Shaping the Postwar Balance of Power: Multilateralism in NATO', in Ruggie (ed.), *Multilateralism Matters*.

of subordinate states to enter institutions in which they would have minimal control while forgoing opportunities for free-riding and dependence reduction. Extreme hegemony thus led to a system of bilateral relations between states rather than a multilateral system that emerged in the North Atlantic area around the North Atlantic Treaty Organization (NATO) and the European Community.[16]

This view is also consistent with the more recent developments. As American hegemony has declined in relative terms within east Asia and as the United States has developed more specific lock-in goals for the states within the region, its interest in multilateral institutional building has increased somewhat.[17] American support for APEC—which is not an institution that requires much if any real policy restraint by the United States—is emblematic of this new multilateralism in Asia.

Institutionalism on the Cheap

The United States has consistently attempted to get as much institutionalized order building after major wars as possible on the cheap, that is, with as little cost to it as possible in real restraints on its policy autonomy or political sovereignty. This is the basic logic that the model illuminates: the leading state will try to lock in other states and create as stable and favourable a political environment as possible with the least cost possible in policy encumbrances.

This logic is seen in the American impulse after 1919 and 1945. At both moments, the United States did not initially foresee specific or legally demanding American commitments to the rest of the world. Instead, the United States sought to encourage general tendencies in the international system that would work independently to foster a stable and favourable international order. In 1919, Wilson understood that the major leverage that the United States had over the policies of other states was not an offer of American commitments and restraints. The leverage was the worldwide democratic revolution. It was Wilson's optimism about the trajectory of history and the ground swell of world public opinion that was to launch the League of Nations and transform world politics. The democratic structure of the world rather than the legal character of binding ties was to be the source of America's stable and favourable world order.

The American president's view of international law and intergovernmental agreements was firmly rooted in nineteenth-century understandings. The intergovernmental institutions themselves were not the mechanisms that

[16] Peter J. Katzenstein, 'The Cultural Foundations of Murakami's Polymorphic Liberalism', in Kozo Yamamura (ed.), *A Vision of a New Liberalism? Critical Essays* (Stanford, CA: Stanford University Press, 1997).
[17] See Donald Crone, 'Does Hegemony Matter? The Reorganization of the Pacific Political Economy', *World Politics*, 45/4 (1993) and Chapter 8 in this volume.

bound states to each other. It was the democratic disposition to cooperate that was the critical source of institutional cooperation. As a result, Wilson did not think the United States was giving up much policy autonomy to get a desired institutionalized order. The League of Nations treaty had an escape clause that made the American commitment to a post-war collective security system consistent with the United States constitution and the wishes of the American Senate. Wilson ultimately did not object to his antagonists in the Senate—and their proposed 'reservations'—because he thought their proposals would break the American commitment to Europe. His rejection of their reservations was more symbolic: that the Senate would send the world the wrong message. This in turn was consistent with his view of the unfolding post-war political situation. The United States needed to encourage the world democratic revolution because it, not specific agreements to reduce American policy autonomy, was the motor of world-order building.

After 1945, the United States again began its thinking about post-war order with a view of an 'automatic' world order that would require little direct American involvement or specific commitments or restraints on its power.[18] Throughout the war, Secretary of State Cordell Hull and the US State Department anticipated a post-war order built around free trade. This was before the post-war social and economic debilitation and potential for political collapse in Europe were fully apparent to American officials and before the cold war rudely shifted official thinking. But the free trade idea was perfect. The United States would get a stable and favourable post-war order without either directly managing the system or placing restraints on its policy autonomy. An open world economy, once the major states moved in this direction, would be self-generating. It would lock other states into a liberal internationalist policy orientation and the United States would not need to offer concessions or reduce its policy discretion.

What was different after 1945 is that the situation changed quickly. The United States realized almost immediately that more direct and specific institutional commitments would be needed to stabilize and orient Europe. In effect, American lock in goals expanded as a result of numerous developments discussed below. Also, for the Europeans the costs of not securing post-war agreements that restrained and committed the United States would be much greater after the Second World War than after the earlier war. These considerations drove the institutional bargain forward. But even as this rolling process of institutional bargaining proceeded, the United States sought to squeeze out as much policy lock-in from Europe with as few restraints on its policy discretion as possible.

---

[18] G. John Ikenberry, 'Rethinking the Origins of American Hegemony', *Political Science Quarterly*, 104/3 (1989).

The Institutional Bargain with Europe

The post-war order in Europe and across the Atlantic was built around multilateral institutions that created an elaborate system of restraint, commitments, and reassurances. The United States and Europe each attempted to lock the other party into specific post-war institutional commitments. They accomplished this in part by agreeing in turn to operate within those institutions as well, even if sometimes reluctantly.

This institutional bargain between the United States and Europe after the Second World War was a rolling process. The United States saw its goals for Europe expand. It progressively came to realize that the stabilizing and reorienting of Europe would require active intervention and engineering, including the creation of a variety of new multilateral institutions that would bind the United States to Europe. It also increasingly valued this European stabilization and reorientation as tensions with the Soviet Union increased. In both these ways, American lock in goals expanded throughout the 1940s. At the same time, the Europeans drove a hard bargain. They actively sought American institutional involvement in post-war Europe and their institutional agreement with the United States was tightly contingent on specific American commitments and restraints. The order that emerged—the European order, the Atlantic order, and the wider post-war world order—was the result of a complex set of rolling institutional agreements that tightly linked the reorganization of Europe to an expanding American multilateral commitment. Along the way, the United States only grudgingly gave up increments of policy autonomy and restraints on its exercise of power but it did so with the explicit understanding that it would be buying the institutional lock-in of Europe.

The most elaborate and consequential institutional bargain was the security alliance. Although established to respond to a growing Soviet threat, the Atlantic pact was also designed to play a wider role in stabilizing relations and reassuring partners *within* the alliance. The NATO alliance provided a mechanism for the rehabilitation and reintegration of West Germany, an instrument of what has been called 'dual containment'. But it also locked in America's reluctant security commitment to Europe, tied the European states together, and reinforced their movement towards regional integration. In this way, the NATO alliance operated along with other post-war institutions as a multifaceted instrument of 'quadruple containment'.

The most consistent British and French objective during and after the war was to bind the United States to Europe. The evolution in American policy, from the goal of a European 'third force' to acceptance of an ongoing security commitment within NATO, was a story of American reluctance and European persistence. The European search for an American security tie was not simply a response to the rise of the Soviet threat. As early as 1943, Winston Churchill proposed a 'Supreme World Council'—composed of the United States, Britain,

Russia, and perhaps China—and regional councils for Europe, the western hemisphere, and the Pacific. In an attempt to institutionalize an American link to Europe, Churchill suggested that the United States would be represented in the European Regional Council, in addition to its role in its own hemisphere. Reflecting American ambivalence about a post-war commitment to Europe, one historian notes, 'Roosevelt feared Churchill's council as a device for tying the United States down in Europe'.[19]

During and after the war, Britain and France sought to bind the United States to Europe in order to make American power more predictable, accessible, and usable. The NATO alliance was particularly useful as an institution that made the exercise of American power more certain and less arbitrary. Despite the vast differences in the size and military power of the various alliance partners, NATO enshrined the principles of equality of status, non-discrimination, and multilateralism.[20] The United States was the clear leader of NATO. But the mutual understandings and institutional mechanisms of the alliance would reduce the implications of these asymmetries of power in its actual operation.

The security alliance also served to reduce European fears of resurgent and unbridled German military power. The strategy of tying Germany to Western Europe was consistently championed by George Kennan:

In the long run there can be only three possibilities for the future of western and central Europe. One is German domination. Another is Russian domination. The third is a federated Europe, into which the parts of Germany are absorbed but in which the influence of the other countries is sufficient to hold Germany in her place. If there is no real European federation and if Germany is restored as a strong and independent country, we must expect another attempt at German domination.[21]

Two years later, Kennan was again arguing that 'without federation there is no adequate framework within which adequately to handle the German problem'.[22]

The idea was to rebuild Germany's economic and military capabilities within European and Atlantic institutions. This binding strategy was widely embraced at the time by American officials. Secretary of State Marshall made the point in early 1948: 'Unless Western Germany during coming year is effectively associated with Western European nations, first through economic arrangements, and ultimately perhaps in some political way, there is a real danger that whole of Germany will

---

[19] John Lamberton Harper, *American Visions of Europe* (New York: Cambridge University Press, 1996), 96.

[20] See Steve Weber, 'Shaping the Postwar Balance of Power: Multilateralism in NATO', in Ruggie (ed.), *Multilateralism Matters*.

[21] 'Report of the Policy Planning Staff', 24 February 1948, *Foreign Relations of the United States*, i., Part 2 (Washington, DC: US Government Printing Office, 1948), 515.

[22] 'Minutes of the Seventh Meeting of the Policy Planning Staff', 24 January 1950, *Foreign Relations of the United States*, iii. (Washington, DC: US Government Printing Office, 1950), 620.

be drawn into the eastern orbit with dire consequences for all of us.'[23] When Secretary of State Dean Acheson went to the Senate to answer questions about the NATO treaty, Senator Claude Pepper posed the question: 'The Atlantic Treaty has given these Western European nations some confidence against a resurgent Germany as well as Russia?' Acheson replied: 'Yes. It works in all directions.'[24] As cold war tensions made West German rearmament increasingly necessary, the elaborateness of alliance restraints on German power also grew, reflected in the complicated negotiations over an integrated military command and the legal agreements accompanying the restoration of German sovereignty.

If NATO bound both West Germany and the United States to Europe, it also reinforced British and French commitment to an open and united Europe. The United States was intent not only on the rehabilitation and reintegration of Germany, it also wanted to reorient Europe itself.[25] In an echo of Wilson's critique of the 'old politics' of Europe after the First World War, American officials after 1945 emphasized the need for reform of nationalist and imperialist tendencies. It was generally thought that the best way to do so was to encourage integration. Regional integration would not only make Germany safe for Europe, it would also make Europe safe for the world. The Marshall Plan reflected this American thinking as did the Truman administration's support for the Brussels Pact, the European Defence Community, and the Schuman Plan. In the negotiations over the NATO treaty in 1948, American officials made clear to the Europeans that a security commitment hinged on European movement towards integration. One State Department official remarked that the United States would not 'rebuild a fire-trap'.[26] The American goal was, as Dean Acheson put it in reference to the EDC, 'to reverse incipient divisive nationalist trends on the continent'.[27] American congressional support for the Marshall Plan was also premised, at least in part, not just on transferring American dollars to Europe but also on encouraging integrative political institutions and habits.

When Marshall Plan aid was provided to Europe, beginning in 1948, the American government insisted that the Europeans themselves organize to

[23] 'Minutes of the Sixth Meeting of the United States-United Kingdom-Canada Security Conversations, Held at Washington', 1 April 1948, *Foreign Relations of the United States*, iii. (Washington, DC: US Government Printing Office, 1948), 71.

[24] Quoted in Lloyd C. Gardner, *A Covenant with Power: American and World Order from Wilson to Reagan* (New York: Oxford University Press, 1984), 100.

[25] For discussions by historians on American support for European integration, see Geoffrey Warner, 'Eisenhower, Dulles, and the Unity of Western Europe, 1955–1957', *International Affairs*, 69 (April 1993); Klaus Schwabe, 'The United States and European Integration, 1947–1957', and Gustav Schmidt, '"Tying" (West) Germany into the West— But to What? NATO? WEU? The European Community?', both in Clemens Wurm (ed.), *Western Europe and Germany: The Beginning of European Integration, 1945–1960* (Oxford and Washington: Berg Publishers, 1995).

[26] 'Minutes of the Fourth Meeting of the Washington Exploratory Talks on Security', 8 July 1948, *Foreign Relations of the United States*, iii. (Washington, DC: US Government Printing Office, 1948), 163–9.

[27] 'The Secretary of State to the Embassy in France', 19 October 1949, *Foreign Relations of the United States*, iv. (Washington, DC: US Government Printing Office, 1949), 471.

jointly allocate the funds. This gave rise to the Organization for European Economic Cooperation (OEEC), which was the institutional forerunner of the European Community. This body eventually became responsible for European-wide supervision of economic reconstruction, and it began to involve the Europeans in discussion of joint economic management. As one American official recalls, the OEEC 'instituted one of the major innovations of postwar international cooperation, the systematic country review, in which the responsible national authorities are cross-examined by a group of their peers together with a high-quality international staff. In those reviews, questions are raised which in prewar days would have been considered a gross and unacceptable foreign interference in domestic affairs'.[28] The United States encouraged European integration as a bulwark against intra-European conflict even as it somewhat more reluctantly agreed to institutionalize its own security commitment to Europe.

The various elements of the institutional bargain among the Atlantic countries fitted together. The Marshall Plan and NATO were part of a larger institutional package. As Lloyd Gardner argues: 'Each formed part of a whole. Together they were designed to "mold the military character" of the Atlantic nations, prevent the balkanization of European defense systems, create an internal market large enough to sustain capitalism in Western Europe, and lock in Germany on the Western side of the Iron Curtain.'[29] NATO was a security alliance, but it was also embraced as a device to lock in political and economic relations within the Atlantic area.

Taken together, American power after the war left the Europeans more worried about abandonment than domination and they actively sought American institutionalized commitments to Europe. Multiple layers of multilateral economic, political, and security institutions bound these countries together, reinforcing the credibility of their mutual commitments. The dramatic asymmetries of post-war power were rendered more acceptable as a result. As the post-1945 period unfolded, American lock in goals for Europe expanded. Stabilizing the European economies, solving the German problem, and reorienting British and French security policies required much more 'engineering' than American officials at first expected. To get these institutional concessions by Europe also entailed reluctant American willingness to make an institutionalized security commitment and reduce its policy autonomy.

Post-Cold War Multilateralism

The United States emerged from the end of the cold war in a newly advantaged position and during the 1990s the world increasingly moved toward unipolarity. In these circumstances, and across security and economic areas,

---

[28] Lincoln Gordon in David Ellwood (ed.), *The Marshall Plan Forty Years After: Lessons for the International System Today* (Bolonga: School of Advanced International Studies, Bologna Center of the Johns Hopkins University, 1988), 48–9.
[29] Gardner, *Covenant with Power*, 81.

the United States sought to build and expand regional and global institutions. NATO expansion and the creation of NAFTA, APEC, and the WTO were elements of this agenda. This pattern of policy is consistent with the logic of post-1945 institution building and it is captured in the model of the institutional bargain. The United States employed institutions as a mechanism to lock in other states to desired policy orientations and it was willing to exchange some limits on its own autonomy to do so. Other states also seized upon these institutions as ways to restrain and commit the United States.

In the immediate aftermath of the cold war, the Bush administration pushed forward a variety of regional institutional initiatives. Towards Europe, State Department officials articulated a set of institutional steps: the evolution of NATO to include associate relations with countries to the east, the creation of more formal institutional relations with the European Community, and an expanded role for the Conference on Security Cooperation in Europe (CSCE).[30] In the western hemisphere, the Bush administration pushed for NAFTA and closer economic ties with South America. In east Asia, APEC was a way to create more institutional links to the region, demonstrating American commitment there and ensuring that Asian regionalism moved in a transpacific direction. The idea was to pursue innovative regional strategies that resulted in new institutional frameworks for post-cold war relations.

These institutional initiatives, Baker later observed, were the key elements of the Bush administration's post-cold war order building strategy and he likened its efforts to American strategy after 1945. 'Men like Truman and Acheson were above all, though we sometimes forget it, *institution builders*. They created NATO and the other security organizations that eventually won the Cold War. They fostered the economic institutions...that brought unparalleled prosperity...At a time of similar opportunity and risk, I believed we should take a leaf from their book.'[31] The idea was to 'plant institutional seeds': to create regional institutional frameworks that would extend and enhance America's influence in these areas and encourage democracy and open markets.[32]

An institution-building agenda was also articulated by the Clinton administration in its strategy of 'enlargement'. The idea was to use multilateral institutions as mechanisms to stabilize and integrate the new and emerging market democracies into the Western democratic world. In an early statement of the enlargement doctrine, National Security Advisor Anthony Lake argued that the strategy was to 'strengthen the community of market democracies' and 'foster and consolidate new democracies and market economies where possible'. The United States would help 'democracy and market economies take root' which would in turn expand and strengthen the wider Western democratic

---

[30] See James A. Baker, III, *The Politics of Diplomacy: Revolution, War and Peace, 1989–1992* (New York: G. P. Putnam and Sons, 1995), 172–3.

[31] Baker, *The Politics of Diplomacy*, 605–6 (emphasis in original).

[32] Interview, Robert B. Zoellick, 28 May 1999.

order.[33] The target of this strategy was primarily those parts of the world that were beginning the process of transition: countries of central and eastern Europe and the Asia-Pacific region. Promising domestic reforms in these countries would be encouraged—and locked in if possible—through new trade pacts and security partnerships.

NATO expansion embodied this institutional logic. At the July 1997 NATO summit, Poland, Hungary, and the Czech Republic were formally invited to join the alliance. These invitations followed a decision made at the January 1994 NATO summit in Brussels to enlarge the alliance to include new members from eastern and central Europe. Led by the United States, the alliance embarked on the most far-reaching and controversial reworking of institutional architecture in the post-cold war era.

The Clinton administration offered several basic rationales for NATO expansion but it consistently emphasized its importance in consolidating democratic and market gains in eastern and central Europe and building an expanded Western democratic community. NATO enlargement would provide an institutional framework to stabilize and encourage democracy and market reform in these reforming countries. NATO would help lock in the domestic transitions under way in eastern and central Europe. The prospect of membership would itself be an 'incentive' for these countries to pursue domestic reforms in advance of actually joining the alliance. Once admitted to NATO, the process of alliance integration was further assumed to lock in institutional reforms. Membership entailed a wide array of organizational adaptations, such as standardization of military procedures, steps towards inter-operability with NATO forces, and joint planning and training. By enmeshing themselves within the wider alliance institutions, the ability of the new NATO members to revert to old ways was reduced and ongoing participation in alliance operations tended to reinforce the governmental changes that were made on the way towards membership. As one NATO official remarked: 'We're enmeshing them in the NATO culture, both politically and militarily so they begin to think like us and—over time—act like us.'[34] NATO membership rewarded steps toward democratic and market reform and pushed it forward and locked it in.

NAFTA and APEC initiatives also embodied this logic although the commitments and lock-in mechanisms were less demanding. The Bush administration supported bringing Mexico into the United States-Canada free trade area for political reasons as well as for the anticipated economic gains. Mexico was undergoing a democratic revolution and American officials wanted to lock in these watershed reforms. Mexican officials also championed the trade accord for the same reason: it would lock in their successors to policy commitments and economic relations that would thwart political backsliding. APEC also

---

[33] Anthony Lake, 'From Containment to Enlargement', *Vital Speeches of the Day*, 60 (15 October 1993).

[34] Quoted in Pat Towell, 'Aspiring NATO Newcomers Face Long Road to Integration', *Congressional Quarterly* (7 February 1998), 275.

manifested at least a trace of this same reasoning. A multilateral economic dialogue was possible within east Asia because of the long-term shift in the developmental orientation of the emerging economies of the region. Japan and
Australia were the initiators of the APEC process but the United States quickly lent
its support. At least part of the appeal of APEC within the region was that it was
a counterweight to American unilateral trade tendencies: the multilateral process
would help restrain the worst impulses of American trade policy, symbolized in
the Super-301 authority—the trade authority that Congress gives the executive
under which the United States can act unilaterally to punish other countries for
restrictive or subsidized trade. In return, the United States was able to encourage
an open east Asian economic regionalism and reinforce the market reforms that
were unfolding across Asia and the western hemisphere. The actual ability of
APEC to lock in policy orientations in the region was limited, but the restraints
on American policy autonomy were also more symbolic than real.

This pattern of institution building can be seen as a continuation of the logic
that underlay the Western post-war settlement. Institutional agreements were
pursued in order to reinforce domestic governmental and economic changes
which, in turn, tended to fix into place desired policy orientations. As a leading
State Department official describes the institutional strategy: 'Our intention was
to create institutions, habits, and inclinations that would bias policy in these
countries in our direction.'[35] The United States was able to ensure political and
economic access to these countries and regions and gain some confidence that
they would remain committed to political and market openness. In exchange,
these countries gained some measure of assurance that American policy would
be steady and predictable. The United States would remain engaged and do so
through institutions that would leave it open to market and political access by
these countries.

The new Bush administration has not fully come to terms with the post-war
institutional bargains with Europe and Asia, and the events of 11 September
2001 expose divisions among officials about how rules and institutional agreements fit into its campaign against terrorism.[36] Two distinct strategies are competing for primacy. One is the strategy of liberal multilateralism that generally
characterized the approach of the previous Bush and Clinton administrations as
well as American policy during the post-Second World War era within the West.
But some Bush administration officials embrace a more unilateral, even imperial, grand strategy, based on a starkly realist vision of American interests and
global power realities. In this view, American preponderance allows it selectively to engage Europe and Asia, dominating world politics with military forces
that are both unchallenged and less bound to United Nations or alliance
controls. Cooperative security, arms control, and multilateral cooperation
across the board play a reduced role in this global strategy. But the events of

---

[35] Interview, Robert B. Zoellick, 28 May 1999.
[36] This section draws on G. John Ikenberry, 'American Grand Strategy in the Age of
Terror', *Survival*, 43/4 (2001).

11 September have rendered this strategy deeply problematic. The logic of the Bush administration's war on terrorism, with its emphasis on leading an international coalition of states, creates incentives for the administration's foreign policy to move back in the direction of post-war liberal multilateralism.

Both unilateral and multilateral tendencies exist within the administration.[37] To be sure, it has reaffirmed basic aspects of the multilateral economic and security order and America's leadership position within it. It has moved forward aggressively with freer trade and investment in the western hemisphere and called for a new round of global multilateral trade negotiations. But lurking in some quarters of the government is a deep scepticism about operating within a multilateral rule-based international order. Glimpses are offered of an alternative grand strategy of unilateralism and selective engagement. 'It is not isolationist but unilateralist, unashamed of using military power', one reporter notes.[38] It is a unilateral grand strategy that resists involvements in regional and multilateral entanglements that are deemed marginal to America's own security needs. It envisages American power acting on the world but not being entangled by the world.[39]

The most visible sign of this scepticism about liberal multilateralism and institutional commitments in the Bush administration is the dramatic sequence of rejections of pending international agreements, including the Kyoto Protocol, the International Criminal Court, the Biological Weapons Ban, and the Trade in Light Arms treaty. In pushing national missile defence, the administration also signalled its willingness to unilaterally withdraw from the 1972 Anti-Ballistic Missile Defence treaty, which many regarded as the cornerstone of modern arms-control agreements. In each case, there is serious debate about the merits of various aspects of these agreements. But together the chorus of rejections underscore the misgivings the Bush administration has about the entire enterprise of multilateral and rule-based cooperation.[40]

The vision that lies behind this grand strategy and military posture is deeply rooted in old ideas about the country's place in the world, ideas that over the last 50 years have been pushed to the sidelines.[41] It is a vision of a country that is big enough, powerful enough, and remote enough to go it alone and disentangle itself from the dangerous and corrupting conflicts festering in all the other regions of the world. It is a vision that is deeply suspicious of international

[37] The US State Department's Director of Policy Planning, Richard Haass, has coined the term 'à la carte multilateralism' to refer to the administration's approach, but important differences in thinking exist across the administration. See Thom Shanker, 'White House Says the U.S. is Not a Loner, Just Choosy', *The New York Times* (31 July 2001).

[38] Stephen Fidler, 'Between Two Camps', *Financial Times* (14 February 2001).

[39] For a fascinating survey of these ideas, see Nicholas Lemann, 'A Next World Order', *The New Yorker* (1 April 2002).

[40] See Gerard Baker, 'Bush Heralds Era of U.S. Self-Interest', *International Herald Tribune* (24 April 2001).

[41] See Thomas E. Ricks, 'U.S. Urged to Embrace an "Imperial" Role', *International Herald Tribune* (22 August 2001).

rules and institutions. 'It is the difference between those who would rely on lawyers to defend America and those who rely on engineers and scientists', observed Newt Gingrich in explaining why his Contract with America included a commitment to National Missile Defence.[42] The dream that propels many missile-defence proponents is not a limited missile shield that might stop an errant missile launched by a rogue state, but a national shield that will once and for all do away with the post-war system of nuclear deterrence, based as it is on the ugly logic of mutual assured destruction.

It is unclear whether the Bush administration's discovery of the virtues of a multilateral coalition in fighting terrorism will spill over to its larger grand strategy. But there will be pressures and incentives for it to move back to a more general multilateral orientation. At least, it will be difficult for the US to ask for new forms of cooperation—intelligence, logistical support, political solidarity—from other states and resist their strongly held views on missile defence, global warming, and other major issues. American unilateralism, exhibited in the first six months of the Bush term, was built on ideology and a practical reality. The ideology was the idea of unilateral or imperial grand strategy embraced by a vocal and articulate group of officials swept into office. The practical reality was that the United States could in fact say 'no' to agreements and not pay a huge price. Today, that ideology has not disappeared but it is less credible. More important, the new practical reality is that the United States does want something from its partners, so it will need to give things in return.

3. Conclusion

Several general conclusions can be offered. First, there is a general institutional logic that combines the instincts of both realist and liberal theory. Institutional bargains are driven by concerns about policy autonomy, legitimacy, the exercise of power, and political certainty. The struggle is to promote a predictable and favourable international environment in which to operate. States are self-interested actors who jealously guard their policy autonomy and sovereign authority but which also are willing to bargain if the price is right. Ironically, it is precisely the asymmetry of power that creates the potential mutually beneficial exchange. The leading state has an incentive to take advantage of its newly dominant position to lock in a favourable set of international relationships—institutionalizing its pre-eminence. The subordinate states are willing to lock themselves in, at least up to some point, if it means that the leading state will be more manageable as a dominant power.

Second, this model assumes that institutions can play a role in muting asymmetries in power, thereby allowing the leading state to calculate its interests

---

[42] Stephen Fidler, 'Conservatives Determined to Carry Torch for U.S. Missile Defense', *Financial Times* (11 July 2001).

over a longer time frame with institutions serving as a mechanism to invest in future gains and the weaker states to be confident that there can be credible restraints on the arbitrary and indiscriminate exercise of power. If institutions are unable to play this role, then the calculations and trade-offs that are highlighted in the model will likely not be of much consequence. But American officials themselves have acted in a way that suggests that at least they think institutions can in fact play such a shaping and restraining role.

Third, the actual costs and benefits behind the trade-off between policy autonomy and policy lock-in are difficult to specify in advance. The post-war crisis in Europe and the multiple engineering tasks that the United States saw as absolutely critical were real enough and they justified the restraints and commitments that the United States offered to get these institutionalized arrangements in Europe. But some of the other lock-in goals, such as economic reforms, human rights standards, and war crimes laws, are not easy to evaluate as goals worthy of X or Y amount of reduced policy autonomy. Because of this the institutional model is perhaps better at identifying a dilemma that states face and less effective at specifying in advance how the trade-offs will be made.

American foreign policy after 11 September 2001 illuminates these basic dilemmas. The choices that the Bush administration makes will have important impacts on its institutional bargains with the outside world, beyond the immediate struggle with terrorism. In seeking partners in its struggle, the United States is rediscovering that the alliances and strategic partnerships that have been built over the decades still exist and are useful. Secretary of State Powell remarked after NATO voted its support for the American campaign that 50 years of steady investment in the alliance had paid off.[43] When the United States ties itself to a wider grouping of states it is more effective. But to do so requires some compromise of national autonomy. It must both restrain and commit its power. The logic of this grand strategy is captured by Robert Jervis:

Binding itself to act multilaterally by forgoing the capability to use large-scale force on its own would then provide a safeguard against the excessive use of American power. This might benefit all concerned: the United States would not be able to act on its own worst impulses; others would share the costs of interventions and would also be less fearful of the United States and so, perhaps, more prone to cooperate with it.[44]

The struggle between unilateral and multilateral grand strategies today is a debate over the costs and benefits of binding American power to wider alliance and global groupings. The United States may give up some discretion but gains partners. The coalition-based struggle against terrorism is providing an object lesson in how best to strike the balance.

---

[43] Secretary of State Colin Powell, public statement (10 October 2001).
[44] Robert Jervis, 'International Primacy: Is the Game worth the Candle?' *International Security*, 17/4 (1993), 66.

II

THE US AND GLOBAL ORGANIZATIONS

3

US–UN Relations in the UN Security Council in the Post-Cold War Era

DAVID M. MALONE

After dominating the United Nations completely in its first 15 years through its close political relationships with many of the organization's founding members, the United States of America found itself increasingly on the defensive in the UN General Assembly, against growing majorities of recently de-colonized countries unsympathetic to its views. However, its veto in the UN Security Council provided protection against decisions there inimical to its interests. Consequently, on key security issues, the US increasingly viewed the Security Council rather than the General Assembly as its forum of choice at the UN.

With the end of the cold war, a fading of the superpower confrontation at the UN, directly and through proxies, and the advent of a more values-based foreign policy initiated under President Carter (1977–81) selectively reinforced by President Reagan (1981–9) and strengthened under President Bush (1989–93), the US stance in the UN Security Council during the 1990s veered between decisions seemingly taken for diffuse humanitarian reasons and those which reflected a more instrumental US approach. This inconsistency of approach was particularly significant because it was occurring at a time when the UN was addressing a far larger range of conflicts and doing so in greater depth when it came to conflict resolution. Moreover, the importance of the position that the United States took was further demonstrated as it became apparent that, while the UN's normative activities, in the Security Council and elsewhere, could make progress in the absence of active US support, major peacekeeping operations were unlikely to succeed without strong US backing and, in some cases, participation.

This chapter will first provide some evidence of this US inconsistency of behaviour in the 1990s with reference to conflict resolution—including use of force, sanctions, and peacekeeping matters—and then with respect to such humanitarian issues as human rights, democracy promotion, and humanitarian intervention. It will go on to explain the primary influences on this behaviour, arguing that US ambivalence towards the UN has been more affected by struggles over a New International Economic Order in the 1970s and US perceptions of unbalanced UN approaches to the Arab-Israeli dispute than by the end of the cold war. Having made special reference to America's chequered historical experience of the United Nations, it examines the ways in which negative perceptions of the UN have played out in US domestic politics, particularly since the late 1990s. Finally, the chapter reviews America's experience of the UN's expanded post-cold war security agenda, noting that the inherent tensions between the promotion of values and the promotion of interests, and the difficulties of relating means to ends, have come sharply to the fore during this period. Scepticism about the UN's competence has combined with this deeper distrust of the organization among leading US politicians. The new Bush administration has inherited a legacy of hostility towards the body—especially among leading Republican Senators—and decreased US influence within it, despite America's status as sole remaining superpower.

Devastating terrorist attacks on the World Trade Center in New York and on the Pentagon on 11 September 2001 reoriented, at least in some key respects, Washington's approach to relations with the UN. A new emphasis on multilateralism and coalition-building featured prominently in public pronouncements immediately after those events, and repayment of most UN arrears to the UN was agreed in the days following the attacks. Nevertheless, the US subsequently conducted military action against the Al Qaeda terrorist network and the Taleban regime in Afghanistan in a 'hub-and-spokes' fashion, dealing bilaterally with key NATO and regional allies in prosecuting the campaign. It welcomed UN Security Council resolutions condemning the attacks on the US, but worked to preclude any Council language that might have constrained its margin for military and political manoeuvre. Echoing US plans for 'smart sanctions' against Iraq, one seasoned UN hand described the US approach as 'smart unilateralism'.[1]

1. Use of Force, Sanctions, and Peacekeeping

The 1990s witnessed momentous shifts in the Security Council's approach to conflict and its resolution, and a sharp drop in use of the veto.[2] Events held by the Council as constituting a threat to international peace expanded to include a range of humanitarian catastrophes, particularly those generating large exoduses of displaced persons and refugees, internally and internationally. This

---

[1] Confidential interview.

[2] Only nine vetoes were cast in the 1990s, as opposed to 192 in the previous 45 years: two by China—over Guatemala and Macedonia, but both relating to ties with Taiwan by these two governments; two by Russia—over Cyprus and the Former Yugoslavia; and five by the US—one over its military intervention in Panama and four over aspects of the Arab–Israeli conflict. During the cold war, the Soviet Union had used the veto nearly twice as much as had the US.

allowed the Council to address a range of conflicts, mostly internal in nature, which it would have avoided in the past when the cold war antagonists often played out their hostility through regional proxies and were prepared to frustrate Council involvement. The Council's decisions in the 1990s proved highly innovative in shaping the normative framework for international relations and stimulated several radical legal developments at the international level, notably the creation of International Criminal Tribunals for the Former Yugoslavia in 1993 and Rwanda in 1994. This in turn greatly intensified pressure for a more universal International Criminal Court (ICC), a statute for which was adopted at a diplomatic conference in Rome in 1998 in spite of US opposition.[3]

Nevertheless, late in the decade, serious tensions resurfaced in the Council over issues relating to state sovereignty, legitimization of the use of force, and the growing incidence of unilateralism by the US and some of its allies. Differences crystallized in 1998 and 1999 among the permanent five (P-5) members over conflicting objectives for, and approaches to, Iraq and Kosovo. As well, Council decision-making at times suggested the re-emergence of 'spheres of influence', with trade-offs in 1994 accommodating France on Rwanda, the Russian Federation on Georgia, and the US on Haiti.[4] This latter phenomenon was not long sustained for, by the late 1990s, France was implementing a more arms-length policy towards its former African colonies and Russia was having trouble controlling events even within its own borders, most notably in Chechnya. Only the US survived as a global power. As I argued in 1998:

The debate since 1994 over the revival of spheres of influence among the P-5, while perhaps music to the ears of the Russian Federation (still shaping its approach to its 'near abroad'), needs to be treated with caution. US global leadership in the Security Council is central, and its ability to sway the UN membership on issues critical to it is unique. Only it can project significant political and military clout continents away. It is significant that France insisted on American partnership as a pre-condition for its own participation in a planned multinational force to assist Rwandan refugees in Zaire in November 1996. Many countries follow the lead of the US, while France and the Russian Federation retain the ability to persuade some countries formerly identified with their spheres of influence. The UK relies on strong links to the US, occasional partnership with France, some traditional links (such as those still existing in the Commonwealth), and the strength of its arguments to influence sentiment at the UN and voting in the Council. China is

---

[3] Subsequently, in January 2001, as one of President Clinton's final acts during his term of office, he did sign the treaty for the ICC. However, the US Senate remains reluctant to ratify and the Bush administration has raised the possibility of 'unsigning' the treaty.

[4] See David M. Malone, *UN Security Council Decision-Making: The Case of Haiti* (Oxford: Clarendon Press, 1998), 117.

passive on many questions, but positions itself as a champion of NAM [Non-Aligned Movement] views and interests.[5]

The Council's willingness in the 1990s to involve itself in a broad range of internal conflicts, encompassing inter-communal strife, crises of democracy, fierce struggles for control of national resources and wealth, and several other precipitating causes or incentives for continuation of war, forced it to confront hostilities of a much more complex nature than the inter-state disputes with which it had greater experience. International efforts to mitigate and resolve these conflicts required complex peacekeeping mandates significantly more ambitious than those that the modalities of 'classic' peacekeeping were designed to meet.[6] The most striking features of 'new generation' peacekeeping operations (PKOs) launched by the Council in the 1990s were not so much the large numbers of military personnel involved—several earlier PKOs, such as those in the Sinai, Congo, and even Cyprus, had featured large deployments of Blue Helmets—but rather the important role and substantive diversity of their civilian and police components.[7] Civilian functions discharged by PKOs or otherwise mandated by the Council included civil administration, most notably in Namibia, Cambodia, the Former Yugoslavia; humanitarian assistance; human rights monitoring and training; police and judicial support, training, and reform; and even a degree of leadership on economic revival and development.[8] The ambitious objectives served by these activities proved significantly more difficult to attain in many circumstances than the Council seems to have anticipated. The Security Council's inability to induce compliance with its decisions fuelled two damaging and to some degree contradictory responses: on the one hand, it moved to enforce decisions which had failed to generate consent in the field, notably in the Former Yugoslavia,[9] Somalia,[10]

[5] Malone, *UN Security Council Decision-Making*, 169.

[6] For discussion of the evolution of peacekeeping, see in particular Thomas G. Weiss, David P. Forsythe, and Roger A. Coate, *The United Nations in a Changing World*, 2nd edn (Boulder, CO: Westview Press, 1997).

[7] See in particular Michael C. Williams, *Civil-Military Relations and Peacekeeping* (Oxford: Oxford University Press, 1998). One strikingly new feature of peacekeeping in the era has been growing participation of P-5 troops in UN and NATO-led peacekeeping in such places as Bosnia, Kosovo, Somalia, and East Timor. During the cold war years, P-5 countries only exceptionally participated in large number in PKOs, as did the French in Lebanon and the British in Cyprus, where they had respectively played colonial roles.

[8] See Steven R. Ratner, *The New UN Peacekeeping: Building Peace in Lands of Conflict after the Cold War* (New York: St Martins Press with the Council on Foreign Relations, 1996). See also Elizabeth M. Cousens and Chetan Kumar with Karin Wermester (eds), *Peacebuilding as Politics: Cultivating Peace in Fragile Societies* (Boulder, CO: Lynne Rienner, 2000).

[9] There is a plethora of literature regarding the Former Yugoslavia and constraints and obstacles encountered in the field including: Adam Roberts, 'Communal Conflict as a Challenge to International Organization: The Case of Former Yugoslavia', *Review of International Studies*, 21 (1995); International Crisis Group, 'Kosovo: Let's Learn from Bosnia—Models and Methods of International Administration', Sarajevo, Bosnia (17 May 1999), at www.crisisweb.org.

[10] See John L. Hirsch and Robert Oakley, *Somalia and Operation Restore Hope: Reflections on Peacemaking and Peacekeeping* (Washington, DC: United States Institute for Peace Press,

and Haiti;[11] on the other, in the face of significant casualties, it cut and ran, as in Somalia and at the outset of genocide in Rwanda.[12]

The United States gave free rein to both impulses. In the Former Yugoslavia it chafed at the ineffectiveness of the UN's large PKO, UNPROFOR, particularly in the years 1993–5, advocating stronger measures, notably the lifting of the UN arms embargo against Bosnia and NATO bombing against Bosnian Serb and Serbian targets, to give teeth to Council resolutions. However, as it was unwilling to risk any of its military personnel on the ground where their safety might have been placed in danger by these tactics, US pleas for stronger action were coldly received by European and Canadian allies who had engaged troops within UNPROFOR.[13] And when its own troops came under fire in Mogadishu in October 1993 with severe casualties, it announced its withdrawal from UNOSOM and that country.[14] With Somalia in mind, it also worked hard against any decision to reinforce UNAMIR, the UN's peacekeeping operation in Rwanda after the killing of ten Belgian peacekeepers and Belgium's immediate withdrawal from the force. Until late 1999, when the arrival of Richard Holbrooke as US Permanent Representative to the UN seemed to effect a qualified about-face in the administration's extremely reserved approach to UN peacekeeping, Washington's policies seemed conditioned by a restrictive reading of Presidential Decision Directive (PDD) of 25 May 1994, which set stiff conditions for US participation in, and even support of, UN PKOs. Gary Ostrower explained it thus:

As Albright told the *New York Times* [on 6 May 1994], the UN had been asked to do 'too much'. Noble ambition must be reined in by a sense of the possible, and the

1995) and more recently Mark Bowden, *Black Hawk Down: A Story of Modern War* (New York: Atlantic Monthly Press, 1999).

[11] Malone, *UN Security Council Decision-Making* ; also James F. Dobbins, *Haiti: A Case Study in Post-Cold War Peacekeeping*, ISD Reports III (Washington, DC: Institute for the Study of Diplomacy, Georgetown University, October 1995); and on Haiti and Somalia see David Bentley and Robert Oakley, 'Peace Operations: A Comparison of Somalia and Haiti', *Strategic Forum*, 30 (Washington, DC: Institute for National Strategic Studies, National Defense University, May 1995).

[12] See in particular Gérard Prunier, *The Rwanda Crisis: History of a Genocide* (New York: Columbia University Press, 1995); Michael Barnett, 'The UN Security Council, Indifference and Genocide in Rwanda', *Cultural Anthropology*, 12 (1997), 551; and J. Matthew Vaccaro, 'The Politics of Genocide: Peacekeeping and Disaster Relief in Rwanda', in William J. Durch (ed.), *The UN, Peacekeeping, American Policy and the Uncivil Wars of the 1990s* (New York: St Martin's Press, 1996).

[13] On US policy with respect to UNPROFOR, see Warren Zimmermann, *Origins of a Catastrophe: Yugoslavia and its Destroyers* (New York: Times Books/Random House, 1996), 111–254; David Owen, *Balkan Odyssey* (New York: Harcourt Brace, 1995); Richard Holbrooke, *To End a War* (New York: Random House, 1998); Laura Silber and Allan Little, *Yugoslavia: Death of a Nation* (US: TV Books 1995), 222–318. For a critical view of UNPROFOR itself, see David Rieff, *Slaughterhouse* (New York: Touchstone/Simon & Schuster, 1996) and also Thomas G. Weiss, 'Collective Spinelessness: UN Actions in the Former Yugoslavia', in Richard H. Ullman (ed.), *The World and Yugoslavia's Wars* (New York: Council on Foreign Relations, 1996).

[14] On these events in Somalia, see Hirsch and Oakley, *Somalia and Operation Restore Hope*, 115–48.

limitations of UN activity must be recognized...PDD 25 abruptly reverses Clinton's own campaign rhetoric calling for more American support for UN operations. [It] reflected disillusionment, frustration, and even exhaustion with peacekeeping during a period when such operations exhibited explosive growth...Although the document called for a more selective approach to peacekeeping, some who applauded it, like the ranking Republican on the Senate Foreign relations Committee, Jesse Helms of North Carolina, hoped to end US peacekeeping contributions altogether. Others who applauded it, like the internationalist editors of the *New York Times*, argued that 'there should be a shift back toward more limited objectives like policing cease-fires'.[15]

Doctrinally, the US appeared fearful and inconsistent. It viewed Somalia as a dangerous case of 'mission creep', but its own officers in the field occasionally continued to advocate broad interpretation of Security Council mandates.[16] After the extended hand wringing—legitimized and, to some extent, introduced by PDD 25—Holbrooke's robust approach to African conflicts, particularly in Sierra Leone, in early 2000 was refreshing. He proved highly supportive of a hard-hitting International Panel report on shortcomings in peacekeeping in August 2000 and helped arrange for a P-5 Summit focusing entirely on improvements in peacekeeping funding and operations on 7 September 2000.[17]

The frequent resort in the 1990s to the provisions of Chapter VII of the UN Charter and to enforcement of Council decisions was not new: Council decisions were enforced in Korea and to a much lesser extent in the Congo during the UN's early years, with the US in the vanguard of the Korean effort between 1950 and 1953. Nevertheless, the extent to which the Council adopted decisions under Chapter VII during the 1990s, always with US concurrence and often at its behest, was wholly unprecedented. At first, it was hoped that the UN would prove capable of launching and managing enforcement operations. However, in the face of disappointing, occasionally catastrophic, results in the Former Yugoslavia and Somalia, UN Secretary-General Boutros Boutros-Ghali concluded by 1994 that the UN should not itself seek to conduct large-scale enforcement activities. Consequently, the Security Council increasingly resorted for enforcement of its decisions to 'coalitions of the willing' in Haiti in 1994, in Bosnia after 1995, in the Central African Republic in 1997, and in East Timor in 1999.[18] It also alternately both worried about and supported in

---

[15] Gary B. Ostrower, *The United Nations and the United States* (New York: Twayne Publishers, 1998), 220. The *New York Times* editorial mentioned in this extract appeared on 12 January 1995, A24.

[16] For an account of the flexibility and creativity with which Maj.-Gen. Joseph Kinzer, the American Commander of UN Forces in Haiti, successfully approached his responsibilities in 1995–6, see Malone, *UN Security Council Decision-Making*, 131–2.

[17] *Report of the Panel on United Nations Peace Operations* (A/55/305-S/2000/809) 21 August 2000. For an account of the P-5 Summit see Stephen Fidler and Carola Hoyos, 'US welcomes shift on funding UN operations', *Financial Times* (8 September 2000).

[18] For an excellent reference work covering UN peacekeeping operations from 1947 to the present, see Oliver Ramsbotham and Tom Woodhouse, *Encyclopedia of International Peacekeeping Operations* (Santa Barbara, CA: ABC-CLIO, 1999).

qualified terms enforcement activities by regional bodies, notably ECOMOG, the military arm of the west African economic cooperation arrangement ECOWAS, in Liberia and Sierra Leone, but this was sometimes under pressure from the US, which was seeking to avoid more direct involvement of its own through UN action. One such enforcement technique, employed only once previously by the Council, against Rhodesia, was the resort to naval blockades to enforce UN Security Council-mandated sanctions. These blockades, mostly led by the US, unfolded with varying success against Iraq in the Persian Gulf and the Gulf of Aqaba, against various parties in the Former Yugoslavia on the Danube and in the Adriatic Sea and against Haiti.[19] With the exception of action on the Central African Republic, very much driven by France, and on Sierra Leone, on which the UK retained the lead within the Council, the US was an active proponent of all of these enforcement measures. However, in deference to Clinton administration perceptions of public opinion—which may well have been erroneous but were rarely less than cautious—Washington engaged its own combat troops sparingly after the Mogadishu fiasco, deploying them in Haiti (1994–6), Bosnia (as of 1995) and Kosovo (from 1999 onwards) only where American interests were perceived to be at play. It provided logistical support for multilateral efforts in East Timor, but did not provide front-line personnel of its own.

The US was not opposed to the use of force per se, having marshalled international coalitions to good effect against Iraq in 1990–1 and in Haiti in 1994, but grew increasingly reserved about the UN's coercive capacities. The US advocated a 'lift and strike' approach to the Bosnian conflict during much of the period 1993–5.[20] It preferred NATO air power to UN ground troops to pressure Belgrade and its Bosnian allies into submission, although the US did commit ground troops to the international coalitions monitoring implementation of the Dayton Accord on Bosnia as of late 1995. A preference for NATO air power was again on display in 1999 in action against Serb units in Kosovo and elsewhere. Indeed, US reluctance to commit ground personnel to the fray was seen as an Achilles heel of the operation. However, once again the US did agree to a significant American military deployment in Kosovo, alongside that of other countries within KFOR, to help secure compliance with the terms of Security Council Resolution (SCR) 1244 of 10 June 1999—actually negotiated within the Group of Eight forum—bringing the active hostilities between NATO and Belgrade to a close.

More common than military enforcement decisions by the Council was the resort to mandatory economic—and, increasingly, diplomatic—sanctions under Chapter VII of the Charter (discussed above), a favoured tool of US diplomacy. However, while arms embargoes remained in vogue, imposition of

---

[19] UN Department of Political Affairs, 'A Brief Overview of Security Council Applied Sanctions', *Interlaken*, 2 (1998).
[20] The US wished to *lift* sanctions against Bosnia and to *strike* the Serbs from the air.

comprehensive trade and other economic sanctions, seen as more gentle than the resort to force, faded noticeably once the humanitarian costs of sanctions against Haiti and Iraq became widely known late in the decade. Resistance to their use increased within the UN General Assembly, notably against Iraq, where their humanitarian consequences were well documented. Washington argued that the Saddam Hussein regime was responsible for the humanitarian plight of Iraqis due to misallocation of available resources, but this cut little ice with a General Assembly membership and UN Secretariat increasingly hostile to a policy that was producing perverse results.[21]

The US also favoured more targeted economic sanctions, such as the ban on air flights aimed at inducing Libyan cooperation with Council efforts to address several terrorist aircraft bombings, and diplomatic sanctions against the Sudan in response to an assassination attempt against Egyptian President Hosni Mubarak.[22] Targeted sanctions were also adopted, at the US's behest, against the Taleban in Afghanistan in November 1999 as a result of the protection provided to Osama Bin Laden.[23] These sanctions were strengthened in December 2000.[24] However, US unilateral economic sanctions against Cuba were increasingly condemned by the UN General Assembly as the decade proceeded, with one resolution netting 151 votes in favour, 8 abstentions, and only 2 votes against—Israel alongside the US.[25] The European Union and Canada, meanwhile, had to fend off the effects of unilateral sanctions imposed by the US Congress against not only companies doing business with Cuba but also those engaged in commerce with Iran and Libya.[26]

In sum, the favoured coercive instruments of the US by decade's end were bombing—of Iraq since December 1998 and during short bursts earlier in the decade; of the Former Yugoslavia at the time of the Kosovo crisis in 1999—and sanctions. Neither risked heavy casualties—that is, for the international actors

---

[21] See Jim Wurst, 'Security Council Faces Iraqi Inspections and Sanctions Issues', *Inter-Press-Service (IPS) Terra* (14 April 2000), www.ipsdailyjournal.org. See also the hard-hitting paragraphs on sanctions in the UN Secretary-General's *Millennium Report* of 3 April 2000 at www.un.org/millennium/sg/report.

[22] For a discussion of sanctions and the increasing use of targeted sanctions, see Daniel W. Drezner, *The Sanctions Paradox: Economic Statecraft and International Relations* (Cambridge: Cambridge University Press, 1999). See also David Cortright and George Lopez, *The Sanctions Decade: Assessing UN Strategies in the 1990s*, An IPA Project (Boulder, CO: Lynne Rienner, 2000).

[23] See SCR 1267 of 15 October 1999. The sanctions went into effect on 14 November 1999. US pressure for sanctions against the Taleban coincided with Russia's military campaign against Chechen separatists, repeatedly vilified as fundamentalist terrorists and Islamic extremists by Moscow. Russia's support for Security Council-mandated action against the Taleban was thus consonant with its domestic concerns.

[24] See SCR 1333 of 19 December 2000.

[25] See General Assembly Resolution A/Res/54/21 of 9 November 1999. US legislation imposing severe sanctions on foreign companies and foreign subsidiaries of US companies investing in Cuba were also strongly resisted by the European Union and Canada.

[26] The legislation in question was the Cuban Liberty and Democratic Solidarity Act—the so-called Helms-Burton Bill—signed into law by President Clinton on 12 March 1996 and the Iran and Libya Sanctions Act signed by Clinton on 5 August 1996.

involved—at a time when alarm was rising over growing incidents of violence against UN staffers and related international personnel, including that of non-governmental organizations serving in fields of conflict.[27] Both strategies gave rise to quiet complaints at the UN that these were cowardly means of confronting adversaries, but there were few complaints from the US public or from political circles in Washington.

2. Humanitarian Issues, Human Rights, and Democracy

The US was highly prone, as were some other member states, to concern over humanitarian suffering of civilians in war, particularly refugees. Refugees were hardly a new topic in the Council, the Arab-Israeli dispute of 1947–8 having led to the creation of a UN agency, UNRWA, exclusively dedicated to their welfare. Those displaced by war had long been seen as deserving the care of the international community and were among the prime 'clients' of both the Red Cross system—the International Committee of the Red Cross and the International Federation of Red Cross and Red Crescent Societies—and the UN High Commissioner for Refugees. Nevertheless, in the 1990s as never before, the US invoked the plight of refugees and their implied destabilizing effect on neighbouring states as grounds for Council involvement in conflict. Any threat that the Haitian crisis of democracy in 1991–4 may actually have posed to international peace and security could have arisen only from the outflow of Haitian boat people which might have threatened to engulf a number of Caribbean countries had the shores of Florida not been their preferred destination. The widespread acceptance that refugee flows could actually be a major catalyst of conflict, rather than merely an outcome of it, was new in the Council.

Humanitarian considerations were a driving force in shaping US positions on a variety of conflicts. The so-called 'CNN effect' was pervasive in the US as elsewhere, with audiences witnessing in real time the horrendous conditions endured by victims of war. Indeed, concern over the starvation of large numbers of Somalis, victims of drought and the depredations of Somali warlords, impelled President Bush in late 1992 to call for and mount an international coalition to take over from an ineffective UN peacekeeping operation only partially deployed in that country.[28] This fateful decision led to a complex US military entanglement in Somalia, culminating in the catastrophic battle of October 1993 leaving 18 army Rangers dead and souring the US on

[27] See Jim Wurst, 'UN Flag Goes from Shield to Target', *Inter-Press Service (IPS) Terra* (10 February 2000), www.ipsdailyjournal.org.
[28] For a straightforward and authoritative account of these events, see Hirsch and Oakley, *Somalia and Operation Restore Hope*, 17–47.

'UN peacekeeping' for many years, even though the dead Rangers had not been under UN command at the time.[29]

Civil strife of such proportions was instrumental in promoting Security Council interest in the protection of human rights. Internal conflicts were likely to be even less amenable to negotiated solutions as long as human rights continued to be massively violated. Thus, the protection, promotion, and monitoring of human rights formed an important and uncontroversial part of the mandates of several UN peacekeeping operations in the 1990s, notably in El Salvador and Guatemala.[30] Where this was not the case, as in Rwanda and Haiti, the UN General Assembly, as part of the broader UN strategy, often deployed parallel human rights missions, with strong US support. For the US, action on human rights at the multilateral level—for example, its attempts throughout much of the 1990s to have human rights abuses in China addressed by the UN Commission on Human Rights—relieved pressure on Washington to act bilaterally. Paradoxically, Republican House and Senate committees increasingly as of 1995 castigated the US administration and the UN for insufficient vigilance on human rights in Haiti, complaining of policies allegedly biased in favour of populist and popular President Jean-Bertrand Aristide.

The US also strongly espoused Council action to promote democracy, *inter alia* by mandating the organization and monitoring of elections, a trend as unlikely during the cold war as would have been the driving force of humanitarian considerations and the Council's role on human rights in the 1990s.[31] The US provided intermittent but ultimately strong leadership in the UN Security Council and at the Organization of American States (OAS) to restore Haitian President Jean-Bertrand Aristide to power after a coup against him in September 1991. Indeed, within its own hemisphere in particular, the United States worked hard and effectively in support of democracy, helping to reverse a military coup in Ecuador in January 2000 and generally remaining true to its strong and consistent commitment to the OAS Santiago Declaration of 1991 on the protection and promotion of democracy among OAS member states. Nevertheless, as the decade drew to an end, the US and other Western powers in the Security Council accepted that elections did not provide a sufficient answer to the challenge of democratization: kleptocratic and inept elected

[29] A rich literature dealing with international impulses underpinning the trend towards 'humanitarian interventions' has grown up in recent years. See Simon Chesterman, *Just War or Just Peace: Humanitarian Intervention and International Law* (Oxford: Oxford University Press, 2001); Simon Chesterman (ed.), *Civilians in War* (Boulder, CO: Lynne Rienner, 2001). The most useful current reference volume on this question is the masterfully annotated Adam Roberts and Richard Guelff (eds), *Documents on the Laws of War*, 3rd edn (Oxford: Oxford University Press, 2000).

[30] On El Salvador, see in particular Michael W. Doyle, Ian Johnstone, and Robert C. Orr (eds), *Keeping the Peace: Multidimensional UN Operations in Cambodia and El Salvador* (Cambridge: Cambridge University Press, 1997). On Guatemala, see Suzanne Jonas, *Of Centaurs and Doves: Guatemala's Peace Process* (Boulder, CO: Westview, 2000).

[31] Ratner, *The New UN Peacekeeping*.

regimes in Pakistan and Côte d'Ivoire were overthrown by military coups initially enjoying broad public support in 1999.

These kinds of issues highlighted normative change in the interpretation of state sovereignty at the end of the twentieth century. It became widely although not universally accepted that tyrants could no longer seek refuge behind the walls of their states to shield themselves from international concern and even action over massive human rights violations and humanitarian catastrophes. However, despite the public espousal of humanitarian causes of a kind that threatened state sovereignty as traditionally defined, the US was not prepared to craft or support new doctrines in this area. The ambivalent, although open, US position was best summed up by President Clinton in his remarks to the UN Millennium Summit of 6 September 2000:

Today, there are fewer wars between nations, but more wars within nations. Internal wars—often driven by ethnic and religious differences—took five million lives in the 1990s, the vast majority innocent victims. This trend presents us with a stark, collective challenge. We must respect sovereignty and territorial integrity. But whether it is diplomacy, sanctions, or collective force, we must find ways to protect *people* as well as *borders*.[32]

3. Explaining the US Approach in the Security Council

Those factors that best explain current US ambivalence towards the UN are rooted in the history of US relations with the organization since 1945. These experiences affect the domestic debate to this day, a debate made sharper during the Clinton era for partisan reasons. While the Bush administration that took power in January 2001 was initially dismissive of the UN, the events of 11 September of that year made it relevant once again, even in Washington. Yet the Bush administration remained, as had the previous two administrations, uneasy about the UN's enhanced role in the field of security, the terms of which were now being more broadly defined. For some, it was much to be preferred if the UN was not the forum of first resort when US interests dictated the need to deal with a breach of security.

Historical Experience

The historical seeds of the current ambiguous, troubled relationship between the US and the UN can be seen to arise from two sources with one basic foundation. The shift in the demographics of UN membership in the early 1960s and the strident advocacy of many newly independent states, buttressing the

---

[32] www.un.org/millennium/webcast/statements/usa.htm.

position of traditional non-aligned states such as India, Indonesia, Egypt, and Yugoslavia, led to differences with Western powers over a range of issues, two of which proved highly sensitive in the US.

Western domination of the General Assembly began to be challenged in the immediate post-colonial period of the early 1960s with the emergence of apartheid in South Africa and the continuance of white minority rule in Rhodesia as key international issues that rallied the mushrooming non-aligned movement. Likewise, the question of Palestine became a growing bone of contention with large numbers of newly independent countries supporting Arab positions, and with the US increasingly relying on its veto to protect Israel from binding Security Council resolutions it considered unbalanced or injurious.[33] Over-charged rhetoric, temporarily ascendant Arab diplomacy, and mismanagement by Western powers led to an infamous resolution by the UN General Assembly equating Zionism with racism on 10 November 1975.[34] The US, along with many of its friends, received the adoption of this resolution with dismay and fury. US Permanent Representative Daniel Moynihan eloquently complained of double standards. This resolution was to have profound and lasting consequences in discrediting the United Nations with much of the US population and political leadership. Its repeal by a strong majority in 1991, essentially unopposed by most Arab countries after a sustained diplomatic campaign by the United States, passed largely unnoticed: the damage was done.[35]

The US—although not necessarily all of its allies—was further dismayed when the Palestinian Liberation Organization was granted observer status by the UN General Assembly some weeks after the November 1975 resolution.[36] During these two turbulent decades, America's own prosecution of the Vietnam war was strongly criticized by UN Secretary-General U Thant (1961–71), but effective action by the UN member states to address the conflict was stymied by evolving approaches to 'uniting for peace', the US and Soviet vetoes in the Security Council—with the US and Russia each pursuing outright victory directly or through regional proxies—and the absence of both North Vietnam and the People's Republic of China from the UN for much of the duration of the conflict.[37]

Elsewhere, but driven by the same General Assembly demographics, the Group of 77—a grouping of developing countries on economic and social issues which was soon to number above 130 members—often joined by

---

[33] 'Table of Vetoed Draft Resolutions in the United Nations Security Council', RA Memorandum 2-1999 (London: Global Issues Research Group, Foreign and Commonwealth Office, September 1999), para. 16.

[34] General Assembly Resolution 3379 of 10 November 1975.

[35] General Assembly Resolution A/46/86 of 16 December 1991.

[36] See United Nations, *UN Yearbook 1975* (New York: Office of Public Information, United Nations, 1978), 242–9.

[37] Kurt Waldheim, Secretary-General during 1971–81, greatly toned down U Thant's rhetoric over Vietnam. Indeed, he barely used the Secretary-General's 'bully pulpit' at all.

sympathetic Western countries such as the Scandinavian countries, the Netherlands, France, and Canada, pressed for a 'new international economic order' (NIEO) which envisaged greater redistribution of wealth from the industrialized to the developing countries through regulation and the intermediation of the UN system. The 1970s witnessed intense negotiations on the specifics of a global new economic deal, culminating with the Cancun Summit of 1981, the communiqué of which held some promise for further progress. In fact, however, by that time the NIEO was already dead, killed off by 'Ronald Thatcherism'.[38] Driving a stake through the heart of activism on the part of developing countries in favour of greater international regulation was the misguided 'new international information order' advocated at UNESCO in the 1980s, which many journalists worldwide saw as little more than a licence for censorship to be exercised by governments and international institutions. This bad idea rapidly expired, but not without inflicting serious damage: the United States and the United Kingdom were incensed by the attempts to impose information dirigisme and exasperated by UNESCO mismanagement under its autocratic Director General, Ahmadou Mahtar M'Bow (in office 1974–87).[39] UNESCO adapted disastrously to their departure and the consequent yawning funding gap by cutting programmes rather than staff. Even today, relations between developing countries and the US can be tense at the UN. As Edward Luck has argued:

Too often, the more extreme and confrontational voices in the nonaligned and G-77 caucuses—as in Congress—seem to be the loudest, blocking forward movement on feasible reform steps and bolstering maximalist positions. Congressional demands on the UN, coupled with cutbacks in foreign assistance, have served in turn, to reinforce fears of some developing countries about American priorities and about the dangers of unfettered US power in the world organization.[40]

This overall and generally negative pattern of relations greatly influenced the US approach within the Security Council, where the US frequently and bitterly, in the post-colonial years, pursued a policy of damage limitation, often through use of the veto on Middle East issues. The end of the cold war and its poisonous dynamic at the UN might have provided an opportunity for new departures, particularly as Western—largely US—values appeared resurgent throughout much of the world. However, deeply ingrained negative perceptions of the UN in powerful policy-making circles in Washington and elsewhere in the US frustrated many such hopes.

---

[38] The term 'Ronald Thatcherism' describing the free market philosophy and activism of Margaret Thatcher, the UK Prime Minister (1979–90) and Ronald Reagan, the US President (1981–9), was to my knowledge coined by Sylvia Ostry, head of economics at the OECD and subsequently a senior Canadian trade and economic negotiator.

[39] The US withdrew from UNESCO in 1984, and the UK in 1985. Singapore also left UNESCO citing the organization's chronic mismanagement.

[40] Edward C. Luck, *Mixed Messages: American Politics and International Organization, 1919–1999* (Washington, DC: Brookings Institution Press, 1999), 297.

Domestic Politics and Opinion

The current state of US-UN relations owes much to these past experiences. Contemporary criticism of the UN in Republican circles is no more strident than during the heyday of former US Permanent Representative to the UN Jeanne Kirkpatrick (1981–5). Much of this criticism revolves around the threats that the United Nations is claimed to pose to US sovereignty. As the Chairman of the Senate Foreign Relations Committee, Jesse Helms, had put it in a bald and unprecedented address to the Security Council on 20 January 2000:

If the United Nations respects the sovereign rights of the American people, and serves them as an effective tool of diplomacy, it will earn and deserve their respect and support. But a United Nations that seeks to impose its presumed authority on the American people, without their consent, begs for confrontation and—I want to be candid with you—eventual US withdrawal.[41]

Most US presidential candidates in the campaign of 2000 determined that, on the UN, discretion was the better part of valour. Only Democratic challenger Bill Bradley, whose bid for the presidency soon faded, took a contrarian tack and advocated greater American cooperation on humanitarian crises with other countries through multilateral forums such as the UN.[42] While Al Gore was widely suspected of being a closet UN supporter on the basis of his extensive involvement in environmental issues earlier in the decade and as a Senator, he had little good to say about the UN on the campaign trail. Condoleezza Rice, before her appointment as National Security Adviser for President George W. Bush, saw some uses for the UN, but only when convenient for the US and in support of US interests narrowly defined:

Using American forces as the world's '911' will degrade capabilities, bog soldiers down in peacekeeping roles, and fuel concern among great powers that the United States has decided to enforce notions of 'limited sovereignty' worldwide in the name of humanitarianism. This overly broad definition of America's national interest is bound to backfire as others arrogate the same authority to themselves. Or we will find ourselves looking to the United Nations to sanction the use of American military power in these cases, implying that we will do so even when our vital interests are not involved, which would be a mistake.[43]

As Robert Zoellick, before his appointment as Trade Representative to the new Bush administration, argued:

Republicans judge international agreements and institutions as means to achieve ends, not as forms of political therapy. Agreements and institutions can facilitate

---

[41] Barbara Crossette, 'Helms, in Visit to UN, Offers Harsh Message', *The New York Times* (21 January 2000).

[42] See 'Foreign Policy Town Meeting', 29 November 1999, Fletcher School of Law and Diplomacy, Tufts University', www.billbradley.com. The issue came up in response to a question on criteria for US responses to humanitarian crises.

[43] Condoleezza Rice, 'Promoting the National Interest', *Foreign Affairs*, 79/1 (2000), 54.

bargaining, recognize common interests, and resolve differences cooperatively. But international law, unlike domestic law, merely codifies an already agreed-upon cooperation. Even mechanisms will need negotiations in order to work, and international law not backed by power cannot cope with dangerous people and states. Every issue need not be dealt with multilaterally.[44]

Not too much should be read into what were electoral policy platforms. Republicans should not be viewed as innately hostile to the UN, nor Democrats firm friends of multilateralism—Clinton and his team proved extremely volatile and unreliable patrons and allies for the UN. Indeed, it was George Bush, Senior in 1990 who sought to reverse the Iraqi annexation of Kuwait by working through the UN; and it was this Republican president, ably assisted by his Secretary of State, James Baker, who built an impressive international coalition mandated by the Security Council to this end.[45] However, each candidate during the 2000 election campaign was responding to a perceived negative perception of the United Nations among groups that were attentive to foreign policy issues and, despite public opinion polls, generally supportive of US engagement with the organization.

The Clinton administration, despite an initial policy interest in 'assertive multilateralism', failed to make strenuous efforts to counter this hostility to the UN in Washington, a failure that was compounded by bureaucratic differences. The White House rarely got involved in key UN issues, with the exception, for brief periods, of the Iraq, Bosnia, Haiti, and Somalia crises. The Pentagon and the State Department were frequently at odds over US decisions in the UN Security Council, with the Pentagon more likely to prevail on important ones, given its ability to connect meaningfully with allies in Congress. Officials within the State Department laboured admirably to articulate the US interest in a strong United Nations, but were weakly supported at the political level. In particular, the White House never went to bat seriously on US funding arrears to the UN. It left it to the controversial but energetic Richard Holbrooke, himself confirmed only after a prolonged struggle with the US Senate, and who found US credibility at the UN to be at a low ebb, to mount an impressive campaign on the repayment of arrears in the halls of Congress and elsewhere.[46]

The Sobering Effects of Action

A final factor explaining the apparent ambivalence in US attitudes and inconsistencies in US behaviour with respect to UN Security Council activity relates to the familiar difficulties in trying to relate means to ends, values to interests, order to justice. The early 1990s showed the Council at its most optimistic and activist. With the US in the lead, the Council achieved some notable successes,

[44] Robert B. Zoellick, 'A Republican Foreign Policy', *Foreign Affairs*, 79/1 (2000), 69.
[45] Jim Baker subsequently served the UN as Kofi Annan's Special Envoy on the Western Sahara issue. [46] For further details see Chapter 1.

such as those in El Salvador and Mozambique. The former Bush and Clinton administrations both asserted that US interests could be usefully advanced through the UN Security Council, and the Bush administration provided a spectacular example of this in organizing, under the UN umbrella, the Desert Storm and Desert Thunder coalitions against Iraq in 1990 and 1991. Action through the UN allowed the US to share the burden of international intervention with other countries.

However, US casualties in Somalia led Washington subsequently to block any reinforcement of the UN's operation in Rwanda and to a strict interpretation of PDD 25, the latter not to be reversed until 1999 and Holbrooke's brief term at the UN. The UN itself in its operations and management contributed to this sense of disillusionment in the United States. Wishful thinking on resources, increasing risk, poor planning, the dilution of responsibility inevitable in committee decision-making, and the absence of a powerful and consistently engaged leader among its members—the role the US could have been playing—all contributed to the Council's subsequent decline into recrimination, risk-aversion, and flight from reality.

Nevertheless, often *faute de mieux*, particularly given the limited capacities of most regional organizations, the UN was again called upon, by the US as by others, in 1999 to deploy large peace operations in Kosovo, East Timor, and Sierra Leone, all of which were seen in Washington as serving US interests in a variety of ways. Moreover, the humanitarian impulse to act in support of victims of conflict, at its height in the early 1990s, had provoked a lively debate in the US, not only over the international right to intervene in the internal affairs of countries to save civilian lives but also over a purported duty to do so.[47] President Clinton in an address to the UN General Assembly on 21 September 1999 hedged his bets on humanitarian intervention, making clear that the humanitarian impulse would continue to influence US policy but would also be balanced against other factors as well:

I know that some will be troubled that the United States cannot respond to every humanitarian catastrophe in the world. We cannot do everything everywhere. But simply because we have different interests in different parts of the world does not mean we can be indifferent to the destruction of innocents in any part of the world.[48]

What Clinton did not go on to state—inappropriate anyway in such a venue—but what US behaviour in the 1990s had increasingly made clear was that not every US security interest would be pursued through the UN, and that

[47] Jonathan Moore (ed.), *Hard Choices: Moral Dilemmas in Humanitarian Intervention* (Lanham, MD: Rowman and Littlefield Publishers, 1998) is a good collection of works broaching this debate.
[48] See 'Remarks by the President to the 54th Session of the UN General Assembly', the White House (Office of the Spokesman), www.state.gov.

the country would be increasingly selective in those operations to which it did lend its support.

A New Dawn?

The 11 September 2001 terrorist attacks on the World Trade Center and the Pentagon appeared to open a new chapter in relations between the US and the UN. The day after the attacks, the Security Council adopted, at the initiative of France, a strong condemnatory resolution, terming these assaults a threat to international peace and security and referring to the inherent right to self-defence.[49] Some days later, the Council adopted, under Chapter VII, a US text stigmatizing the harbouring of terrorists and setting out detailed measures. Member states were mandated to prevent financing of terrorism from within their borders.[50] The Council established a committee to monitor implementation of the resolution's manifold provisions.

At the same time, the US worked to preclude any Council language that might constrain its ability to strike back at terrorists or states harbouring them wherever they might be. Furthermore, in pursuing its military campaign against the Al Qaeda network and the Taleban regime, the US ensured that it alone took key decisions, marginalizing the decision-making role of NATO allies and regional partners.[51] In late November 2001, the US clashed publicly with the UK, which had championed the deployment to Afghanistan of international peacekeepers to establish security for the delivery of humanitarian assistance and perhaps to help a transitional Afghan government to take root. Washington argued that its military objectives had to take priority over all else.[52]

In spite of agreement in the US Senate to confirm a new Permanent Representative to the UN—John Negroponte's nomination had been held up for many months—and its action to repay most US arrears to the UN, it was not clear that anything basic in the US approach had changed. The US stuck to its guns in opposing a protocol to implement the Biological Weapons Treaty, continued to reject the Kyoto Protocol, and worked to undermine implementation of the International Criminal Court statute. Thus, there was little to suggest that the international struggle against terrorism would infuse Washington with a more multilateral spirit. To many, it seemed clear that US multilateral engagement on the issue of counter-terrorism alone would not, as a practical matter, work for long.[53] Partners would look for some US 'give' on matters of

---

[49] SCR 1368 of 12 September 2001.   [50] SCR 1373 of 18 September 2001.
[51] Confidential interviews with senior UN delegates.
[52] Michael R. Gordon, 'US and UK at odds over use and timing of peacekeeping troops', *New York Times* (2 December 2001).
[53] See David M. Malone 'How to wage a diplomatic war', Toronto *Globe and Mail* (19 September 2001).

importance to them to recognize Washington's 'take' on counter-terrorism, even though, obviously, Americans would frown on any formal linkage.

4. Conclusion

No country played a greater role in the design of, and in setting early aspirations for, the UN than did the United States. Yet in the following decades and especially over the course of the 1990s relations between the US and the UN deteriorated sharply, and US influence within the body inevitably waned.[54] The Clinton administration's instinctive penchant for UN-bashing whenever in a tight spot from which blame might be delegated, first on view following the Mogadishu fiasco of 4 October 1993, was displayed repeatedly in subsequent years. The assertive unilateralism of the Bush administration in its early months only aggravated matters.

It is not surprising, or necessarily unhealthy, that the US, beyond key bilateral ties, should reserve the right to pick and choose among organizations forming the 'variable architecture' of the international institutional system for decision-making affecting its vital interests. NATO's military campaign against Serbian President Milosevic proved controversial as it was unauthorized by the Security Council. But an international system absolutely precluding the US from acting at critical junctures because of ill-judged veto threats would enjoy no support whatsoever in Washington. A security system lacking the active engagement of the US would serve neither the United Nations as an institution nor the broader community of nations. At the same time, it is natural for the US to seek to avoid being dragged into conflicts which are secondary to its interests, when its custodial responsibility for international security, as the sole remaining superpower, requires it to be able to act rapidly, at any given time, in support of key political and economic interests of its own and of its closest allies.

However, while acknowledging these broader responsibilities and interests, we may safely say that the management of the US relationship with the UN has not been a strong suit of recent US administrations. In a valedictory address to the UN General Assembly on 12 September 2000, Secretary of State Madeleine Albright delivered a fairly optimistic assessment of progress in achieving the US reform goals at the UN and of the UN's role in US foreign policy.[55] These are messages that her successor, Colin Powell, has also articulated but they have not yet won over Washington.[56]

---

[54] For a first hand if self-pitying account of this, see Boutros Boutros-Ghali, *Unvanquished: A U.S.–U.N. Saga* (New York: Random House, 1999). See also David M. Malone, 'Goodbye UNSCOM: A Tale in UN–US Relations', *Security Dialogue*, 30/4 (1999).
[55] See www.secretary.state.gov/www/statements/2000/000912.html.
[56] See Barbara Crossette, 'Powell Pledges Strong Support for Wide Spectrum of UN Activities', *New York Times* (15 February 2001).

The George W. Bush administration has proved fundamentally suspicious of treaty-based approaches to the promotion of international security, fearing encroachments on US sovereignty and freedom of manoeuvre. The UN, of course, lies at the heart of the treaty-based system for management of international relations. However, the administration did discover, in the wake of 11 September 2001, that the UN can be an important instrument for US policy, a key channel through which major international security crises are interpreted for the world. As well, crises of secondary interest to the US, such as those in the Democratic Republic of the Congo and in Sierra Leone, can be addressed there on a burden-shared basis, reducing both the costs and the risks for the US of necessary action.

Since 11 September 2001, the US Administration has come to focus single-mindedly on the fight against terrorism. After many years of division and recrimination at the UN over the definition of terrorism, particularly as it relates to the Arab-Israel theatre of conflict, Washington may have been surprised by the extent and depth of support it received from the world body in its hour of need. Whether its approach to other contentious foreign policy issues handled through the UN will evolve is open to question. It is not strongly apparent that its aversion to a treaty-based approach to the management of international relations and to the promotion of its own interests has subsided.

4

The United States and the International Financial Institutions: Power and Influence Within the World Bank and the IMF

NGAIRE WOODS

The United States enjoys a special position in the International Monetary Fund (IMF) and the World Bank. When the institutions were created, their structure, location, and mandate were all pretty much determined by the United States.[1] The United States had just over a third of the voting power in each institution.[2] No drawing from the IMF was approved without US agreement first being made clear.[3] These observations suggest that the US was set to play a dominant role in the institutions.

Yet neither the Fund nor the Bank can be cast as a mere instrument of US policy. To some extent the institutions were created in order to propound and enforce US-supported aims and policies around the world. It is also true that the Fund and the Bank exist because their 'neutral and apparently technical advice may be less offensive to national sentiments than direct intervention by the United States', in the case of the World Bank 'sparing the USA the unsavory epithets of... "aid with strings", "arm-twisting political pressures" etc.'.[4]

With particular thanks to Andrew Walter for his detailed and extremely useful comments on the first draft of this paper, and also to Rosemary Foot, Neil MacFarlane, and Michael Mastanduno for their helpful suggestions. This chapter introduces arguments further developed in Ngaire Woods, *Ideas from Abroad: The Politics of the IMF and the World Bank* (forthcoming).

[1] See the excellent account of this in Richard Gardner, *Sterling-Dollar Diplomacy* (New York: Columbia Univ Press, 1980); see also Fred Hirsch, *Money International* (Harmondsworth: Penguin, 1969), 266. Even the Fund's mandate was interpreted in light of the narrow US legislation on the Bretton Woods institutions—the US Bretton Woods Agreements Act—as opposed to the international agreement itself: Susan Strange, 'The IMF', in Robert W. Cox and Harold K. Jacobson, *The Anatomy of Influence: Decision Making in International Organization* (London: Yale University Press, 1974), 278.

[2] Joseph Gold, *Voting and Decisions in the International Monetary Fund* (Washington, DC: IMF, 1972), 238.

[3] Brian Tew, *International Monetary Cooperation, 1945–70* (London: Hutchinson, 1970).

[4] William Ascher, 'The World Bank and U.S. Control', in Margaret Karns and Karen Mingst (eds), *The United States and Multilateral Institutions: Patterns of Changing Instrumentality and Influence* (London: Routledge, 1992), 118. See also Louis Pauly, *Who*

However, if the organizations had absolutely no autonomy, they would be redundant, for they would have no greater legitimacy or mobilizing power than government agencies of the US.

The very creation of multilateral organizations reflects the fact that, in order to propound a vision of the global economy, the participation of a large number of states in the world is required. Such participation in turn requires that a wide range of countries believe in the institutions' legitimacy: that they perceive the institutions to proffer a particular technical expertise as well as a certain degree of independence, a genuinely international character, and actions which are rule-based rather than reflecting US discretionary judgements.

Susan Strange once described multilateral institutions serving either as 'instruments of the structural strategy and foreign policy of the dominant state or states' or to provide necessary public goods: 'allowing states to enjoy the political luxury of national autonomy without sacrificing the economic dividends of world markets and production structures.'[5] The IMF and the World Bank doubtless do some of each. In more modern parlance, their activities are circumscribed by their most powerful members, just as realists would predict. However, as institutionalists stress, within these constraints both institutions provide global public goods and for this purpose states have to delegate to them some degree of autonomy.[6]

There are obvious costs—even if they do not equal the benefits—to the United States of participating in multilateral institutions. Once a powerful state creates an institution and a set of rules which serves its overall interests, it has to show itself willing to subject itself to those rules even when they do not further its interests if the institution is to retain legitimacy and usefulness. That said, powerful states sometimes avoid this restraint by making sure that rules are ambiguous in precisely the areas where they expect to run into difficulties; one example is the way in which the IMF's adjustment rules for key currencies were written.[7] Overall, however, a structure of rules and restraints is the essential distinction between a multilateral 'rule of law' and a simpler form of power politics in which 'might is right'.

The incoming administration of President George W. Bush quickly learnt the practical implications of this difference in respect of the IMF and the World

Elected the Bankers? Surveillance and Control in the World Economy (New York: Cornell University Press, 1997).

[5] Susan Strange, '*Cave! Hic dragones*: A Critique of Regime Analysis', in Stephen Krasner (ed.), *International Regimes* (New York: Cornell University Press, 1983), 342.

[6] Lisa Martin, 'Agency and Delegation in IMF Conditionality', manuscript prepared for workshop on Political Economy of International Finance, Harvard University (October 2000) and also 'The Political Economy of International Cooperation', in Inge Kaul, Isabelle Grunberg, and Marc A. Stern (eds), *Global Public Goods: International Cooperation in the 21st Century* (New York: UNDP, 1999).

[7] Andrew Walter, *World Power, World Money: The Role of Hegemony and International Monetary Order* (London: Harvester Wheatsheaf, 1993).

Bank in the sixth months after June 2001. In that month the new Secretary of the Treasury Paul O'Neill was quick to express the administration's hostility towards the multilateral institutions, declaring that 'the IMF, the World Bank and the regional development banks have spent hundreds of billions of dollars to reduce poverty and address financial crises around the globe...Visit some of the poorest nations in the world and you will see that we have too little to show for it'.[8] However, after pushing the IMF to bail out Argentina in August 2001, the new administration soon discovered that 'markets had increasingly begun to look through the IMF to the US Treasury as the decisive decision maker' and this was going to prove very costly to them. Rather than being seen to push the IMF around, the Treasury soon announced: 'We believe that the Fund's success is essential to stability in the international economy, and we wanted to make sure that we did not undermine its credibility.'[9] Taking some distance from the institutions was necessary if the US was to enjoy the benefits of the rule-based system that they embodied.

It bears noting, however, that powerful states usually face choices in respect of multilateralism. They can opt to use different forums or alternative institutions to achieve particular purposes and thereby also weaken the potential autonomy of the international financial institutions. This was starkly demonstrated in the 1970s, when the United States turned not to the IMF but to a small group of industrialized countries—the Group of 7 and the Group of 10—in order to foster cooperation which would stabilize the world economy. The result was to marginalize the IMF from the process of global cooperation, to undermine US domestic support for the institution since it no longer seemed essential to US interests, and to highlight to all other members and officials of the IMF that the organization's status and role in the world economy would depend upon the uses to which the United States would put it. In this context it was unsurprising that the management of the IMF seized, with some alacrity, the chance to take a central role in the Latin American debt crisis in the early 1980s.

In summary, the international financial institutions have a close relationship with the United States which creates tensions for themselves since they must both please their most powerful political master and at the same time maintain their independence and credibility both as technical agencies and as multilateral organizations. In order to be effective, the institutions need to be perceived by their member countries as legitimate multilateral organizations, pursuing internationally determined objectives in a rule-based way. They need

---

[8] Paul H. O'Neill (Secretary of the Treasury), 'Excellence and the International Financial Institutions', speech to the Economic Club of Detroit, Detroit, Michigan. US Treasury Press Release PO-449 (27 June 2001).

[9] Kenneth W. Dam (Deputy US Treasury Secretary), 'Thoughts on the Global Economy', speech to the World Affairs Council of Washington DC. US Treasury Press Release PO-948 (25 January 2002).

recognized credibility and expertise in economic policy based on the scope and depth of their research. In order to enjoy this legitimacy, they also need a visible degree of political independence from interference by the United States— or, indeed, any other major power or bloc such as the European Union.

This poses two questions. First, how much influence does the United States wield in the institutions and through what mechanisms? Second, seen from the opposite perspective, what features of the institutions give them relative autonomy from the United States? The dominant tendency in political science is to say little about the potential and actual sources of influence on the part of the United States, especially as these are exercised informally, nor to examine the actual degrees of autonomy and relative independence that international institutions such as the IMF and the World Bank enjoy, as exhibited in their actual practices.[10]

1. Analysing the Formal and Informal Structures of Power in the Institutions

The terms 'influence', 'dominance', 'independence', and 'autonomy' have all been used up until this point without definition. For the purposes of this chapter, 'influence' refers to the capacity of one actor to modify the behaviour of another. As Cox and Jacobson argued some time ago, influence differs from power in so far as the latter refers to capability or 'the aggregate of political resources that are available to an actor'. Power *may* be converted into influence, but not necessarily and not to its full extent. The interesting question is therefore to explore the sources and mechanisms through which power is translated into influence.[11] 'Dominance' refers to the influence of one actor relative to all others in a system or regime: in other words, the most influential actor or the player exercising 'commanding influence' over all others.

'Independence' characterizes an actor or organization which is not constrained by external forces. Just as 'independent' is used to describe schools or institutions which are self-governing and not supported from public funds,

---

[10] This point is made by Kenneth Abbott and Duncan Snidal, 'Why States Act through Formal International Organizations', *Journal of Conflict Resolution*, 42/1 (1998). Instead, institutions are often seen either as sites of cooperation or as passive embodiments of norms or rules. See Andrew Moravcsik, 'Negotiating the Single European Act: National Interests and Conventional Statecraft in the European Community', *International Organization*, 45 (1991); Robert Keohane, *After Hegemony* (Princeton: Princeton University Press, 1984); Geoffrey Garrett and Barry Weingast, 'Ideas, Interests and Institutions: Constructing the European Community's Internal Market', in Judith Goldstein and Robert Keohane (eds), *Ideas and Foreign Policy: Beliefs, Institutions and Political Change* (Ithaca: Cornell University Press, 1993); and Kaul, Grunberg, and Stern (eds), *Global Public Goods*.   [11] Cox and Jacobson, *The Anatomy of Influence*.

TABLE 4.1. *Tracing influence within the IMF and the World Bank*

---

1. Financial structure
   - proportion of the core budget paid by the United States;
   - how the institution acquires additional resources for special purposes;
   - US approval required for the US to pay or increase its contributions (role of Congress);
   - how regularly US approval sought.
2. Use of resources
   - formal requirements for US approval for lending decisions;
   - informal processes whereby US approval is sought;
   - to what extent do lending decisions reflect US priorities?
3. Staffing and management
   - the composition of the staff, in terms of nationality and training;
   - US approval for which appointments: whether formally required or not) and the terms of senior appointments (power to dismiss etc);
   - ideological mind set, as compared with what alternatives.
4. Formal structures of voting and power
   - US proportion of formal voting power on constitutional issues and formal requirements for any change in mandate;
   - extent of, and US influence over, informal procedures and conventions;
   - to what extent changes in mandate reflect US priorities (which agencies in the US?);
   - role and implications of inclusion of independent advisers, financial sector actors, and non-governmental organizations.

---

likewise in multilateral organizations a dependence on public funds—from member governments—and political control exercised by member states curtail independence. For this reason, an analysis of the 'autonomy' or capacity to act independently of any multilateral organization is more truthfully an examination of relative autonomy.

'Relative autonomy' refers to the extent to which the organization is not entirely dominated by its most powerful member or members. An example of such 'autonomy' in the IMF is the frequently cited 'substantial autonomy' enjoyed by the staff in the design of lending programmes. In some countries the Fund operates fairly independently of the voice or influence of its most powerful shareholders, in others less so.

How might we rigorously trace the degree of influence exercised by the United States within the institutions? Four characteristics of each organization stand out as particularly important (see Table 4.1).[12] These characteristics serve to highlight both formal and informal channels of influence.

The first is: *how is the organization financed?* What proportion of the core budget is paid by the United States? Equally importantly we need to examine by what means the institution can acquire additional resources for special purposes and whether or not US approval, and more specifically Congressional approval, is required for such payments and, if so, how regularly.

---

[12] Cox and Jacobson, *The Anatomy of Influence*, is a useful starting point.

A second important characteristic of the organizations is what shapes their *use of resources*, or, put another way, how much influence the US exercises over the lending and operational decisions taken by the institutions. Legally, both the IMF and the World Bank are governed by articles of agreement which do not permit political considerations to be taken into account. In practice, however, political pressures have played a key role in determining who has access to their resources and on what terms. The influence of the US is illuminated by examining the formal requirements for US approval, the informal processes whereby US approval is sought, and the extent to which the pattern of lending from the institutions reflects US priorities.

A third set of characteristics which may reveal US influence concerns the *staffing and management* of the institutions: the composition of the staff in terms of nationality and training, the need for US approval—whether sought formally or informally—and the relationship between the prevailing training and mind set of the staff and US interests.

A final set of considerations concerns the *representative and deliberative functions* of the organizations, and *how their mandate is formulated.* In tracing the US influence on these processes one needs to examine who is represented and with what voting power, the rationale for the existing structure of representation and the role of the US in shaping it, the requirements for change, and to what extent formal decision-making rules are overridden by informal conventions and norms.

It bears noting that each of the IMF and the World Bank is governed by executive boards comprising representatives of member governments. However, countries do not enjoy equal representation (see below). Furthermore, representation within the international financial institutions is much narrower than the terms 'member states' and 'international officials' suggests.[13] All representatives are drawn exclusively from the treasury, central bank, stabilization fund, or other similar fiscal agency; and, likewise, the Fund and the Bank work only through these agencies in their dealings with member countries.[14] The result is a system in which there is a significant shared mind set between Fund officials and their interlocutors in member countries, many of whom have themselves spent time as Fund and Bank officials. In as subtle way, this point is underscored by a remark in *External Evaluation into IMF Surveillance*, where the evaluators found that 'the most favourable appraisals came from those whose lines of work bore close similarities to the Fund's— central banks, and, to a lesser extent, finance ministries'.[15] Rather more acidly, Susan Strange wrote in the 1970s of the Fund operating as a 'nursery for

[13] Compare this with participation in other international organizations, for example, the US itself. Charles William Maynes and Richard S. Williamson, *U.S. Foreign Policy and the United Nations System* (New York: W.W. Norton, 1996).

[14] See World Bank Article III, section 2; IMF Article V, section 1.

[15] IMF, *External Evaluation of IMF Surveillance*, Report by a Group of Independent Experts (Washington, DC: IMF, 1999), 35.

monetary managers, producing a worldwide old boy network of officials susceptible to its influence'.[16]

Within the United States, the relationship with the Fund and the Bank is complicated by domestic political arrangements. The Treasury formulates and implements virtually all policy towards the IMF, while the State Department has more input in policy towards the World Bank. However, other agencies, and most particularly the US Congress, bring significant pressure to bear on the government positions, both through direct relations with the IMF and the World Bank and through indirect pressure on the Treasury and State Department officials. Some would argue that the US gains in leverage from the uncertainties created by this system of checks and balances, by putting US officials in a position to wield the threat of an intransigent Congress in order to leverage their preferred terms. However, on some issues Congress has placed a real constraint, thereby reducing the scope of the preferences of the Treasury and State Department.

Finally, in deliberations within, and at the doors of, the international financial institutions, the 1980s saw a rapid increase in the participation of non-state actors. Both institutions have for a long time consulted with independent advisers and the financial sector. In the 1990s, both the Fund and the Bank began more actively to engage with non-governmental organizations. This change in the scope of deliberations, as well as the narrow field of representation, raises a further question as to whether or not this has enhanced US influence.

2. The US and the Financing of the IMF and the World Bank

In most of the organizations of the United Nations, the United States has shown a willingness, indeed even a determination, to withhold funding in order unilaterally to impose conditions on the organization.[17] In theory, however, this is not possible in the IMF and the World Bank. Unlike the UN, these organizations do not depend for their core funding on annual subscriptions or levies from members. Nevertheless, the contribution of the United States to the financing of these institutions gives it substantial influence, and changes within the organizations have further magnified that influence.

In the IMF, the United States contributes 17.67 per cent of the capital subscriptions which are the institution's primary source of financing.[18] This gives

---

[16] Strange, 'The IMF', 269.

[17] Benjamin Rivlin, 'UN Reform from the Standpoint of the United States', *UN University Lectures*, 11 (Tokyo: The United Nations University, 1996).

[18] See Graham Bird, 'Crisis Averter, Crisis Lender, Crisis Manager: The IMF in Search of a Systemic Role', *World Economy*, 22/7 (1999) for a detailed and technical analysis of the financing of the Fund.

the United States 17.33 per cent of votes on the Executive Board. Although this is not a majority of votes, it nevertheless gives the United States power to veto major policy changes which require an 85 per cent majority of votes.[19] Normally, all US policy in the IMF is formulated within the US Treasury, since Congressional approval is not required for a continuation of US subscriptions to the institution.

US influence within the IMF, however, is greatly enhanced by the institution's need to increase its resources. At least every five years the quotas determining contributions to the Fund are reviewed and any increase requires an 85 per cent majority of votes on the Executive Board and hence US approval. Furthermore, within the United States an increase in resources allocated to the IMF requires Congressional approval. For this reason, at each quota review the Fund is subjected to particular scrutiny by the United States—and pressure from it. Over the 1990s, the Congress attempted to influence Fund conditionality over issues such as worker rights, the role of the private sector, human rights, and military spending.[20]

Most recently, in negotiations over the US share of a 45 per cent increase in Fund quota—agreed by the Executive Board in September 1997—the US Congress established an International Financial Institution Advisory Commission—the 'Meltzer Commission'—to recommend future US policy towards the IMF as well as the World Bank and other multilateral economic organizations.[21] The Commission took a different line from the US Treasury on many issues. Indeed, the Final Report of the Commission launches several attacks on the US Treasury and its policy towards the IMF: accusing Treasury of 'circumventing the Congressional budget process' by using the Exchange Stabilization Fund to assist Mexico in 1995; of 'commandeering international resources to meet objectives of the U.S. government or its Treasury Department'; and of leading the initiative to create contingency credit lines in the IMF which were 'so poorly designed that, to date, no country has applied'. In these attacks, the Commission's report highlights differences of view which exist not only among scholars but equally within the US government. The question that exercises us here is: do these differences diminish US influence in the IMF? It is not obvious that they do. And for all their differences, the US Treasury and Congress are unified by the belief that the United States can and should set down terms and conditions for the multilateral economic institutions— as indeed the Final Report of the Meltzer Commission does.

---

[19] See Article III, section 2, which was revised upwards to ensure that the US did retain a veto, even as its relative quota declined.

[20] On US successes in promulgating these issues within the Fund in the 1990s, see Timothy F. Geithner, Treasury Assistant Secretary, US Treasury Statement to US House of Representatives, 21 April 1998, www.house.gov/htbin/fe_srchget/comms/ba00/42198tre.htm.

[21] In November 1998, the International Financial Advisory Commission was established. It reported to Congress in early 2000, available at www.phantom-x.gsia.cmu.edu/IFIAC/.

A recalcitrant Congress may even enhance and magnify US influence in two ways. First, it has created a separate and additional channel of communication with the Fund and the Bank (more on the World Bank below): indeed, one of the first acts of the new Managing Director of the IMF appointed in 2000 was to meet with the head of the Meltzer Commission to discuss the recommendations that had been made in the latter's Final Report. Second, the fact that everyone is aware that a feisty US Congress needs to be brought on board can give the US Treasury and its officials within the IMF extra leverage and a credible threat to hold over other shareholders and Fund officials.

The financial structure of the World Bank is somewhat different from that of the IMF. In the International Bank for Reconstruction and Development, the main arm of the World Bank, the United States contributes 16.98 per cent of the capital stock which the Bank uses as a basis for raising money in financial markets, by selling AAA-rated bonds and other debt securities to pension funds, insurance companies, corporations, other banks, and individuals around the world. Assisting the Bank in accessing resources are the guarantees provided by member states—which have never been called upon—which permit the Bank to borrow at the lowest market rates available 'applying the sovereign credit of its rich shareholders—in the form of their capital guarantees of about $90 billion—to market borrowings, $110 billion of which remained outstanding as of 1995'.[22]

For these reasons, unlike the IMF, the World Bank does not rely directly on contributions from its member governments to fund its activities. Indeed, the paid-in capital subscriptions of member governments contribute less than 5 per cent of the Bank's funds, a proportion which is diminishing over time.[23] Nevertheless the US subscription gives it 16.52 per cent of votes on the Bank's Board and a veto over policy decisions requiring an 85 per cent majority, as in the IMF. Furthermore, like the IMF, the World Bank has become susceptible to more direct US influence as its activities and resources have expanded.

In 1960, a new facility was opened in the World Bank—the International Development Association (IDA)—which gives loans at highly concessional rates to poorer developing countries. The funds for the IDA are donated by governments whose agreement is required for periodic replenishments. As a result, the IDA has opened up a new channel through which the Bank can be directly influenced by its wealthier government members, and in particular the United States. The relationships between the US, the IDA, and the World Bank are worth examining.

The US contributes 20.86 per cent of IDA funds, with the next largest contributors being Japan at 18.7 per cent, and the United Kingdom and France

---

[22] Devesh Kapur, John P. Lewis, and Richard Webb (eds), *The World Bank: Its First Half Century*, i. (Washington, DC: Brookings Institution, 1997), 902.

[23] With regard to paid-in capital for the IBRD, there have been three general capital increases—1959, 1979, and 1989—but along with each there has been a decrease in the paid-in portion, from 10 per cent to 7.5 per cent to 3 per cent.

each at 7.3 per cent.[24] On the basis of these figures one would expect some degree of US leverage within the IDA itself. However, US influence exerted through IDA replenishment negotiations has gone further. Even though the IDA itself accounts for only about 25 per cent of IBRD/IDA total lending, there have been several instances where the US has used threats to reduce or withhold contributions to the IDA in order to demand changes in policy, not just in the IDA but in the World Bank as a whole. For instance, during the late 1970s the Bank was forced to promise not to lend to Vietnam in order to prevent the defeat of IDA 6, and in 1993, under pressure from Congress, the US linked the creation of an Independent Inspection Panel in the World Bank to IDA 10. As one writer puts it: 'with the Congress standing behind or reaching around it, the American administration was disposed to make its catalogue of demands not only insistent but comprehensive on replenishment occasions.'[25]

The 'US' in the context of the IMF and the World Bank describes pressures coming both from the Executive—through the State Department—and from the Congress. We have now seen that, in both the IMF and the World Bank, both arms of the US government have been involved in shaping policy. Further strengthening overall US leverage in IDA replenishment negotiations has been a condition which was applied during negotiations on IDA 5: that all other members could reduce their own contributions pro rata by any shortfall in US contributions.[26] Whilst this pro rata provision ensures an evenly shared burden across contributors, nevertheless it also magnifies the impact of any US threat to diminish its contribution: for if the US does so, all other contributors can follow suit.

A final note worth making about political influence within the World Bank group concerns the increase in the use of co-financing and trust funds in the Bank.[27] By the financial year 1999, these arrangements had come to take their place amidst World Bank disbursements, reflecting a 17 per cent increase in trust fund disbursements (see Table 4.2). Both trust funds and other forms of co-financing give a much more direct control over the use of resources to donors whose Trust Fund Administration Agreement with the Bank governs how the funds are used.[28] It bears noting, however, that this does not mean that Trust Funds have become a conduit of exclusively US influence. Indeed, the United States' contribution in 1999 was less than those of the Netherlands and Japan, and it was not initially a contributor to the HIPC Trust Fund—the Bank's largest—which means initially it did not exercise influence over that

---

[24] See IDA, *Additions to IDA Resources: Twelfth Replenishment* (Washington, DC; IDA, 1998).

[25] Catherine Gwin, 'U.S. Relations with the World Bank, 1945–1992', in Devesh Kapur, John P. Lewis, and Richard Webb (eds), *The World Bank: Its First Half Century*, ii. (Washington, DC: Brookings Institution, 1997), 1150.

[26] See IDA, *Additions to IDA Resources*, 29.

[27] I am grateful to Gnanaraj Chellaraj for drawing my attention to this.

[28] See 'Operational Policies', World Bank, *The World Bank Operational Manual* at www.worldbank.org.

TABLE 4.2. *World Bank disbursements in Fiscal Year 1999 ($m)*

IBRD	18,205
IDA	6,023
Co-financing	11,350
Trust funds	1,333

Source: World Bank, *Annual Report 1999*, at www.worldbank.org/html/extpb/annrep99/

fund.[29] Overall, however, the growth of trust funds and co-financing arrangements signals an increase in bilateral and selectively multilateral control over Bank lending.

In sum, the financing of the IMF and the World Bank has opened them up to US influence in spite of their potential autonomy from this influence. Each time an increase in IMF quotas or a replenishment of the Bank's IDA has been negotiated, the Congress has used the opportunity to threaten to reduce or withhold the funds, being yet more prepared than even the Executive agencies—Treasury and State Department—to set down special preconditions for US contributions. As a result, other shareholders and officials within the institutions have grown used to placating not just the powerful Departments of State and Treasury, but also the feisty US Congress. The overall result seems to have enhanced the capacity of the United States unilaterally to determine aspects of policy and structure within both the IMF and the World Bank.

3. The US and Lending Decisions of the IMF and the World Bank

In theory the United States should have no political influence over the lending decisions of the IMF or the World Bank. Both institutions make loans to countries ostensibly where members have satisfied technical considerations set out in their articles of agreement. Indeed, political influence over their

---

[29] The external funding for trust funds in financial year 1999 was provided by—in order of size of donation in millions of $US—the Netherlands 221, Japan 199, USA 94, UK 87, and Sweden 74. The HIPC (Highly Indebted Poor Countries) Trust Fund has $1,233 million made up of: $850 million from IBRD unallocated net income; $90.4 million from the African Development Bank Group (AfDB Group); $1.2 million from the Nordic Development Fund (NDF); $291.4 million from Belgium, Canada, Denmark, Finland, Greece, Japan, Luxembourg, Netherlands, Norway, Portugal, Spain, Sweden, Switzerland, and the United Kingdom. The United States contribution to HIPC has been a major source of tension between the Executive and Congress: see Stephen Fidler, 'US debt relief under fire', *Financial Times* (13 July 2000).

activities is prohibited, as set out unequivocally in the World Bank's articles of agreement: 'The Bank and its officers shall not interfere in the political affairs of any member; nor shall they be influenced in their decisions by the political character of the member or members concerned. Only economic considerations shall be relevant to their decisions, and these considerations shall be weighed impartially in order to achieve the purposes stated in Article I.'[30]

Yet the record of lending from both institutions strongly suggests a pattern of US interests and preferences. Indeed, right from the early days of the IMF 'the US voice in the Fund was decisive . . . The practical question in those years, in any prospective large use of Fund resources, was whether the United States would agree—and the answer was usually obtained by direct inquiry'.[31]

The seemingly direct influence of the United States poses the question as to what ends and how this influence is exercised. Let us deal first with the question of ends. It has often been asserted that the IMF makes loans according to the size of a country's debt and its strategic importance to the United States and other major shareholders, as well, of course, as its economic position. For example, Susan Strange asserted in the 1970s that 'Without its ever being stated in so many words, the Fund's operational decisions made its resources available neither to those in the greatest need nor to those with the best record of good behaviour in keeping to the rules, but paradoxically to those members whose financial difficulties were most likely to jeopardize the stability of the international monetary system'.[32] However, in a recent statistical analysis of IMF lending Strom Thacker argues that special treatment by the IMF may well be due more to political factors than to the size of debt. One must ask, however, whether his depiction and measurement of political factors is plausible.[33]

Thacker sets up a simple macroeconomic model to test two hypotheses about political influence over IMF lending to developing countries in 1985–94, on the assumption that the United States plays the role of principal in the organization. The first hypothesis tested is that the Fund lends to friends of the United States: the 'political proximity' hypothesis. The second hypothesis tested is that IMF loans are used to reward friendly overtures towards the United States and are withheld in order to punish unfriendly behaviour: the 'political movement' hypothesis. In order to test these factors econometrically, Thacker uses voting patterns on 'key votes' in the UN General Assembly as measures of political alignment and movement.

Thacker's results lend stronger support to the 'political movement' hypothesis: that realignment towards the United States improves a country's

---

[30] Article IV, section 5. It is worth bearing in mind that in fact to some degree policy conditionality has always been part of the Bank's work: David Baldwin, 'The International Bank in Political Perspective', *World Politics*, 18/1 (1965).
[31] Frank A Southard, *The Evolution of the International Monetary Fund*. Essays in International Finance, no. 135 (Princeton: International Finance Section, Dept of Economics, Princeton University, 1979), 19–20.   [32] Strange, 'The IMF', 272.
[33] Strom Thacker, 'The High Politics of IMF Lending', *World Politics*, 52/1 (1999).

chances of receiving a loan regardless of the starting position. Statistically this proved stronger in his tests than the simpler 'political proximity' hypothesis, at least until the end of the cold war (1985–9). Since the end of the cold war, however, both hypotheses seem to hold. Thacker interprets this as evidence that the United States is 'playing the realignment game as vigorously as ever and is rewarding the allegiance of those who stay close without necessarily moving any closer',[34]

The results and interpretation are problematic on many counts. Thacker himself notes that UNGA key votes are a rather crude measure of political motivation; however, the distortionary consequences of his model and its weakness in supporting his conclusions may lie deeper than he realizes. To give one example, he deduces that IMF loans to Hungary, Yugoslavia, and Romania all reflected moves by these countries towards the USA in the 1980s—a difficult, to say the least, assumption in the case of Romania—while the absence of loans to Czechoslovakia and Poland reflected the opposite. He is correct that Poland reflected a politically charged decision within the IMF; however, Czechoslovakia was not even a member of the institution at the time, and therefore ineligible for any kind of loan regardless of political circumstances.[35] This example highlights the need to examine descriptively—even if superficially—the circumstances of the cases tested.

The other argument tested by Thacker is whether specific economic interests drive US policy, as argued by modern political economy or neo-Marxian scholars. Thacker uses measures of US exports and foreign investment to test this view; and, although he rejects it too summarily, he does at least accept that a subtler model specification and further research would be needed to untangle the cross-cutting nature of these interests.[36]

At the end of the statistical analysis, we are still left pondering what kinds of political and strategic interests are being pursued through rewarding 'political alignment' and by what means. The statistical testing does not identify the mechanisms through which influence is exercised, nor where it is that other states enjoy or have the potential to exercise influence to counter the US position. On these latter questions case studies and historical research are useful in a number of ways.[37] In particular, the history of the institutions assists in elaborating the strategic objectives the US has tried to meet through IMF and World Bank lending. More specific case studies can assist in explaining how influence is exercised, with what impact, and within what limits.

[34] Thacker, 'High Politics', 64.
[35] I am very grateful to James Boughton for sharing these insights with me. His *Silent Revolution: The International Monetary Fund 1979–1989* (Washington, DC: IMF, 2001) offers a contrastingly rich historical analysis of such examples.
[36] Thacker, 'High Politics', 58.
[37] See Kapur, Lewis, and Webb, *The World Bank*, i.; Tony Killick, *IMF Programs in Developing Countries: Design and Impact* (London: Routledge, 1995); Kendall Stiles, *Negotiating Debt: The IMF Lending Process* (Boulder, CO: Westview, 1991).

The recently published and richly detailed history of the World Bank gives some insight into the political background to lending decisions within that institution. Having created the IBRD in 1944, the first major decision of the United States was to sideline the institution, using the Marshall Plan instead to channel bilateral, conditional funds directly to European governments. This did not, however, leave the Bank immune from cold war pressures elsewhere. Within the Western alliance, the Bank was soon seen as an important means of supporting and reinforcing allies throughout Asia, the Middle East, Central and South America, and Africa.

In 1948, when Yugoslavia broke from the Soviet bloc, the World Bank stepped in with loans, fulfilling the advice of George Kennan—the architect of the US containment strategy—that the West should offer the country 'discreet and unostentatious support'.[38] In Nicaragua, the US-supported Somoza regime received a disproportionate number of World Bank loans[39] while offering the United States a convenient base for prosecuting the cold war in Central America such as the training and launching of the 1954 overthrow of Guatemalan President Jacobo Arbenz—seen as a Communist sympathiser— and the 1961 Bay of Pigs invasion of Cuba.[40] In the Middle East, Iran was heavily supported while it offered an important way to contain Soviet- sympathizing Iraq. Indeed, in the period 1957–74 Bank lending to Iran amounted to $1.2 billion in 33 loans.[41] In Indonesia, after General Suharto assumed power in March 1966 the Bank immediately began a very close and special relationship with the country. The very substantial levels of corruption, the abysmal human rights record, and most significantly the failure to meet World Bank conditions regarding the state oil company Pertamina, were all overlooked. Rather more important in explaining the Bank's relationship with Indonesia was the backdrop of US strategic concerns about south-east Asia and communist insurgency.[42] In this case as in so many others, loans were used to support and win allies in the cold war against the USSR. Significant in all of these examples—and similar examples in the IMF[43]—is the extent to which economic conditions and performance were overridden by strategic motivations and priorities.

Does the experience of lending during the cold war suggest that the Fund and the Bank were merely instruments of the policies of the US Executive? And, if so, how were these policies imposed on the multilateral institutions? This question goes to the heart of the analysis of US influence and the autonomy of the institutions. Answering the question demands a closer reading of

[38] Kapur, Lewis, and Webb, *The World Bank*, i., 103.   [39] Ibid.
[40] Anthony Lake, *Somoza Falling* (New York: Houghton Mifflin, 1989).
[41] Kapur, Lewis, and Webb, *The World Bank*, i., 500.
[42] Marshall Green, *Indonesia: Crisis and Transformation, 1965–1968* (Washington, DC: Compass Press, 1990).
[43] Harold James, *International Monetary Cooperation since Bretton Woods* (Oxford: Oxford University Press, 1996); Pauly, *Who Elected*.

the cases and understanding of how influence was exercised. Several factors emerge. First, it has not always been the case that the priorities of the US Executive have shaped lending, particularly when other US political voices have exercised pressure in a different direction, such as in the case of World Bank loans to India. Second, the effectiveness of loans in securing US preferences, such as consolidating sympathetic regimes or implementing particular kinds of policies in borrowing countries, depends heavily on the relationship established between Fund and Bank officials and their interlocutors within the borrowing government, including a particular technical expertise and mind set. Where this relationship breaks down, or key interlocutors lose their positions in government, so too the influence of the IMF and the World Bank wanes. Third and finally, where US preferences are clear, they influence the staff and work of the international institutions in a number of ways and through informal as well as formal channels and not just through the politics of the Executive Board. Let us deal with each of these aspects of influence in turn.

In the case of India, World Bank lending went ahead throughout the cold war period in spite of being at odds with US strategic priorities. Indeed, the United States had earlier exerted considerable pressure on the IMF to reduce its assistance to India.[44] The explanation given by scholars who have examined the history of loans to India is that the Bank's lending reflected concerns of the US aid community as opposed to US national interests as understood by the US Executive agencies, that is, Treasury and State Departments. The same scholars argue that the limits of the Bank's policy influence in India came not so much from overriding US-defined political priorities foisted on the Bank but rather from the lack of technocratic interlocutors in the Indian government.[45] This highlights another aspect of how the influence of the IMF and the World Bank is exercised.

For Bank and Fund officials successfully to make loans to member governments, staff of the institutions have to forge good working relationships with interlocutors in borrowing countries. In Indonesia, for example, the Brookings project historians explain the high level of Bank activity in terms not only of the US strategic priorities but also the close relationship which developed between the Bank staff and their interlocutors in the Indonesian government, a group of young US-trained economists—or 'technocrats', as they came to be called—who were brought into government by General Suharto. From the Bank's side, the most senior staff member in Jakarta was given unprecedented powers to make loans and report directly to the World Bank President, leading to a rapid expansion of loans and activity.[46] Significantly, once the Bank's technocratic interlocutors lost some of their influence and power, so too Indonesia's relationship with the World Bank became a more distant one.

---

[44] James, *International Monetary*, 138.
[45] Kapur, Lewis, and Webb, *The World Bank*, i., 293–8, 463–7.
[46] Kapur, Lewis, and Webb, *The World Bank*, ii., 467–71.

This story has been repeated in other countries allied to the West with whom the World Bank formed close relations: for example, Turkey, Mexico, Iran—in particular in the late 1970s—and the Philippines.

The Fund and the Bank rely for effectiveness on good relations forged between their staff and interlocutors in lending countries. This is not something that can be, or has been, directly controlled by the United States. Obviously, where the United States can ensure a large speedily disbursed loan is on offer, this can significantly bolster initial relations. Over the longer term, however, decisions to provide—or not—a particular loan offer only a very rough and short-term capacity to influence the policies of a borrowing government.[47] Over the longer term the deeper relationship with officials from the IMF and the World Bank is vital and depends upon a number of factors, including the degree to which officials share an understanding of the economic problems facing a country and their possible solutions, and the technical expertise of the negotiators on both sides. Yet perhaps this is not just a question of competence in negotiation and economics. These factors might also lead one to ask whether or not the ostensibly 'technical' staff of the Fund and Bank are politically influenced by the United States and, if so, how.

In formal terms, the staff of both the IMF and the World Bank are selected for their excellence as economists and, to quote Article 12, section 4c of the IMF's Articles of Agreement, 'owe their duty entirely to the Fund and to no other authority. Each member of the Fund shall respect the international character of this duty and shall refrain from all attempts to influence any of the staff in the discharge of these functions'. In reality, however, this injunction is honoured more by its breach and goes to the heart of the subtle and invisible way in which political influence affects the work of both the IMF and the World Bank. Politics is not confined to the executive board where in theory it belongs. Indeed, a search for explicit US influence in the minutes of board meetings would reveal very little about the way influence is exercised in the institutions.

Much more important is the fact that senior managers in either the Bank or the Fund would virtually never present a recommendation which risked US disapproval. Indeed, if the issue is a sensitive one, any recommendation will be 'run past' the US Treasury as it is being prepared for presentation to the board. The implications of this run deep: because senior managers will be unwilling to take recommendations to the board, their staff know that they are wasting their time preparing recommendations of which the US may not approve. Hence, all work within the institutions is undertaken with one eye constantly trained on the likely reactions of the institutions' largest shareholder. And where officials do take a stance which diverges from the US

<hr/>

[47] Tony Killick, 'Principals, Agents and the Limitations of BWI Conditionality', *World Economy*, 19/2 (1996) analyses the short-term effects and longer term failure of IMF conditionality.

position, it is not unknown, especially if they are US nationals, for them to be asked by US officials to explain their actions or recommendations.[48]

Overall, the use of resources in both the IMF and the World Bank suggests a high degree of US influence. The US interests being pursued are not always clear; they are the result of contestation within the US political system itself. The US exercises influence over the institutions' lending not simply by wielding its voting power on the executive board—discussed at greater length below. Equally, if not more influential, are the subtle and often invisible pressures perceived by staff within the institutions and operating as mechanisms of self-restraint. This poses the question: does the US have much influence in appointing the technical staff of the organization?

4. US Influence in the Staffing and Management of the Institutions

In most multilateral organizations and throughout the agencies of the United Nations, there are strict nationality quotas which ensure that all countries are represented both formally in the governing councils of institutions and informally among the technical staff. Furthermore, the requirement to work in a number of different languages ensures a spread of different nationalities. However, early in the history of the Fund and the Bank the United States successfully resisted pressures for there to be any national quotas for hiring, and established a commitment to English as the working language.[49] Recent historians of the Bank argue that from the start this skewed employment in the Bank significantly, not just geographically—favouring south Asia over east Asia and Britain over other European countries—but also overwhelmingly towards graduates of institutions that taught in English—that is, predominantly the US and the UK.[50] The allegation that follows from this observation is a sociological one: that US 'knowledge' is embedded in both international financial institutions and is yet another instrument through which US economic and political interests are furthered. What does the evidence suggest?

Today in both the IMF and the World Bank the staff are overwhelmingly US or UK trained in economics and finance. In national terms in 1968, an

---

[48] Conversations with officials in both organizations. Note that in the background lies a general unwillingness of the Executive Board to interfere with other members' business: in the words of the External Evaluation into IMF Surveillance, what is supposed to be 'peer pressure' in fact becomes 'peer protection'—a reciprocal agreement not to interfere. IMF, *External Evaluation into IMF Surveillance*, 34.

[49] Although there is a formal requirement that in making appointments, due regard should be paid 'to the importance of recruiting personnel on as wide a geographical basis as possible'. See IMF Articles of Agreement, Article XII, Section 4d.

[50] Kapur, Lewis, and Webb, *The World Bank*, i., 1167.

analysis of senior staff in the IMF revealed that 32 of 54 were from four English-speaking countries: the United States (23), the UK (6), Canada (2), and Australia (1).[51] A much more recent study reports that, although the nationality of staff had been diversified so that 41 per cent of staff were from English-speaking industrialized countries, among those being hired at the time of the study some 90 per cent of those with Ph.D.'s received them from the United States or Canada.[52] Equally, a 1991 study of the World Bank's Policy, Research and External Affairs Departments showed that some 80 per cent of senior staff were trained in economics and finance at institutions in the United States and in the United Kingdom.[53]

Many economists would argue that the facts stated above simply reflect that the best economics departments of the world are to be found in the United States—with the UK trailing close behind—and that the Fund and the Bank hire the best. However, before accepting this rejection of US influence over the composition and work of the institutions, let us briefly review who controls decisions about staffing and management.

The articles of agreement of the Fund and the Bank provide for the head of each organization to be appointed by the executive board. In practice, by long-standing convention the job of President of the World Bank goes to the candidate most favoured by the United States,[54] and the job of Managing Director of the IMF goes to the candidate most favoured by Western European members. The latter appointment is 'balanced' by the convention that the Deputy Managing Director of the IMF is always an American. In theory, the heads of the institutions are then responsible—subject to the approval of the executive board—for the organization, appointment, and dismissal of the staff of their organizations. For all senior appointments, however, the approval of the United States is *de facto* necessary. The influence of the heads of the organization will also to some degree be influenced by their individual capabilities: their charisma, ideological legitimacy, administrative competence, expert knowledge, previous association with the organization, negotiating ability, and ability to persist in intransigence all contribute to the power of the head of an international organization.[55] Below the level of head of department, other staff are appointed at the prerogative of senior management. It bears noting that, even at this more junior level, the United States has gone to some length to ensure that its own nationals have every incentive to work for the institutions.[56]

[51] See Strange, 'The IMF', 269.
[52] Ian D. Clark, *Should the IMF Become More Adaptive?*, IMF Working Paper WP/96/17 (Washington, DC: IMF, 1996).
[53] Nicholas Stern with Francisco Ferreira, 'The World Bank as "Intellectual Actor"' in Kapur, Lewis, and Webb (eds), *The World Bank*, ii.
[54] In the early days this was seen as vital if the institution were successfully to float bond issues within the US markets.
[55] Cox and Jacobson, *The Anatomy of Influence*.
[56] See, for example, the tax arrangements set out in Geithner, 'US Treasury Statement', 4.

In summary, there are several ways in which the United States has shaped, and continues to shape, the staffing of both the IMF and the World Bank. Influence over who becomes the head or senior management in each organization has a vital role in shaping the institutions, although, certainly, it does not amount to hands-on control—as various United States administrations have found in dealing with 'loyal' appointees to the presidency at the Bank who have turned uncomfortably independent.[57] The staffing may not reflect the sociological view mentioned above, namely, that knowledge is controlled to ensure a particular orthodoxy is imposed worldwide. Nevertheless, as was demonstrated during the first Reagan administration, a change in the politically appointed senior management in either institution can quickly redirect and underline a particular political mind set and blueprint for conditionality within the institutions.[58]

5. Formal Structures of Power and Informal Exercises of Influence

Even if used less than the informal influence discussed above, the power of the US in the formal structures of decision making in the IMF and the World Bank is vital to understanding its influence. At the top of each institution is the board of governors which meets once a year and makes overall strategic decisions. In the IMF, the governors are advised by the International Monetary and Financial Committee—formerly the Interim Committee—in which the voting power of each representative is weighted as per the Executive Board which meets twice a year. All other powers are delegated to the executive boards of the institutions. In other words, the United States has more formal power than any other state in all the agencies of oversight and management of the IMF and the World Bank.

In the executive boards of each of the Bank and the Fund all members are represented but not all are directly represented and nor do they enjoy equal voting power. Only the large members have their own executive directors. All other countries are grouped and represented by one director per group. Each member has a percentage of votes reflecting its quota which in turn reflects its weight in the world economy. Not only does the United States have by a wide margin the largest quota and voting share, but, to cite a senior Treasury official's testimony to a Congressional committee examining the IMF: 'Representing the largest, most influential member, the US representatives speak on virtually every issue coming before the Board.'[59]

---

[57] See Kapur, Lewis, and Webb, *The World Bank*, i.
[58] Ngaire Woods, in Chris Gilbert and David Vines (eds), *The World Bank: Structure and Policies* (Cambridge: Cambridge University Press, 2000).
[59] Geithner, 'US Treasury Statement', 5.

The US capacity to speak on all issues derives from the resources it brings to its representation in the IMF and the World Bank. To take the example of the IMF, while many countries have one or two officials at the Fund, the United States has at least three dozen US Treasury officials regularly involved in working with, thinking about, and offering advice concerning the IMF. As well as the Executive Director at the IMF, supported by an Alternate Director, an economic adviser, three technical assistants, and two administrative assistants, there is a Deputy Assistant Secretary of the Treasury who works mainly on the IMF, supported by between four and six Treasury staff. Furthermore, most US Treasury country and regional offices spend time liaising with the IMF about analyses and programmes affecting their particular countries or regions. Additionally, staff working on G-7 coordination, as well as on private sector involvement, capital account issues, crisis management, appropriate conditionality, and so forth work regularly with the IMF. Their influence is seen in the way the US attempts to coordinate positions with other members and build support for its views.

The executive boards of both the Fund and the Bank operate by consensus, which means that formal votes are virtually never taken. However, the voting power of members is taken into account in determining the extent of consensus on any issue. Practically speaking the board secretary keeps a tally of the extent of agreement, in voting power terms, making the voting structure a key 'behind-the-scenes' element in decision-making. The US does not enjoy a majority with which to push through measures it favours; rather, the US delegation needs to garner support. Hence the large staff mentioned above are deployed in making frequent direct contacts with the management, staff, and the Offices of Executive Directors within the Fund, either individually or in groups. The US Treasury also uses bilateral relations, the G-7 framework, and other multilateral forums in which to garner support for positions within the IMF. This behind-the-scenes work means that when the US does raise an issue within the Fund's Board it can do so 'without triggering counterproductive reactions and a hardening of positions'.[60]

The US is more powerful when it comes to blocking decisions. Enjoying 17.35 per cent of votes, the United States is the only state with a capacity individually to veto decisions requiring 85 per cent majorities; indeed, it negotiated the increase in the special majority as trade-off for its decreased voting share—this was the first amendment to the Fund's articles.[61] In theory, Germany, with 6.08 per cent of votes, France—5.02 per cent—and the United Kingdom—5.02 per cent—could vote together to exercise a similar veto; however, the European countries do not, as yet, coordinate their positions on the

[60] Geithner, 'US Treasury Statement', 7.

[61] Frederick K Lister, *Decision-Making Strategies for International Organizations: The IMF Model*, 20/4 (Denver: Graduate School of International Studies, University of Denver, 1984).

IMF.[62] Similarly, a very large coalition of developing countries could—but don't—organize in a similar way.[63] As a result, the United States remains the only member with an effective and practised veto power.

Finally, further enhancing US power has been the new porousness of the Fund and the Bank to 'civil society' and NGOs, and in particular, NGOs with effective lobbies within the US Congress. Over the past two decades, both the US Congress and Executive Office have pushed the IMF and the World Bank into being more responsive to 'civil society'. To quote a recent statement by the US Secretary of the Treasury on reforming the Fund:

It should become more attuned, not just to markets, but the broad range of interests and institutions with a stake in the IMF's work. Just as the institution needs to be more permeable for information to flow out, so too must it be permeable enough to let in new thoughts—by maintaining a vigorous ongoing dialogue with civil society groups and others.[64]

The terms 'civil society' and 'NGOs' can, of course, mean a wide variety of different things.[65] In Washington DC, 'opening up to NGOs' means working with, and through, grass-roots organizations in borrowing countries. It also means paying more heed to lobby groups in Washington DC who mobilize popular—in some cases predominantly US—opinion for or against the institutions or a particular policy or aspect of the institutions. This is where enhanced US influence is an issue and explaining it draws together several points already discussed in this chapter.

Transnational NGOs will logically target the US in their attempts to reform the IMF and the World Bank. This is because the United States is, among states, the most powerful to demand change. In particular, NGOs turn to the US Congress because it has the power—and uses it—to impose conditions on any approval given for the replenishment of the IDA in the World Bank or any increase in IMF quotas. Not all NGOs will be heard and supported by Congress, however. Rather, the Congress will be most sympathetic to issues approved of by its own constituents and positions which best resonate among local voters. Hence, NGO influence on the Bank and the Fund through the US Congress is likely always to be slanted towards US interests, however broadly drawn. This reasoning makes sense of the finding of research into NGOs and the institutions that 'activism by United States NGOs has probably expanded the already

---

[62] Compare this with the WTO, where they do; and note Robert Solomon, *The International Monetary System, 1945–1981* (New York: Harper and Row, 1982) who argues that European states prefer other forums such as G-7 and G-10 because there they enjoy more equality with the US.

[63] The developing countries' coalition, the Group of Twenty-Four, exists but does not use such tactics.

[64] Lawrence Summers, 'The right kind of IMF for a stable global financial system', Remarks to the London Business School, 14 December 1999 (US Treasury: LS-294).

[65] See Jan Aart Scholte, 'Global Civil Society', in Ngaire Woods (ed.), *The Political Economy of Globalization* (Basingstoke: Macmillan, 2000) for an excellent enumeration.

disproportionate role of the United States in the international financial institutions, especially the World Bank'.[66] Examples of the results of such lobbying
abound and have already been mentioned in this chapter, such as the
Independent Inspection Panel in the World Bank and the Meltzer Commission.

6. Conclusions

In sum, the US has substantial capabilities to bring to bear in shaping the mandates, policies, and *modus operandi* of the international financial institutions.
Yet, while neither the IMF nor the World Bank enjoys the independence envisaged for it in its articles of agreement, neither can be said to be 'controlled' by
the United States. With regard to explaining the nature and limits of US
influence, it has been argued that little is revealed by attempts statistically to
model political influence over the lending of the IMF and the World Bank.
More work is done by studies of specific cases and of the practices and anatomy
of influence within the institutions.

At the core of US influence lies the financial structures of the institutions.
The Fund and the Bank do not rely on periodic donations from members in order
to replenish their core resources. This gives both the potential to be relatively
independent of their government members. Yet in recent years both have, on
occasion, fallen into the arms of the US Congress. The IMF's need for additional
resources and the creation of the IDA within the World Bank have forced the
institutions to ask their government members for additional contributions. In
each case the United States contribution has needed the approval of Congress.
In turn, Congress has used the opportunity to impose conditions not just regarding the specific facilities for which the funds have been asked, but on the overall governance and direction of both the IMF and the World Bank.

Preserving some element of autonomy for the institutions is the fact that
neither can effectively lend resources and influence borrowers without establishing technical credibility and a longer-term relationship with interlocutors
within borrowing governments. This limits the uses to which the United States
could put the institutions, even if it were in a position to call all the shots.
However, the exercise of behind-the-scenes influence by the United States
should not be underestimated. It is telling that senior managers in both institutions would almost never present to the board a proposal which risked US
disapproval. Furthermore, it is unlikely that these managers would be appointed
in the face of any US disapproval.

---

[66] Charles Abugre and Nancy Alexander, 'Non-Governmental Organizations and the
International, Monetary and Financial System', *International Monetary and Financial
Issues for the* 1990s, ix. (Geneva: UNCTAD, 1998), 116.

Finally, although the United States enjoys significant influence in both the IMF and the World Bank, this does not mean that the US Executive agencies control the mandate, lending operations, or outcomes of the institutions. The political pressures emanating from the United States do not all converge. The US Congress is often critical of the Executive agencies of State and Treasury in their policies towards the institutions. Adding further to the fray are NGOs, some of whom effectively lobby the US Congress while others play to a wider world stage. The result is that US influence is almost always effective in securing a hearing and some action within the IMF and the World Bank, but it does not always reflect a coherent set of interests.

5

The United States and the GATT/WTO System

GAUTAM SEN

The relationship between the US and the World Trade Organization (WTO) represents the principal political and legal framework for America's international economic relations. The WTO exceeds the North American Free Trade Agreement (NAFTA) in importance because of its much larger purview, since its reach is the global market. The WTO is also more prominent than the GATT, its predecessor, both because it was established as an international organization and because it has a vastly enlarged scope. The assumption of formal responsibility for a wide range of issues by the WTO under the Uruguay Round Agreement (URA) guarantees further expansion of its activities, as they acquire substantive content through the implementation of specific agreements. By contrast, the contemporary IMF and the World Bank, discussed in Chapter 4 of this volume, might be regarded essentially as vehicles through which advanced countries, led by the US, determine the conditions under which balance of payments support and development loans are offered. They have little direct bearing on the conduct of domestic policies of advanced economies.

The international trade relations of the US are a source of contemporary controversy. The growing proportion of US gross national product (GNP) in the traded goods sector is undoubtedly having a significant impact on the US economy and society. Such growing international economic specialization is acknowledged to promote greater economic dynamism and prosperity. But it also precipitates socio-economic change and dislocation because new patterns of comparative advantage and specialization impose costs on shrinking sectors, displacing workers and altering the spatial pattern of economic activity. In addition, there is concern that international trade rules under the rubric of the WTO threaten to undermine national environmental policies because they constrain domestic preferences and intensify resource use through growth. Similar concerns are voiced about the cost implications of large disparities in international labour standards that affect comparative advantage, due to working conditions and practices that are deemed to violate human rights.

The question posed by the interplay between greater international specialization and its domestic impact is: how do democratic societies respond to the conflicting demands of the beneficiaries of higher growth and those who either are not so advantaged or are opposed for other reasons—the displaced and environmental lobbies? Is US society able to reconcile the aspirations of its citizens with international obligations and the economic challenges of globalization? The fundamental question posed in this chapter relates to the nature of the US commitment to the GATT/WTO system. Could the US seek to exit the organization and pursue a bilateral and regional path? A subsidiary but important question is the degree to which the US honours WTO codes. As a corollary, the role of the US in the establishment of the WTO and its subsequent functioning needs to be understood. In examining this commitment, the societal, constitutional, institutional, and economic roots of US trade policy are also relevant.

1. US Domestic Politics and International Trade Policy

The national trade policies of the US have played a pivotal role in the functioning of the international trade regime since at least 1930 when trade barriers raised by the fateful US Smoot-Hawley tariff triggered widespread trade protectionism. Recognition by the US government that another collapse of the international trade order must be prevented and the endeavour to reconcile the economic advantages of international specialization with domestic political imperatives, as well as international accommodation, have conditioned the post-Second World War history of the international trade system. During the later stages of the Second World War the US was the key protagonist in the negotiation of tariff cuts under the aegis of GATT and the abortive attempt to establish the International Trade Organization (ITO). The rejection of the ITO by the US Congress in 1950 made the GATT, which began operating in 1947, the multilateral forum for international trade relations by default. The impetus for subsequent major rounds of the GATT—the Kennedy (1964–7), Tokyo (1973–9), and Uruguay rounds (1986–94)—largely came from the US.

The US had played a prominent role in defining the scope and character of the legal order as well as the evolution of the GATT. The defining principles that informed post-Second World War international trade agreements, unconditional most-favoured nation and safeguards, originate in US practice.[1] Reciprocity and safeguards remain the basis for the international trade regime,

---

[1] Carolyn Rhodes, *Reciprocity, U.S. Trade Policy and the GATT Regime* (Ithaca: Cornell University Press, 1993), 71–7.

despite fragile justification for their economic rationale, because of US support for them. The acceptance of these precepts by European governments reflected the key role of the US, although the purpose of generalized most-favoured-nation treatment (MFN) was to end pre-existing European preferential arrangements. The US has played an even more influential role in determining the outcomes of the URA and the eventual architecture of the WTO that succeeded the GATT system in 1994, though it initially had misgivings about its establishment as an international organization.[2] The US is also the decisive actor determining the fate of ongoing international trade negotiations, as the onset of the Millennium Round of trade negotiations in November 2001 at Doha highlighted.

US paramountcy and the challenge to it from communism defined the politics of the post-Second World War world. The political, economic, and military primacy of the US was the most significant influence on the negotiations over the post-war international economic order. However, the communist challenge complicated US aims in these negotiations because Washington was also pursuing broader foreign policy goals that created the need for trade-offs between a variety of objectives. The US did often succeed in imposing its will on reluctant European allies in the area of international trade reform—for example, on the removal of quantitative restrictions and non-discrimination beyond a transition period—but it had to accommodate their preferences on some issues, like the balance of payments controls and development.[3] In the end the US allowed its allies to suspend basic norms of a liberal international trade order for much of the 1950s to assist their economic revival and elicit their political cooperation in confronting the communist challenge.

Political Basis of International Liberalization

The concept that articulates the post-Second World War institutional compromise between the goal of efficiency associated with economic openness and protectionist societal distributional constraints is 'embedded liberalism'.[4]

---

[2] For a succinct analysis of the URA and the WTO, see Richard Blackhurst, 'The Capacity of the WTO to Fulfil its Mandate' in Anne O. Krueger (ed.), *The WTO as an International Organization* (Chicago: Chicago University Press, 1998); John H. Jackson, *The World Trade Organization, Constitution and Jurisprudence*, Chatham House Papers (London: RIIA Cassel Imprint, 1998); and John H. Jackson, *World Trading System: Law and Politics of International Economic Relations* (Cambridge, MA: MIT Press, 1997).

[3] Richard N. Gardner, *Sterling-Dollar Diplomacy: The Origins and the Prospects of Our International Economic Order*, 2nd edn (New York: McGraw Hill, 1969).

[4] John Gerard Ruggie, 'International Regimes, Transactions, and Change: Embedded Liberalism in the Post-war Economic Order', in Stephen D. Krasner (ed.), *International Regimes* (Ithaca: Cornell University Press, 1983). It might be noted that 'embedded liberalism' has failed to assist countries that are price-takers, subjected to the harsh market disciplines that price-makers were able to escape. And for the economic rationale for

However, it is important to remember that the compromise of embedded liberalism agreed between the principal protagonists who established the post-Second World War international economic order is not a mutually beneficial symmetric compromise between equals. Each political compromise over trade is a zero-sum result in relation to the potential welfare gains and losses of the countries involved. Thus, while curtailing import penetration is the economic cost one country is prepared to incur to ensure domestic political harmony, the potential exporter in another country loses.[5] Nevertheless, in the face of domestic unrest over the adverse consequences of international openness governments apparently prefer the option of legitimate escape clauses. The fact that they themselves might periodically become victims of the protectionist actions of other countries seems a price worth paying.

The underlying domestic socio-economic context within which national trade policies are formulated is critical in shaping the actual compromise of embedded liberalism. It determines the overall political outcome of the interaction between support for and opposition to international openness within countries, although the evolution of this very socio-economic context is itself the outcome of the ongoing dynamic interplay between openness and protection.[6] The compromise of embedded liberalism also effectively encompasses a number of overlapping but analytically distinct policy goals. Thus, national security considerations, strategic industrial competition, balance of payments constraints, and the problems of sectoral adjustment justify derogation from international openness.[7] Such derogations from the international trade regime are not necessarily GATT-legal and also derive from a combination of international custom and acquiescence by the weaker party.[8]

The balance of payments constraint and associated problems of unemployment and competitive devaluation had the greatest immediate historical resonance during the negotiations over Bretton Woods and the ITO because of

these concepts, see Jackson, *World Trading System*, 175–212, 247–8. On the weak economic grounds and the historical basis of reciprocity, see Bernard Hoekman and Michel Kostecki, *The Political Economy of the World Trading System* (Oxford: Oxford University Press, 1995), 66–77.

[5] The averting of a protectionist backlash by acquiescing in a degree of protection does not obviate the fact that the losses incurred arise from subversion of market outcomes, although the form of the import relief—tariff versus quotas—also deployed has a bearing on the scale of absolute loss suffered.

[6] However, the consequences of international economic openness and protectionist domestic imperatives cannot be juxtaposed as opposites because, in the long run, openness benefits most agents. Domestic trade politics also articulates both opposition to and support for international exchange rather than protectionism alone.

[7] For example, ensuring the viability of some sectors of the economy on grounds of national security or forbidding international trade with some countries owing to sanctions imposed for political reasons.

[8] It is worth noting that the overarching conceptualization of international trade relations as the compromise of embedded liberalism ignores proactive market opening measures of the type represented by the US structural impediments initiative (SII) vis-à-vis Japan, as opposed to a defensive reaction to import penetration.

the experience of the 1930s. However, unemployment due to balance of payments constraints has been managed much better by advanced countries throughout the post-Second World War period and has become less prominent as a reason for protectionism. The exchange rate remains a factor in trade protectionism because currency overvaluation is a catalyst for demands for import relief. The problems of sectoral adjustment, though also prevalent before the Second World War, have become a more prominent influence on national trade policies and to a much greater extent following the first oil crisis in 1973.

These societal factors are critical and condition trade policy at the expense of both collective national and global welfare. They also operate within an ideological context and institutional framework that moulds their ultimate form. But it should not be presumed that, because societal factors are important and the idea of a unitary state single-mindedly pursuing some composite national interest is misplaced, the US faces the same trade policy options as other countries. The US is quite clearly able to achieve its goals in the world trade order to a greater degree than most other countries. This privileged position underlines the importance of its power and status within the international political hierarchy.[9] The US government plays the role of 'price maker' in regulating international trade. Most other countries are 'price takers' as smaller economies are more responsive to external factors than domestic ones, though the European Union virtually constitutes a duopoly with the US.

Nevertheless, the US government, like most other national governments, supports the idea of an open international economy because of the benefits that are understood to flow from international trade, as it constantly reaffirms.[10] But the GATT/WTO legal order is not the outcome of an attempt to uncover some mechanical correspondence between the logic of global economic welfare and appropriate methods and rules for its realization. The formal parameters of the international order require interpretation and discretion, which countries negotiate in terms of their national interests and the power to achieve them.

Domestic Sources of International Trade Policies

Domestic political factors define US foreign economic policy and mould the government's scope for manoeuvre to a greater degree than in virtually any

---

[9] See Patrick O'Brien, 'Imperialism and the Rise and Decline of the British Economy 1688–1989', *New Left Review*, 238 (November–December 1999). Also see Chapter 2 in the present volume.

[10] One estimate puts the annual increment to a four-person household's income owing to the WTO at $3,000. See Robert E. Litan, 'The "Globalization" Challenge: The US Role in Shaping World Trade and Investment', *The Brookings Review*, 18/2 (2000). The importance of economic growth for the political support governments enjoy is discussed in Geoffrey Garrett, *Partisan Politics in the Global Economy* (Cambridge: Cambridge University Press, 1998), 28–31.

other advanced country.[11] A specific feature relevant for understanding the contemporary US attitude towards international trade and the WTO is its changed impact on the US economy and society in recent decades. Immediately after the Second World War wider political concerns, as noted earlier, over-shadowed the protectionist options made available by the compromise of embedded liberalism, although US economic primacy also insulated the economy from costly adjustment.[12] Eventually, the US became more assertive as the cost of its generosity rose, as its allies achieved economic success and burden sharing did not seem likely to undermine them.[13]

The social cost of adjustment to international trade has been rising dramatically for the US as the level of economic interdependence has increased and the composition of imports has changed. Unemployment in the US has a much harsher impact on larger numbers of workers owing to the organization of the labour market and welfare policies, provoking stronger resistance from those industries most affected by imports. Although this rising social cost is a major factor in domestic trade policy, its impact has been somewhat counterbalanced by the very reality of growing interdependence because exporters have also acquired greater political influence. Nevertheless, the relative influence of exporters and import-impacted industries is known to be asymmetric because the latter have greater political weight owing to motivational factors and organizational advantages.[14]

There is a large literature on the identity of US domestic interests and their modes of operation in the US political system, as well as how its institutions and ideological predispositions influence international trade policy. It goes back to analyses of late nineteenth century trade politics and E. E. Schattschneider's work on the logrolling that resulted in the infamous Hawley-Smoot tariff of 1930.[15] The commodity-price equalization theorem of Stolper-Samuelson has provided the analytical economic foundations for identifying the winners and losers from

---

[11] The first decades of the cold war were somewhat exceptional because concern for alliance politics assumed greater weight, but concessions occurred in the context of overall US economic primacy. The sacrifices were also less concentrated sectorally. I. M. Destler, *American Trade Politics*, 3rd edn (Washington, DC: Institute for International Economics, 1995).

[12] John Lewis Gaddis, *We Now Know: Rethinking Cold War History* (Oxford: Oxford University Press, 1996), 189–220.

[13] It is worth noting that the US was more concerned about the domestic stability of its allies than keeping them well disposed towards the various alliances of which they were a part, though that too remained an issue. David Baldwin, *Economic Statecraft* (Princeton: Princeton University Press, 1985), 207–17, and Gaddis, *We Now Know*, 189–220.

[14] Their economic consequences should not be counter-posed against each other as opposites because economic welfare improves because of both exports and adjustment to imports.

[15] Elmer Eric Schattschneider, *Politics, Pressures, and the Tariff: A Study of Free Private Enterprise in Pressure Politics, as Shown in the 1929–1930 Revision of the Tariff* (New York: Prentice-Hall, 1935).

increased international openness.[16] Contemporary work by Robert E. Baldwin, Ronald Rogowski, Paul Midford, Helen V. Milner, and others has achieved greater precision in the analysis of interest groups support for both economic openness and demands for import relief and the associated political process.[17]

These studies specify the trade preferences of different types of industry and labour, deriving from relative national endowment, factor ratios, and the degree of factor immobility. Others have analysed the translation of such preferences into policy within a public choice framework. One perspective that captures the overall dynamic of the US political process in trade policy formation argues that the main goal is to reduce adjustment costs to vulnerable groups while seeking to satisfy the median voter.[18] Political difficulties because of domestic socio-economic adjustment due to imports are only one, though critical, determinant of national trade policy. However, if specific problems are poorly managed openness to trade more generally can be compromised.

Two fundamental features of US trade policy after the failure of the US Executive to gain ratification for the ITO provide an explanation for the greater subsequent success in gaining public and Congressional approval. They are (1) the reduction in what John Odell and Barry Eichengreen describe as 'agent slack' and (2) stronger presidential leadership.[19] In contrast to the experience over negotiations in the late 1940s for the ITO, US domestic interests and US negotiators have cooperated intensively since the Kennedy Round, and especially during the URA. They have therefore ensured a trade policy posture that is largely mutually acceptable. In addition, the Executive has played an active role in support of US trade policy at home and abroad, mitigating narrower congressional perspectives.

Empirical Dimensions of the Cost of Trade Adjustment

In recent decades socio-economic developments have been changing the impact of international trade on US domestic politics, which could conceivably provoke greater trade protectionism and scepticism towards the WTO. Such political pressures were already apparent by the mid-1980s when the Reagan administration faced an array of protectionist demands from

---

[16] For a full elaboration see Paul Samuelson, 'International Trade and the Equalization of Factor Prices', *Economic Journal*, 59 (1948).

[17] Ronald Rogowski, *Commerce and Coalition: How Trade Affects Domestic Political Alignments* (Princeton: Princeton University Press, 1989); Paul Midford, 'International Trade and Domestic Politics: Improving on Rogowski's Model of Political Alignments', *International Organization*, 47/4 (1993); Helen V. Milner, *Resisting Protectionism: Global Industries and the Politics of International Trade* (Princeton: Princeton University Press, 1988); Robert E. Baldwin, *The Political Economy of US Import Policy* (Cambridge: MIT Press, 1985), 1–32. [18] Baldwin, *Political Economy of US Import Policy*.

[19] John Odell and Barry Eichengreen, 'The United States, the ITO, and the WTO: Exit Options, Agent Slack, and Presidential Leadership', in Anne O. Krueger (ed.), *The WTO as an International Organization* (Chicago: Chicago University Press, 1998).

import-competing interests hurt by the strong dollar.[20] Similar protectionist sentiment during the early 1990s provoked opposition to NAFTA from environmental and labour interests; and the agreement barely gained Congressional approval. Domestic interests opposed to globalization disrupted the Clinton administration's efforts to launch a new trade round at Seattle in 1999. And the Bush administration has succumbed to protectionist pressures from key States as the economy has slowed in 2001–2. The imposition of hefty duties on steel imports by the Bush administration in March 2002 has provoked the most serious trade dispute since the signing of the URA in 1994, threatening a cycle of retaliation with the European Union (EU). There is also a revival of US disquiet over the WTO and the alleged activism of its dispute settlement mechanism (DSM) since the US has now lost a number of significant cases brought against it.[21] Nevertheless, the prospect of a full-scale trade war can be discounted because it would cause losses to all protagonists that would be far too high in relation to the stakes involved in the dispute over steel.

The first factor accounting for this domestic political pressure is the impact of labour-intensive imports from developing countries on the US economy and US jobs. This impact grew to serious proportions by the decade of the 1990s and is likely to worsen both because of exports by successful new-comers and because of the liberalizing measures of the URA. By contrast, the impact of such imports in the aftermath of the Kennedy Round was much less severe. The vulnerable area of international trade in textiles and clothing—17 per cent of OECD manufacturing employment in the early 1960s—was, for example, subject to a separate protectionist regime in the form of the Long-term Textile Arrangement—subsequently the Multifibre Arrangement—outside the GATT.

The second factor relevant to understanding US domestic political reaction to greater import penetration by labour intensive imports is the identity of the unemployed and the comparatively harsher socio-economic impact of unemployment in the US. Both import penetration, reflected in rising trade/GDP ratios, and its particular consequences for US labour differ from the experience of countries of the EU, which might have been considered vulnerable to similar conditions and comparable responses.

During the 40 years after 1960, US openness to trade rose from 7 per cent of GDP to approximately 20 per cent. For the EU as a whole it rose from 30 per cent to 50 per cent. However, the crucial difference between the US and the EU has been the latter's constant share of non-EU trade. The rising trade/GDP ratio of the EU is mainly due to intra-industry trade with other advanced countries,

[20] Cf. Dominick Salvatore, 'Trade Protectionism and Welfare in the United States', in Dominick Salvatore (ed.), *Protectionism and World Welfare* (Cambridge: Cambridge University Press, 1993), 326–7.

[21] Guy De Jonquières, 'Rules to fight by' in Comment and Analysis, *Financial Times* (25 March 2002); and 'EU curbs raise trade war tensions with US', in International Economy, *Financial Times* (26 March 2002). See also Claude Barfield, *Free Trade, Sovereignty, Democracy: The Future of the World Trade Organization* (Washington, DC: American Enterprise Institute, 2001).

mostly intra-EU. By comparison, inter-industry trade with developing countries accounts for a significant share of the rising trade/GDP ratio of the US. The scale economies of rising intra-industry trade, resulting from increased intra-EU trade, reinforce workers' bargaining strength through greater international specialization—rather than enforcing adjustment through exit—within product categories and also improve national welfare.[22] By contrast, inter-industry trade involving the import of labour intensive products—responsible for a significant share of the increase in US international trade—displaces jobs because it occurs through traditional shifts in comparative advantage. As a consequence, as Dani Rodrik has argued, the demand for the relatively unskilled and immobile labour in the US has become more elastic. Economic shocks have also caused greater instability of earnings and hours worked in the US because its labour markets are more flexible. Between 1970 and 1997, the median *real* weekly earnings of male full-time workers actually fell by $100 to $600 in constant US dollars.[23]

In addition to resistance towards job displacement induced by labour intensive inter-industry imports, flexible labour market conditions in the US reinforce the political backlash against adjustment. In the US, trade-induced lay-offs directly affect primary groups of workers and have become more long-term. Trade adjustment assistance has also been proving insufficient to ameliorate the scale of losses suffered by primary workers; such assistance reached less than 2.3 per cent of long-term displaced monthly workers in 1999. When the Trade Adjustment Assistance (TAA) programme was promulgated as part of the Trade Expansion Act of 1962, imports from low-income countries were insignificant and US labour supported liberalization.

By comparison, trade-related adjustment within the EU results in greater unemployment amongst older workers and youth because labour market rigidities favour the politically active unionized mainstream. In addition, the EU is more egalitarian than the US: the ratios of income of the highest decile to the share of the lowest decile are 8 per cent and 17 per cent, respectively. The percentage of households with incomes below the 50 per cent median income is also higher in the US, 17 per cent compared with 10 per cent in the EU. Labour market rigidities and greater welfare support in the EU mute the political resistance to globalization because key groups are better protected. In the US, there is heightened political resistance because of the bigger impact of labour-intensive imports and the greater vulnerability of salient primary workers.[24]

---

[22] Paul Krugman, 'Intra-industry Specialization and the Gains from Trade', in *Rethinking International Trade* (Cambridge, MA: MIT Press, 1996).

[23] Andre Sapir, 'Who Is Afraid of Globalization? The Challenge of Domestic Adjustment in Europe and America' (2000), 1–13, available at www.ksg.harvard.edu/cbg/trade/sapir.htm. Also Dani Rodrik, 'Globalization and Labour, Or If Globalization Is a Bowl of Cherries, Why Are There So Many Glum Faces Around The Table?', in Richard E. Baldwin, Daniel Cohen, Andre Sapir, and Anthony Venables (eds), *Market Integration, Regionalism and the Global Economy* (Cambridge: Cambridge University Press, 1999).

[24] Sapir, 'Who Is Afraid of Globalization?'.

Despite the developments described above no dramatic diminution of US support for the international trade order and the WTO itself are likely as a result. Labour-intensive manufactures constitute a small percentage of total US imports, most of which originate in other advanced countries. Paradoxically, firms from advanced countries are also better placed to undertake alternative methods of entry into the US market for their products when they encounter import barriers—for example, through foreign direct investment. And the political weakness of countries responsible for the export of labour-intensive products does not suggest the need for dramatic gestures like the threat of exit.[25] The problems posed by such labour intensive import penetration are amenable to anti-dumping (AD) and countervailing duties (CVD) under Article VI of the WTO, that permit wide latitude for action by the importing country. In addition, implicit or explicit grey-area measures like voluntary export restraints (VERs) might reappear despite the understanding reached during the URA to end their use. Thus, there is no rationale for allowing the rather specific and limited problems of labour-intensive imports to jeopardize the overwhelming percentage of unrelated international trade, which is largely with allies, by resorting to a generalized protectionist retreat or undermining the WTO.[26]

Aspects of US trade relations with Japan, especially during the 1970s and 1980s, might provide an indication of future relations with successful developing countries. Japan had similarly penetrated US markets, and US-Japan trade was characterized by inter-industry trade.[27] The US applied sustained pressure against Japan through a range of policy initiatives, ranging from voluntary curbs on its exports, market rigging—in semi-conductors—and applying AD/CVD to market-opening agreements.[28] When that goal could not be achieved by compelling structural changes in Japan's economy, US officials demanded quantitative targets for Japan's imports from the US. The latter evolved into the notion of a 'level playing field' that the trade theorist Jagdish Bhagwati characterized as an attempt to remould socio-cultural differences.[29] For the most part, these actions cannot be justified legally or vindicated on the basis of a cogent economic rationale: essentially, they constitute an exercise in power.[30] The US

[25] The US Congress, for example, has been unwilling to eliminate barriers to apparel exports from Africa. Jeffrey A. Frankel, 'Assessing the Efficiency Gain from Further Liberalization' (2000), 7, available at www.ksg.harvard.edu/cbg/trade/frankel.htm.
[26] Joann Gowa, *Allies, Adversaries and International Trade* (Princeton: Princeton University Press, 1994).
[27] Edward Lincoln, *Japan's Unequal Trade* (Washington, DC: Brookings Institution Press, 1990).
[28] Merit E. Janow, 'U.S. Trade Policy Toward Japan and China: Integrating Bilateral, Multilateral and Regional Approaches', in Geza Feketekuty and Bruce Stokes (eds), *Trade Strategies for a New Era: Ensuring US Leadership in a Global Economy* (New York: Council on Foreign Relations, published with the Monterey Institute of International Studies, 1998); see especially 179. Merit surveys the troubled relationship and then berates Japan over the Kodak-Fuji dispute that the US subsequently lost at the WTO, DSB, much to its chagrin.
[29] For a series of pithy reflections on US-Japanese trade friction see Jagdish Bhagwati, *A Stream of Windows: Unsettling Reflections on Trade, Immigration and Democracy* (Cambridge, MA: MIT Press, 1998), 149–98.   [30] Jackson, *The World Trade Organization*, 93.

public was convinced that Japanese trade practices were unfair, which made them a useful target for politicians.[31] The campaign against Japanese trade practices yielded a rich harvest in the form of inward foreign direct investment flows to the US, as it did for similar reasons to the EU.

Institutional Arrangements for Trade Policy

The principal domestic US actors in the formulation, implementation, and oversight of US international policy are the President, Congress, the United States Trade Representative (USTR), the Department of Commerce, and the International Trade Commission (ITC). The USTR and the Department of Commerce formulate trade policy in consultation with advisory committees that represent industry. The USTR is the lead agency of the Executive on trade policy and chairs deliberations of other sub-agencies of the US government. The ITC and International Trade Administration (ITA) of the Department of Commerce are responsible for the critical area of AD/CVD. The final tier of discretionary trade policy is the National Economic Council, chaired by the President.

The initiative for tariff setting and routine management of trade policy have been delegated to the President since 1934 by the Reciprocal Trade Agreements Act (RTAA) when Congress belatedly sought to insulate itself from constituency pressures following the disastrous Hawley-Smoot Tariff of 1930. During the post-Second World War period US trade policy and direct bureaucratic interaction in the context of the GATT have remained the prerogative of the Executive. Nevertheless, Congress still possesses ultimate constitutional authority over international trade policy because agreements require legislative approval.

Congress created a time-bound 'fast track' rule in the context of the Trade Act of 1974 that authorizes the President to negotiate trade accords that it can either reject as a whole or accept without amendment, within 60 days of an agreement being presented. This 'fast track' provision, which requires renewal by Congress, allows the President to engage in international trade negotiations with confidence in the outcome not being undermined by the expectation of delays and renegotiation when the agreement is put before Congress, as the experience of the Kennedy Round had shown.[32] But Congress sets the parameters for international trade policy negotiations, to which the Executive is bound. Prior discussion and stipulations as well as involvement of Congressional representatives during trade negotiations improve the prospects of a mutually acceptable accord. The 1974 Trade Act also mandated participation by business and civil society groups—the so-called 'social sector'—are now

[31] Ellen L. Frost, 'Gaining Support for Trade from the American Public', in Feketekuty and Stokes, *Trade Strategies for a New Era*, especially 70–1.
[32] It has been renamed the trade promotion authority (TPA) by the Bush administration.

allowed access in an advisory capacity as well, though business interests remain dominant.

The ITC is effectively the buffer between the grievances of interest groups and the Congress and also adjudicates safeguards, the 'escape clause' instituted by Executive Order in 1947 and incorporated in statute in 1951. It was this escape clause that was incorporated in the shape of Articles VI and XIX of the GATT as a means of deflecting US Congressional opposition. Yet even the ability of the ITC to respond positively to claims for import relief is incomplete and reversible. Ultimately, international economic openness has tended to prevail, but legislative processes since the Trade Expansion Act of 1962 reflect a cyclical curbing of presidential authority in the aftermath of each trade round, as well as an underlying trend limiting the scope for Executive discretion in managing trade policy. Although I. M. Destler concludes that 'the consistent pattern has been for legislators to talk tough but follow the Executive lead', it is noteworthy that the US had the worst record of compliance with GATT panel judgements before the URA.[33]

Principles and Legislative Instruments of Trade Policy

Three interrelated principles and procedures are embodied in US trade policy: reciprocity, safeguards, and 'fair trade'—the notion of a level playing field. They reaffirm the dual purpose of Congress to combat unfair foreign practices that harm US economic interests and ensure relief against disruption to domestic industry by trade that is fair and normal.[34]

The notion of reciprocity was enshrined in the US RTAA of 1934. Although unilateral concessions are not usually damaging to a country's economy, reciprocity reduces the scope for free riding by trading partners. It also elicits the political support of domestic exporters to counterbalance the opposition of those working in industries affected by imports. The universal acceptance of reciprocity as a negotiating principle effectively enlarges the international win-set to accommodate US domestic interests because the US wields greater power than other countries in determining both the agenda and outcomes of trade negotiations, as the history of the URA demonstrates.[35]

Safeguards incorporated in the GATT and the WTO as Articles VI and XIX permit sanctions and import relief in the event of 'unfair trade' practices or serious injury to domestic producers due to imports. Weak or problematic

---

[33] I. M. Destler 'American Trade Politics in the Wake of the Uruguay Round', in Jeffrey J. Schott (ed.), *The World Trading System: Challenges Ahead* (Washington DC: Institute for International Economics, 1996), 122; Robert E. Hudec, *Enforcing International Trade Law: The Evolution of the Modern GATT Legal System* (Salem, NH: Butterworth, 1993).

[34] Judith Goldstein, 'International Law and Domestic Institutions: Reconciling North American 'Unfair' Trade Laws', *International Organization*, 50/4 (1996), 57.

[35] On the meaning of 'win-set', see Robert D. Putnam, 'Diplomacy and Domestic Politics', *International Organization*, 42/3 (1988).

domestic sectors like textiles and agriculture were excluded from the purview of the GATT altogether until their incorporation under the URA. The inclusion of Article XIX itself was of more symbolic than practical importance, as a device for mollifying domestic opposition, because the conditions for its use were considered too onerous in practice. There has always been a preference for AD and CVD against unwelcome or 'unfairly traded' goods—often indistinguishable from an economic perspective—under Article VI because it allows wide discretion, unlike the Article XIX escape clause. They were of indefinite duration, until the time limit introduced by the URA, as well as discriminatory and likely to elicit cooperation and voluntary restraint from threatened parties. Observers regard AD and CVD as major threats to the liberal trade order and their uncertain economic basis has attracted widespread condemnation, although the US and other advanced economies vigorously defend their use.[36] These GATT provisions reaffirm the ability to pursue domestic goals that the notion of 'embedded liberalism' encompasses.

Negotiated international rules on safeguards are complemented by domestic legislation authorizing unilateral action in specified circumstances. They date back to the protectionist decades before the Second World War, which were followed by a succession of GATT rounds that lowered tariffs, despite the rejection of the ITO. Congress passed three substantial trade acts in 1962, 1974, and 1988 that have had an important bearing on the conduct and administration of US trade policies. Among other things, the Trade Expansion Act of 1962 allowed tariffs to be cut on a significant scale and instituted tariff adjustment assistance (TAA). The Trade Acts of 1974 and 1988—the Omnibus Trade and Competitiveness Act—instituted Section 201, for import relief due to injury caused by tariff reductions, and Section 301, to punish unfair foreign trade practices. The circumstances in which such action would be justified were not spelled out, but foreign governments were sensitive to the threat of US private interests seeking investigation under Section 301 and usually modified their behaviour—by increasing imports, for example.

The Trade Act of 1988 changed Section 301 and made it more formidable, requiring the President, previously held to be insufficiently vigorous, to investigate formally when complaints were lodged. It also introduced a novel procedure for creating an inventory of unfair practices of foreign countries, followed by the selection of priority items from it and a demand for the cessation of the offending behaviour, ending with penalties for persistence. It contains Section 337 for remedy of violations to Article VI of GATT on dumping and

---

[36] See Anne O. Krueger, *Economic Policies at Cross-Purposes: The United States and Developing Countries* (Washington, DC: Brookings Institution, 1993). For a vigorous US response, see the relevant section of the Trade Policy Review Mechanism (TPRM) 1998 (communication from the Permanent Mission of the United States, February 2000) (WTO, 1999), document reference: WT/TPR/M/56/Add. 1. Also, Brian Hindley and Patrick Messerlin, *Antidumping Industrial Policy: Legalized Protectionism in the WTO and What to Do About it* (Washington, DC: AEI Press, 1996).

illegal subsidies, and the 'Special' 301 provision designed to protect the interests of US intellectual property rights holders.[37] The Trade Act of 1988 also provides a basis in US law, under the so-called Super 301, for unilateral action against practices that deny fair and equitable access to markets—the so called level playing field—to US exporters. US trade officials provoked the resentment of the international trading community in 1989 by designating Japan, Brazil, and India as targeted 'unfair traders' under the auspices of the Super 301 provision.

Quite plainly, unilateral sanctions under Section 301 are illegal in terms of GATT/WTO law and have been suspended since the WTO treaty came into force. But Super 301 and Title VII, pertaining to the government procurement practices of trading partners, were renewed in 1998. The USTR, in conjunction with the Department of Commerce, continues vigorously to investigate malpractices specified by Section 301 as well.[38] Additional examples of unilateral action range from non-tariff barriers like VERs, supposedly abandoned under the WTO, to the notorious structural impediments initiative vis-à-vis Japan and quantitative import targets. The US, therefore, exercises wide latitude of independent discretion to determine and remedy transgressions and injury to US economic interests.

2. The WTO and US Trade Policy

The internationally negotiated legal framework of the WTO, subject to US interpretation of its provisions, has essentially moulded US trade policy since its inception. The WTO system is a binding, contractual system, with provisions for enforcing adjudication. Yet it operates on a consensual basis, despite the system of universal franchise for sovereign members. Dispute settlement in the WTO is no longer subject to a veto and, on issues where majority voting is allowed, there is a tradition of ensuring the concurrence of important countries.[39] Nevertheless, the WTO treaty implies a major political commitment for member states, including the US, which is unprecedented outside the experience of the EU, though NAFTA approaches it in some respects.

The issue of US influence on the WTO resonates with an older debate about hegemons and followers. The scope and procedures of the WTO needed the

[37] Andreas Furst, 'The "Interaction" Mechanism Between Congress and the President in Making U.S. Foreign Trade Policy', in Carl-Ludwig Hotfrerich (ed.), *Economic and Strategic Issues in US Foreign Policy*, iii. (New York: Walter de Gruyter, 1989).
[38] The 'Special 301' annual review of 2000 identifies 59 countries that deny adequate intellectual property rights protection and fair and equitable markets access to US economic interests.
[39] John H. Jackson, *The World Trading System: Law and Policy of International Economic Relations* (Cambridge, MA: MIT Press, 1997), 342–5; Bernard Hoekman and Michel Kostecki, *The Political Economy of the World Trading System* (Oxford: Oxford University Press, 1995), 40–3, 50–1.

overall support of the EU and Japan, the other important actors in international trade relations, although there were some important areas of divergence with the US. In the final analysis, the experience of the URA and previous rounds of the GATT indicate conjoint control rather than exclusive US dominance. According to one senior US participant, the US and EU had retained cordial relations throughout the Tokyo Round and compromised when differences arose. Interestingly, most of the important negotiations occurred in private, outside GATT meetings, and the main obstacle was in finding common ground with developing countries.[40]

For example, the general agreement on trade in services (GATS), trade-related intellectual property services (TRIPS), and trade-related investment measures (TRIMS), as well as further tariff reductions, were common objectives of the US, the EU, and Japan. Negotiations over the liberalization of trade in agricultural products were prolonged and fraught, but specific commitments on export subsidies, tariffication of non-tariff barriers, and price support were extracted from the EU and Japan. Future liberalization of agricultural trade was also agreed, which has been reiterated at the Doha ministerial declaration of November 2001. The EU was an especially active participant on financial services deregulation and remains proactive in relation to the Millennium Round negotiations.

The wish of the EU to strengthen the DSM of the WTO articulated the desire, shared by others, to curb US unilateralism. The US Congress had misgivings about strengthening these procedures, which has indeed occurred, because it still considers domestic law superior to WTO injunctions. The US had been persistent in its refusal to implement GATT Panel rulings prior to the URA, but it has blocked a review of compliance by the WTO recently as well. But dispute settlement has been reinforced and US unilateralism is quiescent. The commitment to international obligations is therefore largely intact and the President continues to prevail on most trade policies, but at the cost of conceding Congressional ability to question and delay.

The US ensured the acquiescence of developing countries on a range of issues through robust diplomacy and cajolery and continues to exercise its persuasive powers.[41] The developing countries agreed to the liberalization of financial services (GATS), a relatively strict regime on intellectual property rights (TRIPS) and the elimination of performance requirements on multinational corporations (TRIMs). In the crucial area of AD and CVD, particularly aimed at their labour-intensive exports, greater latitude has been granted to signatories. As an overall quid pro quo, the anomaly of excluding trade in textiles and clothing from GATT/WTO discipline was ended. But the schedule

[40] Alonzo L. McDonald, 'Organization and Management of a Complex International Negotiation', *The World Economy*, 23/2 (2000).

[41] The Indian side was the last to capitulate and their senior negotiator was offered a suitable post in the WTO! On US lobbying recently, see John Madeley, 'Dangerous Road to Doha', *The Observer* (4 November 2001).

for liberalization is judged unduly favourable to wealthy importing countries, which have thwarted adjustment for a whole generation. Nor have developing countries gained much from the liberalization of agricultural trade. The US has also forced a large measure of 'unilateral' trade liberalization by developing countries during the past decade through its influence over World Bank finance and IMF adjustment loans.[42]

The opposition of developing countries to the inclusion of labour standards within the URA, because they fear its enforcement disciplines, has led to their temporary redirection to the ILO. But the future of 'core labour standards' awaits only an appropriate formulation and form of words, without which unilateral US measures are possible. The US favoured the introduction of environmental standards as an obligation in the URA, but it has been introduced only at a procedural level so far.[43] From the point of view of environmental campaigners in advanced economies like the US, increased international economic specialization endangers higher domestic standards of protection by initiating a race to the bottom with countries that have less stringent regulation.

The identity and functioning of the WTO are, partly, a manifestation of US structural power.[44] A well-specified contractual arrangement reduces the necessity for extensive subsequent bargaining, though surveillance of compliance may continue. Substantive violations of US interests by other signatories are investigated domestically so that they may be brought before the WTO Dispute Settlement Body (DSB) for remedy, if necessary. The US has become the most frequent user of the DSB since the body began functioning in 1995. It has used it to force the other signatories to comply with their obligations and has achieved a high degree of success before its panels. However, its foreign sales corporation (FSC) tax relief to subsidiaries of US firms was declared illegal by a DSB panel and the ruling was upheld by its superior appellate body in January 2002. WTO disciplines constrain other powerful countries too,

---

[42] See David Vines, 'The WTO in Relation to the Fund and the Bank: Competencies, Agencies and Linkages', and the comment by Julio Nogues, in Krueger, *The WTO as an International Organization*.

[43] The objections of developing countries to the formal inclusion of provisions for labour and environmental standards within the framework are threefold. They fear: its capture by protectionist domestic interests in the advanced countries; supranational inspections that will be intrusive and undermine their sovereign rights on issues that are basically domestic; and the imposition of labour and environmental priorities not of their own choosing by self-interested parties. They also greatly resent the bullying tactics that the US deployed against them successfully on issues like GATS, TRIPS, and TRIMS. The intrinsic merit of issues like 'core labour standards' is hardly able to surface from this soured impasse. For a trenchant examination, see Jagdish Bhagwati, 'The Environment, Labour Standards and Trade Policy', in Jagdish Bhagwati and V. N. Balasubramanyam, *Writings on International Economics* (New Delhi: Oxford University Press, 1998). For a legalistic challenge to the defeat of the US in the Tuna-Dolphin case against Mexico, see Robert Howse and Donald Regan, 'The Product/Process Distinction—An Illusory Basis for Disciplining Unilateralism in Trade Policy', WTO Paper (January 2000); rhowse@umich.du.

[44] Susan Strange, *States and Markets*, 2nd edn (London: Pinter Publishers, 1988).

especially the EU, which is in a position to resist US sanctions. The DSM conveys a signal to the domestic constituents of member countries that transgressions carry costs.[45]

Finally, it would not be an exaggeration to suggest that the WTO bureaucracy is sensitive to the views of the US.[46] The US enjoys an unspoken veto over the appointment of the director-general of the WTO and key staff. The US is also an effective negotiator in the WTO framework by virtue of a well-developed national capacity to navigate complex legal systems.[47] Very few countries have comparable administrative capability to deal with the global economic agenda, developed in the US especially since the Trade Act of 1974. Even the EU is often preoccupied with European issues. The economic liberalism of the WTO, combined with a legalistic deference towards 'escape clauses', also suits US needs more than that of other members. It assures a high degree of international openness that the US considers to be beneficial, but permits abrogation of commitments for a wide variety of reasons. Negotiations over China's entry into the WTO, for example, were basically a two-level game, between the governments of China and the US and the US President and Congress.[48]

WTO Obligations and US National Autonomy

One of the critical questions for the US is the impact of the URA and the WTO on national policy autonomy and domestic constitutional arrangements. The conduct of private citizens of signatory countries will have to conform to the judgements of an international body on substantive issues; and this constitutes a novelty, at least for non-EU nationals. The fear of the loss of sovereignty had prompted some in the US Congress to seek reassurance from the President, resulting in the promise of a so-called 'three strikes agreement'. It proposed to establish a panel of five US federal appellate court judges to review WTO decisions, allowing for the possibility of withdrawing from the WTO if it acted unreasonably against the interests of the US three times in a period of five years.[49] Yet the WTO is not fundamentally different from earlier GATT agreements or

[45] Judith Goldstein, 'International Institutions and Domestic Politics: GATT, WTO, and the Liberalization of International Trade', in Krueger, *The WTO as an International Organization*.

[46] See Anne O. Krueger's comments on the World Bank's informal influence in Peter Lloyd and Chris Milner (eds), *The World Economy: Global Trade Policy* (Oxford: Blackwell, 1999).

[47] The formidable 110-page US response to questions of other countries in the context of the WTO review demonstrates this relative advantage (communication from the Permanent Mission of the United States, February 2000) (WTO, 1999), document reference: WT/TPR/M/56/Add.1.

[48] On the procedures see John H. Jackson, *The World Trade Organization* (1998), 47–51.

[49] Alissa J. Rubin, 'Dole, Clinton Compromise Greases Wheels of GATT', in *Congressional Quarterly Weekly Report* (26 November 1994), 3406. The WTO panel ruling of August 2000, declaring the US Anti-Dumping Act of 1916 illegal, can be regarded as the type of provocative decision that this compromise sought to anticipate. But the US has sought to comply with the ruling, though in accordance with its own legislative convenience. This issue has been re-visited recently by Calude Barfield, *Free Trade, Sovereignty, Democracy* (2001).

NAFTA, which does embody a dispute settlement mechanism, inspired by the EU, privileging rule-based adjudication.

The DSM of the WTO allows for the authoritative adjudication of treaty violations and sanctions legitimate retaliation even though it has no instruments for the implementation of its own judgements, which rely on self-help. In the GATT, the adoption of a ruling over a dispute by a panel could be blocked by the failure of an affirmative consensus accepting it. In the WTO, a ruling by the panel can be blocked only by a consensual rejection. The Appellate Body can then consider it and diplomatic accommodation is probable, but already there is speculation that its position could come to be regarded as that of an international court.[50] Despite a poor record of compliance with GATT rulings in the past, the US has honoured rulings of the DSB of the WTO so far. However, it has a greater stake in international trade law as currently embodied in the WTO, which reflects its preferences more closely.

Nevertheless, the dual separation of political power in the US between the federal authorities and States and between the executive and legislative branches creates unusual dilemmas that more unitary governments elsewhere do not encounter. Although the President negotiates international trade treaties, Congress retains ultimate primacy because of its constitutional prerogatives. Congress, which has always jealously guarded its legitimate authority over trade policy, now discovers this very legitimacy in jeopardy because of the DSM, described by its first director-general as the heart of the WTO agreement.[51] As far as individual states in the US are concerned, some aspects of the URA require them to surrender authority over issues to which they have been hitherto entitled. The government procurement agreement (GPA) imposes obligations towards international bidders that would conflict, for example, with local prerogatives favouring affirmative action in considering the award of public contracts.

However, the implications of conformity to judgements of the DSB for the US must be evaluated in relation to specific situations, for which there are historical precedents, and cannot be prejudged purely on abstract grounds. In practical terms the DSM provides satisfaction on the kind of issues for which unilateral sanctions under Section 301 action had historically been deployed by the US. The observation of Pat Choate—running mate to former US presidential candidate, Ross Perot—that the GATT was superior because discretion favoured US power and legal provisions would be equalizing, though an accurate observation, does not justify the inference that outcomes over disputes would necessarily be disadvantageous to the US.[52]

The WTO has shown itself robust in articulating rule-based judgements on these issues, although diplomatic intercession also occurs to a greater degree

---

[50] Jackson, *The World Trade Organization.*
[51] Jackson, *The World Trade Organization,* 59.
[52] See Chapter 1 in this volume.

than under the GATT. Indeed, the TRIPS agreement of the WTO is proving effective for the protection of intellectual property rights because it sets a universal benchmark supported by the EU and Japan as well. Its precision and comprehensiveness have also been reflected in DSB judgements favourable to the US.[53] Such action through the DSB confers legitimacy, in contrast to the unilateral resort to unpopular sanctions under Section 301. Indeed, as already noted, the US has become the most frequent plaintiff before the DSB. However, the EU, Japan, and the rest of the world were more than happy to substitute the DSM of the WTO for unilateral use of Section 301 by the US.

It is true that the US itself has to conform to adverse DSB judgements that challenge domestic regulation, but there have been few panel rulings against the US—for instance, the FSC tax and with respect to the 1916 US Anti-Dumping law—since the WTO dispute settlement mechanism began to operate. The US is also able to invoke AD and CVD against troublesome imports, especially labour-intensive manufactures, which provoke the greatest American domestic political disquiet. Moreover, the US is less likely to find itself in similar trade disputes over market access, dumping, or intellectual property rights. US problems are with less frequent though contentious questions like environmental or other domestic rules that place imports into the US at a disadvantage. It is also possible to apply AD and CVD measures in response to strategic international competition. Thus, the US has been empowered by the DSM overall, although Congress may be nostalgic about the political prerogatives it previously exercised.

The Confluence of Protection and Liberal Trade

The opposition of segments of organized US labour to liberal trade policies has been intensifying since the 1970s, with ongoing industrialization abroad and the adjustment pressures which it transmits to advanced economies, particularly during periods of economic slowdown. However, its long-term impact on employment and wages in advanced countries remains a matter of some controversy.[54] The US was also apparently suffering from a 'diminished giant' syndrome because its absolute primacy in a range of manufacturing activities was dwindling. In reality, the US has been moving up the ladder to higher-value knowledge-intensive sectors and experiencing the more general shift away from manufacturing and into services, a phenomenon common to advanced economies as per capita incomes rise. By the end of the 1990s, US economic buoyancy and Japan's persisting economic difficulties, as well as setbacks

[53] For example, the US won the case against India over the technical dispute regarding adequacy of its filing system for IPR applications, which required the latter government to hastily pass specific legislation regarding how a foreign patent was to be registered.

[54] For a discussion of this literature, see Gary Burtless, 'International Trade and the Rise in Earnings Inequality', *Journal of Economic Literature*, 33/2 (1995).

suffered by emerging Asian economies, dispelled perceptions about US economic decline. But concern with the trade practices of other countries remains
an enduring theme of US foreign economic policy.

Other factors that provoke protectionist policies include currency overvaluation, as it did during the 1980s because of the high interest rates needed to
finance the fiscal deficit during the Reagan presidency.[55] An overvalued currency
can have a bigger impact on the balance of trade—and capital flows—than
changes in product prices and tariff levels and therefore constitutes a significant
backdrop to protectionism. Finally, there is the role of trade policy in assisting
US firms, often oligopolies and duopolies, engaged in strategic competition with
foreign rivals for market shares and rents. Trade policies in such circumstances
are designed to shift profits from foreign firms to domestic ones in imperfect
markets, dominated by few large firms. Anti-dumping actions and countervailing duties help US firms and deter foreign governments from engaging in predatory conduct on behalf of their own firms. As a corollary, the US also puts
pressure on foreign governments for access to their markets. It is this reality,
rather than conventional import relief to preserve jobs, that explains trade policy tensions in some industries between advanced countries; and concomitant
policies are the product of careful reflection and calculation.[56] By the 1980s,
the US was finding the rule-bound multilateral GATT system too unwieldy for
adequate responses to administrative trade protection and investment-related
measures like performance requirements. It encouraged non-cooperative US
behaviour, and bilateralism also seemed an attractive option to US authorities.
The US addressed many of these concerns in the formulation of the WTO
treaty and continues to persevere with them in the context of the proposed
Millennium Round.

The reason for a renewed espousal of multilateral liberalization was the
growing contrary influence on US trade policy formation of US international
corporations and foreign direct investors and their desire to ensure greater
international openness. This had been evident as far back as the Kennedy Round,
but was being inexorably reinforced by the internationalization of US economic
activity, as reflected in rising US trade/GDP ratios.[57] Since 1974, US business has
had a statutory role in trade policy formulation, sanctioned by Congress, and
has participated actively in moulding US preferences in the URA. It argued

---

[55] At its peak in 1985 the dollar was overvalued by 40 per cent on a trade-weighted
basis vis-à-vis the currencies of its major trading partners. This amounted to a 40 per cent
subsidy on US imports. Dominick Salvatore 'Trade Protectionism and Welfare in the
United States', in Salvatore (ed.), *Protectionism and World Welfare*, 327.

[56] For an analysis of their rationale and formulation, see J. David Richardson, 'The New
Political Economy of Trade policy', in Paul R. Krugman (ed.), *Strategic Trade Policy and the
New International Economics* (Cambridge, MA: MIT Press, 1988). See also J. David Richardson,
'The Political Economy of Strategic Trade Policy', *International Organization*, 44/1 (1990).

[57] J. H. Cheh, 'United States Concessions in the Kennedy Round and Short-run Labour
Adjustment Costs', *Journal of International Economics*, 4/4 (1974); Milner, *Resisting
Protectionism*.

successfully for the inclusion of the GATS and TRIPS within the URA. Studies undertaken by Krueger and Deardoff also conclude that the impact of import relief and market-access measures has been reduced or even removed over time by the President.[58] The US government has therefore simultaneously promoted a liberal international order and tried to mitigate the domestic cost of adjustment to international trade.

Counter-posed against the politics of trade policy is the perception of universal norms of trade by decision-makers and the value electorates evidently put on economic growth. International trade is essentially positive-sum and protectionism benefits only particular interest groups in the short-to-medium term at the expense of global welfare. Adjustment, in fact, imposes political costs rather than welfare losses, since welfare should improve in aggregate. Conflicts between countries therefore pertain to a circumscribed set of international exchanges. Adversarial national goals, which the US is in a stronger position to pursue if not always achieve, are exceptional in light of the totality of mutual benefits of world trade. Countries therefore have no reason to wish to exit the international trade order, although that could happen because of a nationalist backlash owing to economic collapse or war. As a consequence, the question of the dominance of the US ceases to be central to an understanding of what the pay-offs from international trade are for other countries. International trade is essentially variable sum and institutionalized collective efforts to regulate its flows are primarily required to avert Prisoner's Dilemma-type situations. The relative significance of any actor in the WTO, beyond participation in a joint positive-sum endeavour, is largely expressed in its ability to achieve specific additional goals on behalf of domestic interests within the trade order. In the end, individual countries cannot be seeking to systematically maximize their aggregate national gains at the expense of the rest of the world since joint gains are intrinsic to international commerce.

Is the compromise of embedded liberalism now able to reconcile the demands of economic efficiency and world welfare with resistance from both domestic labour and environmentalists? Underlying the partisan, as well as anti-capitalist ideological, motives of some protestors against the WTO lurks the deeper question of national sovereignty. An inescapably symbolic and politically significant turning point has apparently been reached in the regulation of international trade. Domestic constituents are becoming subject to the juridical processes of the DSM of the WTO; and the potential expansion of its reach is considerable. It is this situation that causes widespread unease even among the supporters of liberalization.[59]

---

[58] Anne O. Krueger and Alan V. Deardoff, cited in Robert Stern, 'The WTO Trade Policy Review of the US', in Peter Lloyd and Chris Milner (eds), *Global Trade Policy 1998* (Oxford: Blackwell, 1998).

[59] Robert Keohane, 'The Club Model of Political Co-operation and the WTO: Problems of Democratic Legitimacy' (2000), available at www.ksg.harvard.edu/cbg/trade/keohane.htm. For useful discussions of the impact of globalization on government

3. Conclusion

US protectionism before the Second World War echoed the mercantilism of an earlier era and public debate on the economics of international commerce was much less enlightened than its counterpart in nineteenth century Britain. The US was guilty of free riding on the relatively open British economy while pursuing trade accords in Latin America that discriminated against it. Protectionist domestic political imperatives dominated trade policy and Congress formulated tariff policy as if comparative advantage did not exist. Protectionism reached a nadir in the high economic and political cost inflicted on the world economy by the Hawley-Smoot Tariff of 1930. It was only after the economic depression of the 1930s that realization dawned of the reality of economic interdependence; and a more liberal policy began to take shape, particularly due to the efforts of Secretary of State, Cordell Hull. Paradoxically, reciprocity was enshrined in the RTAA of 1934 as much to balance mutual concessions with other countries as to articulate the need to deflect perverse US domestic unilateralism, best exemplified by the protectionist absurdities of the 1922 Fordney-McCumber Act.[60] The subsequent grudging acceptance of interdependence between exports and imports was conditional and subject to 'escape clauses' embodied in the GATT and an ultimate congressional veto that is a product of US federalism. However, cold war imperatives and overwhelming US economic primacy, underlined by the prolonged era of dollar shortage, advanced the cause of international economic liberalism.

Changes in the balance of US economic interests over time, favouring greater international openness, did not suppress the ability of protectionist interests to lobby more effectively than consumers and exporters. In the post-Second World War period, Congress has sought to constrain the President's discretion by introducing various limitations on his scope for manoeuvre. Permissible tariff concessions were subject to so called 'peril points' in the 1950s to protect domestic industry from competition, resonating with the inward-looking rationale of an earlier era. Agriculture was excluded from international trade by resort to the waiver provision of the GATT in 1955. The aggressive unilateralism of US trade policy, demanding policy changes in other countries not required by treaties, is the expansionist outward counterpart of import relief to protect domestic constituents. Congress also imposed 'sunset' clauses on the

welfare policies, see Rodrik, 'Globalization and Labour', 141–6, and Geoffrey Garrett, *Partisan Politics in the Global Economy* (Cambridge: Cambridge University Press, 1998), 51–128.

[60] It sought to cancel foreign price advantages with a duty equivalent to the differential and subject goods entering the US market at a price below the US cost of production to anti-dumping action. Even the RTAA remained wary of concessions, but, significantly, coupled the MFN principle with reciprocity, allowing for automatic multilateralization of reciprocal bilateral agreements to reduce restrictions. Rhodes, *Reciprocity*, 62–6.

'fast-track' innovation of 1974 that had been designed to ease international tariff negotiations. But more recently, 'fast track' authority, now called the Trade Promotion Authority (TPA), that had been denied since 1994 and voted down in 1998, the last occasion it was presented to Congress, was unexpectedly approved in December 2001.

US trade policy has been poised between protection and liberalization since the 1970s, transmuting into the widened scope of the URA and aggressive market-access negotiations.[61] The net contemporary outcome has been to ensure liberal international trade policies. The President and the Congress are conscious of the benefits to the US from an open international economy, but the structure and dynamics of US politics require sensitivity to demands for import relief. In a sense, the US managed to internationalize its domestic political constraints by putting them firmly on the international agenda, especially during the URA and now the Millennium Round as well, apparently. But the need to prevent excessive damage to relations with economic partners and political allies encourages a substantial measure of cooperation. Fundamentally, in a world in which the production of a growing proportion of high-value goods and services is characterized by increasing returns to scale, the US is in a strong position by virtue of market size alone, even discounting its advantages in R&D and productivity.

Finally, the WTO remains the unavoidable forum for the negotiation of international trade relations on grounds of practicality alone. Its significance has undoubtedly increased because of its vastly enlarged coverage and stronger avenues for pursuing grievances and resolving disputes. The US, of course, prefers the legitimacy of international law for its policy actions, especially when that does not rule out additional quasi-legal means for achieving objectives. The steel dispute that erupted in March 2002 illustrates the violation of the spirit, at the very least, of WTO injunctions when pressing domestics imperatives arise, despite overall US commitment to a multilateral trade order that is necessarily legalistic in its operation.[62] But the US remains indispensable to the WTO because, at minimum, it is the major market for many countries. Not much need be said about the capacity of the WTO to constrain US behaviour given the political power of the latter, except that the WTO system does not merely preside over a conflictual, zero-sum game. International trade results in joint gains, an endeavour that requires participants to cooperate with each other. On the question of the relationship between political power and the functioning of international

---

[61] An overblown sense of grievance against other countries' trade policies is reflected in the recommendation of one US trade policy analyst that: 'The United States must insist that for the WTO to enjoy American support, it must produce real market openings and a tangible balance of benefits from trade and investment liberalization.' Bruce Stokes, 'A Geoeconomic strategy for the 21st Century', in Feketekuty and Stokes, *Trade Strategies for a New Era*, 170.

[62] The US government anticipates, no doubt, a compromise with its trading partners once the shrill recrimination has receded, by which time the restructuring of the steel industry, evidently in need of temporary import relief, will be well under way.

institutions, it may be reaffirmed that neither naked political power nor outcome-neutral procedural rules prevail when disputes do occur.

Cooperation between countries is the rational policy for achieving gains from international trade, which may be asymmetric but still articulate a joint-sum game. The use of political power is not a routine necessity to achieve such gains, although it undoubtedly eases the attainment of specific goals for countries able to wield it. The Marxist view that capitalist exploitation engenders the extraction of relative surplus, as opposed to the struggle for the distribution of relatively fixed absolute surplus under feudalism, offers a useful analogy for the logic of international trade relations and the absence of coercion as a norm. The US and other large players in international trade are able to increase their share of the gains from trade in some situations by resort to forms of optimum 'tariff', owing to market size alone. However, the use of political power, in violation of trade policy principles and norms, to satisfy domestic constituents is almost certainly at the cost of both international and domestic economic welfare. The market norms and principles of international trade regimes like the WTO are, therefore, in fact a reasonably reliable guide to actual trade outcomes. Power political capabilities of member states also inform the setting-up of such a regime, enhancing their ability to manipulate, should they wish, although not necessarily increasing their welfare.[63]

[63] Maurice Dobb, *Studies in the Development of Capitalism* (London: Routledge and Kegan Paul, 1963); Rodney Hilton, *The Transition from Feudalism to Capitalism* (London: NLB, 1976). Also see Jock A. Finlayson and Mark W. Zacher, 'The GATT and the Regulation of Trade Barriers: Regime Dynamics and Functions', in Krasner (ed.), *International Regimes*. For an elucidation of the policy choices that may be induced by such conditions of mutual gain, see John Ikenberry, *After Victory* (Princeton: Princeton University Press, 2001).

6

Looking Beyond the 'K-Word': Embedded Multilateralism in American Foreign Environmental Policy

STEPHEN HOPGOOD

President George W. Bush's announcement in March 2001 that the Kyoto Protocol was 'dead' as far as the United States was concerned makes the title of this chapter seem optimistic to say the least. That this is not so will become clear. The many pressures which now face the President on this issue render his decision to abandon, not modify, Kyoto less rather than more comprehensible. Indeed, I will argue it is a question of how and how soon, not whether, the United States rejoins the multilateral environmental fray.

The United States is neither pro- nor anti-environmental in foreign policy terms in any permanent or unanimous sense. It is split, at the very highest reaches of the state, by an enduring factional struggle between *activists* and *sceptics* based on fundamental ideological disagreements about the appropriate role the United States ought to play in international environmental politics. This dispute is not about the most effective means for securing a given end, but about the value of those ends themselves. These two groups of state officials are united against each other by their positions on three basic questions: the extent of the environmental threat, the proper relationship between state and economy, and the role that the United States, as a hegemon, ought to play in international environmental affairs. Despite these differences, activists and sceptics can and frequently do coexist within the same administration. It is the activist position, however, which has been responsible for fostering engagement in environmental multilateralism in American foreign policy since 1968.

The nature of international environmental issues has helped sustain this long-running split. Unlike policy-making during crises, where intense short-term pressures put a premium on a high degree of intra-state agreement, the problems posed by international environmental issues are long-running, complex, and highly structured. As a result, the intra-state struggle has become

The author would like to express his thanks to this volume's editors and contributors and also to Robert Falkner.

deeply embedded within well-established and formally entrenched institutional positions. This institutional struggle hides a further fact: over the long term, the multilateralists are winning.

The evidence suggests that pro-multilateral activists have slowly but surely advanced their cause to the point where the United States is now so deeply enmeshed in legal, political, and economic obligations monitored through formal institutional procedures that the most vigorous efforts at resistance must eventually fail. As Reaganite attempts to roll back environmental regulation during the early 1980s achieved very little in the end, so the anti-regulatory vigour of President George W. Bush is likely to be diluted, modified, and reformed over the next three years. Activists are, in effect, *always* pressing for the next step forward while the sceptics try to hold them back. Much of the time the sceptics are reasonably successful at slowing advance, but they can never frustrate it permanently and when they weaken the activists push on, policy success for them measured in terms of decades rather than four-year terms.

The current administration can be seen in the same light, regardless of initial appearances. The US has still signed Kyoto—thus a future Democrat could push for ratification—and its major allies and competitors are committed to ratifying it. President George W. Bush came under sustained pressure from senators and many corporations to make domestic emissions-limiting proposals of his own, which were announced in February 2002, *and* to formulate an alternative multilateral climate change regime. Re-engagement may come through renegotiated terms of entry to Kyoto, through a 'bilateral' agreement between the US and the Parties to Kyoto, through the US 'shadowing' Kyoto, or through a major US effort to move beyond Kyoto to an agreement which it finds more accommodating. In all these scenarios, environmental multilateralism is the future, even if Kyoto per se is not.

In his February 2002 proposals to 'limit' domestic carbon emissions, the President argued: 'I reaffirm America's commitment to the United Nations Framework [Climate Change] Convention and its central goal, to stabilize atmospheric greenhouse gas concentrations at a level that will prevent dangerous human interference with the climate.'[1] While some environmentalists allege the plan was effectively 'written by ExxonMobil', it was in part a response to pressure from many members of Congress, corporations—including Dupont, General Motors, Ford—and numerous environmentalists and voters for the US to reconnect with climate-change issues. The Bush administration's search for 'better science' or an 'alternative market-based regime' seems unlikely to yield a solution that can at a stroke replace more than a decade of complex multilateral negotiations on a climate change convention with binding emissions limits.[2]

---

[1] 'Economy Promised Front Seat in Bush Climate Plan', *Environment News Service* (20 February 2002) at www.ens-news/ens/feb2002/20021-02-14-07.html.

[2] For a view of the specific inadequacies of the Kyoto Protocol, see David G. Victor, *The Collapse of the Kyoto Protocol* (Princeton, NJ: Princeton University Press, 2001).

Yet this search is central to President George W. Bush's environmental credibility. Otherwise what Environmental Protection Agency (EPA) Administrator Christine Todd Whitman called 'the only game in town'—Kyoto—remains just that: flawed, perhaps, but the only serious option available. The fact is that international environmentalism is one area where the United States needs multilateral agreement to achieve its *own* goals, thereby giving other states something with which to bargain. It is in this 'gap' between domestic and international pressures that the activists have worked to entrench international cooperation, as we see now in section 1.

1. Politics Inside the American State

Concerted multilateral action on the international environment dates back to the late 1960s and a Swedish proposal to hold a UN environment conference because of fears about transnational industrial pollution, especially acid rain.[3] Thus, the unrivalled scale of domestic environmental politics in the United States at this time was *not* the catalyst for international action. As a result, the international agenda was framed in a very different way from the domestic American agenda, the latter much less clearly reflected in the former than is apparent in other issue areas like international trade, terrorism, or drug-trafficking. In other words, international environmental politics were multilateral from inception, centred as they were on the UN.

The Nixon administration initially preferred to discuss international environmental issues in the OECD and NATO. In both organizations the United States was dominant, and all members suffered the environmental problems of pollution—over-industrialization—not poverty—under-industrialization. In contrast, the scale and scope of the United Nations Conference on the Human Environment, held in 1972 in Stockholm, entailed the loss of these crucial advantages for the United States. The agenda was harder to control. Alliances were fluid in such a new issue area and didn't always map easily on to existing commitments. There were numerous other states involved possessing highly diverse interests. Chinese participation overlaid East–West politics with North–South politics. The centrality of the UN ensured that any post-Stockholm organizational developments would remain multilateral, like the founding of UNEP. In sum, the multilateral nature of international environmental negotiations played relentlessly on the activist-sceptic split from the very beginning.

At this early stage, neither business nor environmental groups within the United States were well organized to pressure the state and both internationalized

---

[3] See John McCormick, *The Global Environmental Movement: Reclaiming Paradise* (London: Belhaven Press, 1989), Ch. 1.

their lobbying efforts in response to Stockholm. As the 1970s unfolded, the relatively straightforward, if contentious, understanding of environmental issues in general, and their links to development, gave way to three progressively more complex and wide-ranging problems: the depletion of stratospheric ozone, the heating of the atmosphere, and the loss of species biodiversity—and the emerging business of biotechnology. As these issues evolved, the central cleavage within US national institutions persisted in remarkably similar form.

This persistence does not come as such a surprise if we see state officials as more than simply delegates for societal—including business—interests. The views of activists like Al Gore or sceptics like George W. Bush long predate their periods in office, as they have done for public officials in this area since the early 1970s. In differentiating activists from sceptics, we can isolate three broad areas of divergence: the reality and implications of the environmental threat, the proper link between state and economy, and the appropriate international role for the United States.

For the sceptics, the environmental threat lacks credibility. They view the science as unconvincing, and suspect that the proponents of greater environmental commitments are pursuing another political agenda entirely, one to do with redistribution and regulation. This has been one plank of the current Bush administration's objections to Kyoto—that the science is still too uncertain and that, although global warming may be happening, 'the policy challenge is to act in a serious and sensible way, *given the limits of our knowledge*'.[4] This concern ties in with the second dimension. As exemplified in the early Reagan years, sceptics share an ideological objection to economic regulation, both domestic and international, which leads them to champion free-market solutions to collective action problems rather than any form of state intervention. A key sceptic under both Reagan and Bush, C. Boyden Gray, viewed the climate change convention, for example, as 'an international clean air act' which posed just as much a threat to US prosperity as the domestic one.[5]

This leads sceptics to support as much devolved government as possible, a far cry from formal international organizations with meaningful autonomy. Fears for US prosperity and concerns that developing countries, and even the EU, will use Kyoto to constrain the US economy form a second plank of the current Bush administration's rejection of the Protocol. The use of market-based methods is also paramount once again. As Christine Todd Whitman told an environment ministers meeting in Italy: 'We can work together with our

[4] White House speech on climate change by President George W. Bush, 11 June 2001, at www.whitehouse.gov/news/releases/2001. Emphasis added.
[5] William K. Reilly, 'I'm Gonna Make You a Star: A New Approach to Protecting the Environment in America and Around the World', lecture text (Institute for International Studies, Stanford University, 9 February 1994). See also Boyden C. Gray and David B. Rivkin, 'A "No-Regrets" Environmental Policy', *Foreign Policy*, 83 (1991).

international friends and allies and neighbors and come up with market-based incentive solutions that can get us to the end of the day with this issue.'[6]

Finally, sceptics see no real interest for the United States in participating in, much less leading, international collective efforts in 'social' areas of this sort. For them, the guiding principle of US foreign policy is the best outcome for 'the United States' understood as a territorial entity whose citizens' welfare has priority over that of non-American nationals. And because they mistrust the science underlying predictions of environmental danger, they are keen to protect Americans from the redistributive implications of responding too vigorously to it. Hegemony thus gives rise to limited interests and responsibilities in this area. Certainly, environmental problems are not taken as seriously by sceptics as many other more traditional issues of national security.[7]

These three dimensions reinforce each other. Believing the environmentalists' scientific claims mask a redistributive political agenda, and believing that agenda to be shared by many other states in 'competition' with the United States, the sceptics resist multilateral commitments and precedents, rhetorical or otherwise, which might permanently entangle the United States. This is clearest from the period when the sceptics came nearest to dominance: the early 1980s, and Republican control of both Congress and the White House. The ideological position of the sceptics was undiluted at home and abroad. As Lynton Caldwell remarked: 'The policy positions taken by members of [Reagan's] administration appear to be largely fallout from domestic interests and issues. To a large extent, foreign policy has reflected domestic politics, and world environmental affairs are no exception.'[8]

Caldwell notes six areas where the Reagan administration reinterpreted or reversed US commitments on the international environment, most importantly trying to cut US contributions to UNEP's budget by at least 80 per cent.[9] Indeed, the formation of federal environmental policy in the 1970s was one of the dynamics identified by Reaganites as largely responsible for the expansion of state regulation.[10] Thus, environmental statutes became a prime candidate for repeal and many were undermined.

---

[6] 'US stance on warming puts Whitman in tense spot', *New York Times* (30 March 2001).

[7] On the environment and national security, see Daniel H. Deudney and Richard A. Mathews (eds), *Contested Grounds: Security and Conflict in the New Environmental Politics* (New York: SUNY Press, 1999). See also Karen Litfin, 'Environmental Security in the Coming Century', in TV Paul and John A. Hall (eds), *International Order and the Future of World Politics* (Cambridge: Cambridge University Press, 2000).

[8] Lynton K. Caldwell, 'The World Environment: Reversing US Policy Commitments', in Norman J. Vig and Michael E. Kraft (eds), *Environmental Policy in the 1980s: Reagan's New Agenda* (Washington, DC: Congressional Quarterly Press,1984).

[9] Caldwell, 'The World Environment', 330–5.

[10] On this expansion see Joseph F. Zimmermann, *Contemporary American Federalism: The Growth of National Power* (Leicester: Leicester University Press, 1992); Charles O. Jones, *Clean Air: The Politics and Policies of Pollution Control* (Pittsburgh: University of Pittsburgh Press, 1975).

There is some evidence of tendencies in this direction under the current administration, George W. Bush's reversal of a campaign pledge to cut US power plant emissions and his reluctance to follow through on a Clinton-era 'roadless rule' for 58 million acres of America's forests being prime examples. This must be balanced, however, with the fact that, far from undermining environmental legislation *in principle* as a restriction on US business, President George W. Bush vigorously protested that the US intends to control carbon dioxide (CO_2) emissions anyway because it takes the environmental threat seriously. This is one indication of a shift towards the activists: that only the most hawkish sceptics now publicly deny the claim that harmful climatic change is under way. Congressmen from both sides of the political spectrum have been urging the President to accept that, while Kyoto may not be the answer, greenhouse gas emissions must be cut, and they have been introducing legislation to try to achieve it. In this way, President George W. Bush represents a much less hostile force where environmental regulation is concerned than President Reagan.

Although not exclusively so, sceptics do tend to be Republicans for whom 'conservation' and 'wise use' rather than 'environmental protection' constitute the core of their environmental philosophy.[11] More than anything else, they affirm national ownership of natural resources and rights of exploitation for national gain as normative principles. It is worth noting, therefore, that many of those involved in the Reagan administration from 1981 onwards resurfaced under President George Bush, constituting a sustained period of high-level sceptic influence (1981–92). This is less true for President George W. Bush, with some high-profile figures from his father's administration—Cheney, Zoellick—now accompanied by a few new faces who represent a post-cold war, generational shift from the older stalwarts of the 'New Right' in the 1980s.

Substantively, the activist position is very different from that of the sceptics. Many activists have been lifelong environmentalists and have often served in some official capacity with an environmental NGO prior to national public office. They take the environmental threat much more seriously than the sceptics, seeing real dangers to the quality of life of Americans and other nations posed by both domestic and international environmental problems. As a key activist, former Under-Secretary of State for Global Affairs, Tim Wirth, told a climate change meeting in Geneva in 1996: 'let me make clear the US view: the science calls on us to take urgent action'.[12]

More than this, the transnational nature of environmental problems dictates, for activists, that there exists a transnational interest in their solution. In other words, what's good for the international environment must be good for

[11] On 'conservation' versus 'environmentalism', see Henry P. Caulfield, in James P. Lester (ed.), *Environmental Politics and Policy* (Durham: Duke University Press, 1989).
[12] Michael Grubb, with Christiaan Vrolijk and Duncan Brack, *The Kyoto Protocol: A Guide and Assessment* (London: RIIA, 1999), 54; Al Gore Jr, *Earth in the Balance: Forging a New Common Purpose* (London: Earthscan, 1992).

individual states as well. There may be trade-offs required for poorer states, but improving the international environment is perceived to be in the interests of all states. Thus, international regulation of one sort or another is unavoidable: doubly so, in fact, because *unregulated* industrial production is considered to be largely responsible for the problems in the first place. The state must act, both in the domestic economy and internationally, to solve environmental 'collective good' problems.

Collective goods, like air and water for example, are subject to both non-rivalness—supply does not diminish as more people use them until a 'congestion point' is reached—and non-excludability—no one can be prevented from consuming them regardless of contribution to their provision.[13] 'Free riding' is therefore rational for states because they will benefit from a cleaner environment *whether or not* they contribute to its clean-up, an insight which lies at the core of neo-liberal claims about the role of institutions in establishing and sustaining international cooperation.[14] But the calculation is different for a hegemonic state—and 'hegemonic polluter'—like the United States. It faces a choice between: free riding—which because of its size hampers hopes for collective action; making up the shortfall caused by other free-riders—benevolent hegemony; and forcing compliance with multilateral accords—coercive hegemony.[15] Given that its compliance or defection is enough on its own to make or break effective multilateral cooperation, US activists' reasoning on this question has two elements: that some form of 'regulation' is required to bind everyone into common agreements which provide collective benefits over time and deter and expose free riding, and that US hegemony, politically and as a polluter, carries with it special responsibilities. This leads us to the United States' role in the world.

The difficulty of fostering trust, managing conflicting interests, and exercising persuasion undergirds activists' sense of a US obligation to provide 'leadership'. First, the United States is more able to generate collective action because of its huge political and economic resources. Second, the United States has, for activists, an ethical responsibility to take a leading role in clean-up negotiations because of its contribution to global pollution and its unrivalled per capita emissions. Third, the scientific prowess of the United States in this

---

[13] Wilfred Beckerman and Joanna Pasek, *Justice, Posterity, and the Environment* (Oxford: Oxford University Press, 2001), 139–40; Russell Hardin, *Collective Action* (Baltimore, MD: Resources for the Future/The Johns Hopkins University Press, 1982); J. Samuel Barkin and George E. Shambaugh, 'Hypotheses on the International Politics of Common Pool Resources', in J. Samuel Barkin and George E. Shambaugh (eds), *Anarchy and the Environment: The International Politics of Common Pool Resources* (New York: SUNY Press, 1999).

[14] See Peter M. Haas, Robert O. Keohane, and Marc A Levy (eds), *Institutions for the Earth: Sources of Effective Environmental Protection* (Cambridge, MA: MIT Press, 1993); Robert Axelrod and Robert O. Keohane, 'Achieving Cooperation under Anarchy: Strategies and Institutions', *World Politics*, 38 (1985).

[15] J. Samuel Barkin and George E. Shambaugh, 'Hypotheses on the International Politics of Common Pool Resources', in Barkin and Shambaugh (eds), *Anarchy and the Environment*, 16–17.

area makes it an obvious candidate for prominence in framing international environmental agreements. We can see this very clearly in the case of ozone depletion, for example, where activists used US science and diplomatic power to try to generate collective action over chlorofluorocarbons (CFCs).[16]

In addition to the 'domestic' ideological roots of the activist-sceptic divide, there are also instructive linkages with theories of international relations. There is, as we can see, the spirit of realism about the sceptic position, and that of liberal internationalism about activist beliefs, whether or not either faction is self-conscious of this or always acts in the way the theory would predict. Sceptics, for example, see the interests of the United States as easily distinguishable from those of other states, regardless of the 'noise' of multilateralism, and they see the United States as in permanent competition with those states.[17]

Activists, meanwhile, see a kind of transnational interest in environmental security in which the interests of the United States cannot be analytically divorced from the more general international interest in a sustainable environment. Further, the moral responsibility which many activists feel given the size of US per capita pollution, and the capacity the United States possesses for generating cooperation, is not shared by sceptics for whom the only obligation national public officials owe is to their *own* populations. The estimation of the environmental threat speaks directly to understandings of what constitutes the 'national interest' of the state, something sceptics define much more narrowly than activists.[18]

Furthermore, the activists have a progressive vision of international environmental multilateralism where permanent and lasting cooperation will improve the quality of life for all. This links directly with neo-liberal claims about the value of international institutions and can be contrasted with sceptic wariness about formal international arrangements which they fear make it harder for 'American' interests to be fully realized.[19] The activists, by contrast, see long-lasting and meaningful cooperation with other states as both desirable and necessary—although they also seek to retain control of international organizations to ensure implementation in a manner they desire.

We can now look briefly at how the split between sceptics and activists has played itself out in three principal international environmental issues: ozone depletion, climate change, and biodiversity.

---

[16] Richard Elliot Benedick, *Ozone Diplomacy: New Directions in Safeguarding the Planet* (Cambridge, MA: Harvard University Press, 1991), 51–4.

[17] Joseph M. Grieco, 'Anarchy and the Limits of Cooperation: A Realist Critique of the Newest Liberal Institutionalism', in David A. Baldwin (ed.), *Neorealism and Neoliberalism: The Contemporary Debate* (New York: Columbia University Press, 1993); John Mearsheimer, 'The False Promise of International Institutions', *International Security*, 19/3 (1994).

[18] Beckerman and Pasek, *Justice, Posterity, and the Environment*, 191.

[19] Stephen D. Krasner, *Structural Conflict: The Third World Against Global Liberalism* (Berkeley: University of California Press, 1985).

Ozone Depletion

With remarkable speed, the United States had banned non-essential CFC use in domestic aerosols by 1978.[20] Despite fierce industry resistance, which included the world's largest CFC producer, Dupont, the aerosol ban represented concerted domestic action with little or no regard to international agreements or scientific certainty about actual ozone depletion. When it came, however, the move to internationalization was initiated by UNEP, not the United States, and was *supported* by US industry representatives who hoped international regulation would avoid them being placed at a further competitive disadvantage. In 1980, therefore, Dupont prompted the establishment of a CFC producer and user lobby group, the Alliance for Responsible CFC Policy, a guiding principle of which was that any further regulation should be multilateral, not unilateral.[21]

This drive to 'level the playing field' coincided with the arrival in Washington of the first Reagan administration with its deep hostility to all facets of the environmental movement.[22] It was soon apparent, however, that the US CFC industry feared unilateral Congressional legislation would hamper it and not its international competitors, and that growing public unhappiness about environmental degradation would give an important boost to activists arguing for even tougher environmental laws.[23] After 1983, more activist administration officials, especially in EPA and inside the State Department, worked together to place the US in a position of leadership on the question of banning CFCs.[24] The first major step, the Vienna Convention on Substances that Deplete the Ozone Layer (1985), amounted to little more than an agreement to cooperate in monitoring and research, and to negotiate more restrictive protocols if and when necessary.[25] Even this low level of multilateralism was nearly derailed by sceptics, who managed to get authority for the US delegation to sign withheld by arguing that it promised to reintroduce by the back door regulation of US industries which the Reagan administration was trying to

---

[20] On the early science, see Sharon L. Roan, *Ozone Crisis: The 15-Year Evolution of a Sudden Global Emergency* (New York: Wiley Science Edition, 1990); Edward A. Parson, 'Protecting the Ozone Layer', in Haas, Keohane, and Levy (eds), *Institutions for the Earth*, 27–73.

[21] Joanne M. Kauffman, 'Domestic and International Linkages in Global Environmental Politics: A Case Study of the Montreal Protocol', in Miranda A. Schreurs and Elizabeth C. Economy (eds), *The Internationalization of Environmental Protection* (Cambridge: Cambridge University Press, 1997), 79; see also Parson, 'Protecting the Ozone Layer', 36.

[22] Philip Shabecoff, *A Fierce Green Fire* (New York: Hill and Wang, 1993), Ch. 10.

[23] Kauffman, 'Domestic and International Linkages', 80.

[24] They broadly formed the kind of network Peter Haas describes as an 'epistemic community'; Peter M. Haas, 'Banning Chlorofluorocarbons: Epistemic Community Efforts to Protect Stratospheric Ozone', *International Organization*, 46/1 (1992), 195; also Karen Litfin, *Ozone Discourses: Science and Politics in Global Environmental Cooperation* (New York: Columbia University Press, 1994).

[25] Parson, 'Protecting the Ozone Layer', 39.

eliminate. It was only when the industry itself said it was not alarmed by the Convention that the US signed.[26]

From this moment on, however, things changed rapidly. With support from the Alliance, and definitive proof of an ozone hole over Antarctica, activists began to have more success in pressing for the United States to take the lead in negotiating an international protocol on eliminating CFC use and production. Congress even threatened unilateral legislation to phase out CFCs while proposing trade retaliation against states which didn't follow suit.[27] The Reagan administration produced a negotiating position called Circular 175 which called for short-term freezes on ozone depleting chemicals, long-term reductions, and trade restrictions for states which defected from this regime.[28] With this plan in hand, activists then launched a wide-ranging diplomatic offensive to negotiate the Montreal Protocol to the Vienna Convention which included arrangements to eliminate certain industrial chemicals.

Still the sceptics resisted; claiming lack of consultation, they managed to reopen Circular 175 to rehash basic scientific and economic questions just as the US was poised to reach international agreement. This resulted in Cabinet disarray, with the two factions even arguing against each other in Congress: the 'ideological dispute' pitting EPA, State, and to some extent the Office of Management and Budget against Commerce, Interior, and the President's science adviser, William Graham.[29] The President eventually sided with the activists, especially after signals from firms like Dupont that they were increasing their research and development into alternatives to CFCs. This showed the sceptics, not the activists, to be at odds with the industry position. Multilateral restrictions were seen by the Alliance as doubly necessary because European firms were taking a bigger and bigger share of the CFC production market. This led to tense negotiations over the Montreal Protocol, the Europeans wanting any cap to be on production, the US wanting bans on certain uses.[30]

Climate Change

The politics of climate change really began to feature on the international agenda only in the 1980s.[31] By this stage, the United States was one of the few countries which had actually given serious attention to the issue.[32] International efforts centred on the World Metereological Organization (WMO) and, as the science became a more prominent issue in the mid-1980s, on UNEP.

---

[26] Benedick, *Ozone Diplomacy*, 46. [27] Benedick, *Ozone Diplomacy*, 29.
[28] Benedick, *Ozone Diplomacy*, 51–4. [29] Benedick, *Ozone Diplomacy*, 59–63.
[30] Daniel F. McInnis, 'Ozone Layers and Oligopoly Profits', in Michael S. Greve and Fred L. Smith Jr (eds), *Environmental Politics: Public Costs, Private Rewards* (New York: Praeger, 1992), 144–5.
[31] See Matthew Paterson, *Global Politics and Global Warming* (London: Routledge, 1996), Ch. 2, for a general history.
[32] Ian H. Rowlands, *The Politics of Global Atmospheric Change* (Manchester: Manchester University Press, 1995), 67–70.

By 1988, these two organizations had established an Intergovernmental Panel on Climate Change (IPCC), bringing together national climatologists under the auspices of the United Nations to establish some scientific consensus. This body worked in parallel with an Intergovernmental Negotiating Committee (INC) which was established in 1990 to develop a climate change convention in time for signing at the Rio conference in June 1992.[33]

Having ultimately failed to halt agreement on ozone depletion, things looked better for the sceptics on climate change.[34] Ambiguous science, higher potential costs, and the lack of industry support for regulation in the early stages all gave a boost to those arguing that climate change would simply be used by America's competitors to make relative gains at the US's expense. Although UNEP had played a role, along with the WMO, in setting up the IPCC, it was marginalized in the climate change negotiations—which in part explained its strenuous efforts on biodiversity.[35] The INC was the principal forum for negotiating the climate change convention, meeting five times between early 1991 and June 1992 in Rio. Although there was much disagreement, three main areas of contention stood out: the refusal of the United States to agree to binding emissions targets for CO_2 or to agree a timetable for emissions reductions; the refusal of developing countries to be tied to commitments on CO_2 reductions, and the use of the World Bank's Global Environmental Facility (GEF) for dispersing funds.[36] Compromise was reached on the GEF—while the refusal of developing countries to be bound by CO_2 limitations is at the heart of President Bush's rejection of Kyoto. In the run-up to Rio, however, the principal sticking point was US intransigence on a proposal to stabilize CO_2 at 1990 levels by the year 2000.

This goal was feasible for the United States, and at one time appeared likely to happen anyway.[37] Nevertheless, sceptics in the administration urged the President to refuse to go to Rio unless targets and timetables were dropped; even the resignation of arch-sceptic John Sununu did not moderate the US position.[38] Clayton Yeutter, who coordinated climate policy within the White House after Sununu, remained equally sceptical, agreeing that the President ought not to go.[39] Eventually the US struck a deal with the Europeans, agreeing to intentionally vague language on the 'aim' of stabilization—1990 emission

[33] Formally the United Nations Conference on Environment and Development (UNCED).
[34] See Rowlands, *The Politics of Global Atmospheric Change*, 76–7, for Bush's scepticism about the science of the IPCC.
[35] Daniel Bodansky, 'Prologue to the Climate Change Convention', in Irving M. Mintzer and J. A. Leonard (eds), *Negotiating Climate Change* (Cambridge: Cambridge University Press, 1994), 60; Mattias Finger, 'Environmental NGOs in the UNCED Process', in Thomas Princen and Matthias Finger (eds), *Environmental NGOs in World Politics* (London: Routledge, 1994), 195.
[36] Bodansky, 'Prologue to the Climate Change Convention', 61.
[37] *Washington Post* (25 April 1992), A1, A11.
[38] Bodansky, 'Prologue to the Climate Change Convention', 68.
[39] Interview with author, 5 April 1994, at Stephen Hopgood, *American Foreign Environmental Policy and the Power of the State* (Oxford: Oxford University Press, 1998), 162.

levels by 2000. Yeutter later told Congressmen the US would do its share only because of domestic policy and not '... because of any compulsion arising from this proposed document'.[40] President Bush agreed to go to Rio where he was, as predicted, assailed from all sides.

Biodiversity

The initial push for a treaty to protect global biodiversity was started, ironically, by the United States itself, although the original idea was to rationalize existing international agreements in areas like endangered species and tropical forests.[41] On biodiversity, the catalytic role of UNEP and international scientific bodies like the International Union for the Conservation of Nature (IUCN) repeated the pattern by which international sources for agenda setting played an important *initial* role. Indeed, it was UNEP which provided the first draft of a negotiating treaty. Under Executive-Director Mostafa Tolba, the more pedestrian process of the 1980s was galvanized into a drive for an intergovernmental treaty for signing at Rio. The draft treaty became more ambitious, expanding to include issues like bio-safety and biotechnology, so playing directly on the activist-sceptic cleavage within the American state.[42]

Sceptics in Washington feared that the US-dominated biotechnology industry would lose billions of dollars.[43] They were also alarmed by G77 demands that the GEF be replaced by the 'parties to the convention' as the channel for any biodiversity-related funds, giving each member state one vote and thus depriving the US of leverage. These concerns meant that White House sceptics, especially officials in the Department of Interior and on Vice-President Dan Quayle's Council on Competitiveness, watched State Department negotiations in Nairobi carefully. In a notorious memo for the Vice-President's chief of staff, Bill Kristol, for example, two Competitiveness Council members tried to derail the prospects for agreement by detailing 'major problems' with the biodiversity convention, including concerns about the need for domestic legislation, biotechnology regulation 'in a manner totally unacceptable to the US', preferential transfer of technology, and an inadequate funding mechanism.[44]

---

[40]   *Boston Globe* (13 May 1992), 1, 9.

[41]   Abby Munson, 'The United Nations Convention on Biological Diversity', in Michael Grubb *et al., The Earth Summit Agreements* (London: RIIA/Earthscan, 1993), 75.

[42]   Kal Raustiala, 'Domestic Institutions and International Regulatory Cooperation: Comparative Responses to the Convention on Biological Diversity', *World Politics*, 49/4 (1997), 490. On the initial biodiversity process at the international level, see Munson, 'The United Nations Convention', 75–6.

[43]   Gareth Porter, *The US and the Biodiversity Convention* (Washington, DC: EESI, 1992), 13; Kal Raustiala, 'The Domestic Politics of Global Biodiversity Protection in the United Kingdom and the United States', in Schreurs and Economy (eds), *The Internationalization of Environmental Protection*, 46–8.

[44]   David McIntosh and John Cohrssen, 'Major Problems with the Draft Convention on Biological Diversity', White House Council on Competitiveness Memo to Bill Kristol (14 April 1992). McIntosh was the director of the competitiveness council, and Cohrssen an expert on biotechnology.

Although the multilateral nature of these negotiations aids the activist cause in the long term, the strong views of other delegations and international administrators actually hindered the chances of agreement. State Department officials negotiating on biodiversity, for example, found many G77 states content with a convention they knew the US would not sign.[45] Thus, having lost on climate change, the sceptics successfully blocked the activists on biodiversity, leaving EPA Administrator and delegation head William Reilly stranded.[46]

Because the sceptics and the activists cohere around an ideological rather than an institutional consensus, they exist and persist within a wide variety of formal and informal institutions. Indeed, one is struck by the similarity of arguments on both sides from the early 1970s, the early 1990s, and in 2001. The sceptics who opposed the biodiversity convention under the first Bush administration were often the same people who opposed action on climate change and ozone depletion.

Over time, however, it is the activists who have made the more impressive gains. In section 2, we consider six reasons for this underlying shift towards embedded multilateralism: the importance of reputation, perceptions of the United States' responsibilities as a liberal hegemon, transnational networks of scientists and officials, pressure from multinational corporations, the cultural role of the environment and scientific research *within* the United States itself, and the precise nature of particular international environmental issues.

2. The Quiet Triumph of Multilateralism

As section 1 made clear, activists and sceptics have *coexisted* within most national settings over the last 30 years, at some times 'capturing' powerful institutions and at others fighting a rearguard action. The permanency of this struggle ensures a kind of dynamic equilibrium such that no one position can ever dominate for an extended period of time. And when this equilibrium cannot be forged in private, the result is Kyoto—in effect, *two* foreign policies hopelessly at odds with each other and there for all to see.

Yet, over time, the activists have managed successfully to embed the United States in a web of complex multilateralism. They have done this not with a shout but with a whisper, developing policy, scientific research, and strategic alliances with other states, international organizations, NGOs, and sympathetic corporations. Thus, even when sceptics do prevail, as currently seems the case, they are apt to discover unilateralism is not a feasible long-term option. The question for them, as for international relations theorists more generally, is whether or not there is really any way back from multilateralism

---

[45] Porter, *The US and the Biodiversity Convention*, 8.
[46] *International Herald Tribune* (3 June 1992), 2.

in this area. Nothing seems like a better test of this bold claim than the first few months of George W. Bush's presidency. What, then, does the 'background scenery' look like? The answer is: surprisingly green.

Whereas the first Reagan administration's objections to environmentalism were deep-seated and arose from a market-based, anti-regulatory philosophy that was the hallmark of the early 1980s in most policy areas, the current Bush administration has spent its time since March 2001 protesting just how thoroughly it remains committed to combating climate change. By 11 June 2001, just three months after Kyoto was rejected, the President was saying that while the Protocol was 'fatally flawed', '. . . the process used to bring nations together to discuss our joint response to climate change is an important one'. He went on: 'I am today committing the United States of America to work within the United Nations framework and elsewhere to develop with our friends and allies and nations throughout the world an effective and science-based response to the issue of global warming.'[47]

In addition to a greater acceptance that 'the science' pointed to the need for *some* action on CO_2 emissions, the necessity for continuing engagement with the climate change issue was reinforced by other pressures, some of which predated Bush's announcement. The most important industry body opposed to Kyoto, the Global Climate Coalition (GCC), had already seen many blue-chip US corporations leave its ranks, some even accepting voluntary reductions of their own emissions. Indeed, some of these corporations joined the Business Environmental Leadership Council founded by the Pew Center on Global Climate Change which was headed by a senior environmental activist from the Clinton years, Eileen Claussen. Corporations which deserted the GCC included BP, Shell, Dupont, Ford, Toyota, Chrysler, Texaco, and General Motors.[48] This left 'Big Coal' and US-based oil companies like ExxonMobil as the most vigorous opponents of emissions restrictions.[49]

If the news from the corporate sector contained ammunition for activists, the same was true in Congress. In July 2001, the Senate Foreign Relations Committee voted 19 to zero in favour of a resolution urging the President 'to return to the bargaining table this fall with specific proposals for either revising the Kyoto global warming treaty or negotiating a new binding agreement for reducing greenhouse gas emissions'.[50] In a telling comment, one of the staunchest critics of Kyoto, Republican Chuck Hagel of Nebraska, told the Committee that Senate criticism was 'never intended as a withdrawal or pass

---

[47] White House speech on climate change by President George W. Bush, 11 June 2001, at www.whitehouse.gov/news/releases/2001.

[48] 'The Rise and Fall of the Global Climate Coalition', Lester R. Brown, Worldwatch Issue Alert (July 2000), at www.worldwatch.org/chairman/issue.

[49] 'Some energy executives urge US shift on global warming', *New York Times* (1 August 2001). See also 'Economy promised front seat in Bush climate plan', *Environment News Service* (20 February 2002), at www.ens-news/ens/feb2002/20021-02-14-07.html.

[50] 'Bush urged to negotiate global warming treaty', *Washington Post* (2 August 2001).

from US obligations to negotiate an agreement'.[51] The problem was with Kyoto, yes, but not with environmental multilateralism as such. As Paul Harris has shown, with more flexibility from developing countries—which the Clinton administration constantly urged upon them—Kyoto might even have been ratified by the Senate.[52]

That the Senate will keep up the pressure on the new president is clear. In the words of Independent Senator James M. Jeffords of Vermont, Chairman of the Environment and Public Works Committee: 'The administration can refuse to commit the United States to the Kyoto accord; that is their choice... But this Congress, this Senate, and especially this committee will not let our international partners down... We plan to take steps to reduce our nation's contribution to this growing problem by working with industry to reduce carbon emissions.'[53]

Finally, within the White House itself environmental multilateralism remains an important issue. A Cabinet review of US options through 2001 culminated in the President's speech on 14 February 2002 announcing proposals for cutting, by 18 per cent over ten years, greenhouse gas 'intensity' in the United States. The President continued to reject Kyoto, but reworked his objections to suggest the Protocol really was unfair to developing countries— that is, their resistance to it was justified—and that the US would therefore work with them to enable growth along a 'more efficient, more environmentally responsible path'.[54] The Cabinet review, led by Dick Cheney, took place alongside a final meeting on Kyoto in Marrakesh in November 2001 at which the EU, Japan, Canada, and Russia all agreed to ratify the Protocol, after major concessions were made in the final stages. Its entry into force is difficult without US participation, yet the treaty is now even more fully 'the only game in town' with no further negotiations planned.

This necessarily brief review establishes that the 'background scenery' is different even from the era of the current president's father. If Kyoto can be ditched by the US, it is clear multilateral negotiation of climate change issues cannot, even by a hegemon: it must cooperate to get its own way. Domestic restrictions on carbon emissions in the US will, as with ozone, push corporations with global markets to look for international regulation. In such circumstances, activists rather than sceptics thrive. As EPA Administrator Whitman tried to tell the President in March 2001: 'We need to appear engaged

---

[51] Ibid.
[52] Paul G. Harris, 'International Norms of Responsibility and US Climate Change Policy', in Paul G. Harris (ed.), *Climate Change and American Foreign Policy* (New York: St Martin's Press, 2000).
[53] 'Members of Congress begin effort to get US to join in fighting global warming', *New York Times* (27 July 2001).
[54] 'Intensity' refers to emissions per unit of economic activity. The plan also included initiatives to cut various other air pollutants domestically; 'Economy promised front seat in Bush climate plan', *Environment News Service* (20 February 2002), at www.ens-news/ens/feb2002/20021-02-14-07.html.

and shift the discussion from the focus on the K-word to action, but we have to build some bona fides first.'[55]

Climate change specialists were drawn from the ranks of existing government officials to help the Cabinet review and these people are likely to be long-term activists.[56] The puzzle we need to explain is therefore long-term activist success. There are at least six reasons for this: the role of reputation, perceptions of the United States' global role, transnational networks of officials and scientists, pressure from multinational corporations for a 'level playing field' internationally, the importance of scientific research within the United States, and the precise nature of particular international environmental issues.

The first point concerns the importance of a state's reputation for keeping its commitments internationally. Whether or not one sees reputation as 'instrumental' or 'constitutive', the international system rarely tolerates bad faith from major powers for long.[57] This reputation does not necessarily have to be 'good', it has to be consistent. States have to mean what they say, even if what they say is illiberal.[58]

This reputation for consistency at the public level is vital for a hegemon like the United States which is busy promoting an increasingly transnational and liberal world order. To abandon well-established attempts to prevent widespread environmental deterioration—attempts to which the United States is already committed—would over time seriously undermine the United States' authority, and so its power, in international environmental politics. If the US can no longer be trusted to comply on issues which involve long term commitments (CO_2 emissions to 1990 levels by 2008–12, for example), the risks of US withdrawal become so high for other co-operators as to deter meaningful agreements. Multilateral cooperation is hard to sustain where others fear the hegemon might defect. Both activists and sceptics know this, and know other interests may suffer as a result.

For example, Kyoto has been mentioned since 11 September 2001 as an illustration of the sort of US unilateralism which upsets allies and foes alike. The unapologetic decision to reject Kyoto outright rather than 'fix' the treaty through negotiation looks less and less well-grounded and there have been suggestions that with hindsight the administration would do things differently.[59] Sceptics may seek to evade the obligation of meaningful implementation, but

---

[55] 'US going empty handed to meeting on global warming', *New York Times* (29 March 2001).

[56] 'After rejecting climate treaty, Bush calls in tutors to give courses and help set one', *New York Times* (28 April 2001).

[57] These questions bear deeply on the rationalism/constructivism debate about 'identity': see, for example, Alex Wendt, *Social Theory of International Politics* (Cambridge: Cambridge University Press, 1999); Peter Katzenstein, Robert Keohane, and Stephen Krasner, *International Organization at Fifty* (Cambridge, MA: MIT Press, 1998).

[58] A more ambitious argument could be made that a reputation for adherence to substantively liberal norms is integral to 'success' in modern world politics.

[59] 'After rejecting climate treaty . . .', *New York Times* (28 April 2001).

they fight hardest to avoid taking on such obligations in the first place. Once commitments are made—and they have been made in principle to mitigating climate change and saving the ozone layer—then the costs of breaking these assumed responsibilities may be higher than maintaining them for the sake of a state's reputation for promise-keeping.

The second reason expands on the self-perceptions of the United States about its role in the international system. The United States has been more responsible than any other state in the post-1945 period for constructing a global system in which American interests are seen as consistent with the interests of all in more rather than less security, wealth, democracy, and human rights. Environmental problems are frequently constructed in much the same way, as neutral or apolitical issues, everyone presumed to prefer a better—cleaner, healthier—environment to a worse one. Given the central role the United States plays in all these areas, it would be inconsistent with the general American commitment to be a liberal and progressive force internationally if it were to withdraw from international environmentalism just when the number of issues, their complexity, and their implications are expanding. More than just damaging its reputation abroad, this would create a deep incongruence between the perception of the United States as a modernizing, rather than conservative, hegemon and the reality. Furthermore, the near impossibility of having meaningful international environmental agreements without the United States means that US withdrawal from 30 years of environmental multilateralism would, effectively, condemn future environmental regimes and organizations to failure.

Third, because activists have established multilateral cooperation and funding in many related environmental areas, and because influential Americans—politicians, scientists, public figures, academics—are heavily involved in transnational organizations dealing with these issues, the setting of a 'rolling' international agenda under constant review and discussion presents the United States, as other states, with a permanent need to respond to international environmental developments.

This incremental development anchors environmental multilateralism in a wide array of continuous processes—meetings, negotiations, reviews, reports—which generate publicity and implicit if not explicit pressure. The diversity of this institutionalized multilateralism gives the sceptics two options: a head-on assault, as tried by the Reagan administration, which may stifle environmental policy activism but raises a wider, more mobilized opposition at large; or constant efforts to restrict funding or deny ratification to formal legal developments like protocols. The latter, however, still requires abiding by a commitment in principle to multilateral regulation.

Fourth, the degree to which US hegemony has allowed American firms to build global consumer and labour markets for their products ought not to be underestimated. In the area of biotechnology, for example, it is clear that a refusal by EU countries to allow unrestricted access for genetically modified products has important implications for US business, implications with which it cannot deal without the help of the US state. As environmental problems begin to touch on trade and commercial issues more centrally, US firms realize that multilateral negotiations are an indispensable part of the process of opening up markets and protecting their investments. On climate change, to take a further example, there is a substantial split in the US's 'economic interest'. Insurance companies and more and more mainstream US corporations see the dangers of adverse climate changes, while 'energy' companies—as BP and Shell now style themselves—see the opportunities of new technologies if oil and coal consumption are restricted. Major fossil-fuel producers, especially the US coal industry, and many American consumers take a very different view. Nevertheless, both sides are well aware that the US state needs to be involved in detailed multilateral negotiations if their interests are to be protected from restrictions on market access elsewhere. This works against sceptic efforts to resist multilateralism.[60] Indeed, more ambitiously, Leslie Sklair has argued that among the world's top 500 companies—he conservatively lists 30 per cent as US-based—most accept that any firm which hopes to be globally competitive must consider itself as a 'globalizing corporation'.[61]

Fifth, the size and impact of domestic environmental politics in the United States dwarfs that anywhere else. In terms of modern environmentalism, the United States moved earlier, more quickly, and further than any other state. Thus, as the era of modern, large membership-based environmental groups began in the late 1960s, the extent of research and issue awareness in the United States was considerable. In other words, the identification of problems through scientific research and the need for effective public policy to combat them was already attended by an extensive institutional architecture in the US: legislation, congressional committees, case law, government agencies, experienced environmentalists, and so on.[62]

Faced with the same problems, now identified as global in scope, and requiring policy and technical solutions already worked on and discussed for many years in the United States, it is unsurprising that the US would be central. The opposite would be harder to understand, especially in an area where the safety of the planet, a seemingly apolitical and neutral question, is concerned. The rolling back of the myriad transnational connections between organizations, corporations, and individuals in the environmental field is difficult to imagine, as the responses to President George W. Bush's rejection of Kyoto seem to

---

[60] See Robert Falkner, 'Business Conflict and US International Environmental Policy: Ozone, Climate and Biodiversity', in Paul G. Harris (ed.), *The Environment, International Relations and US Foreign Policy* (Washington, DC: Georgetown University Press, 2001) on diversity in the 'business' position.

[61] Leslie Sklair, *The Transnational Capitalist Class* (Oxford: Blackwell, 2001), 37, 47–51.

[62] On the raising of environmental consciousness, see Paul Wapner, 'Politics beyond the state: environmental activism and world civic politics', *World Politics*, 47 (1995), 311–40.

confirm—in drafting experienced climate change specialists into the Cabinet review, for example.

This leads us, finally, to the specifics of the issues under consideration. Quite apart from the collective good-like nature of ozone depletion, climate change, and biodiversity loss, the scientific complexity of these problems and the potential implications they have for traditional industrial growth strategies and natural resource development open them up to a bewildering variety of interested parties. The relative lack of certainty about both the causes and the implications of environmental degradation means that arguments about the reality of the 'threat' continue permanently: the issue cannot be settled once and for all as new research and new discoveries may fundamentally change the way an issue is understood. At the rhetorical level, environmental policy-making becomes a kind of free-for-all.

For the activists this may be frustrating, interfering with effective policy development and implementation, but it serves to keep environmental problems in the public spotlight, offering endless opportunities to revive them or push them forward by alternative routes. For these reasons, activists have enjoyed substantial success over four decades. This has always been slow and incremental: sceptics are often powerful opponents. But they have never been able to derail the process or *permanently* halt its momentum. Sceptics would judge the United States' awkward position at Kyoto in 1997 and the Protocol's ultimate rejection by President George W. Bush as examples of success, but as we have seen this is far from the end of the story. When they were in the ascendant under Clinton, activists pushed for the US to sign internationally, waiting for the right moment to build a coalition or strike a deal domestically.

Kyoto remains, awaiting a Democratic administration or a Republican one under pressure from globalizing corporations. There are limited resources for sceptics internationally because those with whom they might make common cause in other states are, by the very nature of their beliefs, suspicious of the power of the United States. However effectively the sceptics get the United States to say 'no', it only ever means 'no' *for the time being*. The same questions come round again and again, the international agenda impossible to structure in such a way as to permanently privilege sceptic interests. In the final part of this section, we see how multilateralism has progressed in each of the three main international environmental issue areas with which we have been concerned.

Ozone Depletion

The US was firmly committed to multilateralism on ozone by 1987 after the sceptics were overcome, if not persuaded, by an alliance of activists and business groups. The US had even been instrumental in forging the Montreal Protocol, enacting the first real cuts in the production of various ozone-depleting chemicals including eliminating CFC production by developed countries by 2000. This Protocol was then strengthened by the London Amendments in 1990, a central part of which was the establishment of a multilateral fund to aid developing countries in phasing out ozone depleting substances.[63] Before leaving office, President George Bush, aware that Dupont had now developed substitute chemicals, unilaterally brought forward the CFC elimination timetable for the US to the mid-1990s. Between 1986 and 1995, the production of so-called ozone depleting potential (ODP) tonnes fell by 75 per cent in industrialized countries.[64] The principal task which now remains involves the elimination of ozone depleting substances in the developing world, an aim it is hoped will be achieved by 2010.

The story of multilateral negotiations on ozone shows success for which the diplomatic weight the United States deployed after 1985 was crucial. The negotiating model—a very general initial convention, then specific protocols with real teeth—helped the activists by establishing *principles* which were hard to resist—for example, preventing massive skin cancer increases, saving the polar ice caps—followed later by *specific agreements* about real production or consumption cuts. This incremental process made the target for the sceptics harder to hit, and locked the United States into years of detailed multilateral bargaining following the commitment in principle, the prevention of which was the sceptics' main aim. Ozone, indeed, set the scene for the policy battle on climate change and biodiversity, one of the sceptics' main hopes on ozone having been to avoid establishing precedents which could be taken up in multilateral negotiations on climate change.

Climate Change

The Clinton administration entered office in early 1993 with many activists, most notably Al Gore, in senior positions, raising the hopes of environmentalists everywhere.[65] Almost immediately, Clinton announced he would accept binding targets and timetables and sign the biodiversity convention.[66] The commitment to stabilization on climate change entailed a 7 per cent reduction in emissions but the necessary energy tax was rejected by Congress, leaving the administration appealing to industry for 'voluntary compliance'. That the administration could not meet its international commitments because of Congress should have come as no surprise, the activist and sceptic factions straddling governing institutions. As the decade unfolded, the administration's activists, most notably the Vice-President and Tim Wirth, became more vocal in support of stronger multilateral agreements. They made it clear they

---

[63] Robert Falkner, 'The Multilateral Ozone Fund of the Montreal Protocol', *Global Environmental Change*, 8/2 (1998); Elizabeth P. Barratt-Brown, 'Building a Monitoring and Compliance Regime under the Montreal Protocol', *Yale Journal of International Law*, 16 (1991).   [64] Falkner, 'The Multilateral Ozone Fund', 174.

[65] Mark Dowie, *Losing Ground: American Environmentalism at the Close of the Twentieth Century* (Cambridge, MA: MIT Press, 1995), 177.

[66] This decision had required overcoming sceptics in his own administration; see *New York Times* (22 April 1993), 1.

believed in the science and saw the US as having special responsibility to lead due to the disproportionate impact Americans had on the environment around them. As Wirth announced in 1996: 'The US recommends that future negotiations focus on an agreement that sets a realistic, verifiable and binding medium-term emissions target...met through maximum flexibility in the selection of implementation measures, including the use of reliable activities implemented jointly, and trading mechanisms around the world.'[67]

This statement and others made to a meeting of the parties to the climate change convention showed Wirth, who headed the US delegation, establishing activist priorities as US foreign environmental policy and reclaiming leadership for the US.[68] Further, the selection of 'flexible mechanisms' for reaching agreed goals was crucial precisely because it opened up room for manoeuvre in relation to Congress. This allowed existing legislation to be combined with less controversial policy in diverse ways to provide a variety of avenues to reach the emissions reductions agreed at Kyoto.[69]

The need for this flexibility was evident from Wirth's exchanges with Congressmen prior to the 1995 Berlin Conference when he sought to persuade them that binding protocols were good for American business.[70] Just as evident is the depth of suspicion in remarks made to Wirth after Berlin by sceptic Congressmen like Michigan's John Dingell, who alleged the State Department had accepted 'wonderful language' that:

... usually binds us and usually does not fine the foreigners, and it leaves the United States in the rather embarrassing position not only of having commitments made to do things and spend money that others are not compelled to do, but also creates a floor upon which further expectations of further actions by the United States, usually adverse to the American interest, must be taken at some future time.[71]

In this way, Dingell perfectly captured the degree to which policy momentum aided increasing multilateral obligations. As Kyoto approached, the Senate took pre-emptive action, with support from the Departments of Commerce, Energy, and Defense, passing a resolution 95-0 that it would not ratify any protocol emerging from Kyoto that did not explicitly include emissions restrictions for developing countries.[72]

Rather than strike a deal with Congress, the administration announced it would support legally binding reductions in emissions to return levels to those of 1990 sometime in the period 2008–12. Thus, it signed up to Kyoto without

---

[67] Grubb *et al.*, *The Kyoto Protocol*, 54.
[68] Grubb *et al.*, *The Kyoto Protocol*, 55.
[69] Activists and sceptics are acutely sensitive to how much *new* legislation—which is always easier to block—is required to meet Protocol obligations.
[70] Timothy E. Wirth, 'Developments in US Policy Toward Global Climate Change', statement to the Subcommittee on Energy and Power of the House Committee on Energy and Commerce, 26 May 1993.
[71] 'International Global Climate Change Negotiations', hearing before Subcommittee on Energy and Power of House Committee on Commerce, 21 March and 19 May 1995, 60, 142–3.   [72] Grubb *et al.*, *The Kyoto Protocol*, 59.

being able to secure any mention of developing-country commitments. If this should seem an act of weakness, one of the points made by analysts of the Protocol is how successful the US negotiators were in framing an agreement which closely mirrored the administration's aims.[73] Even though there was no prospect of this Protocol being submitted to Congress at the time, a precedent was established that, in more favourable times, activists in the White House could have sought to ratify. This may have happened if Al Gore had been elected president. As it was, President Bush's decision to renounce Kyoto left the United States on the sidelines of the international climate change regime. We have seen, however, that things look much more promising for US re-engagement than a cursory examination of American foreign environmental policy might suggest. Given its size, and centrality to the regime, when the US wants to talk other states will be forced to listen and to try to be accommodating, if not servile, to US demands to either reopen Kyoto or to alter it in some fundamental way.

Biodiversity

While the decision not to accept the biodiversity convention left the US isolated and embattled at Rio, President Clinton's decision to sign it in 1993 was also preceded by arguments within the administration about the wisdom of signing, with speech-writers uncertain about exactly what to put in the speech up to the last minute. Indeed, Clinton voiced misgivings about some of the same issues as the first Bush administration and attached 'interpretations' to the US signature on biodiversity.[74]

Once the biodiversity treaty disappeared into Congress for ratification it did not, and has not, re-emerged. The sceptics, especially after sweeping Republican gains in Congress in 1994 and the rise of biotechnology issues in the 1990s, have been able to prevent the US from moving further.[75] Even though the Senate Foreign Relations Committee approved ratification, the Republican leader in the Senate, Robert Dole, made it clear that a blocking coalition of at least 34 Senators existed to prevent the treaty being finally approved.[76] These sceptics argued that the treaty was too expensive for the

---

[73] Grubb *et al.*, *The Kyoto Protocol*, 112.

[74] *New York Times* (22 April 1993), 10. On the role of biotechnology companies in drafting the interpretations, see Raustiala, 'Domestic Politics', 52.

[75] Robert Paarlberg argues that President Clinton felt his interpretative statements and support from the biotechnology industry would be enough to ensure ratification and so he did not invest much effort in the process. Robert L. Paarlberg, 'Earth in Abeyance: Explaining Weak Leadership in U.S. International Environmental Policy', in Robert J. Lieber (ed.), *Eagle Adrift: American Foreign Policy at the end of the Century* (New York: Longman, 1997), 138–9.

[76] Robert L. Paarlberg, 'Lapsed Leadership: U.S. International Environmental Policy since Rio', in Norman J. Vig and Regina S. Axelrod (eds), *The Global Environment: Institutions, Law, and Policy* (1999).

United States and entailed an erosion of sovereignty, and that the interpretative statements were not binding on other states.[77] This may seem a successful case of sceptic resistance, without even an agreed commitment in principle forthcoming. But this is to presume that the multilateral process has ceased with the absence of US ratification.

According to Kal Raustiala, the Clinton White House appeared to abide by the provisions of the treaty without formal ratification. In other words, although Congress prevented formal assent being given, it could not stop the Executive from behaving as if ratification would one day be a reality. As with Kyoto, the role of US multinational corporations with global consumer markets does not make regulatory unilateralism a viable strategy. The Clinton administration remained heavily involved in biodiversity negotiations, an informal observer that nonetheless took an active part in discussions on a Biosafety Protocol with far-reaching implications for US biotechnology business. Under Clinton, the US was even party to confidential meetings held between those who had ratified the convention, and it continued to try steering the process in its preferred direction. This included wanting the WTO to be more involved through the establishment of a WTO working group on biotechnology.[78]

This informal multilateralism had obvious implications. Activists in the Clinton administration saw themselves as only *temporarily* excluded from the formal biodiversity process and remained committed to being part of the evolving regime. It is also worth noting that if a state like the US withdraws from such negotiations they do not cease, the EU, Japan, Canada, and more powerful developing countries continuing to fashion the multilateral institutions to deal with biodiversity issues—as with Kyoto. Once again there are dangers to being on the outside when the institutional framework of an issue like this is being developed, even for a hegemon. Activists therefore remain involved in the process even when formal ratification is absent; the US sent observers to Marrakesh, for example, and participated in many discussions.[79] Nevertheless, one further and potentially crucial point must also be made: the complexity of these issues and of politics more generally after the end of the cold war does suggest some fragmentation of the two factions, both activist and sceptic.

While the underlying activist-sceptic split is evident from the first three decades of international environmentalism, on biodiversity things appear to be more nuanced. While Congressional sceptics were concerned that the biodiversity convention might regulate US biotechnology firms in a detrimental manner, the Clinton White House continued to advance an agenda not entirely unacceptable to the sceptics. What differed was that it was a

---

[77] Paarlberg, 'Earth in Abeyance', 139.
[78] Robert Falkner, 'Regulating Biotech Trade: The Cartegna Protocol on Biosafety', *International Affairs*, 76/2 (2000), 107.   [79] Raustiala, 'Domestic Politics'.

multilateral agenda—to shift biotechnology, and so bio-safety, issues into the WTO, thereby putting the accent as much on trade liberalization as on biodiversity protection.[80] While the biodiversity convention may be lost in Congress without prospect of ratification, the new Bush administration will be forced to engage on biotechnology issues in a multilateral forum like the WTO. It will have to negotiate because unrestrained unilateralism threatens to undermine the very global markets and production networks which sceptical Congressmen and others want US multinationals to dominate. Biodiversity regulation is multilateral in its very essence; the economies of scale, sources of raw materials, costs of production, and markets on which biotechnology companies depend are transnational and must be dealt with as such. An EU-US trade war over genetically modified organisms (GMOs) for example, will do nothing for an industry which is so lucrative only because of the size of the *global* consumer markets in which these products can be sold.

This has a double-edged implication. On the one hand, the embedding of international environmentalism is complete and even sceptics must accept the need to deal with issues of this sort in multilateral ways. On the other hand, redefining issues of this sort as 'trade' issues pushes them towards institutions which have an agenda for *reducing* international regulation across sectors and so the substantive part of the sceptic agenda may still be realized. The science side still matters, and arguments about how certain the risk from GMOs needs to be to impose restrictions go on. Nevertheless, multilateralism is effectively a fact of life in this area; and even though the WTO's agenda is trade liberalization, the need for market access on which a freer trade regime depends requires continuous international negotiation.

In many ways we may see this as the activists' final triumph, even as the beginning of a new phase in international environmental politics. Although trade issues have always been central to sceptics' concerns about regulation, their protectionist impulse is no longer a viable option. The future is international regulation: of economies, the environment, terrorism, drugs trafficking, and so on. Multilateralism is here to stay because it is increasingly central to the way a powerful state like the United States can achieve policy goals in areas where costs and benefits are diffuse, where interests are harder to quantify, and where the compliance of other states is *integral* to the policy goal in the first place—a cleaner environment, or a wide enough, patent-protected market to reward investment in biotechnology research and development.

3. Conclusion

In the words of John Ruggie, '...rarely if ever has it been American policy to endow multilateral institutions with significant independent powers', a fact he

---

[80] Falkner, 'Regulating Biotech Trade'.

explains by reference to the capacity of great powers to get their way by other means.[81] And it is true, even for activists, that giving autonomy to multilateral institutions is a big step, especially for a hegemon with so many international options. However, rather than sovereign states devolving authority to multilateral institutions, we can conceive of this process as one in which aspects of the liberal-capitalist state are being, effectively, *internationalized*. Crafting multilateral agreements which privilege a particular understanding of environmental problems and their most appropriate solutions can be understood, in this sense, as a highly effective way of projecting power. Whether in the environment or in other areas where international cooperation is advancing equally quickly, the benefits of transnational responses to transnational 'problems', however these problems are constructed, are clear.

Far from debating the prospects for environmental multilateralism in the future we can look for the ways and means by which the United States, with support from a variety of other liberal states, seeks to mould international issues and institutions to reflect its own priorities. The decision by President George W. Bush to withdraw from Kyoto must not be interpreted as a decision to withdraw from environmental multilateralism for, as we have seen, non-engagement is available only at a prohibitive cost—environmentally, economically, and politically—as many Senators and US corporations are already telling the new president. In order to manage its territory—what goes in and out, who gets what and how much, what the air and water are like—the US state must involve itself in a variety of multilateral practices. To understand this, we need to be able to conceive of a 'gap' appearing between the 'territorial' and the 'sociological' state, one a fixed location, the other a set of mechanisms and arrangements for controlling social affairs.[82] There is no physical reason why the *sociological* state cannot extend its reach beyond its territory, projecting power through transnational institutions of various sorts. Indeed, it may see this as the most effective way to protect the 'territorial' state and its citizens.

Overall, therefore, the activists might be viewed as part of a larger historical tradition, one which sees the United States as a liberal progressive force whose manifest destiny is to transform the world around it. Although the environment is not an area in which many headlines are made, its mix of science, development, and capitalism makes it a model issue for studying the evolution of long-term incremental policy-making on an international scale. Each new convention or protocol pushes the United States to embrace multilateralism more fully, more permanently, opening up the opportunity for this most powerful of all states to remake the world according to its liberal designs. Ironically, the potential for the full commitment of the American state to multilateralism may one day lead to a certain fondness among some for the days of US scepticism. It is easier to

[81] John Gerard Ruggie, *Winning the Peace: America and World Order in the New Era* (New York: Columbia University Press, 1996), 21.
[82] Hopgood, *American Foreign Environmental Policy*, Ch. 1.

mobilize resistance against an immediate and menacing threat than against the slow advance of persuasion and argument backed by monetary sticks and carrots. Power is no less power when it is exercised multilaterally through the full deployment by the hegemon of incentives to other states to agree with a regime which, in the long run, benefits itself. The case of biotechnology regulation might be an instance of this, with the EU the only plausible political entity able to frustrate US designs.

With the anti-regulatory scepticism of the Reagan era long gone, modern-day sceptics must realize that they need a strategy *for* multilateralism that doesn't amount to George W. Bush's disavowal of Kyoto. Rather than a dawn, in retrospect this may well come to be seen as a sunset: the end of the dream of unilateralism in relation to the politics of the environment and trade. The debate between 'isolationism' and 'internationalism' can then be seen not as a cyclical and enduring feature of American foreign policy but as an historical anachronism. The choice is between, perhaps, 'coercive' and 'benevolent' multilateralism, between conceptions of 'interest' which contrast the 'national' interest of the US and its allies with the 'public interest' more widely conceived. Either way, the US will become more, not less, involved in the fine detail of international relations.

III

THE US AND REGIONAL ORGANIZATIONS

7

Making Africa Safe for Capitalism: US Policy and Multilateralism in Africa

PHILIP NEL

The purpose of this chapter is to trace and assess the ways in which the United States has used multilateral institutions and multilateralism itself[1] to pursue its interests on the African continent. This is not such a straightforward endeavour as might be assumed. The topic of 'the US, multilateral institutions, and Africa' is ambiguous. Does it refer to how the US has used multilateral institutions of which it itself is a member—such as the United Nations, the World Trade Organization, and the International Monetary Fund, for example—to pursue its objectives in Africa? Or does it refer to how the United States interacted with and influenced those multilateral institutions on the African continent itself and of which the US is not a member—such as the Organization of African Unity (OAU), for example? If we prefer to focus on the first, the degree of overlap with the chapters in this book dealing with US policies towards the UN, and with the WTO and the IMF, may be excessive. For that reason, I will limit references to how the US uses institutions of which it is a member in its policy towards Africa only to those instances and trends that are relevant for the broader evaluative argument of this chapter.

A choice in favour of the second option—namely, to focus on Africa's multilateral institutions and how the US interacts with them—is not without its problems either. US policy towards Africa was very much a bilateral, country-to-country affair for most of the period from 1946 to 2000. During the cold war, the US cultivated bilateral relations with specific African states as a counter for a perceived Soviet threat on the continent.[2] Overall, selective

---

[1] 'Multilateralism' I take to refer to activities or initiatives that involve coordination of policies between three or more states. See R. Keohane, 'Multilateralism: An Agenda for Research', *International Journal*, 45 (Autumn, 1990), 731. For a discussion of the distinction between multilateral institutions and multilateralism as an institution, see J. Ruggie, 'Multilateralism: The Anatomy of an Institution', in J. Ruggie (ed.), *Multilateralism Matters: The Theory and Praxis of an Institutional Form* (New York: Columbia University Press, 1993), 12–13.

[2] See P. J. Schraeder, *United States Foreign Policy Toward Africa: Incrementalism, Crisis and Change* (Cambridge: Cambridge University Press, 1994); D. A. Dickson, *United States Policy towards Sub-Saharan Africa: Change, Continuity and Constraint* (Lanham &

bilateralism provided a much higher degree of strategic certainty for the US, and supplied the context within which to exercise its preponderant relational power. Collectively, Africa was not perceived as a potential US ally, given the propensity of Africans to bring out bloc votes against the US in the UN General Assembly. African multilateral institutions were, for the most part, perceived as opponents of US interests because of their tendency to criticize 'the West' for its tacit support for white-minority regimes, and for the forms of cultural, political, and economic neocolonialism perpetrated, according to Africans, by the US and its allies. The same was true of regional bodies in Africa, such as the Southern Africa Development Coordinating Conference (SADCC), which later became the Southern African Development Community (SADC). The SADCC saw as its main goal the liberation of southern Africa from white minority rule; and, to the extent that the US did not want to participate fully in this liberation struggle, it was perceived to be an ally of the enemy.[3] The scope for US involvement with multilateral institutions on the African continent was thus extremely limited.

This situation changed dramatically after the cold war era. With the end of the cold war, and with the transition to a post-apartheid era, the obstacles to closer involvement between the US and the multilateral institutions in Africa largely fell away. In addition, closer integration of African economies with the global economy during the 1990s created new opportunities for the US and Africa jointly to develop multilateral initiatives. Similarly, the development of complex humanitarian crises on the African continent made it imperative for the US to find ways to cooperate with African multilateral conflict-resolution initiatives if it wanted to make good its desire for a new world order in which a collective search for security and shared responsibility for conflict resolution would be the guiding principles.

The 1990s and the early years of the twenty-first century, therefore, turned out to be a busy decade for multilateralism on the African continent, and the US used this opportunity not only to reaffirm its willingness to pursue long-standing interests in Africa but also to explore ways of sharing some of the costs for conflict resolution with African institutions. This latter aspect grew in importance as the American public, and its representatives in Congress in particular, became reluctant to support policies that would embroil the US in costly foreign entanglements. The pursuit of close relations with African institutions and with a number of so-called pivotal states in Africa became part of a cost- and risk-sharing strategy, while also giving effect to the desire to be seen during Bill Clinton' presidency by his domestic constituency to be highly present and active on the African continent. Despite initial expectations that the

New York: University Press of America, 1985); P. Duignan, and L. H. Gann, *The United States and Africa: A History* (Cambridge: Cambridge University Press, 1984), 284–99.

[3] See A. Guelke, 'Southern Africa and the Superpowers', in Stephen Chan (ed.), *Exporting Apartheid: Foreign Policies in Southern Africa, 1978–1988* (London: Macmillan, 1990).

arrival of George W. Bush in the White House would herald a reversal of Clinton's proudly touted 'partnership with Africa', there has actually been much continuity. What has changed, as Peter Schraeder rightly points out, is that the Bush team has drastically toned down the heavy, but often empty, rhetoric on Africa that Clinton was fond of using, and instead has focused on promoting private sector initiatives in Africa to further the gains made in terms of the Africa Growth and Opportunity Act (AGOA), consolidating US ties with pivotal states such as Nigeria and South Africa and promoting African solutions to Africa's problems of conflict resolution.[4]

This chapter situates the emergence of a noticeable multilateral dimension to American policy towards Africa against two backgrounds. The first, provided in section 2, deals with the general features of American policy towards Africa since the Second World War and the role that multilateralism in general has played in that. The second background deals with the rise of multilateralism on the African continent as a process that has a dynamic of its own. This perspective on Africa as an agent, and not simply as an object, of US policy is an important one if we are to maintain a critical perspective on the successes but also the contradictions and failures of US policy towards Africa.

In the final two sections, I turn to a detailed description and evaluation of the dimensions of multilateralism in post-cold war US policy, and in particular the Clinton era which, in many respects, encapsulates much of what is right and wrong with US policy towards the continent. Early indications are that, despite the obvious differences in style between Clinton and George W. Bush, the latter's policy towards Africa is beset by very much the same problems and tensions that plagued Clinton's. My evaluation, and the general assumptions with which I approach the theme of US policy towards Africa, are informed by a broadly neo-Gramscian appraisal of the hegemonic function of the US in the current global political and economic order, and of the place of multilateralism within that hegemonic function.[5]

1. Continuity and Change in US African Policy, 1946–1989

Throughout the post-Second World War era, the US has had limited but real interests in Africa. Its foreign policy goals have included the desire to promote

---

[4] See Peter Schraeder, '"Forget the Rhetoric and Boost the Geopolitics": Emerging Trends in the Bush Administration's Policy towards Africa', *African Affairs*, 100 (2001).
[5] See Robert Cox, 'Multilateralism and World Order' (originally published in 1992), in Robert Cox and Timothy Sinclair (eds), *Approaches to World Order* (Cambridge: Cambridge University Press, 1996); and E. Augelli and C. Murphy, *America's Quest for Supremacy and the Third World: A Gramscian Analysis* (London: Pinter, 1988).

human rights, racial justice, and democratic values; to secure African diplomatic support at the United Nations and in other multilateral institutions; to guarantee US access to a range of important raw materials produced by African states; and to promote trade with and investment in the continent.[6] As in the rest of its foreign policy, in Africa the United States has acted largely as a status quo-oriented power, interested in securing the stability of a global postwar system largely of its own making.

Fearing that growing African resentment of continued European colonial oppression could boil over, the US encouraged an orderly decolonization process in Africa, but it would be an exaggeration to claim that the US was ever a very strong supporter of African independence and thus a 'transformative' actor. The US chose to abstain when the UN General Assembly in 1960 passed the Declaration on the Granting of Independence to Colonial Countries and Peoples.[7] The US also encouraged newly independent African states to maintain links with European capitals and thus to perpetuate the established commercial and financial channels forged during the colonial era.

The concerns of the US over maintaining the status quo are also evident in its approach to conflict on the continent. On the one hand, it has tried to discourage extra-constitutional political change aimed against authoritarian governments, even if the incumbents were clearly violating human rights norms promoted by the US itself. Much of US policy towards white minority governments in southern Africa, at least since the Nixon presidency and up until the start of the second Reagan term of office, shared the basic premise of National Security Study Memorandum 39, namely, that stable change must accommodate the interests of the white oligarchies.[8] Elsewhere, as in the case of Zaire, the US also preferred the devil whom it knew to the one it did not, hoping that it could retain the loyalty of anti-communist leaders. Because these authoritarian figures were an embarrassment in view of expressed US policy on human rights, the US also tried to stimulate orderly, piecemeal change in these authoritarian states. Overall, the priority given to the promotion of human rights, accountable governments, and democratic practices has been geared towards promoting stability in the hope that the elimination of possible sources of political resistance and economic deprivation would prevent the rise of virulent anti-Western nationalisms and communism.

---

[6] D. Rothchild and J. Ravenhill, 'From Carter to Reagan: The Global Perspective on Africa Becomes Ascendant', in Kenneth A. Oye, Robert J. Lieber, and Donald Rothchild (eds), *Eagle Defiant: United States Foreign Policy in the 1980s* (Boston: Little, Brown and Company, 1983), 338.

[7] D. Rothchild and J. Ravenhill, 'Subordinating African Issues to Global Logic: Reagan Confronts Political Complexity', in Kenneth A. Oye, Robert J. Lieber, and Donald Rothchild (eds), *Eagle Resurgent? The Reagan Era in American Foreign Policy* (Boston: Little, Brown and Company, 1987), 397.

[8] See Mohamed A. El-Khawas and Barry Cohen (eds), *The Kissinger Study of Southern Africa* (Westport: Lawrence Hill, 1976), 105.

Washington has consistently viewed violent intra- and inter-state conflict in Africa not only as a threat to trade and investments but also as a source of instability that could spill over onto the global scene and so endanger the relations between major powers. Throughout the last four decades of the twentieth century, the US's overt policy has therefore been to contain conflict on the continent and to prevent it from spreading from Africa to the wider geo-political arena and to pursue peaceful solutions to African conflicts. It has, from time to time, used its considerable diplomatic resources to good effect in this regard, both on its own and in conjunction with the efforts of others. Thus, the US played an important supportive role in the 1979 British-led Lancaster House Agreement on Zimbabwe. In the case of the negotiations that led to Namibian independence in 1990, and the linked withdrawal of Cuban troops from Angola, the US played a leading role in the multilateral effort. When the politics of the United Nations Security Council eventually allowed it to do so, Washington threw its weight behind multilateral peace operations on the continent, and was even prepared to carry the brunt of the burden, as was the case with United Nations Operation in Somalia (UNOSOMII).[9]

The downside of America's strong status quo predilection for negotiated solutions at all costs has been a sometimes inordinate haste to accept any agreement, no matter what its longer-term implications might be.[10] The US has also been prone to lose interest in a conflict once it has proved to be intractable and a 'solution' has not readily emerged, as in Sudan, for instance. Of course, when larger policy goals are at stake, the US can rapidly rekindle its interests in these not-ripe-for-resolution conflicts, as has happened in the case of Sudan as part of the George W. Bush 'war on terrorism'.[11]

Perhaps the most important dimension of the status quo orientation of the US in its dealings with Africa has been Washington's unwillingness to contemplate structural changes in North–South economic interaction. Apart from a short spell during the late 1970s when the Carter administration tried to engage the developing countries on a New International Economic Order,[12]

---

[9] See D. Rothchild and T. Sisk, 'US-Africa Policy: Promoting Conflict Management in Uncertain Times', in Robert J. Lieber (ed.), *Eagle Adrift: American Foreign Policy at the End of the Century* (New York: Longman, 1997).

[10] One example is the way in which the Clinton administration railroaded a deal through in 1999 compelling the government of Sierra Leone to recognize and accommodate the brutal leader of the Revolutionary United Front, Foday Sankoh, leading to the resumption of a civil war in 2000. For a scathing critique of this incident, see Ryan Lizza, 'Where Angels Fear to Tread', *The New Republic Online* (24 July 2000), at wysig://55:///www.tnr.com/0724000/lizza0724000_print.html

[11] George W. Bush was under pressure also from Christian pressure groups, one of his main support bases, to do something in Sudan about the perceived persecution of Christians in the south by the Muslim government in Khartoum. See in this regard Schraeder, ' "Forget the Rhetoric and Boost the Geopolitics" '.

[12] See Donald Rothchild, 'US Policy Styles in Africa: From Minimal Engagement to Liberal Internationalism', in Kenneth A. Oye, Robert J. Lieber, and Donald Rothchild (eds), *Eagle Entangled: US Foreign Policy in a Complex World* (New York: Longman, 1979).

any idea of a redistributive transformation of the global economy has been systematically opposed and disparaged by the US. Instead, Washington has consistently tried to persuade the developing countries, and Africa in particular, of the 'magic of the market,' as President Reagan called it.[13] Whenever African states have resisted, the US has used its considerable power resources, both directly and indirectly, to try to influence the views of the continent's leaders.

As the main architect of the multilateral global economic order that emerged after the Second World War, the US has sought to undermine African demands for structural reform of the global economy by encouraging African states to seek the benefits of membership of the GATT—such as the lowering of trans-action costs in trade negotiations—the IMF—access to credit facilities on favourable terms in times of crisis—and the World Bank—access to multilat-eral developmental funding—and so bind them into the global political-economic status quo. At the same time, though, Washington has used the coercive epistemic and ideological apparatus of these multilateral institutions to 'persuade' African leaders of the 'correct' macroeconomic policies to pursue. While there were credible macroeconomic alternatives available, most African states joined other developing countries in what Krasner has called a 'structural conflict' against the liberal economic regimes promoted by Washington.[14] However, the devastation of African economies during the 1980s made it easy for the ideological forces of global neo-liberalism to convince African leaders that there was no alternative to neo-liberal prescriptions. By the early 1990s, the US had seemingly achieved one of its major foreign policy goals in Africa: making the continent safe for capitalism.

For much of the period under review, the pursuit of this status quo-oriented set of interests on the African continent was coloured by two strands or policy approaches: the accommodationist and the rejectionist. Although the differ-ences between the two should not be overly emphasized, and while it is true that every administration since Kennedy has been influenced by a mixture of the two, the differences between them are real and important.[15]

The fact that Africa is marginal to vital American interests implies that US policy towards Africa has been influenced largely by global concerns. In this sense, American policy towards Africa has been characterized by an overall internationalist tendency seeing Africa as a site of contestation in a global struggle for hegemony. Here, 'hegemony' is used in the Gramscian sense.

---

[13] See R. Feinberg, 'Reaganomics and the Third World', in Oye, Lieber, and Rothchild (eds), *Eagle Defiant.*

[14] S. Krasner, *Structural Conflict: The Third World against Global Liberalism* (Berkeley: University of California Press, 1985).

[15] I find the common distinctions between 'pragmatism' and 'ideological fervour' and between 'globalism' and 'regionalism' in US policy towards Africa not very useful. US policy is always ideological, and always has a global orientation, I would argue. The term 'accommodation' is suggested by Rothchild, 'US Policy Styles in Africa'.

It refers not only to a preponderance of material sources of power or the exercise of sheer coercive force but also, and perhaps more crucially, to 'ideological leadership', the ability to determine which ideas and values will become the norm, the 'common sense', and which not.[16] The drive towards an internationalist hegemony has not disappeared with the end of the cold war, but has become more subtle and less obvious. The ability to lead in such a way that the led follow willingly remains a functional requirement for effective superpower status in a unipolar world. This can be achieved only by means of a constant process of legitimizing those ideas, structures, and institutions that support its right to lead, and the simultaneous delegitimizing of ideas, structures, and institutions that challenge that right.

While this internationalist, hegemonic focus is a constant feature, variation has occurred in the ways in which policy makers have dealt with the concerns, wishes, and interests of black Africa. The US at times appeared prepared to accommodate African concerns and wishes in its policy, without, of course, relinquishing Washington's overall hegemonic objectives. This I call the 'accommodationist' approach in US policy. In the accommodationist approach, hegemony is achieved via attempts at accommodating the legitimate interests of Africa by stressing the degree of complementarity of US and African interests and by stimulating the development of institutions of cooperation and of collaboration.

More often, however, US policy makers have treated African interests—in a fairer distributive arrangement in the global political economy, for instance—with suspicion as being unauthentic, inspired by communist agitation or other un-American forces, or have regarded these interests as unimportant. In this 'rejectionist' approach, African interests in securing a more equitable global political economy are relegated to the category of ideas, structures, and institutions that have to be rejected and delegitimized in order to protect 'US values' from contamination and erosion.

It is important, however, to understand that both these approaches have the maintenance of US hegemony in mind. They differ on the means to be employed. The accommodationist approach can be associated with American liberalism, emphasizing the complementarity of, on the one hand, US interests in the global establishment of national and global human rights regimes, racial harmony, and 'just' free market economies and, on the other hand, African concerns about racial and economic justice. The rejectionist approach has strong links with US conservatism, which remains sceptical about attempts to undermine the autonomy of market forces and openly hostile to state-led redistributive policies.

These are ideal types and cannot be neatly identified in the hustle and bustle of real policy-making and execution. However, it is possible to identify eras in which one of the two became a dominant tendency. The first Reagan

---

[16] Augelli and Murphy, *America's Quest.*

term, for instance, was clearly dominated by the rejectionist approach. Economically the whole Reagan era was one of malign neglect of Africa. The pursuit of supply-side macroeconomic dogmas, aimed at halting and turning around what many perceived as a decline in US hegemony and alarming rates of global inflation, not only led to a global economic recession but also drained capital from developing countries as they struggled to repay their dollar debts whose interest payments rose with interest hikes in the US.[17]

The accommodationist approach in US policy towards Africa is advocated by those policy makers, interest groups, and observers who believe that US policy should attempt to deal with the continent on African terms and be sensitive to its historical and cultural uniqueness. This approach emerged during the Kennedy era, when attempts were made to develop relations that were not exclusively determined by the ideological concerns of anti-communism. It also played a significant role in attempts by Henry Kissinger, when Secretary of State in the Ford administration, to reverse some of the damage to US standing among African leaders by its earlier close association with white minority governments in southern Africa. However, it was only in the highly moralistic and pro-black inclination of Jimmy Carter that the attempt to accommodate African concerns on their own terms came to fruition. The principled accommodationism of the Carter administration

meant a more concerted effort to reconcile the symbols of idealism with fundamental status quo purposes. In striving to project a positive and supportive image to black Africa, good intentions became more than moral imperatives; they were also resources that enabled a Vietnam-weary America to find renewed faith in itself and helped to restore America's liberal reputation around the globe.[18]

It would be reasonable to expect the US to be more supportive of African multilateralism and to be willing to engage Africa more on a multilateral footing during eras in which the accommodationist tendency has the upper hand in US policy-making circles. There is, indeed, evidence to corroborate such an expectation. The appointment of Andrew Young, the African-American civil rights leader, as US ambassador to the UN signalled not only the Carter administration's sensitivity to a crucial electoral constituency but also a desire on the part of the US to normalize multilateral relations with black Africa and to seek, in Andrew Young's words, 'African solutions for African problems'. This cooperative and accommodationist stance stood the US in good stead when it assisted in the multilateral attempts to secure Zimbabwean independence in 1980. It also gave the US good standing when it participated in the formation of the Western contact group that met separately with the South West African People's Liberation Organization (SWAPO) and the South African government in 1977 and 1978 to start the process of peaceful South African withdrawal

---

[17] Feinberg, 'Reaganomics and the Third World'.
[18] Rothchild, 'US Policy Styles in Africa', 317.

from the then South West Africa. The contact group managed to secure SWAPO's agreement to a package of proposals, including a UN-supervised election, only to have it rejected by South Africa.

One would further expect that, all else being equal, an accommodationist approach to African interests would be more likely in eras when the level of ideological rivalry between outside forces on the African continent subsides, and that the opposite would hold in times of greater ideological tension. Again, the Carter era is instructive. The earlier accommodationist sentiments of the Carter administration came increasingly under threat in the late 1970s as the Soviet Union expanded its involvement in Ethiopia, and solidified its support for the Cuban forces in Angola, forcing Carter to backtrack.[19] More importantly, the rising stakes in superpower confrontation in Africa and elsewhere in the developing world helped to create the conditions for Ronald Reagan's win over Carter in 1980 and the re-emergence of the rejectionist line.

To extend this argument, it follows that the end of the cold war would again improve the prospects of the accommodationist sentiment. As I relate below, the empirical evidence with which to test this hypothesis is somewhat mixed. While the earlier Bush administration attempted to accommodate African interests in the terrain of conflict mediation, it was not so accommodating when it came to economic aid and debt relief to African states. In contrast, the Clinton administration elevated Africa to a level of importance it never before had in US policy making, but the actions taken by Clinton's Africa team did not always match its rhetoric. Of course, it was not easy for the Clinton administration to deal with a Congress that in 1994 came under Republican control, especially as far as such a marginal region as Africa is concerned. Nevertheless, the promise of a full-blown accommodationist turn in US African policy has not been realized to the extent that many Africanists hoped for during the Clinton years. Early indications are that George W. Bush has neither turned his back on Africa, as many feared early in 2001,[20] nor turned back to the overtly rejectionist approach associated with previous Republican presidents. For the time being, a weak form of the accommodationist approach seems to be becoming a stable feature of US policy.

Meanwhile, there has been a clear evolution in African perspectives starting in the 1990s away from drastic redistributive conceptions of the global political economy towards a mild form of reformism. By 2001, this mild reformism has made way in turn for a growing acceptance among a new brand of African leaders that they should seek greater integration of African economies into the global system, rather than changing this system. This has contributed to the institutionalization of the accommodationist approach on the part of the US. This approach is encouraged by a new generation of African leaders, such as

---

[19] Rothchild, 'US Policy Styles in Africa', 329–32.
[20] See 'Powell Tour Dispels Backburner Doubts', *Africa Research Bulletin* (15 May–16 June 2001).

Nigeria's Obasanjo and South Africa's Mbeki, who accept and laud the US as a potential partner, hoping among others things to lock post-Clinton administrations into the accommodationist pattern that Clinton helped to establish.

2. The Main Features of Africa's Multilateral Project

Multilateralism in Africa Before the 1990s

With the founding of the OAU in May 1963, African leaders regarded African unity as a means to secure internal political security and to protect Africa from a perceived predatory international economic order. The OAU regime was a mutual political pact, insulating state elites from internally and/or externally induced change. Thus, multilateralism became a vehicle for state-building in the broader sense, but also for securing the power of post-independence authoritarian regimes.

On the economic front, ideas of African self-reliance and inward industrialization, facilitated, among others, by the UN Economic Commission for Africa, were promoted to shield Africa from 'external economic exploitation'. Regional cooperation among groups of African states was promoted as part of this programme of self-reliance.

African participation in international regimes such as commodities agreements and Lomé Conventions was aimed at offsetting perceived inequalities in trading relations, institutionalizing aid, and generally creating protective barriers. Membership of the GATT was limited, and African members used their membership to plead for exceptional treatment rather than as a force for integrating Africa into the world economy.

Conflict resolution on the continent was hardly an issue, although the Biafra war and the struggle against colonialism did elicit some regional responses from African states; for instance, the formation of the SADCC in 1980 served an economic purpose but also assisted the so-called frontline states in their struggle against white minority governments in Zimbabwe and in South Africa. For the most part, 'conflict resolution' was conducted on the initiative of individual African leaders and by ad hoc OAU 'good offices' initiatives. The OAU Charter makes provision for a Committee of Mediation, Conciliation and Arbitration (Article 3), but it remained dormant, without funding, and without a mandate. The management of conflict was often left in the hands of the main cold war rivals and ex-colonial masters.

These early instances of African multilateralism can be characterized as counter-hegemonic but not post-hegemonic behaviour. Early forms opposed the political and particularly economic hegemony of extra-African actors, but with the purpose of legitimizing the exclusionary rule of a first generation of

African state builders. This form of 'established' multilateralism,[21] which leaves no room for broader societal involvement in decision making, dominates African multilateralism to this day. Nevertheless, a number of innovations within this specific qualitative format of African multilateralism have characterized the 1990s.

Evolution of African Multilateralism in the 1990s

Key aspects of the complex of attitudes and concerns that went into stabilizing the earlier form of multilateralism in Africa changed in the early 1990s, for several reasons. Among them were: the end of cold war rivalry, the resultant loss of African bargaining power, the fear of Africa's marginalization, the— partial—acceptance of the failure of self-sufficiency plans such as the Lagos Plan of Action, and the sobering effects of the debt crisis. While old attitudes did not disappear altogether, some new and still contradictory tendencies and emphases did develop.

The following are the main features of African multilateralism in the 1990s:

1. *Regional economic integration*: a renewed push to integrate the economies on the African continent, partially as a continuation of the old belief that 'in unity lies strength' but also in response to the worldwide phenomenon of regionalization that emerged in the late 1980s and early 1990s. The Abuja Treaty of 1991, an ambitious plan of action to create an economically integrated common market of Africa, is the flagship of this trend. Six regional economic groupings are supposed to assist in this programme of market integration:

- Arab Mahgreb Union (AMU);
- Common Market for Eastern and Southern Africa (COMESA);
- Economic Community of Central African States (ECCAS);
- Economic Community of West African States (ECOWAS);
- Intergovernmental Authority on Development (IGAD) in the Horn of Africa; and
- Southern African Development Community (SADC).[22]

The record of the implementation of the Abuja ideal throughout the 1990s is patchy at best. One of the reasons is divergent thinking about whether regional integration serves as a defence against or as a stepping stone towards global integration. However, at the 35th OAU Summit in Algiers (1999), forceful attempts, led by South African President Thabo Mbeki, were made to revitalize the Abuja Treaty, and the Sitre Declaration by African Leaders (September 1999) endorsed the idea of a renewed attempt to institutionalize the economic—and

---

[21] The term is from Michael Schechter, *Innovation in Multilateralism* (Basingstoke: Macmillan, 1999).

[22] T. Mulat, 'Multilateralism and Africa's Regional Economic Communities', *Journal of World Trade*, 32/4 (1998), 117.

political—unity of Africa. This was followed, at the 36th Summit in Lusaka (2000), by the momentous decision to launch the African Union (AU) which is to replace the OAU. Loosely modelled on the EU, it is eventually to create the conditions for the political and economic integration of the member states and to establish common institutions such as a central bank, a single currency, a court of justice, and a pan-African parliament. Although clearly a very long-term project, the AU may have an immediate normative impact on African affairs. In contrast to the non-interference pact among the original OAU elite referred to earlier, AU principles make provision for 'the right of the Union to intervene in a Member State pursuant to a decision of the Assembly in respect of grave circumstances, namely: war crimes, genocide and crimes against humanity', and commits members to 'respect for democratic principles, human rights, the rule of law and good governance' and the 'condemnation and rejection of unconstitutional changes of governments'.[23]

2. *Integration with the global economy.* Economic thinking in the 1990s was torn between continued resistance to the global economy and acceptance that integration into the global economy is preferable. Accepting that integration into the world economy holds the best prospects for developing countries, some 38 African states have joined, and a further two are about to join, the WTO. Various continent-wide initiatives have been launched to cut tariffs, remove non-tariff barriers, and generally improve the trade profile of individual states. This has been accompanied by a—partial and selective—acceptance of the logic, or dogma, of free trade. In some cases, arguments in favour of free trade are being used by African leaders against perceived protectionism by the 'North'. African states are also organizing themselves much better now than they did during the Uruguay Round, in order to participate more effectively in future rounds.

To judge by some of the statements made at the 1999 OAU Summit, some African leaders have doubts about the gains to be had from integration in an era of globalization. Although integration into the global economy was not rejected out of hand, the Algiers Declaration did warn that:

Despite the tremendous efforts invested by our countries to reorganize and restructure their economies at a very high social cost, our economies are increasingly facing a serious deterioration of the terms of trade, a decline in international development co-operation, a continuous fall in official development aid, an exacerbation of the external debt problem and the resurgence of protectionism on the part of the developed countries.[24]

This did not prevent the OAU, however, from accepting what has become known as the New Partnership for Africa's Development (NEPAD) action plan

---

[23] See *Constitutive Act of the African Union* (2000) at www.dfa.gov.za/for-relations/multilateral/treaties/auact.htm.
[24] OAU Assembly of Heads of State and Government, 'Algiers Declaration' issued at the 35th Ordinary Session (12–14 July, 1999), Algiers, Algeria.

in 2001. Based on the Millennium Action Plan drawn up by Mbeki, Obasanjo, and Bouteflika (Algeria) and the Omega Plan of Senegal's President Wade, it acknowledges Africa's complicity in its own economic demise and commits the continent to seeking a more thoroughgoing integration with the global economy through the promotion of direct foreign and domestic investment, a major infrastructural revamping of the continent, and a concerted effort at poverty relief. In return for this broad acceptance of the neo-liberal Washington consensus by African leaders, NEPAD calls on the OECD countries to provide greater access for African exports to their market, increase official development assistance, and enhance debt relief.[25] The plan is a clear indication that a new generation of African leaders looks towards the full integration of their continent into the global economy as their best hope. Whether the terms of this integration will work to the benefit of the poor and marginalized in Africa remains to be seen.

3. *Taking up the burden of conflict management.* In 1993, a heightened sense of African responsibility regarding conflict resolution brought the OAU to create a Mechanism for Preventing, Managing, and Resolving Conflicts in Africa, an underfunded and not very successful endeavour, although it has had some success in mediating in the Eritrea-Ethiopia war. However, as Zartman argues,[26] African negotiators did gain considerable conflict resolution experience during the early 1990s. The creation of regional conflict resolution mechanisms, notably ECOWAS Military Observer Group (ECOMOG) in West Africa, the Organ for Politics, Security and Democracy in the SADC, and the IGAD initiative to broker peace in Sudan all serve as examples.[27] Significantly, NEPAD emphasizes that African institutions themselves have a primary responsibility for managing and resolving conflicts in Africa, and commits leaders to the revitalization of existing conflict prevention and resolution mechanisms.[28]

4. *Disarmament and humanitarian law.* African multilateral innovation in the 1990s also included the negotiation and signing of the so-called Pelindaba Treaty, which turned Africa into a nuclear-free zone; a number of initiatives, leading up to and following the signing of the Ottawa Treaty in 1997 banning the use, stockpiling, and distribution of anti-personnel landmines; strong and coordinated leadership by African states in promoting the 1998 Rome Treaty on the ICC; and, more recently, various regional multilateral attempts to stop the illicit trade in small arms.

---

[25] 'OAU-AU: Economic Visions', *Africa Research Bulletin* (16 June–15 July 2001).
[26] I. William Zartman, 'Inter-African Negotiations and State Renewal', in John Harbeson and Donald Rothchild (eds), *Africa in World Politics: The African State System in Flux* (Boulder, CO: Westview Press, 2000), 154.
[27] See Terrence Lyons, 'Can Neighbours Help? Regional Actors and African Conflict Management', and M. Chege, 'Responsibility and Accountability by International Institutions: Sub-Saharan Africa in the 1990s', in Francis M. Deng and Terrence Lyons (eds), *African Reckoning: A Quest for Good Governance* (Washington, DC: Brookings Institution, 1998).
[28] For the text of NEPAD, see www.dfa.gov.za/events/nepad.pdf.

5. *Linking security, development, and democracy.* In contrast to an earlier phase of exclusive state-building multilateralism, the 1990s have also seen the emergence of African multilateral attempts to place normative restrictions on state builders. One under-appreciated initiative is the Kampala Document, proposed by the Africa Leadership Forum, of 1991. It suggested the formation of a Conference on Security, Stability, Development and Cooperation in Africa (CSSDCA): a 'Helsinki-like' process for Africa, covering four 'calabashes'—security, stability, development, and cooperation—and to be based on the adoption of binding norms, including collective responsibility, good neigh-bourliness, democracy, and the rule of law.[29] Unfortunately, many African leaders resisted it for fear of creating pretexts for external intervention in their—often brutish—internal affairs. The CSSDCA remained dormant until December 1999, when an attempt was made to revive it at a meeting of African foreign ministers in Arusha, Tanzania. The ministers formed a steering com-mittee 'to further this process on the African continent'.[30]

Normatively, these multilateral innovations are somewhat more mixed than an earlier generation of African initiatives were. They do allow more room for civil society involvement, for instance, on landmines, small arms, and the ICC initiatives. Organized multilateral animosity towards unconstitutional changes in government is a welcome new feature. In addition, the CSSDCA process holds the promise that the linkages between democracy, economic openness, and development will come to be recognized much more explicitly in the future. On the other hand, many African states remain suspicious of the role and sources of funding of NGOs, and there is still an unwillingness to expand state-centred multilateralism systematically to allow for the participation of civil society.

3. US Accommodationism and Multilateralism in Africa after the Cold War

1989–1994: The Re-emergence of a Hesitant Accommodationism in US Policy

The end of the cold war in Africa provided the scope for the Bush administra-tion to pursue its vision of 'a new world order'. Although no clear strategic vision for US global leadership emerged during the Bush era,[31] there was a genuine wish not to disengage from Africa altogether and to contribute to the reconstruction of the continent.

Buoyed by the emergence of foreign policy bipartisanship in Washington, Bush could proceed with Congressional support to establish 'regularized patterns

---

[29] See F. M. Deng, 'African Policy Agenda: A Framework for Global Partnership', in Deng and Lyons (eds), *African Reckoning*, 164.
[30] See South African Foreign Minister Dlaminini-Zuma's address to Parliament, 14 March 2000.   [31] Rothchild and Sisk, 'US-Africa Policy', 275.

of political relations'[32] with African states, further explore ways of settling regional and civil conflicts in Africa, and promote governmental reform in Africa. Careful not to confront Congress, and in a spirit of accommodation towards the wishes of the OAU and SADCC, Bush decided to maintain pressure on the South African government, even after President De Klerk's announcement in February 1990 that the resistance movements in exile would be unbanned and Nelson Mandela freed. The accommodationist stance of the Bush administration was also evident in its decision to reverse the Reagan refusal to allow debt cancellation for highly indebted African states. Although the Bush conditions for debt rescheduling and cancellation were stricter than those accepted by most other creditor nations, Bush announced that the US would be prepared to forgive debt that arose from development assistance loans if the debtors agreed to World Bank and IMF structural adjustment programmes.

In the arena of conflict resolution and mediation, the Bush administration showed its willingness to take African interests seriously and to explore the continuities between US and African interests. The Africanists in the Bush administration believed that they could build on their earlier successes in Angola-Namibia to hasten the end of apartheid in South Africa and return war-torn African states to normality. Cautious engagement in unilateral and direct mediating efforts followed in Sudan—leading to the US 'peace plan' of May 1990—in the Ethiopian civil war in 1991, and in the Ethiopia-Eritrean secessionist conflict during the same period; and indirect mediation in Mozambique in 1992.[33]

Multilaterally, the Bush administration gave its support to the spate of UN peace missions in Africa after the demise of the cold war made it possible for concerted UN Security Council action in Africa. Bush supported the deployment of the UN Transition Assistance Group in Namibia (UNTAG) in 1989, the first UN Angola Verification Mission (UNAVEM I) in 1989, UNAVEM II in 1991, and the UN Mission for the Referendum in Western Sahara (MINURSO) in 1991.

While there were some continuities in the African policies of Bush and Clinton—for example, general engagement in Africa, support for conflict resolution, promotion of free enterprise and 'good governance'—Clinton soon elevated Africa to a rhetorical level it had not had before, in a strong declaratory form of accommodationism. His call to reform aid programmes for Africa 'to ensure that the assistance we provide truly benefits Africans and encourages the development of democratic institutions and free market economies' provides an eloquent example.[34] In particular, Clinton wanted to explore the multilateral route, both globally and regionally, as a means to

---

[32] D. Rothchild and John Ravenhill, 'Retreat from Globalism: US Policy towards Africa in the 1990s', in Kenneth Oye, Robert Lieber, and Donald Rothchild (eds), *Eagle in a New World: American Grand Strategy in the Post-Cold War Era* (London: Harper Collins, 1992), 393.

[33] D. Rothchild, 'The Impact of US Disengagement on African Intrastate Conflict Resolution', in Harbeson and Rothchild, *Africa in World Politics*, 170.

[34] Rothchild and Sisk, 'US-Africa Policy', 275.

establish a Partnership for Economic Growth and Opportunity between the US and Africa. His underlying priority was to create the conditions domestically and in the world as a whole, Africa included, for the revival of US economic fortunes on which US hegemony ultimately depended.

In the run-up to the presidential election in 1992, it became clear that the Democrats would focus on 'getting the domestic economy going', believing that that gave them the best chance to undercut the popularity of George Bush.[35] Sticking to his best suit, Clinton focused everything, including foreign trade and investment policy, on the one major goal that could cement his future popularity with the American people: rebuilding American prosperity by making sure that American industries stayed ahead in the new post-Fordist 'knowledge economy' and that American companies could aggressively trade and invest in global markets shorn of protective coatings. Foreign policy became the servant of foreign trade and investment policy.

In this context, parts of Africa did gain some importance via Secretary of Commerce Ron Brown's 'Big Emerging Markets' initiative which identified a post-apartheid southern Africa as one of ten global growth points for US trade and investment. In addition, the Clinton administration was quick to support the new South Africa of Nelson Mandela. While it is clear that Clinton also exploited for domestic consumption his good fortune of being the 'first post-apartheid American President', the initiatives that he took towards the new South Africa showed a commitment to building a 'partnership' with this 'pivotal state'. Similar strategies, but not always for exactly the same reasons, were pursued towards other emerging pivotal states in sub-Saharan Africa, such as Ghana and Uganda.

However, Africa as a whole did not achieve the prominence during the first Clinton term that many accommodationists had hoped for. Given the disastrous outcome of the UN peace-enforcement operation in Somalia in 1993 (UNOSOM II) and the growth of 'Afro-pessimism' in the American media, no American politician could convince the voters that much time and money should be spent on African issues. With the tragic death of Ron Brown in an aircraft accident in 1996, Africa lost one of its strongest spokespersons in Washington. The growing domestic battle that Clinton had on his hands with a Republican majority in Congress after the 1994 mid-term elections left him with little scope to pursue his own, apparently genuine, interest in Africa. In addition, key Africa committee and subcommittee chairs were lost by the Congressional Black Caucus in those elections and the foreign policy agenda for the next two years was set by Afro-pessimists. The result was a virtual standstill in Clinton's Africa policy. Two events illustrate this, perhaps involuntary, neglect of Africa during the first Clinton Administration: the total inaction of the US with respect to the genocide in Rwanda in 1994, and the belated tour of Secretary of State Warren Christopher to selected African states in 1996.

---

[35] M. Bridgman, 'Between "Partnership" and Disengagement: Mapping the Contours of US Policy towards Post-Apartheid South Africa' (unpublished D.Phil. dissertation, University of Stellenbosch, 1999), 99.

Accommodationism and Multilateralism Resurgent?

This hesitant accommodationism made way during the Clinton administration's second term for a return of Clinton's original vision of a closer African-US partnership that would build on an assumed continuity between US and African interests in (1) the liberalization of African economies and their integration with the global economy; (2) US-African cooperation in conflict management; and (3) the consolidation of democratic practices in a growing number of fledgling African democracies. Growing bipartisanship in Congress after the implosion of the Gingrich challenge allowed him to push through new appointments of African-Americans such as Assistant Secretary of State Susan Rice. New interest group alliances emerged, such as the bipartisan African Trade and Investment Caucus formed in 1996 to promote 'broader discussion' of US policy towards Africa.[36] Banking on support from such groups, Clinton could risk new initiatives such as the African Growth and Opportunity Act. In these new coalitions, the African-American-led Constituency for Africa, formed in the early 1990s to build support for aid to Africa, joined forces with groups of African-American and other business people who wanted to exploit the opportunities for trade and investment in the emerging markets of Africa. This led to a flurry of commercial, diplomatic, and other initiatives, both in the US and on the African continent, over the period 1996–2000. Some notable episodes in this range of initiatives were:

- An unprecedented series of three visits to Africa by a US Secretary of State within the spate of two and a half years (1998–2000) and numerous visits by other members of Clinton's Cabinet and US Ambassador to the UN, Richard Holbrooke;
- the high-profile US-African ministerial conference in March 1999 (see below);
- the appointment of an Assistant United States Trade Representative for Africa in 1998;
- the decision by the US government to make use of the US Presidency of the UN Security Council in January 2000 to stage an official Security Council 'Month of Africa'; and
- three visits during 1998 and 1999 by Clinton's 'AIDS czar', Sandy Thurman.

Although the heightened attention to Africa cannot be doubted, there is little doubt that this heightened commitment came on the cheap. Given the delicate balance of forces between the White House and the foreign policy establishment in Congress, the administration knew that Congress would approve only a few of the commitments made by the Executive branch. The administration used Jesse Helms quite effectively as a diplomatic tool, both in terms of telling interlocutors that they could not expect too much while Helms was still the Chair of the Senate Foreign Affairs Committee, and also as an excuse for why delivery was not always as forthcoming as were rhetorical initiatives.[37] Also,

---

[36] Bridgman, 'Between "Partnership" and Disengagement', 159.
[37] Simon Barber, 'US plays Jesse Helms as a pawn in the diplomacy game', *Business Day* (26 January 2000).

Africans could indeed be concerned that the high-profile attention accorded in the UN Security Council to AIDS might become a substitute for substantial US—and other major power—involvement in effective peace operations. Nevertheless, there was a strong wish on the part of the Clinton administration to make good the unintended neglect of its first term.

Two features of Clinton's active African policy stood out. The first was the multilateral nature of many of the US's initiatives. US policy towards Africa in the period 1996–2000 was geared towards involving groups of two or more African states, either via existing institutions or by creating new arrangements to facilitate the coordination of policies. To some extent, this reflected an appreciation on the part of US policy makers that there had been a revival of African multilateralism, and that US policy, to be effective, had to take note of this. This implied that the multilateral nature of US policy towards the African continent in the late 1990s could not be attributed to US initiatives alone. African decision-makers themselves were important authors of multilateralism in US African policy.

The second notable feature of African policy during the second Clinton term, however, was not such a novelty. In fact, it represented a basic continuity in US policy, at least throughout the whole Clinton era. In both its first and second terms the Clinton administration had as its goal the opening of African markets for aggressive US trade and investment. This was probably the core aim of US policy in the 1990s. Before 1996, it was conducted mostly by means of bilateral initiatives, including Trade and Investment Framework Agreements with Ghana and with South Africa. During the second half of the 1990s, however, there was a shift towards multilateral initiatives. Pursuing this goal was important ideologically but also in terms of improved US-African trade and investment relations. US officials during the second Clinton term were fond of pointing out that the returns on investment in Africa were consistently higher than in any other part of the developing world.[38]

As we noted above, the theme of 'partnership with Africa' was a leitmotiv in US policy during the Clinton period. Apart from the important, and I would argue overbearing, commercial sense that this slogan had, it also implied the sharing of responsibilities between African states and the US—resulting, thus, in fewer demands on the US. It also flowed from a perceived willingness to engage Africa in a more equal and less patronizing way than before. African reactions to Warren Christopher's suggestion of a standing African Crisis Response Force, and Clinton's experiences during his trip, cautioned the administration against paternalism.

[38] Susan Rice, 'The United States-Africa Partnership: One Year After the President's Visit', Address before the Morehouse College, Andrew Young Center for International Affairs, Atlanta, Georgia (25 March 1999); Susan Rice, 'Briefing on the Secretary of State Madeleine K. Albright's Upcoming Trip to Africa', Washington, DC: Department of State (15 October 1999); W. Schneidman, 'President Clinton's Partnership Initiatives for Africa', *Economic Perspectives*, electronic journal of the USIS, 4/3 (1999) at www.usia.gov/journals/ites/0899/ijee/toc.htm.

The best example of how this partnership was operationalized multilaterally was the Ministerial Meeting of March 1999. Eighty three ministers from 46 African states, representatives from four North African nations, and the heads of eight African regional organizations met with Clinton, eight of his Cabinet, and four agency heads. A 13-page blueprint for multilateral cooperation between the US and African states, via the OAU, was issued at the end of the meeting. The OAU obviously regarded this initiative as important. At its 1999 summit, the Secretariat was instructed to follow up on the blueprint and the practical steps set out in it. The eventual emergence of NEPAD can in part be attributed to the Clinton team's emphasis on 'partnership' as a preferred mode of interaction between Africa and outside actors.

4. What is the US Multilateral Agenda?

Judging by US policy statements about and behaviour towards Africa, the following can be regarded as the main goals pursued by the Clinton and Bush administrations:

- integration of African economies into the global system and thus enhanced trade and other commercial opportunities for US businesses and investors, particularly in identified promising emerging markets on the continent;
- ensuring greater stability on the continent, particularly by means of promoting democratization and the rule of law, improving civil-military relations, enhancing African peacekeeping capacity, and promoting disarmament;
- combating terrorism and the narcotics trade; and
- addressing the HIV/AIDS epidemic in Africa.

Most of them featured in one way or another in multilateral forums such as the Ministerial Meeting of March 1999. A brief overview of the most important multilateral initiatives taken by the Clinton administration follows.

1. *Conflict resolution.* US multilateral activity centred on the African Crisis Response Initiative (ACRI) which is fundamentally a capacity-building programme. Since 1997, 12,000 soldiers from Senegal, Uganda, Malawi, Mali, Ghana, Benin, and Côte d'Ivoire have been trained with the assistance of the EU, France, Belgium, and the UK. The US spent $55 million between 1997 and 1999. Although still far from the standing rapid reaction force foreseen by Christopher—and rejected by African states—ACRI focused attention on the need for training for peacekeeping and inspired African initiatives such as the Operation Blue Crane exercise in southern Africa. By 2000 the US was seeking South African and Nigerian involvement in the ACRI, as 'pivotal states'.[39]

---

[39] See Rothchild, 'The Impact of US Disengagement', 180–3; Council for a Liveable World Education Fund, 1999, 'ACRI: A Peacekeeping Alliance in Africa', a Project on Peacekeeping and the UN, at www.clw.org/pub/clw/un/acri.html.

The US also supported OAU conflict resolution by donating $8 million between 1993 and 1999 to the OAU Conflict Management Centre, with a further $6 million going to the ECOMOG operations. The US also actively supported the multilateral peace processes in the Democratic Republic of Congo—$1 million to the Joint Military Commission in 1999—and in Angola, including helping to institute sanctions against the rebel movement UNITA. It was instrumental in setting up the African Centre for Strategic Studies in Senegal. Forty African states, along with regional organizations, participated in the first workshop on civil-military relations (1999).

The level of US commitment to conflict resolution under Clinton was probably as high as is possible in view of Congressional opposition, but a strong case can be made that it should be increased considerably if the US wants to make any difference in Africa.[40]

African states were not fully in accord with the approach to conflict resolution taken under the Clinton administration. While the US wanted to shift more responsibility to Africa, under the heading of 'partnership', Africa expected the UN Security Council, and specifically the permanent members, to bear the main responsibility for conflict resolution in Africa, and specifically its call for a 'renewal of multilateralism': a coded phrase for, among other things, keeping the international community involved in the conflicts of Africa. Although there has been a growing acceptance among African leaders of Africa's prime responsibility in this regard, there remains some resentment among African leaders that the US is not committing more resources to conflict resolution in Africa (see the Algiers Declaration of the OAU Summit Meeting, July 2000).

2. *Global economic integration.* Broad attempts by the Clinton and subsequent Bush administrations to encourage market liberalization and other features of 'openness' in Africa took on many forms. There was a persistent attempt to get African states to liberalize their capital accounts. Major attempts under the guidance of Secretary of Transportation, Rodney Slater, were made to draw more African states into 'open skies' air-traffic and other 'open-transport' agreements.[41] However, it was on the trade front that the Clinton drive to 'create opportunities', partly for African exporters but predominantly for US commercial interests, has been most prominent.

The African Growth and Opportunity Act (AGOA), passed in May 2000 by Congress, became the lodestar of Clinton's Partnership with Africa drive.[42] It contained a mixture of bilateral and multilateral initiatives, representing an attempt to ensure the further liberalization of African markets and to shift attention away from aid and towards trade. Despite increased levels of trade

---

[40] J. Stremlau, 'Ending Africa's wars', *Foreign Affairs*, 79/4 (2000).

[41] R. Slater, Address by the Secretary for Transportation at the National Summit on Africa, Washington, DC (18 February 2000).

[42] T. Friedman, 'US protectionism is a blight on Africa', *Sunday Independent* (4 March 2000).

between the US and Africa[43] and large-scale African involvement in the WTO, US officials in 1999 still complained that African states were not liberalizing their trade practices fast enough and that they had made fewer commitments in terms of WTO agreements than any other regional group of countries. These officials were especially concerned that few African states had joined agreements on telecommunications, financial services, and information technology.[44] Apart from the pressure applied by the stipulations of the AGOA, the Clinton administration also provided technical assistance to help gear African states better for full WTO participation. WTO-related workshops were held in Uganda, Zimbabwe, and South Africa, and the United States Agency for International Development (USAID) held regional workshops, with OAU and regional organizations involved, in Côte d'Ivoire and Senegal. USAID also launched the African Trade and Investment Program (ATRIP) in 1998 to provide training and technical support for African countries.

Because of the bipartisan support that the AGOA has, George W. Bush has continued to promote it as the core of US commercial interaction with Africa. During a much publicized Forum of African Trade Ministers and US Officials in October 2001, which was followed by the Corporate Council on Africa, US-Africa Business Summit, he announced the launch of a 'support facility' of $200 million for US investment in sub-Saharan Africa and the appropriation of $15 million to launch the Trade for African Development and Enterprise Program 'to help [African] governments that are trying to improve the investment environment and loosen their trade laws'.[45] Both Bush and his Secretary of State, Colin Powell, made it clear that the administration would focus on private investment in and trade with Africa as the primary goals of their African policy, emphasizing that the private sector has a central role and that their interests would be carefully nurtured.[46]

Thus, the pursuit of market liberalization in Africa through conditionalities in the form of IMF structural adjustment programmes—the favoured approach by the two administrations preceding Clinton—has now been transformed into liberalization more through engagement and incentives. However, conditionalities were not totally absent from the Clinton approach, nor is it from the Bush incentives, and the AGOA was bitterly criticized for the high requirements it set before its benefits could accrue to a specific African state.[47] Furthermore, much of the hard bargaining about the opening of African markets and other

[43] In 1998, the US exported 45 per cent more to African states than to all countries of the former USSR, and 16 per cent of US oil comes from Africa. For an overview of US-Africa trade relations, see Stremlau, 'Ending Africa's Wars', 121–3.

[44] See R. M. Whittaker, 'Integrating Africa into the world trading system', *Economic Perspectives*, electronic journal of the USIS, 4/3 (1999), at www.usia.gov/journals/ites/0899/ijee/toc.htm.

[45] Charles Cobb, 'Bush unveils new US initiative to boost investment', allAfrica.com (30 October 2001) at http://allAfrica.com/storis/printable/20011030001.html.

[46] See the text of Powell's remarks at www.state.gov/p/af/rls/rm/2001/index.cfm?docid=5780, and that of Bush at www.state.gov/p/af/rls/rm/2001/index. cfm?docid=5781.

[47] See Friedman, 'US protectionism is a blight on Africa'.

liberalization steps still took place bilaterally between the US and individual countries. Bilateralism had always been an important bargaining ploy between greater Washington—including the World Bank and the IMF—and Africa.

In line with new economic thinking in Africa, as embodied in NEPAD in particular, African leaders, despite earlier resistance, have come to share US insistence on global economic integration. This acceptance was encouraged by steps taken by the Clinton administration to soften the bitter pill of liberalization, such as the following:

- During the period 1998–2000 the US extended additional General System of Preferences (GSP) privileges on 1,783 tariff items for less developed countries (LDCs), and took the lead in the G8 to commit $90 billion to an extended HIPC debt-relief programme. In 1999 Congress, however, agreed to only about a third of the amount of $370 million requested by the administration to finance the initial debt-relief contribution in fiscal year 2000.
- During the Ministerial Meeting of March 1999, the US agreed to support demands of the Group of African, Caribbean, and Pacific countries (ACP) for a continuation of the current WTO Lomé waiver for 'a sufficiently long transitional period' so as to allow non-reciprocal trade preferences to continue in a post-Lomé IV period. The US was also willing to support the granting of permanent WTO observer status to OAU/ECA (Economic Commission for Africa).
- US official development assistance to Africa has declined since 1993, both in real terms and in comparison with other donors. To offset some of this decline in bilateral aid flows, the US in 1998 and 1999 consolidated its support for the African Development Bank; the US is the largest external stock owner in the Bank.

As we saw above, Bush has followed this with some pill sweeteners of his own. So, overall, liberalization of African economies was pursued under Clinton and is continued by Bush by means of 'partnership', that is, incentives, technical assistance, and—qualified—support for broader African trade-regime concerns. Conditionalities-linked pressures are still being applied, however, in the AGOA and the HIPC debt-relief packages.

3. *US cooperation with regional multilateral bodies.* US support for African regional initiatives was also part of the US programme of promoting liberalization of African economies and their integration into the global economy. US focus during the second Clinton term was very much on SADC, COMESA, and on the Horn of Africa (IGAD). Cooperation with regional groupings also served other purposes, though, such as conflict resolution in the Horn of Africa, humanitarian assistance, democratization initiatives, building up infrastructure—especially transportation networks—and AIDS-related activities. Important initiatives during the latter part of the second Clinton term included:

- The Regional Economic Development and Services Office for East and Southern Africa, through which USAID assisted in getting states to reduce tariff levels in COMESA. USAID also started a so-called 'Investor Road Map', presenting African decision makers with blueprints of investor-friendly policies. Uganda received considerable attention as a potential full trading partner.

- The Greater Horn of Africa Initiative was launched in 1994 to coordinate conflict management and humanitarian assistance actions.
- SADC was widely singled out in US policy circles as the 'prospective economic leader of the continent'. US trade with the SADC region between 1994 and 2000 grew faster than with the rest of the continent, and US officials made it clear that they expected much from the creation of a free trade zone in southern Africa. A US Special Representative to SADC has been appointed, and a Trade and Investment Initiative for SADC is being negotiated. In April 1999 the first ever US-SADC Forum was held in Botswana to promote US-SADC cooperation in trade and trade-related legal reform, as well as in monitoring HIV/AIDS, and environmental protection. In September 1999, a follow-up agreement was signed in which the US committed $3 million to these projects, and USAID also launched an Initiative for Southern Africa promoting 'growth-oriented reforms' in the region.

4. *Democratization*. While African states and the US agreed at the March 1999 Ministerial Meeting to 'the mutually reinforcing nature of economic development and democracy', and agreed on the importance of increased accountability and the importance of human rights, including workers' rights, the US is perhaps more enthusiastically pursuing these matters than are some African states.[48] Resentment over US interference in domestic affairs, among others in heavily subsidizing democracy-oriented NGOs, is very much present. Concerned African states did not publicly express themselves on this matter, hoping not to give a hostile Congress the excuse it was looking for to cut economic benefits to African states. Moreover, the tide in Africa in the late 1990s was slowly turning in favour of broader acceptance of liberal democracy and human rights.

Most US activities in the late 1990s in support of democratization were bilateral in nature, but there were examples, such as the Great Lakes Initiative—an attempt to strengthen the rule of law in that troubled region—that were multilateral. Continent-wide US programmes include the setting up of 'Radio Democracy for Africa', based on the example of Radio Liberty and Radio Free Europe, promoting both the acceptance of OECD anti-corruption standards and IMF best-accounting-practices standards. To date, the Bush administration has not taken any specific measures of its own to promote democratization in African states, choosing instead to focus on commercial links. Some of these links are with African states such as Angola, where the absence of full-blown democratization has not restrained companies with which the Vice-President (Halliburton) and the National Security Adviser (Chevron) were associated

---

[48] See US-Africa Ministerial Joint Communiqué (18 March 1999) at www.state.gov/www/regions/africa/communique.html.

from exploring the fabulous return on investment about which Walter Kansteiner (Assistant Secretary for African Affairs) waxes so eloquent.[49]

5. Conclusions

The post-cold war evolution of American policy was characterized by a growing prevalence of the accommodationist approach towards Africa. This was exemplified by attempts to explore continuities between US and African interests, by the gradual replacement of US pressure with forms of inducements to effect change, and by the cultivation of forms of partnership that entail cost-sharing in return for a willingness by the US to engage Africa more on the latter's terms. Despite being marginal to US interests, and despite signs of a growing weariness with Africa on the part of the US public, the Clinton administration kept the continent and its concerns high on the agenda and used various bilateral and multilateral avenues to address these concerns. This was done partly because of the debts incurred by the Clinton team towards the African-American community in two presidential elections, but also because of a genuine interest by Clinton and his advisers in Africa. Bush's appointment of Colin Powell has ensured that Africa for the time being continues to receive policy attention at the highest level. Powell's visit in May 2001 to South Africa, Mali, Kenya, and Uganda refuted the expectations that Bush would turn his back on Africa. During the Secretary of State's trip to Africa, and during the visit by Nigeria's Obasanjo to Washington during that same month, Bush and Powell highlighted the 'energetic' exploitation of the opportunities provided by the AGOA to enhance trade and investment, continued support for regional integration and African peacekeeping efforts, and US funding to tackle the AIDS pandemic, all very much an extension of initiatives taken during the Clinton years but with a clear emphasis on the first, commercial goal.

The accommodationist approach adopted by the Clinton administration and continued by Bush coincides with a growing ideological consensus between a new generation of African technocrats and the US leadership. Despite remaining differences, there was, on the surface at least, broad agreement on a number of fundamental goals and means to achieve them. The Ministerial Meeting of 1999 was a significant multilateral meeting of minds, and early in his term of office George W. Bush has made it clear that he wants to continue with this form of multilateral engagement. The endorsement that Bush's 'war against terrorism' has received from the OAU and from an important moral figure such as Nelson Mandela illustrates the ideological reciprocity between Africa and the US that has emerged during this accommodationist phase of US policy evolution.

---

[49] According to Kansteiner, the return on investment in Africa stands at 31 per cent, the highest in the world. See his comment at the Corporate Council on Africa, US-Africa Business Summit (1 November 2001), at www.state.gov/p/af/rls/rm/index.cfm? docid = 6191.

In general terms, the current generation of African leaders has come to commit itself individually and multilaterally to global system stabilization and maintenance, which has been the US position since the end of colonialism. Gone are the days when African leaders proposed and defended a range of non-capitalist roads of development. Today, the most influential among them—Mbeki, Obasanjo, Bouteflika—seem to have convinced the rest that nothing less than the full integration of Africa into the global economy, on the terms prescribed by neo-liberal economic ideology, is necessary. US hegemony is thus safe and well in Africa, it seems. That this neo-liberal merging of minds between African leaders and US ideologues was initially presided over by a Democrat in the White House is but one of the many ironies of the post-cold war era.

The growing ideological consensus between African leaders and the powers that be in Washington, DC, does not mean that there are no remaining differences of opinion between Africa and the US. Again, if we take the NEPAD as a reflection of the current multilateral consensus in Africa, it is obvious that African leaders expect the US to be a much more active participant in conflict resolution on the African continent, particularly within the UN context. The benefits accruing from the ACRI programme are restricted to a small band of African states, and do not as yet make a significant contribution to the major conflicts in the Democratic Republic of the Congo, Sierra Leone, Liberia, Angola, and Somalia.

In addition, the 2001 OAU Summit made it very clear that Africa is affronted by the fact that sanctions against Libya have not been lifted despite the conclusion of the Lockerbie trial. African leaders are also pleading with the US to use its influence in multilateral financial institutions to speed up the HIPC Initiative and to lower the onerous preconditions that candidates have to comply with before relief is forthcoming. Finally, shrinking levels of US aid to the continent are of growing concern, specifically in view of NEPAD's calculation that sub-Saharan Africa will need an annual mustering of $64 billion in the form of domestic and foreign investment, debt relief, and official aid if the goal of sustained economic growth at 7 per cent a year is to be attained.

Yet these and other items of remaining disagreement are overshadowed by the growing consensus between the African and US leaderships. What about the longer-term consequences of this consensus, specifically as far as promoting 'openness' of African economies is concerned? What is at stake is not that the 'opportunities' referred to in the 'partnership for economic development and opportunity' and AGOA doctrine ultimately represent a wider scope for US commercial concerns in Africa. The promotion of trade opportunities is part of modern-day statecraft, and the Clinton and Bush administrations can hardly be faulted for doing their job well in this regard. However, the consequences of policies that blindly promote trade and capital account openness without consideration of factors other than better opportunities for US trade and investment remain matters of concern.

While few analysts doubt that open economies tend to do better over the longer term than closed ones, there is a growing unease in African policy circles that the short- to medium-term social costs of economic openness have not been considered sufficiently.[50] Although questions of causality are not clear, one cannot but note that the two decades of structural reform towards openness have not improved the lot of the African rural poor, specifically women, and in many instances have exacerbated it. While faster growth has resulted, it is mostly inequality enhancing rather than inequality reducing growth. US official thinking is very thin when it comes to narrowing gaping income gaps in Africa, as is the NEPAD programme.

Initiatives by the US to promote democracy—prominent under Clinton, but less so under Bush—should also be welcomed, but the type of democracy promoted by US in Africa—and elsewhere—can and should be questioned. The socio-economic impact of this form of democracy must be considered, and no attempts to separate economics from politics should be allowed to obscure this. William Robinson makes a good point when he calls this type of democracy 'polyarchy', characterized by 'elite minority rule and social inequalities alongside formal political freedom and elections involving universal suffrage'.[51] The blind pursuit of policies that reflect basic US values, without considering their impact in conditions of growing socio-economic inequality and high levels of poverty, is not what one would expect of a true 'partnership'.

Attempts launched by Clinton, and enthusiastically continued by Bush, to support the commercial activities of US firms in Africa are clearly also a bonus for a continent that receives less than 2 per cent of global direct foreign investment. However, as William Reno has pointed out, African leaders and warlords whose very existence as leaders depends on continuing conflict in their countries or regions, and the fostering of corrupt patron-client relationships, have been known to use commercial contacts with multinational firms, some of them headquartered in the US, to prop up their rule and link them with the global political economy.[52] Far from promoting democracy and openness, the privatization of US policy towards Africa may be contributing to entrenching patterns of power abuse in the weak states of Africa. As is the case with the other concerns mentioned above, the major problem is that the current US accommodationist approach to Africa is sidelining the major political challenges of the continent for the sake of a commercially oriented hegemonic ideology. This may eventually undermine the very goals of stability, transparency and good governance that everyone, even the African leaders themselves, are so enthusiastic about these days. Africa is getting safer for capitalism, yes; but for how long?

---

[50] See J. M. Rao, *Development in the Time of Globalization* (New York: UNDP Poverty Elimination Programme, 1998); D. Rodrik, *The New Global Economy: Making Openness Work* (Washington, DC: Overseas Development Council, 1999).

[51] W. Robinson, *Promoting Polyarchy: Globalization, US Intervention and Hegemony* (Cambridge: Cambridge University Press, 1996), 16.

[52] William Reno, 'Africa's Weak States, Non-State Actors, and the Privatization of Interstate Relations', in Harbeson and Rothchild (eds), *Africa in World Politics*, 286–307.

8

US Approaches to Multilateral Security and Economic Organizations in the Asia-Pacific

RALPH A. COSSA

Since the end of the cold war, the United States has become—in principle if not always in practice—a strong, if somewhat uneven, advocate of multilateral security and economic cooperation in the Asia-Pacific region. This was particularly true during the Clinton administration but appears to continue to hold true for the George W. Bush administration as well, charges of 'American unilateralism' notwithstanding.

Washington has taken an active role in establishing some regional institutions and its concurrence and active participation have been instrumental to the success of many of those proposed by others. This support for multilateral institutions in the Asia-Pacific has one important caveat, however: Washington will not allow such institutions to be seen as substitutes for or as threats to US bilateral efforts and arrangements. This is especially so in the security field, where several key bilateral security alliances—with Japan, South Korea, and Australia—provide the foundation for the US security strategy in the Asia-Pacific region. As this chapter argues, the US does not see bilateral and multilateral efforts as being in tension; rather, they complement one another. East Asian multilateral organizations are seen as useful tools in pursuing US national security objectives.

Nevertheless, unlike Europe, where multilateral institutions like the North Atlantic Treaty Organization (NATO) play a critical role in the US national security calculus, in Asia bilateral relationships still retain pride of place by a large margin. Any multilateral organization that appears to restrain or threaten US bilateral alliance relationships will not be supported by Washington. As the post 11 September 2001 US-led international war on terrorism demonstrates, while Washington is willing, indeed eager, to develop a multilateral approach in combating global terrorism, it has made it clear that this will not deter America from pursuing its objectives unilaterally if necessary.

It is not a coincidence that the two most developed, far-reaching, and thus far—modestly—successful regional multilateral organizations—the ASEAN

Regional Forum (ARF) on the security front and the Asia Pacific Economic Cooperation (APEC) forum linking regional economies—do not carry a 'made in the USA' label.[1] The Association of SouthEast Asian Nations (ASEAN) is credited with founding the security forum that bears its name, while Australia, with significant Japanese input, is generally viewed as being APEC's instigator. We should not be surprised by this: in a region with several major states that frequently do not see eye to eye with one another, organizations promoted by so-called middle powers have the greatest chance of seeing the light of day. Nonetheless, without support from Washington, and acceptance by China and Japan, it is hard to envisage that either the ARF or APEC would have been established. And proponents of these and other successful multilateral organizations have made it clear that they intend to complement and not replace or diminish the current US alliance network which most nations in the region—with the notable exception of the PRC which is ambivalent, and North Korea which is overtly critical—support.

In this chapter, I examine US policy towards and participation in several key multilateral organizations, with the aim of establishing how central these organizations are to the overall development of US policy and the extent to which, and how, they influence or constrain US behaviour. The study begins with a review of US strategic goals and briefly discusses some of the domestic and external factors that have led to the development and implementation of these goals in East Asia. An overview of regional multilateral security organizations is provided, focusing primarily on the ARF, given its all-encompassing nature and relatively advanced—by Asian standards—stage of development. I also touch briefly upon a few other US-instigated multilateral institutions and initiatives to assess how these more narrowly focused approaches also serve American interests. In terms of economic organizations, APEC provides the centrepiece of the discussion. I look at its role both in creating an Asia-Pacific economic community and, more recently, as a vehicle for political cooperation through the institutionalization of the US-instigated 'Leaders' Meetings' which bring many of the region's heads of state and government together annually, ostensibly for economic discussions. Included also is an evaluation of the advantages and disadvantages of these organizations from a US perspective in order better to understand how security and economic multilateralism fits with the largely bilaterally-oriented US national security strategy.

---

[1] Nor do they carry a 'made in China', 'made in Russia', or 'made in Japan' label, although the Japanese deserve a certain amount of credit for inspiring both organizations. For an argument that accords Japan a far greater role than is suggested here in APEC's founding, together with the perspective that the United States was more supportive than has hitherto been acknowledged, see Ellis S. Krauss, 'Japan, the US, and the Emergence of Multilateralism in Asia', *The Pacific Review*, 13/3 (2000).

1. US Strategic Goals and Objectives

Before we look at Washington's approach to multilateral security and economic mechanisms, it is useful briefly to review overall American strategic goals and objectives in both the security and the economic realms as they apply both globally and, more specifically, within the Asia-Pacific.

One generalized treatment of these goals, laid out by the Clinton administration but unlikely to be superseded any time soon by the Bush administration, can be found in the White House's annual statement titled *A National Security Strategy for a New Century*. This document noted that America's national security strategy for the new millennium had three core objectives: to enhance America's security, to bolster its economic prosperity, and to promote democracy and human rights abroad.[2] The Bush administration's National Security Strategy statement of September 2002 is not significantly different—other than including references to fighting international terrorism—just as the Clinton National Security Strategy report did not differ significantly from George H. W. Bush's statement. America's overall national security objectives do not change with every change in administration, even though presentational features sometimes make it appear so.

While the first two core objectives were stated in US-centric terms, they were preceded by an acknowledgement that, in an interconnected world, events halfway around the earth can profoundly affect US safety and prosperity. As President Clinton put it in 1999:

Americans benefit when nations come together to deter aggression and terrorism, to resolve conflicts, to prevent the spread of dangerous weapons, to promote democracy and human rights, to open markets and create financial stability, to raise living standards, to protect the environment, to face challenges that no nation can meet alone.[3]

Despite this US recognition of global interdependence, this chapter focuses on the first two objectives relating more directly to US security and prosperity, with the understanding that both aims are perceived in Washington as helping to create conditions that foster democracy and promote human rights. The presumed link between promoting economic prosperity at home and abroad on the one hand, and the promotion of democracy and human rights on the other, is made particularly clear. For example, one of the primary reasons used to support the granting of normal trade relations[4] with China and to justify Chinese entry into the World Trade Organization (WTO) was that such actions would result in greater economic liberalization and that this, in turn, would help bring about political liberalization. WTO accession would 'help spread

---

[2] William J. Clinton, *A National Security Strategy for a New Century* (Washington, DC: White House, December 1999), iii.   [3] Ibid.
[4] Formerly known as most favoured nation or MFN status.

the message and the tools of freedom to the Chinese people', even as it created jobs and opportunities for Americans.[5] It is an argument that continues to have appeal, even within a Bush administration that has adopted a somewhat firmer stance towards China than the previous Clinton administration.

The 1999 National Security Strategy paper, like its predecessors, also noted that US security and economic interests are inextricably linked, observing that: 'Prosperity at home depends on stability in key regions with which we trade or from which we import critical commodities, such as oil and natural gas. Prosperity also demands our leadership in international development, financial, and trade institutions.'[6]

Washington has traditionally placed considerable stress on the argument that multilateral security and economic institutions are mutually supportive and invariably have a relationship with each other. Without a certain level of cooperation and political stability, economic interactions become strained and progress towards common goals becomes difficult. Likewise, economic cooperation serves political purposes and the process of economic liberalization is seen as an important step towards the larger goals of political security and social well-being. Given this reasoning, it is unsurprising that, as multilateral organizations in the Asia-Pacific have developed since the ending of the cold war, they have been afforded a prominent role in US policy.

This perception of the intertwined nature of economics and security has been reinforced in the US-led international war against terrorism, which has combined an ad hoc military force, drawn primarily from Washington's traditional allies, with a global financial effort aimed at crippling the international terrorist network by cutting off its sources of funding. While the bombing campaign in Afghanistan garnered the bulk of international media attention, the first 'shots' to be fired were financial ones, and it is in this area where multilateral cooperation has been at its strongest.

2. Multilateral Security Cooperation

US security strategy in Asia is centred on its bilateral security alliances and the forward military presence that both underscores US alliance commitments and is made possible by them. As the 1999 National Security Strategy put it, 'our military presence has been essential to maintaining the peace and security that have enabled most nations of the Asia-Pacific region to build thriving economies for the benefit of all'.[7] However, the document also pointed to direct benefits for the United States itself, which continues to maintain about

[5] Clinton, *A National Security Strategy*, 38.
[6] Clinton, *A National Security Strategy*, 21.
[7] Clinton, *A National Security Strategy*, 34.

100,000 military personnel in the region 'to deter aggression and secure our own interests'.

This argument was spelled out even more clearly in the Pentagon's December 1998 *East Asia Strategy Report* (EASR),[8] which asserted that 'maintaining an overseas military presence is a cornerstone of US National Security Strategy and a key element of US military policy of "shape, respond, and prepare"'.[9] This Report, the final one for the 1990s in a series of four Pentagon pronouncements on East Asian military strategy dating back to 1990, and produced by both Republican and Democratic administrations, discussed the 'critical practical and symbolic contributions to regional security' that bilateral alliances and forward deployed forces play, again stressing their deterrence role, but noting also that the alliances and stationing of forces contribute to 'shaping' the security environment.[10]

However, a change of emphasis was evident in the first Clinton administration EASR document, produced in February 1995, which had a section referring to 'The Desirability of Exploring New Multilateral Security Initiatives'.[11] The 1998 EASR devoted less space to multilateral organizations, but nonetheless praised the 'cumulative effect of bilateral, minilateral, and multilateral security relationships as establishing a diverse and flexible framework for promoting common security'. It specifically commended the ARF's efforts.[12] While it made clear that multilateral approaches complemented but were of lesser priority than bilateral alliances, these two reports reflected a significant warming in US attitudes during the Clinton period towards multilateral cooperation and dialogue mechanisms, projecting them as useful vehicles for promoting confidence and greater understanding in ways that supported American national security interests in East Asia.

No Bush administration Asia strategy report has yet been undertaken, but early pronouncements make clear that Washington will, first and foremost, follow an alliance-based strategy in East Asia.[13] This was clearly evident in Secretary of State Colin Powell's January 2001 confirmation hearing before the US Senate. After talking about the central role of NATO in US European security strategy, Secretary Powell noted: 'To our west, a similar bedrock exists. It is our strong relationships with our Asia-Pacific allies and friends, particularly Japan. Weaken those relationships and we weaken ourselves. All else in the Pacific and East Asia flows from those strong relationships.'[14]

Powell's comments, since endorsed by President Bush and other senior administration spokesmen, replay the pronouncements about the 'centrality'

---

[8] Officially titled *The United States Security Strategy for the East Asia-Pacific Region* [*East Asia Strategy Report, EASR*] (Washington, DC: US Department of Defence, 1998).
[9] *EASR* (1998), 9. [10] Ibid. [11] *EASR* (1995), 12–14.
[12] *EASR* (1998), 66.
[13] See Ralph A. Cossa, 'U.S. Asia Policy: Does an Alliance-Based Policy Still Make Sense?' *Pacific Forum, Issues and Insights*, 3-01 (Honolulu: Pacific Forum, September 2001) available on the Pacific Forum web site www.csis.org/pacfor.
[14] See the State Department web site www.state.gov/secretary.

of America's Asian alliance network to US security strategy in Asia contained in the Clinton and former Bush administration's East Asia strategy documents. This does not equate to an abandonment of the multilateral process, however. As will be addressed below, Secretary Powell's participation in and praise for the July 2001 ASEAN Regional Forum meeting in Hanoi and President Bush's personal endorsement of the APEC process—and his participation in the Shanghai Leaders' Meeting during the height of the Afghan bombing campaign—suggest that multilateral mechanisms will not be abandoned by the Bush administration.

The Evolution in US Attitudes Towards Multilateral Security Cooperation

It was not that long ago that most Asia-Pacific policy-makers viewed multilateral security dialogue mechanisms with a great deal of apprehension and suspicion. As recently as 1991, when then Japanese Foreign Minister Nakayama suggested at an ASEAN Post-Ministerial Conference (PMC) gathering that a forum be established to discuss regional security issues, his remarks were not well received by either the ASEAN states or their other dialogue partners.

The US, in particular, was cool to such an idea. More comfortable with the one-on-one approach to security issues in Asia, US officials at the time were reluctant to embrace multilateral approaches, especially for addressing security concerns. This was no doubt prompted, in part, by memories of previous failed efforts, specifically the ill-fated SouthEast Asia Treaty Organization (SEATO), officially disbanded in June 1977.[15] Even the long-standing trilateral ANZUS alliance among Australia, New Zealand, and the US proved impossible to sustain, given New Zealand's 'nuclear allergy' which resulted in US nuclear-powered ships being prohibited from visiting New Zealand ports.[16] Sponsorship of Asian multilateral initiatives by various Soviet leaders during the cold war was widely seen as a thinly-veiled attempt to dilute or eliminate American influence and to contain China, while enhancing Soviet influence in Asia. These added to the earlier cautious approach towards multilateral security initiatives, both in Washington and in Asia.

With the end of the cold war, there has been a decided shift in regional attitudes towards more senior-level, issue-oriented multinational security initiatives. On the US side, the first clear signal of this shift was presented

---

[15] Other less ambitious multinational efforts have been quietly effective in Asia for decades, however. For example, the Five Power Defence Arrangement (FPDA) linking Australia, Malaysia, New Zealand, Singapore, and the United Kingdom was established over 20 years ago and has helped create a level of understanding and military complementarity between its Asian and Western members. It also provides an indirect link, via the Australian common denominator, between the US and the ASEAN members of the FPDA.

[16] As a result, New Zealand remains 'suspended' from what is now a bilateral US-Australia alliance.

during the April 1993 Senate confirmation hearings of Assistant Secretary of State for East Asian and Pacific Affairs Winston Lord, when he identified a commitment to enhanced multilateral security dialogue as one of the Clinton administration's ten priority policy goals for Asia.[17]

This change of attitude in favour of multilateral dialogue was solidified at the 1993 ASEAN PMC meeting when the assembled foreign ministers met informally over lunch to talk about security matters. The group decided that they would reconvene the following year in Bangkok for the inaugural meeting of the precedent-setting ARF, which now brings together annually, for security-oriented discussions, 23 foreign ministers from the Asia-Pacific region, together with European Union representation.[18]

US receptivity to these signals and at the highest levels was underscored when President Clinton, during his July 1993 speech in Seoul before the Korean National Assembly, called for the creation of 'a new Pacific community, built on shared strength, shared prosperity, and a shared commitment to democratic values'. He identified four priorities for the security of this new community: continued American military presence and commitment, stronger efforts to combat the proliferation of weapons of mass destruction, support for democracy and more open societies, and the promotion of new multilateral regional dialogues on the full range of common security challenges.[19]

The Development of the ARF

Out of this policy speech came a new-found American interest in multilateral approaches to security cooperation in East Asia, although one that was plainly built upon the foundation provided by America's enduring bilateral security relationships. This manifested itself most directly and immediately in US support for the ARF, an organization that, at its first meeting in 1994, proclaimed its commitment 'to foster the habit of constructive dialogue and consultation on political and security issues of common interest and concern' in order to make 'significant efforts toward confidence-building and security cooperation in the Asia-Pacific region'.[20]

---

[17] For more information see 'Excerpts from Ambassador Winston Lord's Confirmation Hearings', disseminated in Pacific Forum CSIS, *PacNet* (7 April 1993). *PacNet* is a weekly newsletter published by the Pacific Forum CSIS at www.csis.org/pacfor.

[18] Current membership includes the ten ASEAN states—Brunei, Cambodia, Indonesia, Laos, Malaysia, Myanmar, the Philippines, Singapore, Thailand, and Vietnam—plus Australia, Canada, China, India, Japan, Mongolia, Papua New Guinea, Russia, South Korea, North Korea, New Zealand, the United States, and the European Union. For a helpful analysis of the ARF and its origins, see Michael Leifer, *The ASEAN Regional Forum*, Adelphi Paper 302 (Oxford: Oxford University Press, 1996).

[19] William J. Clinton, 'Remarks by the President in Address to the National Assembly of the Republic of Korea', Seoul, Korea, 10 July 1993, The White House (Office of the Press Secretary).

[20] See the Chairman's Statement issued at the end of the first ASEAN Regional Forum meeting in Bangkok, 25 July 1994. For the complete text and a review of the

There was not much in that inaugural statement to alarm the United States. But there were also clear limitations to the organization as well which served to shape Washington's attitude towards the body. While the ARF seemed well-suited to serving as the consolidating and validating instrument behind many security initiatives proposed by governments and at non-official gatherings in recent years, from a US perspective its contribution to the regional security order was severely constrained. For example, Taiwan has not been permitted to participate and the PRC has insisted that 'internal Chinese affairs' not be on the agenda, effectively blocking ARF discussion of cross-Strait tensions despite their obvious broad regional implications.

There were also few illusions regarding the speed with which the ARF would move. The agreement at the second ARF meeting to 'move at a pace comfortable to all participants' was aimed at tempering the desire of more Western-oriented members for immediate results in favour of the 'evolutionary' approach preferred by the ASEAN states, which see the process as being as important as its eventual substantive products. The Asian preference for 'non-interference in internal affairs' also has placed some important topics essentially off limits. The Chinese have even been reluctant to address conflicting claims in the South China Sea at the ARF, insisting instead on talks with ASEAN or with the other claimants on an individual basis.

Meanwhile, the need for consensus ensured that the ARF would move ahead only as fast as its most cautious members desired. This suggested that the evolution of the ARF from a confidence building measures' 'talk shop' to a true preventive diplomacy mechanism, as called for in its 1995 Concept Paper, would be a long and difficult one, since several members—China and India in particular—have feared that moving ahead with preventive diplomacy could open the door for ARF interference in domestic affairs.[21] The dominant ARF approach has also underscored the utility of 'track two' mechanisms—that is, meetings that include officials who participate only in their private capacities—to tackle the more difficult or more sensitive problems while focusing on mid- to long-range solutions.

Despite—or perhaps because of—the constrained nature of ARF deliberations, the US has seen the body as a generally useful and positive vehicle for promoting American interests—and values—in the Asia-Pacific region: it provides a low-cost way of satisfying some ASEAN security goals while doing preventive maintenance on key relationships within ASEAN, especially with bilateral treaty allies—Thailand and the Philippines—and with Singapore, which quietly houses US military forces. It also aims to promote unobjectionable developments such as confidence building, dialogue, and overall stability.

---

proceedings by the Thai Foreign Ministry's ARF coordinator, see Sarasin Viraphol, 'ASEAN Regional Forum (ARF)', Pacific Forum CSIS, *PacNet* (14 October 1994).

[21] This despite the fact that all working definitions of the process used in Asia stress that preventive diplomacy requires the *voluntary* participation of all involved parties.

The ARF additionally permits Japan to become more actively involved in regional security matters in a manner that is non-threatening to neighbouring countries. This serves US interests in encouraging Japan to be a more assertive security partner and a greater contributor to regional security affairs. It provides, too, a useful vehicle for greater interaction between China and its neighbours while promoting greater transparency regarding Chinese capabilities and intentions.

Ironically, the one development that initially caused the United States some unease turned out to be short-lived. This was the decision to allow India to become a participant in the ARF, one consequence of which has been that New Delhi has blocked serious debate—or condemnation—of South Asian nuclear proliferation. However, as India has expressed outspoken support for US missile defence plans and also signed up early for the struggle against terrorism, India's presence in the ARF in the end proved to be advantageous for Washington.

Various ARF study groups, called Intersessional Support Groups or ISGs, have also provided a vehicle for the US to move the multilateral process along in areas important to Washington, such as maritime cooperation, search and rescue, and confidence building, all of which help promote greater transparency and military-to-military cooperation. Progress is slow, however, and the ARF has been compelled to turn to track-two mechanisms, including the non-governmental Council for Security Cooperation in the Asia Pacific (CSCAP) to tackle more contentious issues such as the development of both a Working Definition and Statement of Principles of Preventive Diplomacy and Guidelines for Maritime Cooperation.[22]

As a result, it is hard to argue that the ARF really enjoyed high priority within the Clinton administration or is likely to gain enthusiastic support during Bush's reign. True, US Secretaries of State, including Colin Powell, have attended most—but not all—of the annual ARF ministerial-level meetings, Powell describing his first such meeting as 'very, very useful' and noting with approval the way that participants linked economic development with a stable security environment.[23] But, even before the war on terrorism, southeast Asia has traditionally been seen as a generally low-priority area and the ARF is seen, rightly, as an ASEAN/south-east Asian initiative, whereas Washington's major security interests lie in north-east Asia.

---

[22] CSCAP links regional security-oriented institutes and, through them, broad-based member committees comprised of academics, security specialists, and former and current foreign ministry and defence officials; all participate in their private capacities. CSCAP committees have been established in Australia, Brunei, Cambodia, Canada, China, the European Union, India, Indonesia, Japan, South and North Korea, Malaysia, Mongolia, New Zealand, Papua New Guinea, the Philippines, Russia, Singapore, Thailand, the United States, and Vietnam. Taiwan scholars participate in their private capacities. For more information see the CSCAP web site www.cscap.org.

[23] Colin Powell, Press Briefing, Hanoi, Vietnam, 26 July 2001, available on State Department web site www.state.gov/secretary.

North-east Asian Institutions

Part of the reason for the US casting of the ARF as a predominantly south-east Asian organization is that there have been other important sub-regional mechanisms for dealing with security issues in north-east Asia. In this part of the region, the proposal for Four-Party Talks among North and South Korea, China, and the US had the specific aim of replacing the 1953 Armistice Agreement with a formal Korean Peninsula Peace Treaty, ending the state of war that has existed on the peninsula for almost five decades. The talks were also intended as a means to develop and pursue confidence-building measures between North and South Korea.

The proposal for Four-Party Talks was a direct response to Pyongyang's persistent demand for direct bilateral negotiations with the United States. The US-South Korean Joint Presidential declaration of April 1996 flatly stated that the current Armistice Agreement should be maintained until it was succeeded by a permanent North-South peace treaty and that 'separate negotiations between the United States and North Korea on peace-related issues cannot be considered'. The Four-Party Talks effectively put the ball back in the North's court by refusing to accept its unilateral declaration regarding the Armistice regime and by definitively ruling out any hope of a separate peace agreement solely with the United States. The aim was to use the multilateral process, in the first instance, as a substitute for bilateral US-DPRK talks that would isolate and alienate South Korea, while at the same time using this four-party process to facilitate eventual bilateral North-South direct dialogue. Now that direct North-South dialogue has commenced, albeit somewhat shakily, the future utility of this forum is questionable, although the South Korean government has repeatedly endorsed its validity and the Bush administration's Korean Policy Review supports a continuation of this effort, if and when the North Koreans assent.

Another multilateral effort of significance to US policy-makers in north-east Asia has been the Korean Peninsula Energy Development Organization (KEDO). KEDO was established by the US, South Korea, and Japan to implement the October 1994 bilateral Agreed Framework between the United States and North Korea. Its two primary objectives have been arranging for fuel oil deliveries and, by negotiating the supply agreement and necessary support contracts, organizing the construction of two nuclear light water reactors (LWRs) to replace the North's graphite nuclear research reactors, which supposedly can be used to develop a nuclear weapons capacity.[24] In March 2002, the Bush administration raised questions about its commitment to the Agreed Framework on the grounds that it had still to verify whether North Korea has lived up to its side of the bargain.

---

[24] *The U.S.-DPRK Agreed Framework: Is it Still Viable? Is it Enough?*, Pacific Forum CSIS Occasional Paper (Honolulu: Pacific Forum, CSIS, April 1999).

Of equal importance to these material and security goals, the establishment of KEDO has provided a creative way for the ROK to be directly and meaningfully involved in the Agreed Framework process. From its inception, the ROK has been a member of KEDO's Executive Board and has had a direct role in KEDO's decision-making process. ROK officials have been involved in all KEDO meetings with the DPRK. As a result, KEDO has become an important vehicle for quiet but direct North-South contact. One of the unsung successes of KEDO is that it has transformed the bilateral US-DPRK Agreed Framework process into a multilateral dialogue in which the Republic of Korea now plays a leading role. This has also helped restore South Korean confidence in the United States, confidence that was shaken during the negotiating process leading up to the Agreed Framework. Thus, KEDO has also bolstered the bilateral alliance between Washington and Seoul at a time of structural change and delicate negotiations.

KEDO has also successfully brought Tokyo into the Agreed Framework process. Japan is one of the three co-founders of KEDO and also sits on the Executive Board. In addition to the most obvious benefit—Japanese financial contributions—this direct participation has helped to ensure a more coordinated approach towards North Korea among the US, South Korea, and Japan.[25] Japan's involvement here has been particularly important since it is not a part of the Four-Party process and would otherwise feel cut out of decision making in areas which directly affect its national security interests. The US, then, has used this multilateral mechanism to help avoid problems in its key bilateral security relationship with Japan as well.

There is also one quasi-official multilateral mechanism that merits brief mention, namely the NorthEast Asia Cooperation Dialogue (NEACD). The NEACD's aim is to enhance mutual understanding, confidence, and cooperation through meaningful but unofficial dialogue among China, Japan, Russia, the United States, and both South and North Korea. While North Korea has thus far refused to participate, the NEACD has regularly brought together senior officials, along with a small group of academics, from the other five countries for dialogue on political, security, and economic issues of concern to all parties.[26] The NEACD has enjoyed strong US government backing since its inception. As noted earlier, at his confirmation hearings to become President Clinton's first Assistant Secretary of State for East Asia, Winston Lord laid out a US commitment to multilateral dialogue. The NEACD was a direct manifestation of this US commitment, Secretary Lord becoming intimately involved in

---

[25] This has now been formalized within the Trilateral Coordination and Oversight Group (TCOG) which periodically meets to coordinate policy and has, as a significant side benefit, helped to bring the ROK and Japan closer together.

[26] For background information, see Susan Shirk and Christopher Twomey, 'Beginning Security Cooperation in NorthEast Asia: A Report on the First Meeting of the Institute of Global Conflict and Cooperation's NorthEast Asian Cooperation Dialogue', *PacNet* (5 November 1993), 33.

its formation and in obtaining US government funding for this effort.[27] This programme continues to enjoy full support from Washington despite the change in administrations, with recent meetings being well attended by both State and Defence Department representatives.

The NEACD serves several useful purposes for the US, even at its quasi-official level. Most importantly, it has acted as a convenient way for facilitating Japanese and Russian involvement in the broader north-east Asia security process, while also providing a convenient excuse or justification for keeping both out of the more sensitive and narrowly focused Four-Party Talks. It has also offered the US, together with Japan and the ROK, an opportunity to explain and defend their alliance relationships to ever-suspicious Russian and Chinese officials.

The successful establishment and generally productive, if relatively non-constraining, results to date of the ASEAN Regional Forum and other security dialogue mechanisms provide evidence of both US and broader regional acceptance of, and official governmental support for, multilateral security dialogue. As noted at the onset, however, American policy-makers continually stress that US support for increased regionalism is based on the premise that such multilateral efforts complement or build upon, and are not seen as a substitute for, enduring bilateral relationships. That message has been even more loudly proclaimed in the George W. Bush era; witness Secretary Powell's earlier-cited comment that 'all else in the Pacific and East Asia flows from those strong [bilateral alliance] relationships'. In short, multilateral security regimes will grow out of the US bilateral alliance structure; it is not an 'either-or' proposition from a US perspective. Bilateral alliances remain at the base of a network of overlapping and interlocking institutions that contribute to regional stability in Asia.

Some US policy-makers, especially within the Defense Department, remain concerned that a few regional proponents of multilateral security organizations see these as alternatives to the American bilateral alliance structure. Chinese officials in particular have questioned the relevance of these US bilateral alliances— 'leftover vestiges of the cold war'—and claim multilateralism as the new security paradigm. From a US perspective, however, bilateralism and multilateralism are not mutually exclusive but mutually supportive. Washington believes, that without solid bilateral relationships, few states would have the confidence to deal with one another in the broader context. This view is shared by all US allies in the region and by most other states that also see the US bilateral alliance structure as providing the foundation for regional security. Moreover, some problems

---

[27] The ROK, Japan, and Russia have also proposed the creation of a more formal, governmental six-party dialogue mechanism. The US has been generally, but not enthusiastically, supportive of these initiatives, the Chinese much less so. China has claimed that it is 'premature' to hold official six-party talks and cites North Korean reluctance as a reason. One also suspects a lack of eagerness on China's part to involve Japan more intimately in regional security affairs. For its part, North Korea has rejected all six-party proposals—governmental or non-governmental—out of hand.

can best, perhaps only, be solved bilaterally. It was with this one caveat firmly in mind and clearly articulated that the US became engaged in multilateral security dialogue in earnest with the advent of the ARF. But there is no question that, if forced to choose between its bilateral and multilateral relationships, multilateralism would finish last.

Benefits of Multilateral Security Cooperation

This is not to imply that support for such multilateral security organizations is low in the United States, however. From a US perspective, emerging multilateral security mechanisms such as the ARF can be useful vehicles for promoting long-term peace and stability. They are seen as most valuable when they serve as confidence-building measures aimed at avoiding, rather than reacting to, crises or aggression. In time, regional multilateral security organizations also might be capable of dealing with somewhat less politically sensitive non-traditional security concerns such as disaster relief, coordination of refugee problems, or pollution and other environmental issues, all matters that have been recognized in Washington's broader post-cold war definition of security. In this regard, the decision by the ARF to establish a study group to discuss multinational cooperation in the area of search and rescue seems particularly noteworthy. ARF study groups have also provided a vehicle for uniformed military participation in this track-one effort in a positive, non-threatening context, again a move that is supportive of US goals to enhance the transparency of the military in states such as China. Even before 11 September 2001, another ARF study group had been looking at transnational crime issues; and this group can be expected to look more deeply into terrorism issues as well, a topic now at the top of the Bush administration's agenda. The various CSCAP Working Groups have also been examining the phenomenon of transnational terrorism, including the impact of the war on terrorism on regional stability.

American participation in East Asian multilateral security organizations such as the ARF has also served to reassure regional states of its continued commitment to regional security in the post-cold war era. There was considerable concern expressed in East Asia in the early 1990s, especially after the troop withdrawal from the Philippines—at the request of the Philippine government—that the US was going to abandon the Asia-Pacific. Full participation in the ARF was aimed at combating this concern. And even if multilateral efforts do not always directly serve US needs or interests, such organizations impose few, if any, constraints on the United States. Broad-based institutionalized multilateral forums like the ARF are useful vehicles for discussing potential problems, but seem ill-equipped—and not very eager—when it comes to resolving crises once they have occurred. In the event of military hostilities or a clear threat to US national security interests in Asia, the US probably would prefer, and is more likely, to act in concert with its existing allies or through an ad hoc grouping of like-minded states similar to the current coalition assembled to deal with the war in Afghanistan.

From time to time there have been suggestions about the need for a broader NATO-like multilateral security arrangement in the Asia-Pacific region. As the failed SEATO/CENTO attempts demonstrated, this proved impossible to achieve, even during the cold war. The prospect for such a formal multilateral military alliance evolving in a time of relative peace thus seems remote. However, multilateral military cooperation *per se* is not unthinkable in Asia; in fact, it is alive and well and spreading. For example, military-to-military cooperation, largely spearheaded by the US Pacific Command (USPACOM), has led the regular US bilateral exercises often to become multilateralized, both to create habits of broader cooperation and for cost reasons through more efficient use of military personnel and resources. For example, COBRA GOLD 2001, the 20th iteration of a US-Thai military exercise, included participation for the first time by Singaporean forces. Nine other nations—including US allies Australia, Japan, South Korea, and the Philippines—sent observers; China was also invited as an observer but declined. Similarly, CARAT 2000 involved sequential US exercises with naval forces from the Philippines, Malaysia, Indonesia, Brunei, and Thailand, while the US Pacific Fleet's annual RIMPAC exercise has for years brought allied and other friendly navies together for combined training off Hawaii.

One thing many of these multilateral military training exercises have in common is participation by America's various Asia-Pacific allies. Thailand, for one, has been increasingly receptive to broader cooperative efforts; and the Philippines has also shown more enthusiasm following the passage in 1999 of a new Visiting Forces Agreement that paved the way for renewed exercise activity with US forces. Japanese military forces have also been observers at such exercises, despite Tokyo's self-imposed collective defence prohibition, and have routinely participated in bilateral training with the US Navy coincident with RIMPAC, in effect providing the Japanese Maritime Self Defence Force with exposure to the operations of other navies beside the US.

No attempt has been made to try to further institutionalize multilateral military cooperation among the US, Japan, ROK, and Australia, much less with America's two south-east Asian allies Thailand and the Philippines, and none is likely to be attempted. But the degree of inter-operability established by frequent contact between the US and its Asia-Pacific allies, both bilaterally and in broader settings, can allow them to form the core of cooperative 'coalitions of the willing' in the event of future crises, whether they be caused by military confrontations or natural disasters. Australia's own multilateral cooperative effort with New Zealand, Singapore, Malaysia, and the UK—the Five Power Defence Arrangement—also serves to provide an informal linkage between American forces and those of several other south-east Asia states, as do concerted efforts by several ASEAN states—Singapore in particular—to increase military cooperation with the United States. For example, Singapore has provided facilities for a modest US logistics presence in that city-state since the time of the US base closures in the Philippines and has recently developed a new deep-water pier to facilitate visits by American aircraft carriers.

In short, America's Asia-Pacific bilateral alliances and the extended military-to-military contacts both with US military forces directly and with the forces of America's allies have created an enhanced capability as well as a growing inclination to cooperate in the military arena, especially for operations other than war. While it is doubtful that this expanded cooperation will result in a more formalized military structure in the Asia-Pacific region similar to the enlarged NATO in Europe, it has increased habits of cooperation and the ability of those nations so inclined to form coalitions of the willing as they individually and collectively deem appropriate in the future. It was no coincidence that it was America's bilateral allies in Asia who were quick in offering military support to the war on terrorism's *ad hoc* coalition.

3. Asia-Pacific Multilateral Economic Cooperation

Multilateral economic cooperation and the promotion of open markets and free trade have long been priority objectives for Washington, regardless of administration. This was clear when the first Bush administration actively promoted APEC at its creation in 1989 and remains true today: witness George W. Bush's decision to go to the October 2001 APEC gathering despite the ongoing war against terrorism. As Democratic and Republican administrations have made clear, a prosperous and open Asia-Pacific is seen as crucial to the economic health of the United States. Statements by the Bush administration have underscored the enduring nature of the US economic objectives in Asia, as outlined in the 1999 National Security Strategy, including:

- continued recovery from the post 1997 East Asian financial crisis;
- further progress within APEC towards liberalizing trade and investment; and
- increased access for US exports to Asian countries, through market-opening measures and new and non-discriminatory opportunities for US businesses.[28]

The Bush administration has pursued all these objectives, and has built upon Clinton administration agreements, for example, finally helping to bring about Chinese and Taiwanese accession into the WTO. Support for multilateral efforts notwithstanding, it must also be acknowledged that the most important factor in ensuring Asia's economic rebound in the eyes of most US economic—and political/security—officials is not APEC's efforts but Japan's economic recovery. Hence the US focus is on the need for continued Japanese

---

[28] Clinton, *A National Security Strategy*, 37.

economic reforms aimed at stimulating the Japanese economy as an engine of growth in Asia.[29] This has been a constant message from Democratic and Republican administrations, as well as a bipartisan opinion shared by most members of the US Congress.

APEC's Origins

The Asia Pacific Economic Cooperation (APEC) grouping of regional economies was created in the waning days of the cold war with the tacit approval of the first Bush administration, which saw greater economic cooperation in the region as a useful, low-cost way to promote free markets and democracy.[30] There was also a concern, as the 'Asian economic miracle' was hitting high gear, that US influence was declining over time as faster Asian growth decreased the relative importance of the US in Asia. As one APEC specialist has observed:

> As a consequence [US policy-makers believed] it was important to try to infuse our economic processes and values during the window of opportunity that we had. APEC seemed to be one way of ensuring that the US had an influence over the future direction of the Asian economies as opposed to a possible arrangement in which Asian countries were by themselves and primarily influenced by Japan.[31]

APEC started out as an informal dialogue group, growing from an original 12 members to 15 in 1991—when China, Hong Kong and Chinese Taipei joined as member economies—to a strength of 21 at the beginning of the twenty-first century.[32] Institutionalization began in February 1993, when the APEC Secretariat was established in Singapore, shortly after President Clinton's inauguration. The Clinton administration, with its emphasis on 'it's the economy, stupid' seized the initiative as a way of internationalizing its domestic economic recovery goals. The Bush administration likewise saw the value of APEC as a vehicle 'to achieve free and open trade and investment in the Asia-Pacific region' and committed itself to APEC's revitalization through its active role in promulgating the 2001 APEC Shanghai Accord.[33]

---

[29] For an account of how Japan's economic malaise affects broader Asian economic health, see the January 2002 issue of *The Oriental Economist*.

[30] APEC has to be referred to as a 'gathering of economies' rather than a gathering of states due to the presence in its ranks of Hong Kong and Taiwan, which members have agreed remain part of 'one China'. Taiwan's head of state is specifically not invited to attend the annual Leaders' Meetings, even though Hong Kong's chief executive regularly attends.

[31] Interview with Dr Charles Morrison, President of the East-West Center, Honolulu, and former head of the Center's APEC Study Group, 23 August 1998.

[32] Founding members were Australia, Brunei, Canada, Indonesia, Japan, the Republic of Korea, Malaysia, New Zealand, the Philippines, Singapore, Thailand, and the United States. Additional members include China, Hong Kong, Taiwan (Chinese Taipei) plus Mexico and Papua New Guinea (1993), Chile (1994), Peru, Russia, and Vietnam (1997).

[33] White House, 'Fact Sheet on APEC's Free Trade Goals (The Shanghai Accord: US Leadership in Achieving APEC's Free Trade Goals)', 21 October 2001, available on the White House web site www.whitehouse.gov/news/releases/2001/10/print/20011023-10html.

While aimed first and foremost at managing the effects of growing economic interdependence, APEC has had important political and security consequences as well. This has been especially true since the 1993 Seattle meeting when President Clinton invited the APEC heads of state and government to the first of what have now become regular annual Leaders' Meetings designed to elevate the importance of this economic gathering. The Leaders' Meetings have become an important vehicle for fostering political relations in addition to raising the level of economic dialogue and putting pressure on the region's leaders, and especially the host state, to move the process forward.

APEC's Evolution and Progress

The ambitious agenda at the 1993 Seattle meeting was aimed at capitalizing on the so-called 'Asian miracle' and ensuring that such states committed themselves to the pursuit of free markets and economic liberalization.[34] According to Charles Morrison, the Clinton administration, and especially APEC 'eminent person' Fred Bergsten, believed that APEC could be a catalyst for world economic liberalization because the Europeans 'would be forced to come along or be left out'.[35] The Clinton administration thus hoped to use the high-profile APEC gathering to pressure the existing GATT and emerging WTO negotiations to move forward on trade liberalization.

Largely through the efforts of APEC's Eminent Persons Group, APEC got off to a good start. The Seattle free trade objectives were institutionalized in the agreement at the 1994 meeting in Bogor, Indonesia, which set a fixed target of 2020 for developing states and 2010 for industrialized states to create free and open trade among the member economies. How to implement the Bogor Declaration was divisive, however, and at the 1995 Osaka meeting the US, Canada, and Australia lost the battle to make trade liberalization binding. Members agreed only to establish a set of common principles that all APEC member economies would adhere to in achieving Bogor's goals. At the 1996 meeting in Subic Bay, the Philippines, members agreed to the Manila Action Plan for APEC (MAPA) which required individual member economies to submit details on market liberalization measures that they would voluntarily undertake. The 1997 Vancouver meeting saw only limited progress in even these voluntary measures to implement the original 1994 goals.

If APEC was already having difficulty in maintaining momentum prior to the Asian financial crisis, that event further exacerbated the problem. The failure of the leaders or ministers at the 1998 Malaysia meeting adequately to address the financial crisis, much less promote remedial measures, raised serious questions about APEC's future relevance—questions which APEC's

[34] For a more detailed review of APEC, including an accounting of the meetings referenced below, visit the APEC Secretariat's web site www.apecsec.org.sg. See also Chapter 5 in this volume on the GATT and WTO for additional information on US economic policies in the Asia-Pacific. [35] Interview with Morrison.

critics contend remain unanswered. As political economist Jane Skanderup noted just prior to the 1998 meeting, 'if the financial crisis can't galvanize regional political will to jointly address problems that hit APEC shores especially hard, then APEC will continue to squander the opportunity to develop a real voice for Asia-Pacific interests in the global community'.[36] Her conclusion was that APEC had 'lost its inspiration, and is in serious danger of becoming an irrelevant player in international economic dynamics . . . and useless to members to boot'.[37]

There are also potentially difficult matters of adjustment between APEC and ASEAN's proposed Free Trade Area (AFTA). The United States, among other governments, has additionally been wary of Malaysian Prime Minister Mahathir's calls for an exclusionary East Asia Economic Caucus (EAEC) which keeps reappearing in various forms. Its latest iteration, the ASEAN Plus Three—Japan, China, and South Korea—body, appears considerably less objectionable since it does not appear aimed at creating an exclusionary block and has put the creation of an AFTA on its agenda. As a result, it has received general support from the Bush administration, and other APEC members, such as Australia and New Zealand, have sought to join this gathering.

At the end of the twentieth century US officials were still professing support for APEC as an important body for encouraging East Asian states to open their markets and as a means to underline Washington's own strong commitment to economic cooperation with the states of the region. However, enthusiasm for APEC had clearly waned by the closing days of the Clinton administration as it became progressively harder to move the liberalization process along, especially after the economic downturn in East Asia. Nonetheless, the Bush administration, while not as enthusiastic about APEC as Clinton had been at the start of his first term, seems intent on breathing new life into the organization. It is promoting a trade policy as part of the Shanghai Accord 'that commits APEC economies to pursue trade policies on services, intellectual property, and tariffs that will encourage development of the New Economy'.[38] The White House APEC 'Fact Sheet' also highlights Washington's commitment to 'capacity building', that is, 'to reaching out to developing countries to ensure that they have the capacity to benefit from open markets'.[39] In short, the Bush administration has sent clear signals that it is intent not only on supporting but also on broadening the APEC vision.

Benefits of Multilateral Economic Cooperation

As is the case with multilateral security dialogue mechanisms, and despite obvious limitations, Washington still sees some utility in economic gatherings

---

[36] Jane Skanderup, 'The 1998 Asia Pacific Economic Cooperation Meeting: Opportunity for Relevance?' *PacNet* (6 November 1998).
[37] Skanderup, 'The 1998 Asia Pacific Economic Cooperation Meeting'.
[38] White House, 'Fact Sheet on APEC's Free Trade Goals'.   [39] Ibid.

such as APEC as useful tools in advancing its economic policy objectives. It is unlikely that the US would ever give up using direct bilateral approaches or pressure, including the threat of unilateral sanctions, to help achieve these objectives, but there is a recognition that couching the call for economic reforms in multilateral terms takes some of the sting out of the demand and perhaps lessens the degree to which the message of opening markets is identified solely with the United States.[40]

As APEC's annual meeting has become more high-profile, it also puts increased pressure on each year's host to deliver at least some of the goods, again relieving the US of certain of the expected leadership obligations. Some APEC hosts have risen to this challenge better than others, but the Leaders' Meeting has made a demonstration of progress a matter of national pride to the host country, providing some impetus to policy development.

APEC's future agenda also remains important to the US. Most importantly, Washington wants the 2010/2020 objectives for free and open trade—the Bogor Declaration—to be met, and APEC remains one—and a relatively less abrasive—means of ensuring that this process moves forward. This, in and of itself, warrants continued US participation. The APEC 2000 (Brunei) Priorities, which called for a focus on the development of human resources and of small and medium enterprises, also meshed nicely with US economic and political objectives for the region,[41] as did the 2001 Shanghai Accord.

In addition, after an admittedly slow start, APEC has been trying to deal with the aftermath of the Asian financial crisis and to promote continued recovery. The organization has called for greater transparency and predictability in corporate and public sector governance, enhanced competition to improve efficiency, and improved capacity of regulators to design and implement policies for sustainable growth: all measures that are being promoted independently by the US, and by the IMF.[42]

Many of the process-oriented benefits outlined as pertaining to multilateral security cooperation are similarly realized through cooperation in the economic sphere. For instance, as noted earlier with respect to security organizations, multilateral settings can facilitate bilateral, or sub-regional, dialogue among states and their official or unofficial representatives who, for a variety of reasons, may be unable or ill-prepared to make arrangements directly with one another.

APEC's Evolving Political/Security Role

This facilitation of dialogue on divisive political issues has been made plain at several of the APEC meetings since 1993 that have brought together heads of

---

[40] This is only partially true, however. Since the US is powerful within some multilateral organizations, the IMF in particular, in many instances the US is the assumed initiator of a particular policy even when a multilateral organization is in the lead. See Chapter 4 in this volume.   [41] 'Brunei Priorities in 2000', www.apecsec.org.sg.
[42] 'Financial Recovery', www.apecsec.org.sg.

state or government. Of course, APEC is not a security forum per se, and is not likely to become one in the near future, at least not explicitly, since most if not all members would regard this as unhelpful. The presence of Taiwan in the organization would also ensure a Chinese veto of any overt moves in this direction. Nonetheless, APEC annual meetings have added a significant, if implicit, political-security dimension to the organization. Even if security matters are not on the official agenda, leaders frequently discuss such issues in the corridors, and their mere meeting has implications for political relations, as do the side meetings between many of the heads of state or government. Even not attending has a political cost, as the US learned the hard way. In 1995, for example, President Clinton felt compelled to skip the Osaka APEC Leaders' Meeting due to a budget stand-off with the Republican-led US Congress. This came on the heels of the US Defense Secretary William Perry's comment indicating that America wanted to turn APEC into some type of security arrangement, a comment which had already offended most, if not all, the other APEC members, while further feeding the suspicions of those who believed from the outset that American support for APEC had hidden motives.

Making matters worse, Secretary of State Warren Christopher, already in Japan, cut short his visit to rush home to monitor the Bosnian peace talks, rekindling memories of his earlier absence from the first ARF gathering in Bangkok in 1994. The Japanese hosts and most of the assembled leaders generously expressed 'understanding' about President Clinton's last-minute regrets. But damage to US credibility was done. With Clinton nowhere in sight—Vice-President Gore did attend—Chinese President Jiang Zemin grabbed the spotlight, underscoring the Chinese message that America might not always be around but China was a permanent fixture in the Asian landscape.[43]

The political and even strategic significance of the Leaders' Meetings was most dramatically underscored in Auckland in 1999, a gathering that was significant more for what happened outside the APEC venue than inside the meeting. Security issues dominated the side discussions and the talk in the corridors. Not the least of these was the growing, and well-founded, concern over the deteriorating security situation in East Timor. The Auckland meeting was well-timed in that it provided an opportunity for regional leaders, including President Clinton and Australian Prime Minister Howard, to work out arrangements for the Australian-led multinational peacekeeping mission (INTERFET) that was subsequently sent to East Timor. Obtaining on-the-spot Chinese approval of this effort, made possible by Indonesia's reluctant acceptance of the intervention, helped assure UN Security Council authorization of the

---

[43] Clinton's subsequent visit to Korea and Japan the following spring helped to restore US credibility, but Clinton's snub of the Malaysia APEC meeting in 1998 during the heart of the financial crisis was once again seen as a diplomatic setback, one made worse by Vice-President Gore's uninhibited attack on Malaysia's human rights and domestic political behaviour.

subsequent UN operation, the United Nations Transitional Authority in East Timor (UNTAET).[44]

In similar fashion, APEC 2001 provided an important vehicle for President Bush to explain Washington's war on terrorism to his Asian colleagues and to garner their support. In addition to the aforementioned Shanghai Accord and the usual annual APEC Leaders' Meeting, the assembled leaders also issued an APEC Leaders' Statement on Counter-Terrorism—the first political document to be issued in APEC's 13-year history—which unequivocally condemned the September 11 attack and deemed it 'imperative to strengthen international cooperation at all levels in combating terrorism in a comprehensive manner'.[45] This was considered a real victory for President Bush and no doubt helped to increase APEC's—or at least the Leaders' Meeting's—relevance in his eyes.

The APEC Shanghai meeting also provided President Bush with his first opportunity to meet directly with Chinese President Jiang Zemin, which helped to end the downward slide in Sino-US relations under way since Bush's inauguration, especially after the collision between a US reconnaissance plane and a Chinese jet fighter over the South China Sea in April 2001. The two leaders were able to put the relationship back on track, aided by China's willingness to cooperate in the battle against terrorism. APEC 2001 also provided President Bush with another opportunity to build upon Washington's growing post-cold war cooperation with Russia[46] and to meet Malaysian President Mahathir and Indonesian President Megawati, leaders of the two south-east Asian nations with predominantly Muslim populations. This allowed him to emphasize that the war on terrorism was not aimed at Islam.

4. Conclusion

American policy-makers generally believe that Asia-Pacific multilateral organizations are useful vehicles both for promoting greater political and economic cooperation and for enhancing regional security. Efforts that build upon and seek to complement, and not to replace, existing bilateral relationships that already exist in Asia are of particular value from a US perspective. Any effort that is perceived to undermine US bilateral dealings, and especially those that seek to diminish or replace America's key bilateral security alliances, are sure

[44] Neither ASEAN nor the ARF was a major player in the East Timor crisis, demonstrating their limited utility as crisis-response mechanisms. For an analysis of the ASEAN role, see Alan Dupont, 'ASEAN's Response to the East Timor Crisis', *Australian Journal of International Affairs*, 54/2 (2000).
[45] APEC Leaders' Statement on Counter-Terrorism, at http://tyr.apecsec.org.sg/virtualib/econlead/AELM_Counter_Terrorism.html.
[46] For more on this emerging relationship, see Ralph A. Cossa, 'Toward a Post Post-Cold War World', *PacNet* (12 October 2001).

to be rejected by Washington both today and by any future administration. This fact places constraints on the future agenda of such organizations, as well as signalling clearly US policy priorities.

While multilateral organizations hold many promises for Asia, it is import-ant to understand their limits as well as the opportunities they present. In the security arena, a comprehensive security arrangement or NATO-type alliance aimed at containing or responding to a specified threat simply does not apply to a post-cold war Asia. Rather, emerging security mechanisms should be viewed more as confidence-building measures aimed at avoiding or dampen-ing the possibilities of, rather than reacting to, crises or aggression. Economic gatherings are also seen as important confidence-building mechanisms that have positive security implications while also supporting broader US economic goals of free trade and more open markets.

There is much in US behaviour and articulation of its interests to suggest that this limited role for region-wide multilateral security and economic organizations meshes well with its preferences. While these organizations maintain their current consensus-based form and undemanding agenda, the US can be expected to remain an active and reasonably supportive participant for reasons already outlined. Undoubtedly and comparatively, for some time to come Washington will remain more active and involved in north-east Asia, where it has long been dominant in shaping the multilateral negotiations that involve its two most significant bilateral allies in the region.

In sum, the US sees multilateral bodies in the Asia-Pacific as essentially sup-plementary rather than primary vehicles for achieving US national security and foreign policy objectives in the region. Washington's policies, though influenced by the existence of the organizations, are not fundamentally constrained by them, whereas the organizations themselves are shaped by US preferences.

9

Trouble in Pax Atlantica? The United States, Europe, and the Future of Multilateralism

DAVID G. HAGLUND

If there existed one defining feature of America's involvement with the world during the second half of the twentieth century, it was the strong preference given to what George Kennan once labelled 'particularistic' variants of internationalism over 'universalistic' ones.[1] Equally marked has been the geographical focus of this particularism, the North Atlantic region broadly conceived so as to embrace not only North America above the Rio Grande but also Western Europe and such portions of southern Europe as those countries in the Mediterranean basin.

This region had been the cynosure of American grand strategy for half a century, even if it had not been the exclusive concern of that strategy. In large measure, then, it was the security commitments made to allies in the North Atlantic community, as well as the relationships it has forged with important Western European states, that constituted the standard of America's post-1945 internationalism and provided a litmus test of the country's orientation towards that institution known as 'multilateralism'. The latter had been, and possibly still remains, very much a function of the 'Pax Atlantica'.[2]

In recent years, many have concluded that America has been growing less committed to multilateralism as a method of statecraft.[3] Unless the next few decades of American foreign policy are to represent a fundamental departure from the pattern of the past five decades, and they may, America's

---

[1] John Lewis Gaddis, *Strategies of Containment: A Critical Appraisal of Postwar American National Security Policy* (New York: Oxford University Press, 1982), 29. See also Robert W. Tucker, 'The Triumph of Wilsonianism?', *World Policy Journal*, 10 (Winter 1993/94). On the ups and downs—mainly the latter—of America's universalistic internationalism, see Edward C. Luck, *Mixed Messages: American Politics and International Organization, 1919–1999* (Washington, DC: Brookings Institution Press, 1999).

[2] Michael Lind, 'Pax Atlantica: The Case for Euramerica', *World Policy Journal*, 13 (Spring 1996).

[3] The interpretative trend appears to have started in the immediate aftermath of the Reagan administration, when scholars found it easy to discern a flagging American

internationalism will continue to be heavily dependent upon the quality of the security and political bonds—and to a lesser extent, the economic ones—between it and its European allies. Therefore, attention to the trends in transatlantic relations might repay dividends for a broader, global, inquiry into America as a multilateral actor.

Accordingly, in what follows I am going to attempt to account for what can only be considered a souring of the transatlantic mood over the past few years—a process that seemed to have been accelerating up until the attacks on America of 11 September 2001.[4] In particular, I will try to determine to what, if any, extent this change in mood might be said to suggest a transformation of basal significance, as opposed, say, to merely reflecting the normal bickering that has always characterized transatlantic security relationships—a state of affairs whimsically captured many years ago by one American defence policy-maker's response to being told the alliance was in disarray: 'When has NATO ever been in array?'[5] But, to know how to interpret the contemporary transatlantic mood, we need to pose a pair of questions. How should we understand American behaviour towards multilateral security organizations in the transatlantic arena—primarily NATO and also, to an extent, the EU? And what has been and likely will be the impact of American behaviour on these multilateral organizations?

These two questions will carry much of the interpretative burden of the remainder of this chapter. However, before I inquire into the sources and implications of American involvement in transatlantic multilateral organizations, something should be said about the foreign policy dispensation that so often figures as the logical antithesis of multilateralism, namely, 'isolationism'. While many experts claim its recurrence would be as impossible to conceive

commitment to multilateralism; more recently, and notwithstanding the initial predisposition of the Clinton administration towards 'assertive multilateralism', the trend has accelerated. See Margaret P. Karns and Karen A. Mingst, 'The United States and Multilateral Institutions: A Framework for Analysis', in Margaret P. Karns and Karen A. Mingst (eds), *The United States and Multilateral Institutions: Patterns of Changing Instrumentality and Influence* (Boston: Unwin, Hyman, 1990); David Rieff, 'Whose Internationalism, Whose Isolationism?', *World Policy Journal*, 13 (Summer 1996); and Stewart Patrick, 'America's Retreat from Multilateral Engagement', *Current History*, 99 (December 2000).

[4] Martin Walker, 'What Europeans Think of America', *World Policy Journal*, 17 (Summer 2000); Michael Getler, 'Growing Split with Allies Feeds Anti-Americanism', *International Herald Tribune* (25 January 2001). The list of items said to be contributing to the allies' anti-Americanism was a long and expanding one in the months leading up to the attacks on New York and Washington, and included: American gun-control and penal practices, global warming, the International Criminal Court, payment of United Nations dues, arms control treaties, genetically modified crops, and national missile defence. William Pfaff, 'The U.S. Misreads the Causes of Anti-Americanism', *International Herald Tribune* (31 March–1 April 2001).

[5] Quoted in François Heisbourg, 'Europe/États-Unis: le couplage stratégique menacé', *Politique étrangère*, 52 (Spring 1987). Although Heisbourg did not name the American official, it is believed the remark was made by Harold Brown, Secretary of Defence during the Carter administration.

of as it would be absurd to advocate, the spectre nevertheless has a way of intruding upon most of their discussions about the durability of America's commitment to its allies, especially the Europeans. At the very least, arriving at a sensible understanding of the historical and conceptual significance of isolationism should also enable us better to comprehend what might be implied by its mooted antithesis, multilateralism. But it is not just its value as a potential definition *a contrario* that commends isolationism to our attention; for it seems, as I argue below, that some in Europe were prepared to believe that the new Bush administration boded ill indeed for the future of multilateralism, suggesting that the earlier dispensation might not be so obsolete, after all, to those who were contemplating US foreign policy in the first half of 2001.[6]

1. Isolationism as Multilateralism's 'Other'?

Though it is a commonplace among scholars to decry, and usually to deny, isolationism as either a behavioural or a historical datum in American foreign policy, it nevertheless ranks as another in a long list of concepts that resist disappearing from policy debates. It is also one of those concepts that have had critical significance for the quality of American relations with Europe: to the extent isolationism has possessed any meaning at all in US foreign policy, it has done so first and foremost in respect of Europe. The first thing to note is that, while 'isolation' and its derivative, 'isolationism', are relatively recent additions to the lexicon of American grand strategy, dating only to the 1890s, they stand for an orientation towards *parts* of the world that has a pedigree going back to the founding of the United States. Walter McDougall regards what is customarily called 'isolationism' as being the second great tradition in the country's foreign policy, superseded in America's bible of geopolitical doctrines only by the anterior tradition of liberty, 'or exceptionalism, so called'.[7] Because isolationism, like all other political concepts, is essentially contested, it is subject to interminable debate about its 'true' meaning. That being said, a large part of the problem with this particular concept has stemmed from a confusion between the product of isolationism—that is, American policy or 'grand strategy' especially during the inter-war years—and the domestic sources,

---

[6] Martin Kettle, 'If We See Bush as a Joke, It'll End in Tears', *Guardian Weekly* (11–17 January 2001).

[7] Walter A. McDougall, *Promised Land, Crusader State: The American Encounter with the World Since 1776* (Boston: Houghton Mifflin, 1997), 39. It is sometimes thought that 'exceptionalism' must entail a special presumption towards leadership, but I think McDougall's sense of it as being rooted in liberty is closer to the mark. See also the deft treatment of the concept in Michael Kammen, 'The Problem of American Exceptionalism: A Reconsideration', *American Quarterly*, 45 (March 1993).

ethnic, regional, ideological, or otherwise, of the isolationist sentiment that was so widespread during those years.

It is isolationism as American grand strategy that concerns us in this section. In this respect, it is important to dispel the confusion associated with this policy orientation and to start by saying what isolationism as strategy has *not* meant historically. It is frequently claimed that the US could never again 'go isolationist' [*sic*] because the extent of its economic interdependence with the world, and with Europe in particular, is simply so vast that it cannot afford to cut itself off from that intercourse.[8] This claim, I think, misses the point about isolationism.

Why? For the good reason that isolationism has *not* meant economic self-containment or autarky. With the exception of one 15-month interlude during the presidency of Thomas Jefferson, in 1807 and 1808, the US never tried to cut itself off from commerce with the outside world.[9] It did, for many generations, follow policies of economic protectionism as well as of export promotion; but, then, so did just about everyone else in the international system until fairly recently.

What else has isolationism as a policy injunction not meant empirically? It has never implied the general renunciation of political, or even military, engagements abroad.[10] An examination of the historical record reveals that proscriptions on political, including military, connections with other lands had consistently been applied before the Second World War to only one continent—Europe—with the important exception of 1917–18.[11] Towards Latin America, particularly towards its nearby neighbours in the Caribbean area, the US had been nothing if not interventionist from the early nineteenth century on. In East Asia, more self-restraint may have characterized American activity but, by comparison with its behaviour towards Europe, Washington followed policies there that could only with difficulty be branded 'isolationist' in its demotic sense.[12]

Acting abroad without the encumbrance of potent allies: it was precisely this that constituted the defining characteristic of isolationism as grand strategy.

---

[8] Kenneth Waltz used regularly to deny that systemic, and American, economic interdependence really was very high throughout most of the twentieth century, and he continues to make this case; see his 'Globalization and American Power', *National Interest*, 59 (Spring 2000).

[9] Martin Borden, *Parties and Politics in the Early Republic, 1789–1815* (New York: Thomas Y. Crowell, 1967).

[10] This does not mean that advocacies for such a renunciation have been, or are, non-existent. Consider Eric A. Nordlinger, *Isolationism Reconfigured: American Foreign Policy for a New Century* (Princeton: Princeton University Press, 1995). But even Nordlinger's desired national security strategy that overturns the longstanding posture of 'strategic internationalism' is complemented by a 'fully activist economic diplomacy on behalf of free trade'; *Isolationism Reconfigured*, 3–4.

[11] And even during that contest, Washington insisted that it was participating as an 'associated' not an 'allied' power.

[12] Selig Adler, *The Isolationist Impulse: Its Twentieth Century Reaction* (New York: Collier Books, 1961), 24; and Bernard Fensterwald, Jr, 'The Anatomy of American "Isolationism" and Expansionism: Part I', *Journal of Conflict Resolution*, 2 (June 1958), 115, 118.

And if there is any life left in this policy dispensation, it inheres in the desire to minimize security entanglements in pursuit of maximum policy autonomy. Although many political scientists seem to have conceptual difficulties with it, historians have fared much better at understanding isolationism. Take as an example the best work on the isolationism of the inter-war years, in which Manfred Jonas concludes quite sensibly that the hallmark of the strategy was the preference for *unilateralism* as the modus operandi of American diplomacy.[13]

Compared with the diversity of interpretations about the source of isolationist sentiment, there is a surprising degree of convergence among historians regarding isolationism's meaning as *strategy*. Echoing Jonas, Warren Kimball has observed that a more accurate name for isolationism as grand strategy would be 'unilateral internationalism'.[14] To Kalman Silvert, 'the functional distinction which should interest us is between acting alone and acting in concert with others, and not the misleading words "isolationism" and "internationalism". The former involves working abroad with no entangling alliances'.[15] Probably no one has expressed the matter more succinctly than McDougall: 'Let us dispense with the term [isolationism] altogether and substitute for it a word that really describes the second great tradition in American foreign relations: Unilateralism.' This latter implied that the US would avoid 'permanent, entangling alliances'.[16]

Isolationism in the historical context was a strategy that had meaning only in respect of Europe, which is where the sources of entanglement, not to mention danger, lay; as such, it makes little sense to distinguish it from unilateralism. From this follows the observation that the future of America's multilateralism could be argued, as has Samuel Huntington, to depend primarily upon the quality of the relationship it experiences with its NATO allies. The 'lonely superpower' of his fears may not become a narcissistic superpower, it might not even 'leave' Europe, but it would be an international actor that had slipped whatever constraints it has had, and allowed itself to have had, imposed upon it by the multilateral institution known as the Atlantic alliance: 'Healthy cooperation with Europe is the prime antidote for the loneliness of American superpowerdom.'[17]

In the event of a parting of the ways with its long-standing Atlantic partners, and on the assumption that it could not forge something akin to the Atlantic

[13] Manfred Jonas, *Isolationism in America, 1935–1941* (Ithaca: Cornell University Press, 1966).
[14] Warren F. Kimball, *The Most Unsordid Act: Lend-Lease, 1939–1941* (Baltimore: Johns Hopkins Press, 1969), 1.
[15] Kalman H. Silvert, 'The Kitsch in Hemispheric Realpolitik', in Ronald G. Hellman and H. Jon Rosenbaum (ed.), *Latin America: The Search for a New International Role* (New York: John Wiley and Sons, 1975), 31.
[16] McDougall, *Promised Land, Crusader State*, 40.
[17] Samuel P. Huntington, 'The Lonely Superpower', *Foreign Affairs*, 78 (March/April 1999), 48. Also see the similar argument of David Calleo, 'A Choice of Europes', *National Interest*, 63 (Spring 2001).

alliance elsewhere in the world, might America become, once again, an 'isolationist'—though hardly stay-at-home—power? Geo-political correctness would doubtless oblige us to use the softer descriptive 'unilateralist' to capture that policy dispensation. But is such a parting of the ways likely to happen? To answer this, we need to ask a prior question: why did the US opt in the first place to become a part of the European balance of power via a multilateral security institution?

2. Sources of America's Eurocentric Multilateralism

To account for US behaviour in and towards Eurocentric multilateral structures, we need some prior knowledge about why the US acts abroad. As this volume's introduction makes obvious, it is far from easy to pronounce definitively on 'why' American foreign policy is the way it is; some writers even go so far as to deny that we can theorize foreign policy at all and argue that we must instead content ourselves with the more modest 'analysis' of policy, sustained by assessments that invariably rest upon the invocation of relevant 'factors'.[18]

Two such variables, suggested as having some explanatory power in determining US behaviour, are taken from the domestic—second image—and systemic—third image—levels of analysis. By the former I have in mind 'national character', a subset of political culture; by the latter, I mean the distribution of capabilities and diffusion of norms. Moreover, I take it for granted—though I could be wrong—that American foreign policy behaviour depends upon, and is reflective of, 'rationality' in the dual sense of (1) effort consciously aimed at the optimization of some value(s), and (2) effort that is also the product of a coherent entity, the state, which can be allowed to define and defend action in the context of 'national interests'.

I assume that forging multilateral security bonds with European allies made sense for the US after the Second World War, and preserving those links still makes sense today, even though their preservation may not be as necessary for protecting American 'vital' interests as it once was. My approach can be called 'realist' of the sort suggested by the modifiers 'classical' or 'neo-classical': that is, I take policy-makers' beliefs about the contemporary global balance of power to be a necessary point of departure, but I regard the distribution of capability to be only one among several variables that must be invoked to account for that American policy behaviour. David Lake has put it well in conceiving of multilateral security cooperation as a choice whose rationality can be and is tested against expectations of gain and loss across the three dimensions of (1) joint production economies: how much more security can

---

[18] For a good discussion of foreign policy as a theorizable field, see Gideon Rose, 'Neoclassical Realism and Theories of Foreign Policy', *World Politics*, 51 (October 1998).

be had through tapping the assets of partners?; (2) costs of opportunism: to what degree might allies complicate or otherwise frustrate one's purposes?; and (3) governance costs: how much would it take to maximize gains in the first, and minimize losses in the second, of these dimensions?[19]

Where I relax the rationality assumption that figures so centrally in Lake's 'relational contracting' theory is in the manner in which certain other variables, internal as well as external, enter into play. Some categories just do not yield readily, if at all, to value-optimization assumptions, nor should it be said that realism *has* become just another form of cost-benefit analysis.[20] 'Identity', an implicit datum of the national character variable listed in this volume's introduction, is clearly one such non-rational category. And identity, as social constructivists have reminded us, is and must be constitutive of 'interest', including the national interest.[21]

To put this discussion into historical context, let us say that America opted for multilateral security cooperation with European allies at the onset of the cold war for at least two important reasons. The first had to do with the cost-benefit calculation of a country whose leaders understood such cooperation to be required, and not just convenient. And the second inhered in the kind of country America was imagined to be by foreign policy elites.

In light of both these factors, it can come as a surprise to no one that Europe should have occupied such an important place in American multilateralism once the old, isolationist, carapace had been discarded. Because of them, Eurocentrism could be even said to have been over-determined in American foreign policy. By mid-century a new axiom of strategy had become the touch-stone for a rising generation of American geo-strategists, not a few of whom were themselves European imports: no piece of real estate, outside of North America itself, could be of such basal significance to US strategic interests as that land mass often referred to as 'Eurasia'. Control of this terrain by a single adversary or league of adversaries would pose a fundamental, perhaps insur-mountable, challenge to US security and prosperity, and do so for a very long time. Such control, however, could be gained only if an adversary were able to dominate Western Europe, the dynamic 'rimland' of Eurasia within which was concentrated enormous industrial and therefore military power and potential.[22] If there ever was a rational-actor construction of American strategic orientation, then this was it.

---

[19] David A. Lake, *Entangling Relations: American Foreign Policy in its Century* (Princeton: Princeton University Press, 1999), 11–16.
[20] The case that it has is argued in Richard Rosecrance, 'Has Realism Become Cost-Benefit Analysis?' *International Security*, 26 (Fall 2001).
[21] See Jutta Weldes, 'Constructing National Interests', *European Journal of International Relations*, 2 (September 1996).
[22] For the fullest elaboration of this perspective, see Nicholas John Spykman, *America's Strategy in World Politics: The United States and the Balance of Power* (New York: Harcourt, Brace, 1942).

But there was more to America's embrace of multilateralism than cool ration-alist calculation derived from perceptions of the international distribution of capability—and of threat. The second source of Eurocentrism in American strategy owed more to ideological than to balance-of-power inspiration, and for this reason was possibly even more significant in shaping the policy of a country whose home-grown leaders never had been consistently good realists, and who in the post-war era sought guidance as often in ideational as in relative-power assessments—and not just any sort of ideational assessments, but 'liberal' or 'Wilsonian' ones.[23] For, as James Kurth argues, 'the liberal tradition is not only *in* America, it *is* America. The realist tradition, in contrast, not only is rarely in America, it is un-American'.[24] On this view, it is not just that liberalism constitutes the cardinal feature of American 'exceptionalism'.[25] More than this, liberalism had come to represent a standing injunction for many American policy elites to conceive their country's place in the world in interventionist and multilateralist terms.

Liberalism—though hardly an unambiguous term in its own right—was said by many not only to predispose America to multilateralism; it predisposed it towards Europe, the seed-bed and, to some, fundamental core of the West's security community as well as of its 'democratic alliance'.[26] According to this way of looking at things, the ideology has shaped the identity of the country, and the identity has generated the interests: America, then, was born multi-lateral in the late eighteenth century and, historical appearances to the con-trary notwithstanding, it has had and retains a geo-political soul marked by a strong preference for multilateral norms and processes. It took some time, of course, for it to reclaim its true soul, only doing so definitively after 1945.[27]

Not only was post-war America's liberal political culture, depicted as being open, transparent, and predictable, beneficial to Europe's political, security, and economic prospects, but so too was American involvement in European multilateral arrangements beneficial to the country's own domestic order, keeping at bay retrogressive and parochial tendencies as expressed often by

---

[23] See Mary N. Hampton, 'NATO at the Creation: U.S. Foreign Policy, West Germany and the Wilsonian Impulse', *Security Studies*, 4 (Spring 1995).

[24] James Kurth, 'Inside the Cave: The Banality of I.R. Studies', *National Interest*, 53 (Fall 1998), 40.

[25] See Seymour Martin Lipset, *American Exceptionalism: A Double-Edged Sword* (New York: W. W. Norton, 1996).

[26] Thomas Risse-Kappen, *Cooperation Among Democracies: The European Influence on U.S. Foreign Policy* (Princeton: Princeton University Press, 1995).

[27] On this postulated politico-genetic predisposition towards multilateralism, see John Gerard Ruggie, 'The Past as Prologue? Interests, Identity, and American Foreign Policy', in Michael E. Brown *et al.* (eds), *America's Strategic Choices*, (Cambridge: MIT Press, 1997); David C. Hendrickson, 'In Our Own Image: The Sources of American Conduct in World Affairs', *National Interest*, 50 (Winter 1997/98); and Daniel H. Deudney, 'The Philadelphian System: Sovereignty, Arms Control, and Balance of Power in the American States-Union, circa 1787–1861', *International Organization*, 49 (Spring 1995).

Congressional partisans and their backers—the 'special' interests—and serving to enshrine an institutional bargain within which America's self-interest—enlightened and 'national' instead of selfish and 'special'—could attain maximum flowering.

Finding European partners who were willing, after the Second World War, to join with America in security multilateralism and to follow its lead required that it exercise what one author has called 'strategic restraint'.[28] It had to do this so as to provide a level of comfort on the part of its weaker allies, in whom it would instil the conviction that it would refrain from taking advantage of the power differential in its favour, thereby reducing the returns to—its own—power and simultaneously enhancing its long-term ability to exercise leadership.

3. Systemic Change and American Behaviour: The Case of NATO

During the bipolar era of cold war, America certainly managed to preserve and even extend its system of 'stakeholder hegemony'.[29] Central to this undertaking was the Atlantic alliance. Is there any reason to imagine that what worked in one systemic context—bipolarity—might not be able to function in another—unipolarity? Put differently, is there any reason to assume that American multilateralism cannot coexist with American unipolarity as ably as it did with bipolarity? Or must multilateralism require multipolarity, as many today seem to believe, or at least bipolarity?

Given that it is widely accepted that during the cold war there were only two superpowers, and hence the system was 'bipolar', the demise of the Soviet Union must have wrought a 'systemic change'.[30] Few deny that this occurred; where there is a contest, it has taken place between those who now call the system unipolar and those who regard it as multipolar. Given the number of schemes that are currently making the rounds for re-equilibrating global power, it would appear that even foes of American pre-eminence are prepared to concede the system must be unipolar. Certainly this would also apply to

[28] G. John Ikenberry, 'Institutions, Strategic Restraint, and the Persistence of the American Postwar Order', *International Security*, 23 (Winter 1998/99). See also this same author's *After Victory: Institutions, Strategic Restraint, and the Rebuilding of Order After Major Wars* (Princeton: Princeton University Press, 2001), especially Chapter 7, 'After the Cold War'.

[29] G. John Ikenberry, 'Getting Hegemony Right', *National Interest*, 63 (Spring 2001).

[30] For this meaning of change, see Robert Gilpin, *War and Change in World Politics* (Cambridge: Cambridge University Press, 1981), 42: 'Systemic change involves a change ... within the system rather than a change of the system itself. It entails changes in the international distribution of power, the hierarchy of prestige, and the rules and rights embodied in the system ...'.

some of the allies, above all France; else why bother to strive to *make* the system—not *keep* it—multipolar?

But does it follow that multipolarity correlates positively with multilateralism in American foreign policy? Hardly. We need simply recall from the discussion earlier in this chapter about the meaning of isolationism in American foreign policy that this pre-eminently unilateralist dispensation flourished during a long era when the system was characterized by multipolarity. Moreover, there are some, including one of this volume's editors, who are prepared to claim that unipolarity should, all things being equal, predispose Washington towards optimal security multilateralism, for the very good reason that, if it wished to preserve its grand strategy of 'primacy', America would have to understand that in security matters it was necessary for it not just to be polite but to proceed multilaterally, meaning to listen to and take seriously the opinions of allies.[31]

Nothing written above should constitute a prima facie case that America cannot be multilateralist in a multipolar world; it is simply to remark that in the multipolar world(s) we have had, America never used to be particularly inclined towards multilateralism. Whether we are even moving towards a multipolar world must depend, of course, on the relative increase in capabilities of other countries or on the merging of other countries into a larger political ensemble, irrespective of whether the relative capabilities of the parts are increasing. In this latter context, the European Union is often posited as a candidate vehicle for the transformation of the system into a multipolar one or at least a bipolar one. It is not the only such candidate, of course, and in the past few years a second systemic challenger has been imagined: China.[32]

Whether unipolarity disappears as a result of any challenge mounted by the European Union must in large part depend upon the future of the Atlantic alliance; for, if NATO can continue to assure the security of Western Europeans both from outside threats and even from internal ones, why should the Europeans bother to invest much of their scarce resources in defence, a policy area in which they have been content to under-invest for decades?

Let us take a look, then, at the current state and future prospects of the alliance in a search for clues as to the sustainability of America's particularistic, half-century old, variant of internationalism. On the topic of NATO's current state, it must be acknowledged that the scholars are divided, and they are not the only ones. Two extreme visions serve neatly to bracket the debate. At one pole are found those who believe NATO to be nothing other than the extension of American unilateralism, in essence the indispensable military component of

---

[31] For this argument, redolent of Ikenberry's 'strategic restraint', see Michael Mastanduno, 'Preserving the Unipolar Moment: Realist Theories and U.S. Grand Strategy after the Cold War', in Brown (ed.), *America's Strategic Choices*.

[32] 'Whatever model America chooses to adopt for its foreign policy in the twenty-first century ... China seems destined to present the most testing challenge'. Martin Walker, 'Bush's Choice: Athens or Sparta', *World Policy Journal*, 18 (Summer 2001), 7.

the Pax Americana, judged if at all only in terms of the effectiveness with which it serves Washington's interests. This is not, obviously, a NATO-friendly hypothesis, but neither is it propounded solely by critics of America. Some analysts, such as French anthropologist Emmanuel Todd, do figure among those opponents; but others with this perspective are anything but critics of America, and instead are nationalists for whom the only good alliance is a subservient one.

In an interview published shortly after the ending of the war with Serbia by the Madrid daily, *El País*, Todd drew an analogy between NATO and the Delian League. The latter, it will be recalled, was an Athenian-led alliance constructed in the fifth century BC for the initial purposes of amassing Greek power against the Persian empire; over time, it grew into an Athenian empire, which ultimately would go to war, in 431 BC, against a rival Greek grouping of states, the Peloponnesian Confederation, or League, led by Sparta.[33] The war against Serbia, Todd suggested, revealed how much NATO itself had come to resemble the Delian League. America had become the new Athens, the imperial protector of the interests of lesser allies, from whom little might be required or expected militarily, yet much was demanded politically and economically. This arrangement, to Todd, posed an obvious threat to the other allies, however much they may have thought their display of unity against Slobodan Milosevic in 1999 had advanced their interests.[34]

Walter McDougall shares, up to a point, Todd's view. McDougall makes no secret of the fact that he would greatly prefer an America that stuck closer to home and, heeding the wisdom contained in the country's earliest foreign policy traditions, dedicated itself to perfecting the 'promised land'. Instead, McDougall gazes out upon an America that is incapable of resisting the siren song of crusading on behalf of ideals that besmirch rather than ennoble the country's geo-political soul, which he takes, contrary to John Ruggie, to be a unilateral not a multilateral one. Still, he does not believe America need decamp from NATO, given that 'our core alliances today should be thought of less as violations of Unilateralism than as extensions of the American System to the opposite shores of the two American oceans'.[35]

On the opposite interpretative shores can be found those who regard the alliance as anything but a vehicle designed for the simple purpose of projecting American interests and power. To the contrary, these analysts consider it to be the means of allowing allies, whatever their size, to advance as well as to *conceive* their own interests through the norms and processes of multilateralism. So penetrated does every alliance country, even and particularly the US, become by the workings of multilateralism that it grows increasingly problematical to try to

---

[33] F. S. Northedge, *The International Political System* (London: Faber and Faber, 1976), 43–5. See also Adda B. Bozeman, *Politics and Culture in International History* (Princeton: Princeton University Press, 1960), 80–2.

[34] Octavi Martí, 'No existe una conciencia común europea', *El País* (11 August 1999), available at www.elpais.es/cgi-bin/ELPAIS.

[35] McDougall, *Promised Land, Crusader State*, 212.

distinguish the individual allies' national interests. Instead, a collective, Western interest is argued to exist, one that is constituted from a collective Western identity and set of shared values.

Among some alliance watchers, the 'new NATO' that had been in constant evolution throughout the 1990s[36] has so transformed itself as to overstep the traditional boundary between international organization and domestic institution. As a result, NATO 'should be viewed as an evolving civic community whose pacific relations are the institutionalized norm rather than the calculated preference of states'.[37] Put differently, NATO has been a major factor contributing to the shaping of a collective identity among Western policy elites—and presumably their publics.

Collective identity is a relatively new addition to the vocabulary of international security, taken, in the words of Alexander Wendt, to refer to 'positive identification with the welfare of another, such that the other is seen as a cognitive extension of the Self rather than as independent'.[38] No longer just a clearing house of national interests and a valued forum for consultation and even coordination, as 'classical realists' and 'neo-liberal institutionalists' alike would have it,[39] the alliance was being regarded by a different, constructivist breed of theorist as something truly new under the international security sun. To Wendt, who pushed this argument to its furthest point, NATO looked like being something much more grandiose than a military alliance; it could be, he speculated, nothing other than the first, best, example of post-Westphalian governance by means of the 'international state', that is, a transnational structure able and willing to assume certain traditional functions previously fulfilled, if fulfilled at all, only by the territorial state.[40] Among those functions, Wendt argued, none was as crucial as the provision of security, which is what he said NATO did, by dint of its being a 'collective security system' characterized by its 'joint control of organized violence potential in a transnational space'.[41]

---

[36] David S. Yost, *NATO Transformed: The Alliance's New Roles in International Security* (Washington: United States Institute of Peace, 1998).

[37] Michael Brenner, 'The Multilateral Moment', in Michael Brenner (ed.), *Multilateralism and Western Strategy* (New York: St Martin's, 1995), 8. See also Jaap de Wilde, *Reversal in the International System? The Long Peace Debate in the Present*, Working Papers 21/1994 (Copenhagen: Centre for Peace and Conflict Research, 1994), 8–9; and John S. Duffield, 'NATO's Functions after the Cold War', *Political Science Quarterly*, 109 (Winter 1994/95), 777.

[38] Alexander Wendt, 'Identity and Structural Change in International Politics', in Yosef Lapid and Friedrich Kratochwil (eds), *The Return of Culture and Identity in IR Theory* (Boulder: Lynne Rienner, 1997), 52.

[39] See John W. Holmes, 'Fearful Symmetry: The Dilemmas of Consultation and Coordination in the North Atlantic Treaty Organization', *International Organization*, 22 (Autumn 1968).

[40] Wendt borrows this concept from Robert Cox, *Power, Production, and World Order* (New York: Columbia University Press, 1987), 253–65.

[41] Alexander E. Wendt, 'Collective Identity Formation and the International State', *American Political Science Review*, 88 (June 1994), 392. Also see John Gerard Ruggie, 'Territoriality and Beyond: Problematizing Modernity in International Relations', *International Organization*, 47 (Winter 1993).

According to this view, NATO is more than a marriage of security conveni-ence between partners possessed of interest-based reasons for cooperation; it is a community of shared values, the foremost of which are human rights, the rule of law, and especially democratic governance. As such, it can be expected to persist: 'If the Western Alliance is based primarily on shared values, norms, and a collective identity rather than on the perception of a common threat, one should expect the transatlantic security community to persist in one institutional form or another.'[42]

What is striking about the recent literature on NATO as a community of values, for many of its supporters, is the uniform claim that neither an enemy nor a boss is required to keep the allies allied. Their norms and values inform their interests, and the latter in turn become ever more congruent, to the point where one can speak of them not as a summed, and negotiable, set but rather in the singular, as *a* collective interest emerging from *a* collective identity. 'Discourse analysis', it is said, allows us to recognize the collective identity as it is revealed in the perceptions, ideas, and words of those who constitute the Western alliance's effective decision-makers.[43]

Whatever else the American public might think about NATO, it is unlikely to conceptualize it in terms such as those above, nor does the discourse of US policy pundits betray much of a tendency so to conceive the alliance. 'Interests', American ones to be exact, continue to dominate the real-world debates of the policy community, even if the ivory tower may have taken the discussion to a much higher, though not more relevant, plane.[44] At the very least, one can say that NATO in particular and allies in general are held in reas-onably high regard by the American public, no more so than when the issue of military intervention gets broached. But while the American public and their leaders, according to a recent survey of the Chicago Council on Foreign Relations, may continue to be committed to their country's engagement with the world, the mood had been one of 'a "guarded engagement" by a largely satisfied superpower'[45]—up until 11 September 2001, that is.

Not only was there no hearty appetite for military interventions at a time when no one was attacking American territory, but the public strongly pre-ferred that, whenever military force had to be employed, it be done with

[42] Risse-Kappen, *Cooperation Among Democracies*, 194–5.

[43] Thomas Risse-Kappen, 'Democratic Peace—Warlike Democracies? A Social Constructivist Interpretation of the Liberal Argument', *European Journal of International Relations*, 1 (December 1995), 511. For a critique of this values-based approach that also stresses the centrality of group identification, see Michael Spirtas, 'French Twist: French and British NATO Policies from 1949 to 1966', *Security Studies*, 8 (Winter 1998/99–Spring 1999).

[44] For a depiction of the self-erected barriers that keep so many of the academics at the margins of policy-making, if even there, see David D. Newsom, 'Foreign Policy and Academia', *Foreign Policy*, 101 (Winter 1995/96). Also see Stephen M. Walt, 'Rigor or Rigor Mortis? Rational Choice and Security Studies', *International Security*, 23 (Spring 1999).

[45] John E. Rielly, 'Americans and the World: A Survey at Century's End', *Foreign Policy*, 114 (Spring 1999), 97.

allies—mainly, though not exclusively, NATO allies. 'Seventy-two per cent think the United States should not take action alone in international crises if it does not have the support of allies. Leaders are more evenly divided: Forty-eight per cent prefer not to act alone and 44 per cent are willing to take action without allied support.'[46]

NATO has remained popular among public and leaders alike in the US; this seems to be apparent. But, beyond this, what in particular can we deduce even from the pre-September evidence in so far as it concerned America's commitment to multilateralism? One inference, and one only, seemed to suggest itself: America would continue, unless the European allies forced it to act otherwise, to be 'multilateralist' in respect of transatlantic security arrangements, but it would not be offering the kind of multilateralism they wanted, nor would it be the kind of multilateralism they thought, perhaps wrongly, they had become accustomed to over the past several decades.

More and more, American multilateralism was demonstrating a decidedly 'instrumentalist' flavour. This was not a process that began with George W. Bush, but it was certainly intensified in his administration's first nine months in office. Nor should it be thought that it was just the French who were objecting to a variant of multilateralism bordering on the ersatz—in fact, for the French, instrumentalism is not such a bad thing; increasingly, it was the *ur*-multilateralist Germans, so far among the best students in the Atlanticist classroom, who had been grumbling about the quality of American leadership, some to the extent that they began to doubt whether America's erstwhile commitment to multilateralism ever *did* reflect anything other than 'instrumental multilateralism [in which] international institutions are useful as long as they help to reduce costs, lend legitimacy to foreign policy actions, and do not constrain the United States'.[47] The German mood was hardly improved in the early months of 2001 when American policy-makers and policy analysts sympathetic to the administration began to extol the virtues of Washington's 'à la carte' multilateralism, and even of its 'consultative unilateralism'.[48]

---

[46] Rielly, 'Americans and the World', 102.

[47] See Peter Rudolf, 'Vision Impossible? The United States as Benign Hegemon', in David G. Haglund (ed.), *The France-US Leadership Race: Closely Watched Allies* (Kingston: Queen's Quarterly Press, 2000), 152, and 'Amerikanische Außenpolitik unter George W. Bush: Eine erste Einschätzung', *SWP-Aktuell*, 5 (April 2001), 3. See also Bernd W. Kubbig, Matthias Dembinski, and Alexander Kelle, *Unilateralism as Sole Foreign-Policy Strategy? American Policy towards the UN, NATO, and the OPCW in the Clinton Era*, PRIF Reports 57 (Frankfurt am Main: Peace Research Institute Frankfurt, November 2000). OPCW is the Organization for the Prohibition of Chemical Weapons.

[48] The first expression is attributed to Richard Haass, director of policy planning at the State Department; the second springs from the keyboard of William Safire. See Stewart Patrick, 'Don't Fence Me In: The Perils of Going It Alone', *World Policy Journal*, 18 (Fall 2001), 2; and William Safire, 'Bush's Missile Shield Can Work', *International Herald Tribune* (4 May 2001), 11.

4. Consequences for Multilateral Organizations: The EU and the ESDP

On the eve of the 11 September attacks on America, there was renewed uncertainty concerning the prospects of transatlantic multilateralism. Rarely in the past half century could 'strategic restraint' have been a less appropriate means of capturing the quality of the US-European relationship than during the first eight months of 2001. Nor was its conceptual sidekick, 'hegemony', faring any better among the Europeans, who were chafing at its implications, no matter how 'benign' these were held to be and notwithstanding that it—or unipolarity—may well be the most appropriate structural framework for their continued prosperity and peace.

As is apparent from the quotations that ended the section immediately above, what some in Europe were objecting to in American multilateralism is precisely what David Lake and others argue constituted, for Americans, multilateralism's appeal in the first place: its utility for *American* interests, registered through some cost-benefit calculation, coupled with the lightness of its constraining embrace. Could the alliance continue to exist if such fundamental disagreement characterized the partners' respective understandings of multilateralism?

The 'lesson' of Kosovo might suggest it could not, especially as such was read by the EU members, who took it to be self-evident that they had best set to work developing a more capable and coherent defence entity, usually under the rubric 'common European security and defence policy' (ESDP) sometimes expressed, in North America, as the European security and defence identity (ESDI). But there was another empirical referent suggesting it could: the allies' experience with 'flexible response' from the 1960s through the 1980s. On that doctrine the US and its European partners showed themselves to have radically divergent views. They disagreed nearly all the time, yet they still won the cold war. Their disagreements over flexible response, it bears recalling, occurred within a certain structural context—bipolarity—in which the alliance was held by many to be virtually immune to fracturing. Glenn Snyder spoke for a legion of structural realists in propounding, during the mid-1980s, the conviction that, transatlantic backbiting to the contrary notwithstanding, NATO 'cannot break up. Since NATO is a product of the bipolar structure of the system, it cannot collapse or change basically until that structure changes.'[49]

From this assertion, it is easy to see why the structural realists were so quick to discover, once the system had changed with the demise of the Soviet Union, that NATO was on life support: what structure gave, structure was poised to take away. None other than the dean of structural realism, Kenneth Waltz,

---

[49] Glenn H. Snyder, 'The Security Dilemma in Alliance Politics', *World Politics*, 36 (July 1984).

managed to conclude that NATO *had* disappeared![50] But the classical realists
have always been a bit more prudent in prophesying, and the most that their
variant of theorizing could have been expected to generate in the way of
'NATO-friendly' prediction were claims to the effect that, should the various
actors have an 'interest' in keeping the thing going, they should be able to find
the means to do so. One thinks, in this respect, of central and eastern European
states demonstrating an interest in joining the alliance, held to be a worth-
while thing to do, either because it is thought to make them more secure—as
in Poland's case—or because alliance membership is a ticket to the West—as in
the case of Hungary and the Czech Republic, as well as Poland. Or one could
even think of France's mid-1990s' rapprochement with the alliance, said to be
good for France because it advanced the day when European defence autonomy could become a reality.[51] The list could be easily extended, given that
there are nearly as many European countries with an interest in NATO as there
are countries in Europe.

The point is that this way of approaching the matter may not be wrong, but
neither is it particularly profound. It can also lead to not so benign expectations
regarding the alliance on a similar logic, namely, that should they diminish their
respective interest(s) in keeping it going the allies could well let NATO lapse,
because they wish it. However, there are some deeper, and for the alliance more
problematical, expectations that can be derived from classical realism. These,
too, stem from classical realism's emphasis upon *raison d'état*, another way of
expressing the national interest. As noted earlier, interest is being increasingly
interpreted as dependent upon identity, which is to acknowledge that national—
'state', really—interest cannot simply be deduced from assumptions about anarchy. If this is so, then there is reason to believe that a European security and
defence identity, should one take tangible form and be backed by concrete
resources, could have implications for the quality of American internationalism
that may not be as positive as some in Europe are wont to believe.

Randall Schweller reveals why this may be so, in drawing our attention to
what he considers the chief shortcoming of structural realism: its amnesia
regarding the sources of state action. Structural realists, in their emphasis upon
the maximization of security as being the state's principal if not only
objective, have strayed from realism's roots. It may well be that security is one
objective of states, and that security might even be a 'positive-sum' value, or a
'public good', such that many can enjoy it without others necessarily being

---

[50] Kenneth N. Waltz, 'Structural Realism after the Cold War', *International Security*, 25
(Summer 2000), 19: 'I expected NATO to dwindle at the Cold War's end and ultimately
to disappear. In a basic sense, the expectation has been borne out. NATO is no longer
even a treaty of guarantee...'.
[51] Hans-Georg Ehrhart, 'Change by Rapprochement? Astérix's Quarrel with the New
Roman Empire', in David G. Haglund (ed.), *The France-U.S. Leadership Race: Closely
Watched Allies* (Kingston: Queen's Quarterly Press, 2000); and Anand Menon, 'From
Independence to Cooperation: France, NATO and European Security', *International
Affairs*, 71 (January 1995).

deprived of it. But it hardly follows that all, or even most, objectives states pursue can be placed into similar public-goods baskets. In fact they cannot, for the objects of states' desire—prestige, status, political influence, leadership, market share—are all 'positional goods', available as are other such goods only in limited supply, thereby engendering among states a 'constant positional competition'.[52]

Evidence of such competition in the transatlantic context was not hard to come by prior to September 2001; and, even though there may be little reason to assume their commercial wrangling must drive a political and military wedge among the allies, the same expectation may not apply to contests that are more directly related to the quest to achieve ESDP. Nor should it be assumed that, once the current war is over, the transatlantic allies will refrain from reverting to their more normal posture, that is, of eyeing each other somewhat warily.[53] Thus it is in this regard that developments in the European security and defence identity merit attention. And as this section's objective is to assess the impact of American behaviour upon European security multilateralism, the first place to look is Washington's claims to provide the positional good known as 'leadership' to the alliance.

Guillaume Parmentier has recently commented, apropos those claims, that the problem with NATO—namely, its sub-optimal multilateralism—inheres in its military not political arrangements. Kosovo is regarded as the proof of this contention, for what the war against Serbia demonstrated was how split NATO's personality really could be: politically it may be an arrangement that constrains the US, as the constructivists and historical-institutionalists maintain, but militarily it is thoroughly dominated by America. The war reminded observers that NATO militarily was run not through Supreme Headquarters Allied Powers Europe but through the US European Command, and therefore ultimately through the Pentagon. Thus the alliance is and remains a hybrid, something whose multilateral political being is contradicted by its unilateral military nature. Bringing the latter into conformity with the former remains key to its future viability, and for many in Europe NATO's health becomes indistinguishable from, and perhaps even dependent upon, the future well-being of the EU's own defence and security arrangements.[54]

American behaviour can play an obvious role in reshaping NATO militarily and bringing it back into the kind of balance Parmentier claims to want. If the problem really is, as alliance elites like to put it, not one of 'too much America

---

[52] Randall L. Schweller, 'Realism and the Present Great Power System: Growth and Positional Conflict over Scarce Resources', in Ethan B. Kapstein and Michael Mastanduno (eds), *Unipolar Politics: Realism and State Strategies After the Cold War* (New York: Columbia University Press, 1999), 28.

[53] See Jessica T. Mathews, 'Estranged Partners', *Foreign Policy*, 127 (November/December 2001).

[54] Guillaume Parmentier, 'Après le Kosovo: pour un nouveau contrat transatlantique', *Politique étrangère*, 65 (Spring 2000), and 'Redressing NATO's Imbalance', *Survival*, 42 (Summer 2000).

but too little Europe', then all the US needs to do is back off from its military presence on the old continent and contemplate with greater equanimity European claims to an enhanced share of leadership. For obvious reasons, during the cold war this was not thought to be a wise strategy, but in the past decade there have been on-again, off-again glimpses of an America that looked as if it wanted to disengage somewhat from the allies, or at least shoulder less of the 'burden' for the common defence. Indeed, supporters of what the EU claims to be building—a more coherent security and defence capability—who are also supporters of the transatlantic link are quick to stress that unless Europe does more for its defence and security the US will leave Europe, in disgust at the allies' inability to fulfil their share of the 'transatlantic bargain'.

Alternatively, the US could take bold, and expensive, steps to help the EU bolster its defence and security capabilities, including such measures as making available to the European allies sensitive technologies associated with the revolution in military affairs (RMA) as part of a package of initiatives intended to close the transatlantic capabilities gap that has been growing wider during the past decades. This America is hardly likely to do, for reasons related to legitimate security worries about sensitive technologies falling into the wrong hands and also because it expects its allies—not *itself*—to be spending and doing more for the common defence; this is not a new expectation, but neither should it be thought that America's 'burden-sharing' grievance against the allies has abated with the events of the past decade.[55]

Of the above two alternatives, the former is more likely to reflect future American behaviour towards the European allies. As I argue below, America is going to figure less in—Western—European security, so that, whether or not the European allies ever do manage actually to attain greater defence capability in any absolute—thus, meaningful—sense, they will assuredly be charged with more relative responsibility for their own security and defence.[56] This will not be a development caused by the Afghan war, but it will certainly have been speeded up by that conflict.

5. The Bush Administration and the European Allies

Nostalgia may not be what it used to be, but it still had a way of tugging at heartstrings, even transatlantic ones, in early 2001. Recall how the administration of

---

[55] David S. Yost, 'The NATO Capabilities Gap and the European Union', *Survival*, 42 (Winter 2001/01).

[56] For a pessimistic view regarding the European allies' ability to generate more effective capability absolutely, primarily because of the inability of the EU's largest country to contribute more meaningfully to ESDP, see Mary Elise Sarotte, *German Military Reform and European Security*, Adelphi Paper 340 (London: International Institute for Strategic Studies, 2001).

Bill Clinton was being re-imagined by the European allies during its final days once it became clear who had actually 'won' the state of Florida: the administration that had presided over a country baptized a 'hyperpower' by France's foreign minister, the same country that had been vilified by anti-Americans throughout Europe during the war with Serbia. That country and that administration were now being recalled, in the closing days of the Clinton presidency, as the very model of multilateral probity.[57] In truth, transatlantic querulousness had been festering during that same Clinton administration that only retrospectively appeared to represent the golden age of American multilateralism.

Nevertheless, personalities and ideologies do matter, and it is useful to reflect on such evidence about America's new president as came to light in the months between his inauguration and the attacks on the World Trade Center and the Pentagon. Was there anything the Bush administration could do so as to enhance the quality of America's security relationship with the allies? The early trends were not promising, and suggested a tilt in the direction of unilateralism. In fairness, so too had the early trends in the first Clinton administration, and we all witnessed the effect that the Bosnia crisis of 1992–5 had on America's—belated—recognition that NATO and the Europeans still remained a 'vital' American interest.

Might the Bush team turn out similarly? Those who worried that it would not had some basis for their fears in the half-year or so following the president's swearing-in. Europeans were quick to recall that George W. Bush was not known for being a world traveller, and what little sojourning he had done usually managed to take him to ports of call located anywhere but on the old continent. As well, he was considered by many Europeans—and non-Europeans— to be intellectually none too subtle, certainly not subtle enough to grasp the intricacies of transatlantic security. The president was regarded as being fundamentally out of touch with European political and cultural sensibilities, with his support for the emphatically 'anti-European' activity of capital punishment seen as proof of this pudding. He was thought to be too attentive to Mexico—more irksome to Canadian than to European officials— and talked as if the Western hemisphere was going to re-emerge as an area of strategic priority for America—although others said it would be Asia that captured his attention even if not his fancy.[58] He surrounded himself with

---

[57] Joseph Fitchett, 'Albright Urges Bush to Calm Fears on Europe and North Korea', *International Herald Tribune* (13–14 January 2001); Ian Black, 'Defence Differences May Push Bush into an Early Transatlantic Crossing', *Guardian Weekly* (25–31 January 2001). See also 'Europe Is Sad to See Clinton Go', *Guardian Weekly* (19 January 2001), in which outgoing President Bill Clinton is roundly eulogized by European leaders as practically one of them: in the words of France's foreign minister, as the president who has been 'the most open to European ideas in 20 years'.

[58] Thomas E. Ricks, 'Rumsfeld Signals Shift to Pacific in Overhaul of Defense Thinking', *Guardian Weekly* (29 March–4 April 2001); Martin Kettle, 'East Asia Now the Only Game in Town', *Guardian Weekly* (29 March–4 April 2001). Also see Marvin C. Ott, 'East Asia: Security and Complexity', *Current History*, 100 (April 2001).

advisers some of whom looked to be too reluctant to countenance using American power for purposes of European security. And, as if all this were not enough, he was determined to try to provide America with a shield against ballistic missiles tipped with nuclear, chemical, or biological warheads.

No doubt there was much hyperbole in the Europeans' criticism of the new president, but there can be no mistaking the unease he triggered in allied countries. Less than a month before the attacks on America, polls were revealing that citizens in the four largest Western European countries were convinced that the president was dreadfully mismanaging foreign policy, with the two biggest sources of their disquiet being global warming and national missile defence (NMD). Incredibly, those polled in the four allied countries of the United Kingdom, France, Germany, and Italy had only slightly more confidence in the American president than in his Russian counterpart, Vladimir Putin.[59]

The feeling was mutual. Europe did matter less to George W. Bush than it had either to his father or to his immediate predecessor. For those in Europe inclined in recent years to criticize an overbearing American presence—the 'arrogance of power'—it was possible to discern a silver lining in the transatlantic storm cloud in that indifference towards the allies looked set to replace the domineering approach of the past. And, even if the Europeans chose not to invest more in their own defence, the relative weight of America vis-à-vis Europe in the old continent's military affairs would have to diminish by dint of the former's doing—and caring—less. After all, was not autonomy—from American tutelage—one of the announced objectives of the ESDP project? Would it not advance the EU's attempt to construct a European identity if its security and defence competence were increased, even if only relatively?

As for America's own identity, it may not have been changing in any objective sense, if such could be said ever to have existed. But it was changing hermeneutically as new interpreters of that identity gained supremacy in policy debates. The Wilsonians, who had so recently been triumphant on the interpretative battlefield, now appeared to be in headlong retreat, with the contest being won by writers such as Walter McDougall, who were stressing the more libertarian aspects of liberalism and singing praises for the virtues of America's 'Old Testament' foreign policy.[60] As anyone familiar with *Promised Land, Crusader State* knows, those virtues do not include multilateralism. Ironically, what many in Europe had felt compelled to criticize over the past

---

[59] Brian Knowlton, 'Bush Gets Low Marks in Europe', *International Herald Tribune* (16 August 2001). The multi-country survey was conducted earlier in August by the International Herald Tribune in collaboration with the Pew Research Center for the People and the Press, and in association with the US Council on Foreign Relations.

[60] For a sample, see Marc A. Thiessen, 'Out with the New', *Foreign Policy*, 123 (March/April 2001), 64–6. Thiessen was a majority—that is, Republican—staff member of the Senate's committee on foreign relations prior to Vermont's James Jeffords's decision to leave the Republican party, which gave the Democrats control of the Senate. Thiessen recommended McDougall's book as an 'excellent primer' for understanding America's geopolitical soul.

quarter-century or so—namely, the 'instrumentalist' cast of American multi-lateralism—bid fair to resembling nothing so much as the good old days of multilateralism.

And then came the attack on America. It is difficult to know the ultimate impact of the attack and the ensuing war upon America's relations with the European allies, and thus upon the future quality of the country's 'particularistic internationalism' that had given sustenance to its post-1945 multilateralism.[61] Policy analysts are, as usual, at odds, though there does appear to be consensus on one point: that 11 September must have some transformative significance for the transatlantic security relationship. Some, noting the speed with which the Atlantic alliance invoked for the first time in its history its collective defence clause—Article 5 of the Washington treaty of 1949—descried therapeutic import in the September tragedy and expected a new era of transatlantic solidarity where shortly before there had been so much evidence of disunity if not hostility.[62] A few went further and took the attack on America to signal the—belated—recognition on the part of the country's political class that there could be no other way to safeguard the country's security interests than through the willing cession of some of its sovereignty to multilateral regimes, including and especially those concerned with arms control and disarmament.[63]

It is certainly possible to read too much transformation into American foreign policy as a result of 11 September; on the other hand, it is foolish to insist that nothing fundamental has changed. As Fred Halliday relates, two things in particular warrant noting: the reassertion of American power and the ability of America to put together a multifaceted coalition.[64] How, though, should we conceptualize this shift in the context of this volume's animating theme of multilateralism and this chapter's focus upon European-US relations? I address the latter in what remains of this section, and the former in my concluding remarks.

In a season of great transatlantic discontent, the late spring of 2001, William Wallace issued a plea for mutual accommodation—'moral disarmament', he termed it—on the part of the transatlantic disputants. Quite simply, he said, Europe and the US were too essential to each other to refuse to adjust to the new reality of an EU that wanted and deserved more decision-making authority. At the root, though not the sole source, of the problem was growing American unilateralism. Washington would simply have to accept that, for it, Europe remained what it had been for decades—the 'necessary partner'—now

[61] See Peter Rudolf, 'Der "Krieg gegen den Terror": Konsequenzen für die amerikanische Außenpolitik', *SWP-Aktuell*, 21 (October 2001), 2.

[62] Robert E. Hunter, 'NATO's Article 5: The Conditions for a Military and a Political Coalition', *European Affairs*, 2 (Fall 2001).

[63] Robert Wright, 'America's Sovereignty In a New World', *New York Times* (24 September 2001).

[64] Fred Halliday, 'Aftershocks to Shake Us All', *Guardian Weekly* (29 November–5 December 2001).

more so than ever. In particular, 'now that the Cold War is past, the United States needs NATO as much as it European allies do', if for no other reason than that American forces in Europe 'now serve as the basis for potential deployment across Eurasia and the Middle East'.[65]

Is this so? Without disputing that NATO and the Europeans do remain important for American interests, we can query whether the evidence of the current war sustains the conclusion that America now needs Europe just as much as, or even more than, it ever did, and that as a result of this necessity it will constrain itself to rediscover its multilateralist path. Some traditional allies—for example, Britain—do seem as valuable as ever, but others, including one that not too long ago was being touted as a future 'partner in leadership' by the Americans, occupy a position that is anything but central, especially when compared with the value of newly discovered 'allies'—for example, Uzbekistan—and even of recent antagonists—for example, Russia.[66]

For if one lesson of the recent past this administration has learned—from the first Bush administration—is the necessity of assembling a coalition for combat in the Middle East and central Asia, there is another, even more recent, lesson that instructs American policy-makers. EU elites were not alone in reading into the experience of the Kosovo war certain implications; in their case, that war emphasized the wisdom of greater autonomy and, if they could pay for it, capability. For the Americans, Kosovo demonstrated how *not* to fight a war; to them, it signalled the wisdom of avoiding excessive constraints imposed by the politics of alliances.[67]

Nor is it even apparent—at least to this observer—that American forces in Europe contribute importantly to the success of missions in the Middle East and that portion of Eurasia in which Afghanistan finds itself. The army division that deployed into Uzbekistan in the early stages of the war did so not from 'nearby' Europe but from near the border between Ontario and New York State: Fort Drum, in upstate New York, which is the home of the 10th Mountain Division. And as for the two marine units that made up Task Force 58 deployed to the south-west of Kandahar in the closing stages of the war, their home bases are in California and North Carolina. The military effort was sustained by carrier task forces stationed in the Arabian Sea. The point is that, while it is obvious that American bases in Europe are useful for operations in or near Europe, it is far from obvious that the European theatre will be the focus of America's strategic attention in coming years.

---

[65] William Wallace, 'Europe, the Necessary Partner', *Foreign Affairs*, 80 (May/June 2001), 25.

[66] As one German news account put it, where George Bush senior had a vision of Germany as America's principal strategic partner, George Bush junior looks upon it as a second-class partner; see Günther Lachmann and Ralf Georg Reuth, 'Deutschland am Katzentisch', *Welt am Sonntag* (Berlin, 30 September 2001).

[67] See Kim R. Holmes, *Responding to the Attack on America: Beware of Constraints Imposed by International Coalition*, Heritage Foundation Backgrounder, 1473 (Washington, DC: Heritage Foundation, 17 September 2001).

6. Conclusion

And this brings me to some final thoughts. I argued in this chapter that American multilateralism was primarily identified with a particularistic form of internationalism that accorded a geo-strategically privileged position to Western Europe. For half a century one could gauge the tenor of America's commitment to multilateralism by studying the quality of its relationship with the European allies. In a word, America's multilateralism was Eurocentric and paradoxically for the same reason that American isolationism had also been Eurocentric: because Europe was where the power and the threat both lay. It was important for generations of American leaders before 1940 to avoid the constraints and risks entailed by involvement in the European balance of power. After 1945, it was judged absolutely necessary to engage with European allies precisely to minimize, through the acceptance of constraint, the prospect of risk.

Will Europe continue to figure as centrally in American foreign policy in the next 50 years as it has in the past 50 years? I suspect it will not. NATO will continue to be useful to both the Americans and the Europeans, but it will not become an institution with global reach, and within its own sphere of competence it will become more 'Europeanized' if only by dint of there being less America in it. Within the context of a more Europeanized NATO, it will not matter so much whether the Europeans manage to succeed in concocting their autonomous ESDP. Indeed, to the degree—high—that it will be British and not French preferences that guide the process, the Europeanized NATO will become less and less easy to distinguish from the 'autonomous' ESDP.

As for America, it will be unlikely to recommit itself to anything like the nostalgic, but false, version of security multilateralism understood in the qualitative not simply the quantitative sense.[68] Its 'multilateralism' will continue to be of a selective, or instrumental, nature. In fact, we may discover that multilateralism obfuscates almost as efficiently as does its supposed logical antithesis, unilateralism, especially as interpreted in this chapter, as constituting the effective equivalent of historical isolationism.

Indeed, in what has to be a sober parting shot to a chapter in a book that addresses multilateralism as unilateralism's 'other', it could turn out that we have been pursuing the wrong rubrics all along. For if nothing else, the recent evidence suggests that America has adopted a grand strategy resembling, in Josef Joffe's words, 'Bismarck' rather than 'Britain'; accordingly, we might profitably forget about, or at least down-play, both multilateralism and unilateralism, and concentrate instead upon what truly could be important: the conceptual orphan known as 'bilateralism'.[69] After all, what does a hub-and-spoke

---

[68] For the distinction, see this volume's introduction.

[69] Josef Joffe, '"Bismarck" or "Britain"? Toward an American Grand Strategy after Bipolarity', in Michael Brown (ed.), *America's Strategic Choices* (Cambridge, MA: MIT Press, 2000), and 'Who's Afraid of Mr. Big?' *National Interest*, 64 (Summer 2001).

model of strategy, dependent as it is upon a hegemonic America providing not just public but also private goods to its security partners, connote if not creative and ambitious bilateralism? And why has so little work been done, of late, on this variant of internationalism?[70]

Joffe's terminology can be confusing, for by Bismarck he does not suggest that American strategy accords any elevated status to Germany; to the contrary, if any country in Europe is likely to derive enhanced benefit from this strategy, it will be Britain!

[70] For one important exception, which argues that the only distinction worth drawing between bilateralism and multilateralism is a quantitative, not a qualitative, one, see Stéphane Roussel, *North America's Liberal Order: The Impact of Democratic Values, Norms, and Institutions on Canadian-American Security Relations, 1867–1958* (Kingston, Ontario: Queen's University School of Policy Studies, 2002).

10

Power Multiplied or Power Restrained? The United States and Multilateral Institutions in the Americas

HAL KLEPAK

The United States is a country of the Americas. Despite its deep British and European roots, US relations with its immediate neighbours to the north and the south, or with their imperial parent states, have deeply marked the evolution of United States foreign policy and affected in important ways its approach to the world. And as in other areas of the world, Washington has sought to use multi-lateralism in the Americas as a profitable approach to international affairs offer-ing a number of advantages for the achievement of national aims. The first permanent multilateral organization of which the United States was a member was the Pan American Union, precursor of the Organization of American States. From the beginning of its membership the US sought specific national advant-ages from such a multinational forum, in particular in the areas of exclusion of European influence, legitimization of US policy, access to markets, and mobil-ization of hemispheric resources in the service of US aims.

At the same time, smaller states of the Americas have sought to use multi-lateralism and multinational institutions to restrain the influence of the United States and its behaviour in the western hemisphere. They have often hoped to use such forums to stop US initiatives which they saw as harmful, to anchor the principles of non-intervention in the domestic affairs of states and the equality and sanctity of the nation-state, as well as to slow or halt US tend-encies towards unilateralism in hemispheric matters.

The central argument of this chapter is that United States power, once estab-lished as predominant in the hemisphere, has been nothing short of decisive in the founding, nature, and functioning of the multilateral institutions in the Americas in which it has taken part. The examples of the Pan American Union (PAU)/Organization of American States (OAS) and of the North American Free Trade Agreement (NAFTA) will be used to show this state of affairs in play. The bulk of the chapter will deal with the OAS because of the lessons one can derive from the very long history of US membership. In another case, that of Mercado Común del Sur (Mercosur, or Common Market of the South), it will be shown how, even where the United States is not a member of a multilateral organization in the hemisphere, its weight is still felt in terms of the aims and behaviour of that body.

At the same time, it will be seen that such organizations may indeed on occasion be useful for the smaller states in restraining to at least some extent United States behaviour. But in general one will note that such a restraining role is reserved for moments when US vital interests tend not to be involved and where Latin American or more recently Canadian actions to limit US unilateralism do not negatively affect goals perceived to be key by Washington.

I will attempt to show in the case of each institution studied answers to a series of questions:

- How does the United States dominate the organization?
- How does that domination express itself over time?
- How does the organization serve US interests?
- How does that service change over time?
- How does the US role change the organization over time?
- How does Latin American, West Indian, and Canadian experience with the organization affect their use of it over time?
- Where do US domestic issues play into the US and the organization? What are their effects?

These questions will be addressed, first, by an overview of the United States and the hemisphere over the more than two centuries of its diplomatic and related action therein. With this context in place, we then turn to the specific experience of the PAU and then the OAS. In contrast to the other cases in this volume, this approach places the importance of history squarely to the fore and does so because in the inter-American system one has the longest US experience in the world with a multilateral institution. For well over a century Washington has used this system to further its own interests; and thus its story can help give deeper insights into longer-term US approaches to such multilateral bodies.

This unabashed emphasis on the historical record is necessary here in order to demonstrate the richness of the US experience in the hemisphere and to provide therewith a better sense of the US use of multilateralism in this region. By examining these longer-term elements, it will prove possible to compare this experience with that of the more recent NAFTA and with an organization of which the US is not a member but for which it plays a central role: Mercosur.

1. The United States and its Approach to the Hemisphere

The United States enjoys at the present time asymmetries of absolutely extraordinary dimensions in the Americas. It has a larger GNP than all other countries of the hemisphere combined, the greatest agricultural production, the greatest industrial base, the largest population, the most powerful armed forces, and the richest population. But this has not always been the case.

In colonial times, the population of the 13 colonies was small when compared with Spanish America. But the English-speaking colonists already had connections with their southern neighbours, especially the *bostonenses*, merchants and sailors of New England who found their way south for commercial reasons.

The British colonists drove out both Dutch and French contenders for a role in North America. That same expansion brought the colonies up against Spanish possessions to the west and south. Important for the future of the relationship were British views of the Spanish that were inherited to an extraordinary degree by the New World colonists. This perception of the neighbours to the south tended to be highly negative, infused with a Protestant ethic of great moral superiority and reflecting a view of things Spanish as obscurantist, reactionary, slow, and unproductive.[1]

With Independence Yankee traders became even more active in Spanish America. Those early years were dominated by westward expansion of the US population, largely at the expense of the Indians but soon also spilling over into Spanish territory. The frustrated attempt to seize the British territories to the north during the Revolution rankled, and within two decades Jefferson and many others were openly talking of taking over Cuba and moving both west and south at Spanish territorial expense.[2]

Poor relations with Britain encouraged a US tacit alliance with France and an attack on Canada in 1812. But successive US invasions were beaten back, and Britain, freed of the worst in Europe by Napoleon's defeat, invaded the United States in 1814, seizing huge areas of the country. Ambitions of conquest in the north took a hard blow.

At the same time, US attempts to profit from the European situation at Spanish expense were much more successful. Both Spanish Floridas, including what were to be the southern portions of Mississippi, Georgia, and Alabama, were seized while Spain was busy with its own national survival struggle between 1810 and 1815. The message seemed to be clear to US expansionists: go south and not north. As these events were unfolding, revolutions broke out in Spanish America. From 1808 until 1826, war raged at often ferocious levels in much of the region. Nonetheless, the US was less keen on weakening Spain elsewhere in the Americas, where its own territorial advance was not going to

---

[1] See the work of Angela Moyano Pihassa, *La Resistencia de las Californias a la invasión norteamericana 1846–1848* (Mexico: Consejo Nacional para la Cultura y las Artes, 1992),15–27; Juan Ortega y Molina, *Destino manifiesto: sus razones históricas y su raíz teológica* (Mexico: Alianza Editorial Mexicana, 1989); and Frederick B. Pike, *The United States and Latin America: Myths and Stereotypes of Civilization and Nature* (Austin: University of Texas Press, 1992), 44–132.

[2] Demetrio Boersner, *Relaciones internacionales de América Latina* (Caracas: Nueva Sociedad, 1990), 81–7.

benefit. Washington proved slow to recognize the new nations of Spanish America. Fear once again of the ineffectual Spanish being replaced by more strident powers doubtless played a major part in stimulating this reticence.

The wars ended, however, with a geo-political situation from which it would have been difficult for the United States not to profit. While liberators such as Simón Bolívar had dreamed of a great Latin American independent state capable of defeating European and United States attempts to dominate them, in fact what resulted from the conflict was a series of unstable, weak, and poor nations, incapable of collective action.[3] The United States, through the Monroe Doctrine of 1823, intended to do its best to ensure that no such attempts at reconquest or domination came from Europe, and Royal Navy power made sure this proved the case.

It was with this geo-political environment that the strident nationalist and expansionist philosophy that came to be known as 'Manifest Destiny' was born. This school of thought believed that it was the obvious God-given future of the US to expand into the empty or unproductive lands around it and to bring US civilization, drive, Protestantism, racial purity, and other advantages to bear on those regions. Biding one's time for the proper moment for expansion northwards seemed to be the most intelligent policy while the southern republics were weaker than ever, torn by struggles among their local strong men (caudillos) and among themselves over borders, national organization, and ideology.

The immediate neighbour, Mexico, was in particular trouble, being unable to decide on monarchy or republic, federalism or centralism, conservatism or liberalism, and clericalism or anti-clericalism. Its border regions facing the United States were lightly inhabited and poorly garrisoned. The birth of an independent Texas under overwhelming US tutelage was thus an easy objective. By 1836, this was accomplished and ten years later war broke out between the US and Mexico over the new country's future. US annexation of the State was a fact after two years of war. More important still, other US conquests during the war added almost half of the Mexican national territory to that of the US. Manifest Destiny began to seem very manifest indeed.[4]

Soon Manifest Destiny's proponents were aiming much farther afield than immediate neighbours. Filibustering expeditions, made up of adventurers anxious to repeat the Florida and Texas successes, attacked virtually every independent state in the Caribbean Basin. Rarely officially supported by the US state,

---

[3] Charles Minguet and Annie Morvan, Bolívar: l'unité impossible (Paris: Découverte, 1983).

[4] For a while it appeared the British and Mexicans might combine forces to thwart US expansion, especially when Texas and Oregon crises occurred nearly at the same time in 1846. Palmerston's doubtless correct estimation that Mexico would prove too weak an ally for such high stakes ended such thoughts. See Josefina Zoraida Vázquez and Lorenzo Meyer, México frente a Estados Unidos: un ensayo histórico 1776–1988 (Mexico: EFE, 1989), 51–6.

their successes were nonetheless met with great assistance; and only likely or real failures stimulated no supportive action by Washington.

The US civil war of 1861–5 put paid to these largely private efforts. For the four years of war, and twelve of Reconstruction, national energies were more than absorbed by re-incorporation of the South and expansion westwards. The war had anchored the coastal defence traditions of the navy, reduced the weight of the merchant marine, and permitted French and Spanish adventurism in Mexico with the Maximilian fiasco,[5] off western South America in the form of Spanish naval raiding, and in Santo Domingo with the temporary and much fought-over re-establishment of Spanish direct rule there. The Monroe Doctrine had been put out of action altogether.

In 1867, the new Dominion of Canada was founded out of four of the British North American colonies. Greeted by some in the US as a good thing for the development of North America as a whole, many others tended to see it as a buttressing of the block to US expansion northwards.[6] The US replied to the creation of Canada with the purchase of Alaska from Russia in the same year, virtually excluding the new dominion from the Pacific region even if British Columbia were to join as a new province.

The years to the First World War saw a rapidly increasing US role in the Americas south of the Rio Grande. With the national territory complete and the economy booming, the United States increased its role in Asia and Hawaii as well but nowhere as much as in Latin America. Americans soon became the largest group of investors in Mexico and Central America, rapidly displacing that region's former major source of capital, Great Britain.

While this process was going on, Secretary of State James Blaine called on the countries of the Americas to send delegates to a major international conference to be held in Washington in 1889 to lay the basis for an inter-American system of relations different from those applied in Europe. Latin Americans were invited to consider submitting themselves to an inter-American arbitration court to resolve their disputes. More important than this, however, were attempts to convince them of the wisdom of applying a common external tariff on European imports while lowering tariffs between members of an inter-American customs union. All the countries with close links with Europe rejected this 'America for the Americans' with the countervailing call, coined by Argentina's foreign minister, 'America for humanity'.[7]

---

[5] During the American Civil War, France's Napoleon III attempted to take advantage of US preoccupation with its internal conflict to install Austrian Archduke Maximilian as monarch of Mexico. As Union forces moved towards victory in the United States, they turned their attention to this intrusion and France withdrew. Maximilian was captured and executed by Mexican forces.

[6] The early years of Canadian nationhood, and US reactions to it, are discussed in Charles P. Stacey, *Canada and the Age of Conflict, 1867–1921*, i. (Toronto: University of Toronto Press, 1984), 17–40.

[7] Alain Rouquié, *Amérique Latine: Introduction à l'Extrême-Occident* (Paris: Seuil, 1987), 394.

There was agreement, nonetheless, that there should be further meetings of the governments of the hemisphere. The US had certainly staked out what it felt was a leadership role in what would come to be known as Pan-Americanism, a political belief that the Americas were somehow different from and better than Europe and should have relations among their countries that reflected this superiority.[8] And a major success was the agreement at the conference that there should be an International Union of American Republics—the Brazilian monarchy had fallen the year before and the term 'republic' ensured the exclusion of Canada—whose role would be to compile and distribute economically useful data. A small office was to be set up in Washington to do this work under the US Secretary of State and would be styled the Commercial Office of the American Republics. It was totally dominated by the US from the beginning.[9]

In 1898, the United States arrived on the Latin American stage with a vengeance. This time war with Spain led to the temporary acquisition of Cuba and the permanent occupation of Puerto Rico. Shortly thereafter the 1901 Hay-Pauncefote accord led to British acquiescence to US naval superiority in the Caribbean and to US sole control of the Panama Canal then being planned. Three years later Theodore Roosevelt added his famous corollary to the Monroe Doctrine giving the US the right to police the Latin American region in the name of all civilized nations. All these moves were accompanied by massive United States investment in the Caribbean and 'dollar diplomacy' soon became the model for relations between Washington and its southern neighbours.

Further Pan American conferences were held in Mexico 1901–2 and at Rio de Janeiro in 1906. The Washington commercial office was reorganized but this merely confirmed absolute US dominance therein by ensuring the permanent headship of the bureau by the US Secretary of State. In 1906, US power was even more evident with the recent 'creation' of Panama and a protectorate arrangement established over Cuba. Major Latin American disenchantment with Washington marked the event, but Brazilian diplomacy under the exceptional leadership of Baron Rio Branco began to show the new approach to the United States that was to mark it for most of the twentieth century. Far from confronting the US and opposing its designs for the Americas, as Argentina was doing, Brazilian policy would see the country as the major ally of Washington in the region. It was no surprise to see a more activist secretariat for the Pan American organization come out of this meeting as well as a more standardized system for future meetings.

The First World War saw Latin America further cut off from Europe and its ties with the US develop even more, given the need for industrial imports and markets for regional goods. When the US entered the war in mid-1917, several Central American and Caribbean countries followed suit. The seeds of future

[8] See Arthur Whitaker, *The Western Hemisphere Idea: Its Rise and Decline* (Ithaca: Cornell University Press, 1954).

[9] Ismael Moreno Pino, *Orígenes y evolución del sistema interamericano* (Mexico: Secretaría de Relaciones Exteriores, 1977), 75–6.

inter-American security cooperation were thus sewn. The weakening of the European connection gathered steam and the US was fully present to harvest the fruit of this trend. At the same time, the presence of the US expanded enormously not only in the area of investment but also through military interventions in the Caribbean Basin. While the 14 Points might be official policy elsewhere, there was little reflection of them in US relations with Latin America.

This was all to change the 1930s. President Franklin Roosevelt quickly moved to alter dramatically the US approach to Latin America when he adopted his Good Neighbour Policy in 1933–4. This called for relations based on mutual respect between the US and Latin American nations. In this context, US occupations of Haiti, Nicaragua, and other parts of the Caribbean region were ended and even the US right to intervene in Cuba was abolished. Pan Americanism did seem to be a reality as military interventions stopped and the more ferocious types of arm twisting of governments were abandoned.

The repayment for this policy was soon to be a reality as well. As war in Europe approached, successive hemispheric conferences reflected a much more united approach to regional cooperation and even defence. In the decisive summer of 1940, with most of Europe falling to the fascist Axis powers, the US found unity behind it in the determination not to allow any European colonies in the Americas to be handed over to Germany or Italy. The US also reached out to Canada and each country assured the other that it would not stand by if its neighbour were invaded.

When Pearl Harbor was attacked in December 1941, several Latin American states followed the US in declaring war on Japan. A major defence cooperation conference was held in February 1942 in Rio de Janeiro to decide how to jointly face the challenge; and while Washington was not successful in getting all it wanted in terms of inter-American solidarity, it did achieve a great deal. An Inter-American Defence Board was set up to coordinate regional military efforts.[10] A wide range of economic accords was agreed to, and a body was put in place to coordinate efforts to rid the hemisphere of fascist groups.

The most vital assistance provided by the Latin American nations to the US war effort was the securing of the southern flank of the country; something never entirely achieved during the First World War, as is evidenced by successive twists of the Mexican revolution. In addition, though, Latin America provided valuable mineral and agricultural resources to the US and denied them to the Axis. Mexico sent male farm labourers to the US to release that country's workers for military duty. It also sent an air squadron to the Pacific war. Brazil did even more with a full division in Italy, joint anti-submarine operations in the Atlantic, and US forces *in situ* operating the air bridge to North Africa.

With Europe weakened more than ever, and with Latin America cut off from its major partners, US penetration of the region grew apace. Defence

---

[10] Rodolfo Garrié Faget, *Organismos militares interamericanos* (Buenos Aires: Depalma, 1968).

cooperation with Canada and Newfoundland was even greater than that with Latin America. But throughout the hemisphere US leadership was now a given.

The legacy of inter-American wartime cooperation was a largely positive one. The war for democracy was welcomed by broadened elites more willing to countenance political change. Pan Americanism had stood the test and had benefited both Latin America and the United States. Relations among the countries were not on a zero-sum basis but could benefit both. Policies based on good neighbourly relations worked for all.

Under the impact of this thinking both Latin America and the United States looked forward to extending the wartime arrangements into the peace. To do so, they first met to discuss the post-war region at Chapultepec in Mexico in 1945. Agreements there led to a further meeting at Rio in 1947 leading to the signature of the Rio Pact, or more formally the Inter-American Treaty of Reciprocal Assistance, the first post-war mutual assistance treaty and the model for later ones elsewhere.

The following year, the Pact's main security features were included in a charter for a new organization set up to replace the unwieldy elements of the old Pan American Union. The new Organization of American States was to have economic, political, and security elements and wide political coordination roles. These accords were to be followed with a peaceful settlement of disputes arrangement; but this has never come into force.[11]

2. The PAU and the OAS: Grand-daddy and Daddy of Them All

The above context allows us to begin to ask again in the cold war context the questions raised at the beginning of the chapter. In view of the evolution of the United States in Latin America, what did and does the United States seek from Pan Americanism? Has this always been the same thing? How does Washington act in order to ensure that it gets what it seeks? What does Latin America want? How does it act to try to reach these goals?[12]

The PAU

All of these questions are reflected in any overview of the behaviour of the US and Latin American states in the PAU and later in the OAS. From as early as

---

[11] For this story, see Héctor Fáundez-Ledezma, 'The Inter-American System: Its Framework for Conflict Resolution', in José Silva-Michelena (ed.), *Latin America: Peace, Democratization and Economic Crisis* (Tokyo: The United Nations University, 1988), 168–86.

[12] At this stage the question will not be asked about Canada. That country rejected Pan Americanism from the beginning. And it is so new to the OAS that its revision of ideas on a new Pan Americanism is only now taking shape.

the US invitations to the 1889 conference, one can see the desire in Washington to exclude rival influences in the hemisphere and to push forward US interests, especially economic ones, through bringing Latin American economic behaviour closer to US needs.

The US was in the late 1880s becoming a major industrial power with economic interests pushing for outlets for US production. But it was not easy for US manufacturers to break into markets long dominated by Europeans. While Britain was by far Latin America's most important economic partner, France and Germany were also impressive players there. In most countries the US lagged well behind. There was a widely perceived need to find some means to help US penetration of these markets; and the rather naive objectives of the US callers of the conference bear witness to both US ignorance of the realities of the region and that country's lack of understanding of its own reputation there.

Keeping the British and other Europeans out, or at least finding some way of pushing oneself in more forcefully, was the undeniable objective of US policy at this point, and the selling of an early version of Pan Americanism appeared to be one way to do so. The failure of the conference to reach all the decisions that Washington hoped for showed to what extent the US lack of relative power at this stage hindered Washington from imposing its preferred way forward. Power relations would have to change dramatically before any such gains could be made and before a multilateral institution in keeping with US objectives could be founded.

With the explosion of US economic, political, and security interests in the region in the following 20 years, Washington's desires grew but so did its abilities to influence events. By 1906, at Rio de Janeiro things were beginning to change. As mentioned, Rio Branco believed that Brazil could benefit from a more permanent organization and was willing to accept US leadership of it. He appears to have believed this, first, because of Brazil's size and importance, which suggested that Brazil could fend off excessive US demands; second, because of his belief that European interests were much more powerful and thus threatening to Brazil than those of the still unimpressive United States; and third, because Brazil could use the US, already seen by its rival Argentina as anathema, as a pro-Brazilian pillar in that rivalry.[13]

The result was a strengthening of the organization which took on some of the attributes of a real institution. By the 1910 Buenos Aires meeting, there was a name change reflecting this evolution; and a permanent building in central Washington was given to the new PAU. The growth of US power and influence, but also the perception that such power was not as yet excessively menacing, are vital in explaining what had happened.

When war came to Europe in 1914, it was to signal the beginning of a long process of European decline in Latin American affairs, a decline already signposted by Hay-Pauncefoote, a client state of the US created in Panama in 1903,

---

[13] Alvaro Lins, *Rio Branco* (São Paulo: Alfa-Omega, 1995).

an exclusively US canal in Panama in 1914, and interventions by US marines in much of the Caribbean Basin between 1903 and the war. US exports and investment in Latin America grew enormously, to the point where Britain was superseded now in most of northern Latin America. The costs of the war in Europe were such that the great powers came out of the conflict with their political, economic, cultural, and military influence massively affected. Britain was nearly bankrupt, as was France. Germany was out of the game. Nor was Japan—nor, indeed, the new Soviet Union—as yet in any position to influence events in this far-away region. And while these countries had been at each other's throats, the US had penetrated their markets and sources of raw materials in the region with ruthless but impressive efficiency. Many of the old linkages between Europe and Latin America had been ruptured and many of these were not to be re-established.[14]

By the 1923 Santiago Pan American Conference, the US was able to ensure that a number of clearly political issues were included on the agenda: rights of foreigners operating in the region, closer political coordination among members, and common approaches to non-American actions against an American state. The Latin Americans were able to make some changes in the secretariat at this time including the abolition of the Secretary of State as ex officio head and a provision for the appointment of delegates specifically assigned the representation of their countries at the PAU. The US was, however, more than willing to accept these changes in return for the clearly greater political coordination that would now be occurring.

The Great Depression and the consequent falling back of much of Europe on to its colonial economic linkages furthered the process of loosening the links with Latin America. And the Good Neighbour Policy of the US did much of the rest of the work to be done. At exactly the time Europe seemed to be turning its back on Latin America, a new and positive face was being put on US policy towards the region.

As mentioned, when a second world war came, Washington was superbly placed to harvest the fruits of its policy at exactly the same time as yet another, and in this case the most powerful, shock struck the historic European-Latin American relationship. And in the meantime the US had worked hard to make something much more concrete and much more value-sharing come into being in the reform and improvement of the PAU over the 1930s. The acceptance of those reforms by the Latin American states reflected again the great gains in relative power made by the United States in the years in question, the loss of influence by the Europeans, and finally the reduced fear of the US on the part of the Latin Americans resulting from years of relatively favourable treatment at Washington's hands.[15] By any standards, most Latin American

---

[14] Rouquié, *Amerique Latine*, 395–7.
[15] See the work of David G. Haglund, *Latin America and the Transformation of US Strategic Thought* (Albuquerque: University of New Mexico Press, 1984), 46–50.

nations—Argentina and Chile excepted—proved to be stalwart if not necessarily very effective allies for the US. The bulk of the region was harnessed to the US war effort and Washington had reason to be pleased.

The OAS

In the reinforcing of an inter-American system after the end of the war, one saw a combination of power and mutual interest again at work. The United States was now the undisputed leader of the West and by far the most powerful country in the world, not only in the Americas. Its economic, political, cultural, scientific, and military influence was inescapable. Canada, the West Indies, and Latin America had all ended up cooperating with it during the war, even the reluctant Argentines finally declaring war on the Axis.[16]

At the same time, the 'Colossus of the North' appeared now to be well-disposed towards Latin America and willing to collaborate in peacetime on the basis of the Pan Americanism which had served Latin American interests so well during the recent war and had brought unheard of prosperity as a result of the high prices resulting from the war for so many regional products. Little wonder, then, that the Latin Americans accepted happily the idea of a conference in 1945 to discuss the post-war world and again in 1947 and 1948 to make more concrete inter-American cooperation on a number of fronts.

In general, the Latin Americans wanted to see something like a Marshall Plan for Latin America, a recognition of the regional effort during the war, and a mirror of what was being done in Europe. In response, Latin American states offered the US their collaboration in establishing a new inter-American body where the hemisphere could coordinate its efforts under US leadership. There was a remarkably generalized feeling that such leadership would be good for Latin America but, even if this proved not to be the case, the Latin Americans generally felt that the new body would serve to limit US freedom of action regionally by sanctifying the principles of non-intervention in the domestic affairs of states and of the formal equality of states.

The position of the United States had meanwhile undergone considerable change. While recognizing the value of the Latin American wartime contribution, the US placed even more stock in its European and Asian allies. And after 1945, the US was no longer simply the major partner in the Americas. It was a world power in an increasingly bipolar world, with interests in all continents and priorities far from the hemisphere. Indeed, the major items on key desks in Washington were rarely related to Latin America.

So if the Latin Americans were willing to see US-inspired change in the system, what was driving the US to seek such change? The answer can again be seen in the new scene faced by Washington. Yet there are major elements of

---

[16] John Child, *Unequal Alliance: The Inter-American Military System 1938–1978* (Boulder, CO: Westview Press, 1980), 27–62.

continuity here where US interests are concerned. For if the US were to take on the role of one of two major powers in a global struggle for survival, then it had to choose its battlegrounds. Latin America was far from central to the East-West rivalry then evolving. Europe and Asia were. Thus once again, as during other 'wars' the US had been involved in, the key issue was to have the southern flank secure so as to have one's hands free for more crucial efforts elsewhere.[17]

The US thus needed a new organization in the Americas that kept the lid on matters there while Washington busied itself with more important business in the hot spots of the world. That organization would have to have major security elements embedded in it, even in peacetime. And it would need to have arrangements guaranteeing US access to strategic imports during crises. It also needed a safe and automatically supportive inter-American grouping, one that represented almost a third of the membership of the then key world body—the UN—and would be there when the US needed votes in New York.

In addition, the US wanted to avoid having problems brought to the UN as a result of what might be future US actions in the hemisphere. The US pressed hard at the negotiations on the UN Charter to ensure that there would still be room for regional organizations despite the overall responsibilities of the UN for the whole international community. And the US achieved this to the letter. Chapter VIII not only permitted their existence but made arrangements for regional bodies to deal with issues first and only then pass them up the line to the global level. Thus issues related to eventual unilateral US interventions in Latin America would be dealt with first in a more US-dominated body in Washington before perhaps being sent on to the UN. Lastly, the US needed a grouping that could legitimize Washington's decisions in the coming cold war.

This could hardly have been farther from the Latin American perspective on the new institution. For them, it would coordinate efforts for regional development, would link peace and security with the economic interests of the developing countries of the region, and was to secure such US involvement in order to achieve that development. The Latin American states likewise wanted no regional body that would slow or even block their access to the UN at crucial moments and force them to go through a US-dominated grouping before having such access. And it was finally useful for them to have an OAS in order to act to rein in US unilateralism, rather than giving it free rein and support for whatever Washington decided.

On the other hand, realpolitik obliged. Europe was now a fully spent force where Latin America was concerned. Not even Britain was any longer a major player on the regional scene. No possible counterpoise to US power could be conceived of in the post-war era.

---

[17] This way of thinking is well discussed in Lars Schoultz, *National Security and United States Policy toward Latin America* (Princeton: Princeton University Press, 1987), 37–9.

Thus the confrontations in the OAS of the long years of the cold war could be seen coming virtually at the rebirth of the PAU in its new form. And the likelihood that Latin America would usually have to buckle under, in the last analysis, to US power seemed clear. It is hardly surprising that Canada was little tempted by the organization as of these years. While Ottawa had shown some shy interest during the war, as part of its desire to multilateralize the relationship with the US as British power waned, Washington had moved once again with alacrity to stifle such thoughts, suggesting once more that Canadian membership in the PAU, or indeed the OAS, would somehow be letting the British in by the back door. This rejection of its interest was increasingly acceptable to Canada, which saw where the organization was likely to go given the almost diametrically opposite goals for it in the minds of Latin Americans and the United States.[18]

The US got virtually everything it wanted on the key issues of the day. A security treaty which enshrined collective defence in the Americas under absolute US leadership was soon combined with bilateral accords with most Latin American countries—Mutual Assistance Pacts—which ensured considerable links between the vast US military and the infinitely smaller defence forces of Latin America. The US was guaranteed access to strategic products and taken as the model for arms and equipment standardization agreements. Indeed, US equipment and weapons were increasingly accepted as the basis for such standardization and arms sales and other accords ensured US influence in training, logistics, administration, and doctrine.[19]

Latin American countries would concentrate on local defence and leave international security threats to the US. They would thus not need, in US eyes, access to sophisticated weapon systems. In addition, the Bogotá Pact, a system of conflict resolution constituting the third pillar of the new system, would ensure that Latin American states did not make war on one another and thus destabilize the southern flank. However, the United States was not successful in making this last instrument operational. But the weight of US influence was thought more than capable of producing the same results, especially if US control over arms imports could ensure that the best weapons did not reach Latin American hands. In the political sphere the US victory was equally complete: no outside state was to have even the slightest real political role in Latin America. And this went for the Soviet Union as well as the more traditional rivals of the US in the region.

The Latin Americans, on the other hand, got little of what they had expected. The OAS Charter spoke almost dismissively of economic cooperation while

[18] James Rochlin, *Discovering the Americas: the Evolution of Canadian Foreign Policy towards Latin America* (Vancouver: University of British Columbia Press, 1994), 17–24, and the first chapters of Peter McKenna, *Canada and the OAS* (Ottawa: Carleton University Press, 1995).
[19] See the study by Horacio Veneroni, *Estados Unidos y las fuerzas armadas de América Latina* (Buenos Aires: Periferia, 1973).

using all the normal platitudes about how important it was. There was no Marshall Plan for Latin America nor any major attempts at linking US policy interests with development issues. The OAS was to be, if anything, even more dominated by the US than was its predecessor, a state of affairs again reflective of the massive growth in US power combined with the virtual collapse of any potential counterpoise from Europe or elsewhere.

The Cold War

This system stood the test of time very well indeed, from a United States perspective. When the Guatemalan reformist government of Jacobo Arbenz threatened US economic interests in that country, Washington was able to browbeat Latin American governments into accepting that, even though an accusation that the Guatemalan president was a Communist was patently ridiculous, his government was unduly under Communist 'influence'. At the Caracas OAS meeting of 1954, the US obtained a declaration that communism was incompatible with the inter-American community, and was able, with little Latin American criticism, to stage the overthrow of the Guatemalan government.

Cuba after 1959 came closer to causing a problem; but even here the system worked well for the US. As the Castro revolution moved left, Washington was able to orchestrate a general OAS rejection of the regime, its expulsion from the security structures of the inter-American system, and then its suspension from the OAS altogether. From 1962 to 1967, successive meetings of the organization achieved all of this as well as establishing a collective embargo of the country. And while Mexico stood aloof from such attempts to isolate Castro, all other countries in the OAS cooperated even though some kept such collaboration close to the merely rhetorical level. Even so, only Mexico City kept relations with Havana and regional isolation was reasonably complete.[20]

Equally striking, the US engaged in a massive military and economic campaign to defeat the 'export of revolution' activities of the new Cuban government. The Alliance for Progress became, somewhat belatedly, the Marshall Plan the Latin Americans had asked for over a decade and a half before. And the Latin American armed forces were the targets of a huge military assistance programme aimed at preparing them better for the counter-insurgency tasks involved in defeating leftist revolution. An Inter-American Defence College was added to the 22-year-old Inter-American Defence Board, a specialist counter-insurgency School of the Americas began large-scale training of Latin American officers, and annual conferences of the commanders of the armed forces of the Americas were instituted. Joint exercises and increased transfers of equipment and weapons completed the picture for a much more active inter-American security system.

---

[20] F. V. García-Amador, *La Cuestión cubana en la OEA y la crisis del sistema interamericano* (Miami: University of Miami Press, 1987), 13–99.

Not all of this was based on the OAS structure, however. Reticence on the part of some Latin American countries was soon visible where US efforts to coordinate a hemispheric response to the 'communist threat' were concerned. And this slowed US efforts within the OAS to put together a truly inter-American response to what was viewed in Washington as an international communist challenge. Ad hoc or bilateral arrangements increasingly had to serve instead of region-wide ones based on the regional organization. Mexico's unwillingness to countenance OAS initiatives in the military field was seconded in the 1970s by others. Nonetheless, the US was able to use the system remarkably well in bringing a widespread and successful military effort to bear on the Cubans. The 'export of revolution' soon died out as a result of these countermeasures which led most spectacularly to the death of Che Guevara in October 1967 and to the at least temporary defeat of leftist revolution everywhere in the region.

The contradictions between US and many Latin American objectives in the regional body continued to show themselves, and this state of affairs worsened as the years went by. While US policy helped make or break Latin American governments in the 1960s and 1970s, and only rightist governments could expect to receive favour in Washington, with time this changed. Military regimes supported by the US by the end of the 1970s were giving way to civilian democratic governments of a less cold war orientation. In that decade many countries in the Americas re-established their relations with Cuba. At the same time their willingness to play the game at the OAS was also slackening.

The organization was losing what steam it had in its early years under the impact of its inherent contradictions. The 1965 US invasion of the Dominican Republic had found Washington still able to use an OAS fig-leaf to legitimize the action. But by a decade later, Latin American governments received little for their automatic support of the US. In reaction, in the mid-1970s they called for institutional reform and modernization. The consequences of standing up to the US were likewise less massive, given the shaking of that power's self-confidence in the Vietnam War, its failures to unseat Castro, and the returning economic influence of Europe in the region.

The institution could simply not find a role for itself in successive crises. As the Central American civil wars heated up in the late 1970s and early 1980s, the OAS was at best seen as a bystander. When Peru and Ecuador had in 1981 their 'mini-war' the organization had little to contribute. And even more dramatically, the Falklands war saw Argentina and much of the rest of Latin America shocked to discover that the Rio Pact was not actually applicable to a real case of what they viewed as aggression against an American nation.[21] Time and again on the security front, the organization had failed its members, or so they perceived things.

---

[21] Lawrence Freedman, *Britain and the Falklands War* (Oxford: Basil Blackwell, 1988), 42–3, 77–8; and Heriberto Cairo Carou, *La Construcción social del conflicto territorial argentino-británico* (Mos (Pontevedra): Novo Século, 1995), 134–5.

At the same time, US interest in mobilizing the organization waned. The Reagan government found the environment in the OAS unhelpful for its much-vaunted 'roll-back' of communism. There was little shared ground on which to build common approaches to joint problems. Everything pointed to the decline of the organization. Latin American frustration joined to US lack of commitment sealed the fate of the OAS for years and increased US unilateralism resulted.

The End of the Cold War

With the end of the cold war, attempts have been made to make the OAS more relevant. Some of the unwieldy and inefficient bureaucracy has been cut and procedures at least somewhat streamlined. Major current issues such as drugs, the anchoring of democracy, regional security and arms control, regional economic integration, and others have slowly got on to the agenda and agencies of the organization have been set up to move these issues forward. The US national agenda is visible in all that has been done.

The US first priority in the region over more than a decade has doubtless been the anti-narcotics issue. In response, the Inter-American Drug Abuse Control Commission (CICAD after its initials in Spanish), an OAS agency attempting to coordinate approaches to the problem across the Americas, has been set up.[22] Another priority in Washington has been support for democracy. And an OAS Unit for the Promotion of Democracy has seen the light of day in consequence. Security matters such as hemispheric confidence-building measures, education for peace, ecological matters, and others the US could never get on the table during the cold war can now be addressed in the OAS in the new Permanent Committee for Security Affairs. And a number of issues of economic integration raised at summits of the Americas have been handed over to the organization for addressing. There is little doubt, then, that the organization is knowing something of a rebirth at the moment, even if it is easy to exaggerate the health and energy of the reborn infant. It is also clear that US interests have continued to dominate in this region where US hegemony locally has now been reinforced by US unipolarity—at least in security, cultural, and political affairs—more widely on the global scene.

There has been more congruence, however, in recent years between the US and Latin American agendas than at any time since the Second World War or even before. This has been crucial in allowing Caribbean Commonwealth countries to enter the OAS but even more dramatically in opening the door to the long-awaited entry of Canada. All these countries find the OAS a more comfortable place than it could possibly have been at the height of the cold war. Operational areas of cooperation in fields of mutual concern such as

---

[22] See Peter Smith, *Drugs Policy in the Americas* (Boulder, CO: Westview, 1992).

drugs, crime, security, and democracy have also laid more of a basis for a cooperative spirit between the United States and its southern partners. Latin American countries may have priorities where such issues are concerned different from those of the US. But that can often mean that they perceive the challenges posed by them as being shared and dealt with only through joint efforts. This may well be the most hopeful element for a real change in the rather dismal record of hemispheric collaboration over much of the period discussed. That having been said, US power continues to prevail on matters of crucial importance to that country; and Latin American, Commonwealth Caribbean, and Canadian policy in the organization still frequently aims at limiting the age-old tendencies in the US toward unilateralism.

3. The North American Free Trade Agreement

The emphasis in this chapter, as pointed out above, falls on the Organization of American States. But the US has in recent years joined another multilateral organization in the Americas, one whose responsibilities are much more limited than those of the OAS, but which nonetheless has demonstrated patterns of US behaviour useful for a study of this kind.

NAFTA is a free-trade agreement. And while its associated agreements touch on issues such as labour, the environment, and other seemingly non-free trade matters, the reality is that the arrangements centre on trade. Needless to say, however, the accord's importance goes much further, especially in terms of investment but also in political, immigration, international relations, and even some security terms.

It is also true that the main stimulants to the founding of such a grouping are found in the trade field. The United States sought such a thing essentially because of its fear of being cut out in the trend towards trade blocs visible in the years since the success of the European Economic Community (EEC) became evident in the 1960s. US perceptions of its own advantages in the world economy were often not very optimistic at this time and rightly or wrongly many economists felt drastic surgery was necessary to regain competitiveness.[23]

Canada and Mexico felt even greater pulls towards such an agreement. Ottawa had long sought trade diversification not only as a means to ensure the best economic conditions possible for a trading country like Canada but also in order to reduce the drift towards ever greater economic and political dependence on the United States. While this was relatively easy to do for much

---

[23] For this situation in some detail, see Rosa Cusminsky, 'Algunos intereses económicos de Estados Unidos en la firma de un tratado de libre comercio', in Bárbara Driscoll de Alvarado and Mónica Gambrill (eds), *El Tratado de Libre Comercio* (Mexico: UNAM, 1992).

of the time since confederation, with time it became more difficult. For the first eight decades as a dominion, Canada's trade relationship with the United Kingdom ensured that the country was not excessively dependent on its great southern neighbour. But with British decline in the 1940s, concern began to grow.

In trade and investment terms, the British connection weakened rapidly after the Second World War. The UK's weakness was compounded by a vastly reduced economic importance both as a market for Canadian goods and as a source for Canada's imports. The massive struggle of the war meant that the US, as in Latin America, had replaced Britain in many areas of Canadian import needs, and reduced circumstances meant that the mother country was no longer in a position to take such a large percentage of Canadian exports.[24]

The fact was that the two main North American countries were becoming increasingly a single economy. Canadian governments reacted by attempting to diversify trade and investment through government stimulants and programmes of a variety of kinds. Repeatedly, trade missions were sent to the rest of Europe, to Latin America, Asia, and even Africa. The Mackenzie-King government, known for wishing to loosen ties with the UK for most of its long mandate, sought to strengthen them as it realized how weak Britain had in fact become through the titanic struggle of 1939–45.[25] The government of John Diefenbaker (1958–63), faced with statistics which left no doubt about where trends were leading, attempted a rearguard action to stimulate trade with the UK and the Commonwealth. And Pierre Trudeau (1968–84) aimed to place a 'Third Option' at the centre of Canadian trade policy, putting emphasis on staving off US economic influence in Canada through an active policy of stimulating trade with Europe, Asia, and Latin America. In all these circumstances, political factors were at least as important as economic. It was generally thought in Ottawa that economic dominance must necessarily lead to political dominance. And this, it was of course felt, had to be avoided.[26]

In Mexico a similar picture prevailed. Mexican governments since the Porfiriato of 1876–1910 had understood the largely political importance of diversifying trade and investment away from excessive dependence on the United States. President Adolfo López Mateos (1958–64), Diefenbaker's contemporary, was particularly active in this area. He was followed by two further presidents, each sharing the concern, Luis Echeverría and José López Portillo.[27] Only after 1983, and amid a series of shocks to the Mexican economy, did presidents such as Miguel de la Madrid, Carlos Salinas, and Ernesto Zedillo come to accept fully

[24] This situation is fully discussed in Jack Granatstein, *How Britain's Weakness Forced Canada into the Arms of the United States* (Toronto: University of Toronto Press, 1989).

[25] Stacey, *Canada and the Age of Conflict*, ii., 421–5.

[26] Rod Dobell and Michael Neufeld (eds), *Beyond NAFTA: the Western Hemisphere Interface* (Lantzville, British Columbia): Oolichan Press, 1993).

[27] This is discussed in Héctor Aguilar Camín, *Subversiones silenciosas* (Mexico: Aguilar, 1993), 42–6.

that dependence was inevitable and that it was now necessary to abandon the diversification policy, at least the elements which annoyed the US.[28]

The reality of course was that Mexico's economy was becoming as closely tied to the United States as was Canada's, and that despite determined government policies aiming at ensuring that this did not result. Those policies were a failure, as were their Canadian counterparts. Both Prime Minister Brian Mulroney of Canada (1984–93) and President Carlos Salinas (1988–94) were to come to the conclusion that something would have to be done about this.

The Canadians were first to reach the seemingly self-evident conclusion. With growing protectionist sentiment in the United States, and with Europe and several other regions of the world becoming large trading blocs, Canada would simply have to do something. The failure of the Third Option policy to find a place for Canada with the major European entity meant that only the United States itself, despite obvious disadvantages, could offer Canada a partnership which could protect its trade-based prosperity. Hence in the mid-1980s moves began which would end with the signature of the Canada-US Free Trade agreement in 1988. The US negotiated hard with its northern neighbour and most analysts felt Washington got a deal that served it well.[29]

Just after the first months of bilateral discussions between Washington and Ottawa, Mexico and the United States began to have similar discussions about a free trade agreement. In 1990, within two years of the signature of the bilateral Canada-US agreement, Ottawa made clear its interest in joining a trilateral negotiation. Mexico likewise took its time in deciding whether this was a good thing. But in the end both smaller partners gave key importance to the political and economic advantages inherent in the admittedly limited multilateralism of a three-way deal. And in 1992 the NAFTA accords were signed, beginning to come into force in January 1994.

United States public opinion was far from universally in favour of the NAFTA arrangements. While not particularly troubled by the bilateral deal with Canada, the Mexican dimension of the new accord, especially those elements revolving around cheaper labour and the likely movement of firms south, was deeply worrying to many in the US.[30] At the same time, environmental and human rights issues related to the state of the Mexican political and economic system came to the fore.

Be that as it may, Congress approved the deal and NAFTA became a reality. The United States here again had got what it wanted over all even though it is

---

[28] Nora Lustig, *Mexico: The Remaking of an Economy* (Washington, DC: Brookings Institution, 1992), 132–7.
[29] For much of this, see the relevant chapters of Ricardo Grinspun and Maxwell Cameron (eds), *The Political Economy of North American Free Trade* (Montreal: McGill-Queen's University Press, 1993).
[30] Leonard Waverman, 'Post-NAFTA: Can the United States, Canada and Mexico Deepen Their Economic Relationship?', in Jean Daudelin and Edgar Dosman (eds), *Beyond Mexico* (Ottawa, Carleton University Press, 1995).

easy to exaggerate the degree to which the US was united on the matter. Nonetheless, the US became the unquestioned leader of a bloc of three countries who enjoy protection from at least some of the nefarious factors that troubled them about the previous evolution of the international trading system. But selling the deal to the US Congress and people had required that the Clinton administration place the question significantly more in the security area than one might have thought. Opposition was fierce and it appears that only appeals to avoid the chaos in Mexico that the failure of NAFTA would have occasioned pushed many legislators to accept it as needed largely for US national security reasons. Americans were clearly uncertain about whether they really wanted free trade in North America or more widely. But they were certain they did not want a destabilized Mexico on their borders. And this mix of far-from-common economic desires and almost totally shared strategic ones regarding how to deal with a potentially unstable and volatile neighbour proved enough to carry the day.

Representing almost 90 per cent of the gross regional product, the US is able to dominate on most matters of concern to it within NAFTA. Indeed, the major questions being raised by the two other partners relate to that dominance. The first of these is the dispute resolution features of the accords, especially those related to dumping.[31] From the perspective of the smaller partners, when a dispute is judged in favour of them the US shows a tendency simply to ignore the judgement; and with its massive power to 'link' the specific issue to other outcomes in other fields desired by the smaller partner, the latter may feel it wiser on occasion simply to keep quiet or at least muffle its protests. Thus the US can reap the benefits of the relationship without paying the full price for a rules-based system which actually might on occasion hurt the US.[32]

The second question, that of NAFTA expansion, while more political, still sees the US holding all or most of the cards. Here, both Mexico and Canada have profoundly wished the accords to be expanded to Chile and other countries in the Americas. At first the US administration was fully in agreement with this vision. However, in the meantime US public opinion had shifted on the matter, largely as a result of the 1994 Mexican peso crisis 'bail-out', a move usually viewed as extremely unpopular with much of the US public.

---

[31] 'Dumping' is a term used to describe the export of a 'product at a ... price below its "normal value" (usually the price of a product in the domestic market of the exporting country) if such dumped imports cause injury to a domestic industry in the territory of the importing ... party'. See 'Agreement on Implementation of Article VI (Anti-Dumping)', in WTO, *A Summary of the Final Act of the Uruguay Round*, at www.wto.org/english/docs_e/legal_e/ursum_e.htm. States signatories of GATT (Article VI) are permitted to levy duties on such goods. Anti-dumping action does not appear to make much sense with a free trade area but the utility of such acts in curbing trade trends hurtful to one's own country frequently makes its use politically almost irresistible. See Waverman, 'Post-NAFTA', 62–7.

[32] This was to some extent foreseen by specialists. See Waverman, 'Post-NAFTA'.

The result is that Congress refused President Clinton's request to proceed to negotiate with other candidates for NAFTA membership on a 'fast-track' basis.[33] In effect, US Congressional opposition stalled the whole process of NAFTA expansion towards the 2005 deadline for an inter-American free trade area, set by the hemisphere's leaders in Miami in December 1994. Canada and Mexico were thus left without either the economic or the political advantages of multilateralism which they expected when NAFTA was signed. It remains to be seen whether Mr Bush's relative enthusiasm for hemispheric free trade will result in significant progress in this field.

Here again, then, power counts and has indeed been decisive in the foundation of NAFTA, its functioning, and its future prospects. Key elements of the US public, if not the government, appear to be getting what they want from the system as it prevails at this time, without paying much of a price for its advantages. Meanwhile, relations of power ensure that the other two partners, while doubtless benefiting in many ways from the accords, are not harvesting all of the political and economic advantages to which they feel they have a right.

The Bush government, in the wake of 11 September 2001, nonetheless seems to remain keen on the process of an inter-American free trade area. And Congress, while so far too busy with the 'war on terrorism' to give much time to the hemisphere's trading and investment arrangements, does appear to be more likely to concur than it did with the president's predecessor.

4. Mercosur

The United States is not, of course, a member of Mercosur, the free trade and eventual customs union agreement linking Argentina, Brazil, Paraguay, and Uruguay, and having as associate members Bolivia and Chile. However, it is our intention here to show that such are the power relationships in the Americas that, even without membership, the US dimension of inter-American political and economic relations is such that the foundation and functioning of Mercosur is greatly affected by that country.

With the Canada-US Free Trade Area and the European Community only too obvious realities, moves towards greater integration were increasingly seen in Latin America. The disastrous showing of the region during the 1980s, marked not only by the deep debt crisis but also by economic growth at levels leading to the designation of the ten years as the 'lost decade', led most of the region to search desperately for original solutions. New governments, exhibiting an uncharacteristic realism in international affairs, were elected in Argentina,

---

[33] 'Fast track' refers to the authority given to the president to engage in negotiations on expansion on a rapid basis, without constantly referring back to Congress, and present the whole finished negotiated package at one time to the legislature for approval.

Mexico, Peru, and some Central American states. Almost everywhere in the region, governments were accepting new ways of thinking about economic affairs which usually included a rejection of import-substitution policies and their replacement by more orthodox liberal economics. The acceptance of economic multilateralism was thus a result of failure in experiments with other models—as we have seen in the Canadian and Mexican cases as well. And a growing consensus emerged within Latin America itself, based on failure with previous approaches to both political and economic structures, that export-led growth and democracy were the best economic and political routes for the future. Pressures from the international institutions were not absent from this evolution in thought.

Integration schemes that had been moribund, such as the Central American Common Market project and the Andean Pact, were renewed and newer ones begun. The new thinking was dominated by the view that going it alone as individual countries and economies had led to disaster and there was now no choice but to combine efforts if one wished to be taken into consideration when major decisions about the new international division of labour were taken made.

Mercosur is the most dynamic of these initiatives by far. Aiming at a full common market, and with hope for stimulating political and security policy coordination as a by-product of the economic integration process, the four members have set their sights high.[34] The accords must be seen within the context of a long-standing rivalry between Brazil and Argentina dating back beyond independence and involving two wars in the nineteenth century, and arms races and mutual suspicions until the mid-1980s.

The shocks to Argentina resulting from its disastrous performance in the 1982 Falklands war and the subsequent economic crises of the rest of the decade made it possible for the government of Carlos Menem, coming to power in 1989, to propose solutions to national ills which flew in the face of nationalist opinion. In effect, Argentina abandoned the rivalry, accepted Brazilian leadership, and nestled under the wing of the increasingly self-evident regional giant. Cooperation in many spheres resulted, even the thorny nuclear one that had kept both countries so nervous. And when it was seen that cooperation was possible and profitable, even in such difficult areas, the door was wide open for other mutually beneficial initiatives.[35]

Early cooperation and negotiations on a bilateral basis led to the quadripartite Treaty of Asunción of 1991, an accord laying down highly ambitious objectives of freeing up trade, moving toward a common market, and starting

---

[34] Riordan Roett (ed.), *Mercosur: Regional Integration, World Markets* (Boulder, CO: Lynne Rienner, 1999).
[35] Alcides Costa Vaz, 'La política exterior brasileña: prioridades, alianzas estratégicas e implicaciones para el Mercosur', in Francisco Rojas Aravena (ed.), *Argentina, Brasil y Chile: integración y seguridad* (Santiago: FLACSO, 1999).

the process to much greater foreign policy and even defence policy coordination. For our purposes, however, the key elements in all this were the stimulants for it.

The new 'blockism' which was so evident in the northern states was even more so in the southern. The highly sophisticated Brazilian Foreign Ministry (Itamarati) was quick to size up the consequences for a trade-dependent nation like Brazil if the trend continued and Brazil did not find its place. Mercosur was a partial answer to this. But in the inter-American context, it was even more a response to the contemporary drive by the United States to lead a hemispheric movement towards a massive bloc including the whole of the Americas.

Brazilian diplomats, statesmen, and economists were little impressed with the deals Canada and Mexico got from the NAFTA arrangement, which they saw as dominated by the US and serving much more the interests of that country than those of the two minor partners. Brazil's vast trading links with the rest of the world, and especially with Europe, made an exclusivist bloc in the Americas in any case risky. Argentina, also a major trading nation, echoed these concerns.

Buenos Aires and Brasilia wanted to avoid negotiating on an individual basis with the United States in the construction of a new inter-American bloc. They soon came to the conclusion that, if their own integration schemes locally could bring success, not only would this be valuable per se but their hand would be strengthened in future dealings with NAFTA. This would be especially true if trends towards an inter-American bloc continued but would be true in any case since such success would strengthen their negotiating position in many forums, not just those related to inter-American free trade.

Thus one sees that, even in this case, where the US is not even a member of a new multilateral organization in the Americas, its weight in influencing decisions can be massive. Examples of further effects on Mercosur of US policy are legion, but one or two are illustrative.

Chile hoped to be the fourth member of NAFTA quickly following the signing of the tripartite accords. But as mentioned, US presidential difficulties getting permission for fast-track negotiations over Chilean accession prevented this result. Instead, Chile was left at the door, waiting in a rather humiliating posture. The government in Santiago, also linked to Asia, Europe, and increasingly Mercosur, lost little time in leaving the NAFTA option for the distant future while negotiating an association with Mercosur which was to profit Chile greatly and quickly in both a growth in trade and truly impressive breakthroughs in investment. Here again, US views, or rather the results of US Executive-Congressional bickering, prevailed and the preferences of Canada and Mexico, not to mention Chile, were ignored. And once again, US policy had a major impact on the development of an institution of which it was not even a member.

Similar if not so dramatic conditions prevailed in Bolivia's choice of a Mercosur association. And Venezuela's flirting with the grouping also reflects concerns that the US cannot be relied on to actually move forward with an inter-American free trade area, and a growing feeling that other South American countries would benefit as well from getting a united front together before negotiating with the northern giant.[36]

US power is here a stimulus to the coalescing of Latin American states into multilateral organizations of their own, forums which will combine their strengths for future negotiations and provide more direct advantages of their own to their members. US inter-agency and Executive-Congressional battles can frequently have this sort of result, not necessarily beneficial for US interests but illustrative of the continued importance, not to say centrality, of the US on the hemispheric political and economic scene.

That same US influence provides the drive for further linkages with Europe. While it is easy to exaggerate the importance of these links, they exist and show room for developing further. EU-Mercosur meetings are now regularly held and contractual links of a variety of kinds are in the air or already signed. Individual members of Mercosur have been even more forward than the grouping as a whole in seeking special connections with the Europeans. Europe is a larger investor in Mercosur than is the United States itself. And the economic appeal of closer relations is made much more dramatic through the return of the Europeans, albeit in much reduced form, as a potential partial political counterpoise to the United Sates.

5. Conclusions

The story of the United States in multilateral organizations in the Americas is to a great extent the story of that country in the Pan American Union and its successor, the Organization of American States. But interesting light is shed on its behaviour, power, role, and influence by looking at more recently shaped institutions as well. This chapter has tried to trace the role of the US in these organizations to show how asymmetries of power have been central to those organizations' role, functioning, structures, and evolution.

Other countries helped found these organizations and remain in them. Thus, there is proof that they feel that membership is better than staying aloof. They wish to have the advantages of a relationship with the US which is close, while using multilateral organizations to reduce the negative features of an inter-American context where asymmetries of power are the rule and where their effects can be serious indeed for smaller states.

As we have seen, the US may find itself willing to constrain itself through membership of such organizations where the matters at hand are less than

---

[36] Marcelo Cavarozzi *et al.*, *Comunidad andina y mercosur* (Bogotá: Ministerio de Relaciones Exteriores, 1998).

vital for its interests. But when those interests are truly vital, Washington often has shown itself not only unwilling to compromise but more than willing to go outside the organization and act unilaterally. Domination of the PAU/OAS varied over time, largely as a result of the levels of US power able to be brought to bear on it. When Latin Americans benefited from potential counterpoises to US power, they were able to restrain the US more effectively. But when those counterpoises disappeared, the ability to restrain largely did the same.

One is forced therefore to come to the conclusion that power asymmetries have been crucial in defining the role of the United States in multilateral institutions in the Americas, a region in which its relative power position is virtually absolute. Where domestic factors play into that role, they can be either influential or not, or anywhere in between on a broad spectrum. In NAFTA they have been central. In the development of policy towards Latin America, Canada, or the Caribbean, they can be so as well. But they are not necessarily central. Wider issues such as strategic concerns can keep them away from that centre. In the wake of 11 September 2001, both domestic and international issues coalesced to put terrorism and related security issues at the top of the US agenda in the hemisphere, despite the region being relatively unaffected by the international brand of terrorism currently targeted. The bringing into play of the Rio Pact in order to give a rubric for inter-American cooperation against terrorism is merely the latest example of how effective the current inter-American system can be in furthering US interests.

Behaviour in newer organizations does not seem to vary very much from the OAS model. The US is generally very effective in using the institutions to further its own interests. And if it is not, and the interest is important enough, it merely goes elsewhere to do so. Latin America, the Commonwealth Caribbean, and Canada must adjust. Such is the way of small powers facing large. And such small players can only hope that multilateralism can reduce the negative features of such a relationship and maximize the positive. The United States is likely to continue to hope that multilateralism can remain as one arrow in a quiver of options including of course unilateralism as well. And if multilateralism does not deliver the goods, and the issue is important enough, unilateralism will doubtless be brought into play to do so.

The Bush government faces these options in the current context of its relations with the OAS, NAFTA, and Mercosur. US power ensures that its views will be taken seriously even if not always acted upon. But the quiver of options for the United States is an impressive one on the inter-American scene. And inter-American mobilization in support of the United States on the issue of international terrorism, even in states where the matter is far from clear, shows to what extent past experience with the utility of the 'system' may still be reflected in the future.

Conclusion: Instrumental Multilateralism in US Foreign Policy

ROSEMARY FOOT, S. NEIL MACFARLANE, AND MICHAEL
MASTANDUNO

One of the more striking aspects of the evolution of international society since the end of the Second World War has been the multiplication of multilateral organizations linking states in cooperative arrangements to address shared problems. Since these are, by and large, inter-state arrangements, their effectiveness depends on the attitudes and policies of major states within them. Over the same period, the United States has been a dominant force in world politics, even more so in the post-cold war era. Its perspectives and actions thus have had a substantial impact not only on those institutions of which it is a part but on those of which it is not, but with which it interacts. In recognition of the importance of the United States to the multilateral enterprise, our objectives in this study have been twofold: to describe and explain US behaviour in and towards a broad range of global and regional multilateral organizations, and to analyse the impact of the United States on the capacity of these organizations to meet their own objectives.

We undertook this analysis at a time when many commentators had concluded that there was a reasonably well-established trend in the post-cold war era towards American unilateralism, a trend that had been accelerated by the election of George W. Bush and the setting up of his administration in January 2001. The administration's reactions to the events of 11 September 2001 have also been interpreted in two distinct ways. Some have argued that the response to global terrorism would require a deeply cooperative multilateral response on the part of the United States, while others pointed to the American preference for relying on its own capacities, drawing on the resources of others only selectively and on a bilateral basis. It is these kinds of arguments that we have sought to probe in this study.

1. General Findings

The contributions to this volume suggest that there is no clear pattern or trend that signals a growing US rejection of multilateral organizations as venues for the promotion of US foreign policy interests. The United States picks and chooses from a range of possible approaches, depending on the issue, its interests, and changing international and domestic conditions. America can afford to be discriminating in this way. US hegemony affords it broad discretion to use unilateral, bilateral, or multilateral means to obtain its objectives. Hegemony provides it with the privilege of instrumental multilateralism.

The first decade after the cold war was one of considerable variation in the US approach within and between issue areas, a variation that was sensitive to particular circumstances and experiences. Regarding UN peace operations, the United States went from enthusiastic embrace at the beginning of the decade, to deep disillusion subsequent to the Somalia affair, to a more modulated support at decade's end. Scepticism about UN peace operations did not translate into rejection of multilateralism per se in this area. The period of maximal disillusion with the UN was also that of US engagement in multilateral peace enforcement in the former Yugoslavia. The Bosnian and Kosovo cases both involved substantial UN roles.

Turning to variation between issue areas, we see more evidence of unilateralism in the area of security than there is in that of economic cooperation. However, even in the latter case we can see that American attitudes blow hot and cold. President Clinton lost fast-track authority to negotiate trade agreements after the conclusion of the NAFTA Accord in 1993. This was followed, however, by a strong US push for establishment of the WTO. The current Bush administration came into office with a far more substantial interest in American free trade than that of its predecessor, and has expended considerable political capital in persuading the Congress to restore fast-track authority. Nevertheless, the administration has also succumbed to domestic protectionist pressures from key States and has imposed import duties on certain goods important to US domestic producers.

The US has also shown itself willing to rely on the IMF in the post-cold war era, both in the case of Russia, where US officials preferred the Fund to be the body associated with administering 'shock therapy', and in the bail-out of Argentina in August 2001. During the Asian financial crisis of 1997–9, the US again supported a prominent role for the IMF both in responding to the crisis and in efforts to restructure the domestic political economies of the east Asian developmental states. In the area of the environment, American slowness or retreat in some areas of the agenda—for example, climate change—is accompanied by enthusiastic embrace and continued commitment in others—for example, CFCs.

These examples suggest that grand generalizations about America's hostility towards multilateral institutions are overdrawn, especially when one looks broadly across issue areas and regions, and over time. As noted above, the pattern can best be described as instrumental or pragmatic use of such organizations. If institutions do a reasonable job at promoting American agendas and show signs of being effective, they tend to be embraced. If they constrain American pursuit of its perceived interests beyond a point that can be tolerated, or they appear to be ineffectual, they will be avoided or opposed, leading the United States to explore other options. For both Republican and Democratic administrations it seems that multilateral institutions will be supported or created when they can assist in the furtherance of America's policy objectives; otherwise they will not.

Another way of framing this finding is to describe US perspectives towards multilateral institutions as being grounded in issue-specific cost-benefit analysis. Despite American preponderance, institutions may be useful in attaining specific objectives at lower cost than unilateral approaches. Thus, there is no reason to assume that unipolarity leads inexorably to unilateralism, although it does afford the United States a broad discretion that is not available to weaker states. Multilateral institutions may promote US burden-sharing preferences, as is evident from the NATO role in the former Yugoslavia. The existence of UN or regional peacekeeping structures or the IFIs arguably makes it easier for the US to avoid direct engagement on issues it seeks to steer clear of or which might involve substantial costs. International institutions, and particularly the United Nations, also play a role in the legitimization of US power, as, for example, in the intervention in Haiti or the use of force against Iraq. In the case of Cuba after 1959, the United States found it politically valuable that the OAS endorsed a general rejection of the Castro regime. Membership in international institutions makes it easier to influence evolving agendas in world politics, a finding that has even begun to have a powerful conditioning effect in the area of US environmental policy. Even if the Kyoto Protocol is finished as far as the US is concerned, re-engagement with environmental multilateralism is a genuine prospect.

The utility of institutions relates not only to specific policy concerns but also to milieu goals. Institutions serve as a transmission mechanism in the effort to universalize American values, for example, the promotion of democratic and market reforms. The United States also often finds institutions useful in constraining other states, binding these states into sets of policies that promote American conceptions of world order. Where this calculation has been made, the United States when it joins such institutions has been willing to accept some limitations on its own room for manoeuvre in order to embed—or 'lock in', as Ikenberry has put it—other states into institutional arrangements. This purpose may be particularly important in the long run. If American preponderance eventually decays, the lock-in effect may be all the more important in sustaining a world congenial to American preferences. However, the United States also has the capacity to encourage multilateral institutions to form and reform even where it is not a member, as is evident from our discussion of Africa and Latin America.

These descriptors of American behaviour apply to both the universal and the regional organizations and to economic, security, and environmental issue areas. The United States is perhaps more selective in its regional as opposed to its global associations, but this reflects the degree of US engagement in the region as well as the functions of the organizations themselves. American commitment to regional institutions of which it is a member, and its support of those of which it is not, reflect judgements concerning the degree to which these bodies promote or support US objectives. This suggests that difference in level of organization has little significance to the general explanation.

2. Explanatory Factors

The discussion so far, focusing on our generalized findings, has treated the United States as a unitary actor. Yet our chapters make plain that a variety of domestic factors play important roles in shaping policy towards multilateral institutions.

The most important of these internal influences is American exceptionalism, when based on a definition that emphasizes US beliefs that its national values and practices are universally valid and its policy positions are moral and proper and not just expedient. Exceptionalism is highlighted not only in Luck's discussion of peacekeeping, the creation of the WTO and UN arrears, but also in Sen's contribution on the WTO and Woods's analysis of the Bank and the Fund. Woods makes a point that could apply to our other issue areas: there is a US unity of view that America can and should set down the terms and conditions for the IFIs.

Exceptionalism is also evident in each of the regional chapters. The essential element in the regional account is the American effort to *export* indigenous values that it believes can be made universal—particularly apparent in the chapters on Africa, Asia, and Latin America—or to *reinforce* or *magnify*, at least in earlier decades, American liberal values by cooperating with its NATO allies. Of all our domestic factors, exceptionalism appears as the most pervasive explanatory variable, affecting all the issue areas that we have investigated and all of our regionally-based chapters.

Other internal factors, while less pervasive, do nevertheless make their influence felt, of course. Luck demonstrates the key role of partisanship in understanding US policy towards the United Nations, particularly when one party controls the Executive and the other the Congress. Yet, as the above comment on fast-track authority indicates, this effect is not limited to the UN. At another level, Hopgood explains US policy towards multilateral environmental issues and institutions in terms of a contest between activists and sceptics in the United States, with the former tending to be Democrats and the latter Republicans. Nel suggests another dyad in his consideration of US policy towards multilateralism in Africa: in this case it is intimately related to the contest between 'accommodationists' of a liberal persuasion and 'rejectionists' of a more conservative stripe, in successive administrations.

Interest groups appear to be particularly salient in environmental and economic issue areas, probably reflecting the fact that it is multilateral activities in these domains that have a particular impact on the preferences of powerful domestic lobbies. The role of the legislature and the constitutional division of powers in American policy-making features strongly in the evolution of US policy towards the United Nations and its specialized agencies, as is evident in the chapters by Luck, Malone, and Woods. An increase in resources allocated to the IMF requires Congressional approval, for example, which has provided the legislative branch with opportunities to influence the conditions attached to Fund lending. Where a replenishment of the World Bank's IDA has been negotiated, the US Congress has tried to use its leverage over funds here too, to impose its preferences on Bank policies. In addition, and perhaps reflecting the attentiveness of affected interest groups, there is a strong Congressional component to policy formulation on trade in general and the WTO specifically, an attentiveness that is set to increase as a result of more frequent US involvement with the Dispute Settlement Mechanism of the WTO. However, even in our regional chapters, we see how important the separation of powers can be. As Nel notes, with Republican gains after the 1994 mid-term elections, key African Committee and Sub-Committee chairs were lost by the Black Caucus. Thus, Clinton in turn lost significant support in Congress for his African policy.

Competing bureaucratic interests evidently continue to influence the current Bush administration's unresolved debates about the costs and benefits of multilateralism; and in certain specific areas, such as in policy towards the IFIs, trade, and the environment, different agencies have long been awarded different responsibilities in the multilateral negotiating process. These agencies have used such openings to promote particular agency interests. However, serious turf battles do not figure strongly in any of the chapters in this volume.

Turning to the external dimension—or what is more accurately described as an interpenetrated set of domestic and external factors—we see that US policy towards multilateral organizations is strongly informed by the desire to enhance and to sustain power in a way that contributes to US world order preferences. Klepak, for example, argues that relative power and the ingrained assumptions that flow from asymmetry are essential factors in the understanding of the long historical pattern in US foreign policy towards Latin America, as is the effort by weaker states to develop and employ multilateral institutions to constrain American power. Haglund's chapter clearly suggests that one fundamental motivation for US sponsorship and maintenance of NATO is the desire to maintain a position of power in the European region. Relative power considerations also go some distance towards explaining American ambivalence about the emergence of the EU as a powerful political/military as well as economic actor in world politics.

Also powerful in determining US attitudes towards multilateral organizations is the perceived performance or effectiveness of such bodies. This perception is strongly linked to the extent to which these groupings show themselves to be compatible with US objectives, objectives which are themselves informed by US national values. Malone, for example, emphasizes the importance of evolving debates in the UN in the era of decolonization over the Middle East and the new international information order in significantly contributing to US disillusion with the organization. Elsewhere, the weak performance of the OSCE as a manager of security issues in Europe has contributed to its marginalization in America's European policy. The relatively undemanding nature of the ARF, on the other hand, as Cossa shows, facilitates US involvement with the institution because it challenges neither materially nor normatively the bilateral alliance structure that the US long ago established in the Asia-Pacific.

In contrast, international norms that support the idea that interdependent political actors within an international community should operate collectively rather than unilaterally appear to have little causal significance in the explanations of American behaviour. Norms are important in other ways, however, as indicators of the reasons for US acceptance or avoidance of particular international institutions. In some instances, as with regard to the ARF, the United States abides by the community's norms but these do not conflict significantly with US policy preferences. In other instances—for example, the WTO and the IMF—institutional norms reflect American preferences and thereby help to maintain US support for these bodies. The UN in the 1960s and 1970s, on the other hand, came to be viewed as a venue that promulgated norms that conflicted with US values.

It is clear that all of the organizations we have considered—and many state members of these organizations—make efforts to influence US policy towards their organizations. It is equally clear that such efforts have a mixed record of success. There is no case described in our chapters where such lobbying operated as the primary determinant in shaping US policy on an issue of major significance, although it is clear that international or transnational actors have helped to boost an argument that is already being made at the domestic level.

3. US Impact on Multilateral Organizations

The studies in this volume suggest that the impact of the United States on multilateral organizations is also variable, both in intensity and in content. In the first place, American policy exercises an important direct or indirect influence over the formation of international institutions. The direct role played by the United States had a defining effect on the character of the United Nations, the IFIs, and such regional organizations as the PAU/OAS and NATO. The indirect role is evident in the fact that some multilateral institutions have come into being in part to balance American power (Mercosur) or in the hope of reaping financial rewards through conformance to US preferences: for example, Nel's discussion of emerging multilateralism in Africa. In the Asian case, as Cossa notes, APEC and ARF were formed in part out of concerns about US disengagement and to tie the US in to the region's affairs. As Ikenberry argues, institutional bargains not only involve locking weaker states into enduring policy positions but are also attractive for the weaker parties themselves because they place some constraints on the operation of the hegemonic state's power and reduce the prospects for abandonment by the powerful state.

The United States also has profound disabling or enabling effects on the operation of institutions once they are established. Luck's and Malone's discussions of UN funding issues in the 1990s both highlight the significance of the power to withhold resources in American policy towards the organization. Variation in American willingness to pay greatly affects the scope and the consistency of UN action in response to threats to international peace and security. Access to US military assets has an equally substantial enabling effect for NATO in its out-of-area operations. In the IMF, the US contributes 17.67 per cent of the capital subscriptions and therefore has 17.33 per cent of the votes on the Executive Board—an effective blocking power because major policy changes require an 85 per cent majority of votes.

The United States additionally has a major influence both in shaping the agendas of institutions where its interests are at stake and, even more fundamentally, in shaping and reshaping the actual character of the institutions themselves. Woods's analysis of the decision-making of the international financial institutions suggests that the US exercises strong control over what these institutions consider. This may reflect either the ideological hegemony of American understandings or the reluctance of institutional secretariats and members to raise issues that they know will be opposed by the United States. The United States has also used the IMF to promote the values of privatization and financial deregulation. Sen notes that the US enjoys an unspoken veto over the appointment of the Director-General of the WTO and other key staff. More ambitiously on the part of the United States, he shows that it has engineered a shift from a weaker GATT regime to the more powerful WTO which incorporates a binding, contractual, system, with provisions for enforcing adjudication—capable also of constraining the United States. Developing-country agreement to the liberalization of financial services and to the embrace of new issues such as the TRIPS and TRIMS depended significantly on robust US diplomacy. There is evidence in the chapters by Luck and Malone that expected US opposition to new peace-enforcement missions in the aftermath of the 1993 Somali debacle discouraged the UN from serious consideration of a robust and timely response to the genocide in Rwanda the following year. And NATO enlargement has largely been a reflection of American preferences.

Still another dimension of impact is evident in Nel's account of American approaches to multilateralism in Africa. In an analysis strongly influenced by Gramscian notions of power, Nel suggests that the United States is getting its way in the region on democratization and economic reform because key leaders in Africa have come to accept the validity and legitimacy of an ideological agenda promoted by the US. The same phenomenon, Klepak suggests, may be operating in Latin America's embrace of democratization and human rights.

This is not to say that the United States has full control of multilateral agendas and the shaping or reshaping of organizations. Reference to the 1970s NIEO and the ill-starred new international information order of the 1980s, or the ICC, or the Kyoto Protocol today would all indicate that it does not. The fate of the developing-country initiatives of the 1970s and 1980s, discussed by Malone, does indicate, however, what happens when an international organizational agenda gets too far beyond the pale: the United States will withdraw its support and look for other arenas or means in which to advance its policy goals.

Finally, as suggested in the Introduction, the US has often had profound effects on multilateral institutions, not so much as a result of its deliberate pursuit of objectives with respect to, or through, international organizations but as unintended consequences of decisions taken for reasons unrelated to them. The sheer size of the United States economy, for example, means that domestic policy decisions may have large international effects. As Hopgood points out, the decision to ban CFCs in the United States itself had a major enabling effect in the process leading to the conclusion of the Montreal Protocol. Decisions by state and local authorities to insist on targets for the use of recycled paper in newsprint have created substantial disputes within NAFTA, where some see this as an illegal restraint on trade. The continuous upgrading of US military capabilities in the 1990s has fostered inter-operability problems that, in the view of some, undermine NATO.

4. An Instrumental Multilateralist

The finalization of this conclusion followed closely on the heels of the Bush administration's announcement that it had no intention of submitting the treaty on the International Criminal Court for ratification by the Senate, and as the US formally withdrew from the ABM treaty. Both appear to provide further evidence of the Bush administration's preference for pursuing its interests through unilateral means. Nevertheless, as several of our authors argue, in many policy areas multilateralism is central to the way in which a hegemonic state like the United States can achieve its policy goals, whether that is in the struggle against terrorism, for a healthy environment, or in the search for positive-sum gains from international trade. What our chapters suggest is that US power enables it to engage in a careful weighing of the costs and benefits of multilateral cooperation and to be selective about the terms of its engagement with international institutions. The United States may best be described, then, not as unilateralist but as an 'instrumental multilateralist'. America's decisions to cooperate in multilateral forums will be determined predominantly by the extent to which any specific organization is perceived by important US domestic actors to be an effective and congenial vehicle for the promotion of America's objectives. As for multilateral institutions themselves, they will continue to operate within the direct and indirect constraints that US instrumentalism imposes.

SELECT BIBLIOGRAPHY

Abbott, Kenneth and Snidal, Duncan, 'Why States Act Through Formal International Organizations', *Journal of Conflict Resolution*, 42/1 (1998).

Adler, Selig, *The Isolationist Impulse: Its Twentieth Century Reaction* (New York: Collier Books, 1961).

Aravena, Francisco Rojas (ed.), *Argentina, Brasil y Chile: integracion y seguridad* (Santiago: FLACSO, 1999).

Augelli, Enrico and Murphy, Craig, *America's Quest for Supremacy and the Third World: A Gramscian Analysis* (London: Pinter, 1988).

Baldwin, Robert E., *The Political Economy of US Import Policy* (Cambridge, MA: MIT Press, 1985).

Barkin, J. Samuel and Shambaugh, George E. (eds), *Anarchy and the Environment: The International Politics of Common Pool Resources* (New York, NY: SUNY Press, 1999).

Beckerman, Wilfred and Pasek, Joanna, *Justice, Posterity, and the Environment* (Oxford: Oxford University Press, 2001).

Bhagwati, Jagdish, *A Stream of Windows: Unsettling Reflections on Trade, Immigration and Democracy* (Cambridge, MA: MIT Press, 1998).

——and Patrick, Hugh (eds), *Aggressive Unilateralism: America's 301 Policy and the World Trading System* (Ann Arbor: University of Michigan Press, 1990).

Brenner, Michael (ed.), *Multilateralism and Western Strategy* (New York, NY: St Martin's Press, 1995).

Carpenter, Ted Galen (ed.), *Delusions of Grandeur: The United Nations and Global Intervention* (Washington, DC: Cato Institute, 1997).

Cavarozzi, Marcelo, *et al.*, *Comunidad Andiana y Mercosur* (Bogota: Ministerio de Relaciones Exteriores, 1998).

Child, John, *Unequal Alliance: the Inter-American Military System 1938–1978* (Boulder, CO: Westview Press, 1980).

Cox, Robert W. and Jacobson, Harold K. (eds), *The Anatomy of Influence: Decision Making in International Organization* (London: Yale University Press, 1974).

Cox, Robert and Sinclair, Timothy (eds), *Approaches to World Order* (Cambridge: Cambridge University Press, 1996).

Daudelin, Jean and Dosman, Edgar (eds), *Beyond Mexico* (Ottawa: Carleton University Press, 1995).

Deng, Francis M. and Lyons, Terrence, *African Reckoning: A Quest for Good Governance* (Washington, DC: Brookings Institution, 1998).

DeSombre, Elizabeth R., *Domestic Sources of International Environmental Policy: Industry, Environmentalists and US Power* (Cambridge, MA: MIT Press, 2000).

Destler, I. M., *American Trade Politics*, 3rd edn (Washington, DC: Institute for International Economics, 1995).

Dickson, D. A., *United States Policy towards Sub-Saharan Africa: Change, Continuity & Constraint* (New York: University Press of America, 1985).

Dobell, Rod and Neufeld, Michael (eds), *Beyond NAFTA: the Western Hemisphere Interface* (British Columbia: Oolichan Press, 1993).

Dowie, Mark, *Losing Ground: American Environmentalism at the Close of the Twentieth Century* (Cambridge, MA: MIT Press, 1995).

Duignan, Peter and Gann, Lewis H., *The United States and Africa: A History* (Cambridge: Cambridge University Press, 1984).

Durch, William J. (ed.), *UN Peacekeeping, American Politics, and the Uncivil Wars of the 1990s* (New York: St Martin's Press, 1996).

El-Khawas, Mohamed A. and Cohen, Barry (eds), *The Kissinger Study of Southern Africa* (Westport, CT: Lawrence Hill, 1976).

Evans, Peter B., Jacobson, Harold K., and Putnam, Robert D., *Double-Edged Diplomacy. International Bargaining and Domestic Politics* (Berkeley: University of California Press, 1993).

Fawcett, Louise and Hurrell, Andrew (eds), *Regionalism in World Politics: Regional Organization and International Order* (Oxford: Oxford University Press, 1995).

Feketekuty, Geza and Stokes, Bruce, *Trade Strategies for a New Era: Ensuring US Leadership in a Global Economy* (New York: Council on Foreign Relations, published with the Monterey Institute of International Studies, 1998).

Gardner, Lloyd C., *A Covenant with Power: American and World Order from Wilson to Reagan* (New York: Oxford University Press, 1984).

Gardner, Richard, *Sterling-Dollar Diplomacy* (New York: Columbia University Press, 1980).

Gilbert, Chris and Vines, David (eds), *The World Bank: Structure and Policies* (Cambridge: Cambridge University Press, 2000).

Goldstein, Judith, 'International Law and Domestic Institutions: Reconciling North American "Unfair" Trade Laws', *International Organization*, 50/4 (1996).

Gowa, Joanne, *Allies, Adversaries and International Trade* (Princeton, NJ: Princeton University Press, 1994).

Graham, Otis L., Jr. (ed.), *Environmental Politics and Policy 1960s–1990s* (Philadelphia: University of Pennsylvania Press, 2000).

Grinspun, Richard and Cameron, Maxwell (eds), *The Political Economy of North-American Free Trade* (Montreal: McGill-Queen's University Press, 1993).

Grubb, Michael, Vrolijk, Christiaan, and Brack, Duncan, *The Kyoto Protocol: A Guide and Assessment* (London: RIIA, 1999).

Haglund, David G. (ed.), *Latin America and the Transformation of US Strategic Thought* (Albuquerque: University of New Mexico, 1984).

—— *The France-US Leadership Race: Closely Watched Allies* (Kingston: Queen's Quarterly Press, 2000).

Harbeson, John and Rothchild, Donald (eds), *Africa in World Politics: The African State System in Flux* (Boulder, CO: Westview Press, 2000).

Harris, Paul G. (ed.), *The Environment, International Relations and US Foreign Policy* (London: Routledge, 1994).

—— *Climate Change and American Foreign Policy* (New York: St Martin's Press, 2000).

Hoekman, Bernard and Kostecki, Michel, *The Political Economy of the World Trading System* (Oxford: Oxford University Press, 1995).

Hopgood, Stephen, *American Foreign Environmental Policy and the Power of the State* (Oxford: Oxford University Press, 1998).

Hurrell, Andrew and Kingsbury, Benedict (eds), *The International Politics of the Environment* (Oxford: Clarendon Press, 1992).

Ikenberry, John G., *After Victory: Institutions, Strategic Restraint, and the Rebuilding of Order After Major War* (Princeton, NJ: Princeton University Press, 2001).

Jackson, John H., *The World Trading System: Law and Politics of International Economic Relations* (Cambridge, MA: MIT Press, 1997).

—— *The World Trade Organization: Constitution and Jurisprudence*, Chatham House Papers (London: RIIA Cassel Imprint, 1998).

James, Harold, *International Monetary Cooperation since Bretton Woods* (Oxford: Oxford University Press, 1996).

Kammen, Michael, 'The Problem of American Exceptionalism: A Reconsideration', *American Quarterly*, 45 (March 1993).

Kapstein, Ethan B. and Mastanduno, Michael (eds), *Unipolar Politics: Realism and State Strategies after the Cold War* (New York: Columbia University Press, 1999).

Kapur, Devesh, Lewis, John P., and Webb, Richard, *The World Bank: Its First Half Century Volume 1* (Washington, DC: Brookings Institution, 1997).

Karns, Margaret P. and Mingst, Karen A. (eds), *The United States and Multilateral Institutions: Patterns of Changing Instrumentality and Influence* (Boston, MA: Unwin Hyman, 1990).

Kaul, Inge, Grunberg, Isabelle, and Stern, Marc A. (eds), *Global Public Goods: International Cooperation in the 21st Century* (New York: UNDP, 1999).

Keohane, Robert O., *After Hegemony: Cooperation and Discord in the World Political Economy* (Princeton, NJ: Princeton University Press, 1984).

—— *International Institutions and State Power* (Boulder, CO: Westview Press, 1989).

Krasner, Stephen (ed.), *International Regimes* (New York: Cornell University Press, 1983).

—— *Structural Conflict: The Third World Against Global Liberalism* (Berkeley: University of California Press, 1985).

Krauss, Ellis S., 'Japan, the US, and the Emergence of Multilateralism in Asia', *The Pacific Review*, 13/3 (2000).

Krueger, Anne O., *Economic Policies at Cross-Purposes: The United States and Developing Countries* (Washington, DC: Brookings Institution, 1993).

—— *The WTO as an International Organization* (Chicago: Chicago University Press, 1998).

Kull, Steven and Destler, I. M., *Misreading the Public: The Myth of a New Isolationism* (Washington, DC: Brookings Institution Press, 1999).

Lake, David A., *Entangling Relations: American Foreign Policy in Its Century* (Princeton, NJ: Princeton University Press, 1999).

Leifer, Michael, *The ASEAN Regional Forum*, Adelphi Paper 302 (1996).

Lieber, Robert J. (ed.), *Eagle Adrift: American Foreign Policy at the End of the Century* (New York: Longman, 1997).

Lipset, Seymour Martin, *American Exceptionalism: A Double-Edged Sword* (New York: W. W. Norton, 1996).

Litan, Robert E., 'The "Globalization" Challenge: The US Role in Shaping World Trade and Investment', *The Brookings Review*, 18/2 (Washington, DC: Brookings Institution, 2000).

Luck, Edward C., *Mixed Messages: American Politics and International Organization 1919–1999* (Washington, DC: Brookings Institution Press for the Century Foundation, 1999).

Lyons, Gene and Mastanduno, Michael (eds), *Beyond Westphalia? State Sovereignty and International Intervention* (Baltimore, MD: Johns Hopkins University Press, 1995).

McDougall, Walter A., *Promised Land, Crusader State: The American Encounter with the World Since 1776* (Boston, MA: Houghton Mifflin, 1997).

Mack, Andrew and Ravenhill, John (eds), *Pacific Cooperation: Building Economic and Security Regimes in the Asia-Pacific Region* (Boulder, CO: Westview Press, 1995).

MacKinnon, Michael G., *The Evolution of US Peacekeeping under Clinton* (London: Frank Cass, 2000).

Malone, David, *Decision-Making in the UN Security Council: The Case of Haiti, 1990–1997* (Oxford: Clarendon Press, 1998).

Maynes, Charles William and Williamson, Richard S., *U.S. Foreign Policy and the United Nations System* (New York: W. W. Norton, 1996).

Mearsheimer, John J., 'The False Promise of International Institutions', *International Security*, 19/3 (1994/95).

Milner, Helen, *Resisting Protectionism: Global Industries and the Politics of International Trade* (Princeton, NJ: Princeton University Press, 1988).

—— *Interests, Institutions and Information: Domestic Politics and International Relations* (Princeton, NJ: Princeton University Press, 1997).

Mintzer, Irving M. and Leonard, J. Amber (eds), *Negotiating Climate Change* (Cambridge: Cambridge University Press, 1994).

Mulat, Teshome, 'Multilateralism and Africa's Regional Economic Communities', *Journal of World Trade*, 32/4 (1998).

Nathan, James and Oliver, James, *Foreign Policy Making and the American Political System* (Boston, MA: Little, Brown, 1987).

Nordlinger, Eric A., *Isolationism Reconfigured: American Foreign Policy for a New Century* (Princeton. NJ: Princeton University Press, 1995).

Nye, Joseph, *Bound to Lead: The Changing Nature of American Power* (New York: Basic Books, 1990).

—— *The Paradox of American Power* (Oxford: Oxford University Press, 2001).

Ostrower, Gary B., *The United Nations and the United States* (New York: Twayne Publishers, 1998).

Oye, Kenneth A., Lieber, Robert J., and Rothchild, Donald (eds), *Eagle Entangled: US Foreign Policy in a Complex World* (New York: Longman, 1979).

—— —— —— *Eagle Defiant: United States Foreign Policy in the 1980s* (Boston, MA: Little, Brown and Company, 1983).

—— —— —— *Eagle Resurgent? The Reagan Era in American Foreign Policy* (Boston, MA: Little, Brown and Company, 1987).

—— —— —— *Eagle in a New World: American Grand Strategy in the Post-Cold War Era* (London: Harper Collins, 1992).

Patrick, Stewart, 'America's Retreat from Multilateral Engagement', *Current History*, 99 (December 2000).

—— and Forman, Shepard (eds), *Multilateralism and U.S. Foreign Policy: Ambivalent Engagement* (Boulder, CO: Lynne Rienner, 2001).

Pike, Frederick B., *The United States and Latin America: Myths and Stereotypes of Civilization and Nature* (Austin: University of Texas Press, 1992).

Porter, Gareth, *The US and the Biodiversity Convention* (Washington, DC: EESI, 1992).

Princen, Thomas and Finger, Matthias (eds), *Environmental NGOs in World Politics* (London: Routledge, 1994).

Reisman, Michael W., 'The United States and International Institutions', *Survival*, 41/4 (1999/2000).

Rhodes, Carolyn, *Reciprocity, U.S. Trade Policy and the GATT Regime* (Ithaca, NY: Cornell University Press, 1993).

Rielly, John E., 'Americans and the World: A Survey at Century's End', *Foreign Policy*, 114 (Spring 1999).

Risse-Kappen, Thomas, *Cooperation Among Democracies: The European Influence on U. S. Foreign Policy* (Princeton, NJ: Princeton University Press, 1995).

Robinson, William, *Promoting Polyarchy: Globalization, US Intervention and Hegemony* (Cambridge: Cambridge University Press, 1996).

Rochlin, James, *Discovering the Americas: the Evolution of Canadian Foreign Policy towards Latin America* (Vancouver: University of British Columbia Press, 1994).

Roett, Riordan (ed.), *Mercosur: Regional Integration, World Markets* (Boulder, CO: Lynne Rienner, 1999).

Rogowski, Ronald, *Commerce and Coalition: How Trade Affects Domestic Political Alignments* (Princeton, NJ: Princeton University Press, 1989).

Roussel, Stephane, *North America's Liberal Order: The Impact of Democratic Values, Norms, and Institutions on Canadian-American Security Relations, 1867–1958* (Kingston: Queen's University School of Policy Studies, 2002).

Ruggie, John Gerard (ed.), *Multilateralism Matters: The Theory and Praxis of an Institutional Form* (New York: Columbia University Press, 1993).

—— *Winning the Peace: America and World Order in the New Era* (New York: Columbia University Press, 1996).

—— *Constructing the World Polity: Essays on International Institutions* (London: Routledge, 1998).

Schattschneider, Elmer Eric, *Politics, Pressures, and the Tariff: A Study of Free Private Enterprise in Pressure Politics, As Shown in the 1929–1930 Revision of the Tariff* (New York: Prentice-Hall, 1935).

Schechter, Michael, *Innovation in Multilateralism* (Basingstoke: Macmillan, 1999).

Schott, Jeffrey J. (ed.), *The World Trading System: Challenges Ahead* (Washington, DC: Institute for International Economics, 1996).

Schoultz, Lars, *National Security and United States Policy toward Latin America* (Princeton, NJ: Princeton University Press, 1987).

Schraeder, Peter J., *United States Foreign Policy Toward Africa: Incrementalism, Crisis and Change* (Cambridge: Cambridge University Press, 1994).

—— ' "Forget the Rhetoric and Boost the Geopolitics": Emerging Trends in the Bush Administration's Policy towards Africa', *African Affairs*, 100 (2001).

Schreurs, Miranda A. and Economy, Elizabeth C. (eds), *The Internationalization of Environmental Protection* (Cambridge: Cambridge University Press, 1997).

Tew, Brian, *International Monetary Cooperation, 1945–70* (London: Hutchinson, 1970).

Trubowitz, Peter, *Defining the National Interest: Conflict and Change in American Foreign Policy* (Chicago: University of Chicago Press, 1998).

Veneroni, Horacio, *Estados Unidos y las Fuerzas Armadas de America Latina* (Buenos Aires: Periferia, 1973).

Victor, David G., *The Collapse of the Kyoto Protocol* (Princeton, NJ: Princeton University Press, 2001).

Vig, Norman J. and Kraft, Michael E. (eds), *Environmental Policy in the 1980s: Reagan's New Agenda* (Washington, DC: Congressional Quarterly Press, 1984).

Vogler, John and Imber, Mark F. (eds), *The Environment and International Relations* (London: Routledge, 1996).

Wallace, William, 'Europe, the Necessary Partner', *Foreign Affairs*, 80 (May/June 2001).

Walter, Andrew, *World Power and World Money: The Role of Hegemony and International Monetary Order* (London: Harvester Wheatsheaf, 1993).

Weiss, Thomas G., Forsythe, David P., and Coate, Roger A., *The United Nations in a Changing World*, 2nd edn (Boulder, CO: Westview Press, 1997).

Wohlforth, William C., 'The Stability of a Unipolar World', *International Security*, 24/1 (1999).

Yost, David S., *NATO Transformed: The Alliance's New Roles in International Security* (Washington, DC: United States Institute of Peace, 1998).

—— 'The NATO Capabilities Gap and the European Union', *Survival*, 42 (Winter 2000/2001).

Zakaria, Fareed, *From Wealth to Power: The Unusual Origins of America's World Role* (Princeton, NJ: Princeton University Press, 1998).

INDEX

Notes: All references are to United States and multilateralism unless otherwise specified. Most organizations are entered under their acronyms. Page numbers in bold indicate chapters